Between the Rivers

Rev. John Nye, principal author of BETWEEN THE RIVERS, an alumnus of Iowa Wesleyan College and Garrett Evangelical Theological Seminary, also studied at the Universities of Iowa and South Dakota. Received as a full member and elder of the Iowa Des Moines Conference of the Methodist Church in 1940, he served 35 years as a pastor at various charges in the state. During World War II he was a chaplain in the Army of the United States, including 35 months in Europe.

Between the Rivers

A History of Iowa United Methodism

John A. Nye

with special contributions by
Leonard E. Deaver, Louis A. Haselmayer, Miriam Baker Nye

Published by the Commission on Archives and History,
Iowa Annual Conference of the United Methodist Church

Copyright 1986 by The Archives and History Commission of Iowa Annual Conference of The
United Methodist Church.
Library of Congress 86-80106
ISBN Hardback #0-9616298-0-0
Paperback #0-9616298-1-9
Printed by The Graphic Publishing Co., Inc., Lake Mills, Iowa 50450.

BETWEEN THE RIVERS
A History of Iowa United Methodism

List of Illustrations for *Between the Rivers:* History of the United Methodist Church in Iowa

Frontispiece—United Methodist Headquarters Building

Chapter 1

Chapter 2

Chapter 3

Chapter 4

Chapter 5

Chapter 6

Dedication

To the congregation of the Agency United Methodist Church where the writer, as a boy and young man, learned to love the church and its history.

"For all the saints, who from their labors rest,
Who Thee by faith before the world confessed,
Thy Name, O Jesus, be forever blessed,
Alleluia! Alleluia!"
—William H. How (1823-1897)

United Methodist Headquarters Building

Foreword

The story of the United Methodist Church in Iowa is the story of ordinary people living extraordinary lives. The heroines and heroes of our tradition were very much like the persons who make up our communities and churches today. If they were distinguished in any way it was by their faith in Jesus Christ and their near extravagant commitment to God's reign in all the world.

We look back with gratitude to those courageous and committed people who braved an unknown frontier and an uncertain future to plant the church in the rich and productive soil of Iowa. Their offspring nurtured what they had planted and the young, growing church often took enormous leaps of faith to launch still another ministry of Christ in the world.

Today we reap the harvest of their labors. Our congregations, hospitals, colleges, homes, camps and programs are the fruit of their wise, careful, courageous and faithful living. Today we receive from the hands of those who have gone before the rich gifts of their faithful labors. Every time we pass a United Methodist facility, experience a program of the church, or pause to pray in a United Methodist house of worship we are reminded how our lives are enriched daily by the wisdom, courage and sacrifice of our mothers and fathers in the faith. We can experience the nurture and support of the church and a growing relationship with Christ in our journey through life because generations before us were faithful.

What will future generations have to say about us? Let us labor and pray so to live that future generations may know Christ and the church and look back to our age with gratitude.

Rueben P. Job
Resident Bishop, Iowa Area
May 1985

Persons who have served terms on the Conference Archives-History Commission during the period when this history was in preparation (1974-1984):

Helen L. Black	Edward S. Zelley
John A. Nye	Sue Terry
Walter B. Phelps	Dale J. Williams
Marjorie Cloyed	Robert MacCanon
Joseph F. Kissinger	Donald R. Arthur
Helen Snepp	Robert Sands
Elsie Dotisman	Robert V. Gildner
Miriam Baker Nye	Margaret Phelps
Eldon Ogan	David Dunsmore
Donald F. Roberts	J. A. Leatherman
Jerry L. Richards	Louis Frederick
Wilton M. Grant	Gerald La Motte
Leland L. Enke	William Richards
Howard F. Ball	Mary Jane Sweet
M. Stanley Ballard	G. Eldon Haworth
James W. Morris	Raymond Lott
Louis A. Haselmayer	Robert Bostwick
William T. Miller	Robert Fowler
Lucille Morgan Wilson	Mearle L. Griffith
Helen Sutherland	Lorraine Hawley
John Faris	Roy Mayhew
Walter A. Cooper	Lester Moore
Clay Lanman	Jean Heaps
Henry Riegel	Lyle Johnston
Paul H. Heath	Wilda Workman

Preface

For some years before this project was undertaken, persons interested in collecting and preserving our church's history in Iowa had been expressing concern that a new conference history should be written. In 1974, at a meeting of the Archives-History Commission, Rev. Walter Phelps moved that John Nye should begin the work. By unamimous vote of the commission, a decade of research and writing commenced.

During their terms as the commission's chairperson, the late Helen L. Black and Rev. Jim Morris gave much support. Members serving on the Commission 1974-1984 encouraged the effort. Rev. Mearle Griffith, Dr. Louis Haselmayer, Dr. Leonard Deaver, and Dr. Dendy Garrett were the editorial advisors. Rev. Jim Morris, Rev. Mearle Griffith, and Rev. Lyle Johnston served on the publication committee.

Special thanks are due Dr. Leonard Deaver for his chapter on the Evangelical Church in Iowa, Dr. Louis Haselmayer for his chapter on Schools and Colleges, Mrs. Miriam Baker Nye for her chapter on Women's Contributions, Rev. Robert MacCanon for researching the chapter on the United Brethren in Christ, and Dr. Alferd Wilken for the data in the chapter on the Evangelical United Brethren Church. Thanks is also due Miriam Nye for careful editing and re-typing of the entire manuscript.

Rev. Henry Riegel's translation of old hand-written minutes of the Evangelical Association (Iowa Conference) was helpful. Mrs. Helen Volkman rendered invaluable assistance on numerous visits to our conference archives at Iowa Wesleyan College. Dr. Max Volkman helped with translation of some German passages. Rev. Lyle Johnston's indexing makes the book more useful, and Rev. Harvey Walker's chart provides a graphic concept of the predecessor annual conferences (inside covers).

Appreciation is offered to Staves Memorial United Methodist Church for use of their photo-copy machine in some stages of manuscript preparation.

As this writing task is completed, I realize the influence of my seminary professor, Arthur Wilford Nagler, upon my thinking about church history. In his preface to *The Church in History* Nagler stated: "It is hardly necessary to say that the author has written with the conviction that the history of the church is a part of the one great stream of human life. It has its divine origin, its divine guidance, its divine meaning, yet it is never shut off from the common life in which it moves and of which it is a part. In its thought, its activities, and its institutional forms it has been most intimately influenced by the life about it and in this larger setting it must always be studied."

John A. Nye
Moville, Iowa

1
An Introduction

One could say that The History of the United Methodist Church in Iowa began on that autumn day in 1833 when Barton Randle of the Illinois Conference crossed the Mississippi River to the cluster of cabins that was to become Dubuque, and preached to whoever would listen.[1] In a broader sense, the Methodist Church in Iowa really started in Lincoln College, Oxford, England in 1729. There a group of young men met to study and pray together. The results of that student fellowship have been felt around the world.

The entire story of the growth of the Methodist Societies does not need to be retold here, but a few highlights should be remembered. John and Charles Wesley never left the Church of England, and it was never their desire to start a new denomination. They were not preaching any new doctrine, but were merely asking people to take the old ones seriously. The Methodist Societies in America were not intended to be a new church, and only became one when the Revolutionary War broke the ties with England and made it necessary. That small pious sect grew to become one of the largest "main line" American churches.

John Wesley
Portrait by Williams

Francis Asbury

The next spring (1834) after Barton Randle began his work in the Dubuque area, Barton Cartwright was sent to Flint Hills (now Burlington). He organized a class in the home of Dr. William A. Ross. Other former denominations comprising what is now the United Methodist Church were not far behind. It is the largest Protestant church in Iowa.

A few characteristics of Methodism are not always understood by all of its members. First, one should remember that "Methodism" has no distinctive doctrines. The United Methodist Discipline states that

> The pioneers in the traditions that flowed together in the United Methodist Church—the Wesleys, Albright, Otterbein, Boehm—understood themselves as standing in the center stream of Christian spirituality and doctrine, loyal heirs to all that was best in the Christian past. As John Wesley had claimed, theirs was
>
>> "the old religion, the religion of the Bible, the religion . . . of the whole church in the purest ages."
>
> Their Gospel was rooted in the Biblical message of God's gracious response to man's deep need, in His self-giving love revealed in Jesus Christ. Their interest in dogma as such was minimal; thus they were able to insist on the integrity of Christian truth even while allowing for a decent latitude in its interpretation. This was the point to their familiar dictum, "As to all opinions *which do not strike at the root of Christianity,* we think and let think."[2]

Methodists do emphasize some beliefs, held by some Christians more than others, tending toward social activism.

Secondly, Methodism is a "connectional" church. Every congregation is tied to every other congregation by bonds of common organization, traditions, and program. The individual local church does not call and ordain its own minister, as the Baptists do, although consultation is included in the appointment-making process. A person becomes a minister in the United Methodist Church on recommendation of his/her local congregation. The individual Methodist preacher has almost total job security, because the annual conference assumes the obligation to give each an appointment, while the minister agrees to go where sent.

Because of this organization the United Methodist Church has been able to build hospitals, establish colleges and other institutions, and make its voice heard on American social issues. Churches joined together in a big denomination, with each making its own contribution, can accomplish things that a less-organized denomination cannot.

A third emphasis in Methodism has been the application of faith to personal and public life. The United Methodist Church speaks for public morality, for racial and social justice, and against interests such as the liquor traffic, seen as destructive of the public good.

One of the factors enabling Methodism to spread across America and become one of the most "American" churches was its system or organization into "classes" and "circuits." From the earliest days Methodist preachers came together in "annual conferences" to hear reports, make plans, and receive their appointments for the coming year. The preachers, unofficially known as "circuit riders," went to their circuits to preach and to organize classes. The classes, under the leadership of the lay "class leader," met weekly and carried on the work of the church in the local community between visits of the circuit rider.

These characteristics of Methodism—class meetings and the circuit system—made it possible for the Methodist movement to carry the Gospel to the frontier with the first settlers. The circuit riders, whether they preached in German or in English, arrived with the first settlers. They were literally "at the edge of the edge" of the settlements. Methodist, United Brethren, and Evangelical preachers were among the first to move into Iowa and take their place in building the state.

In many ways the growth of the United Methodist Church has resembled the weaving of a tapestry. Varied threads have gone into the evolving picture. Pietism has been an element of Methodism since the time of the Holy Club at Oxford. Classes always emphasized the devotional life. One of the reasons why some Methodist Protestant and Evangelical United Brethren members resisted joining with larger groups in mergers of 1939 and 1968 was a fear that the church was losing its spiritual fervor. Whether these fears were well founded or not is another story.

For many years the weekly prayer meeting and the annual revival were important ingredients in churches that eventually joined to make the United Methodist Church. While Methodists were meeting to pray for their souls, they were also praying for guidance in Christian living. Methodists in Iowa opposed slavery for years before the Civil War. They led opposition to legalized gambling and liquor traffic.

A United Methodist in Iowa has a deep concern for future generations, in the use of God-given natural resources. It is a serious matter to permit a gully to cut its way across a farm field. It is the duty of a Christian to be a good steward.

Not surprisingly many Methodist young men have been conscientious objectors to war, and more especially to the war in Viet Nam. But as some have taken a stand against war, many others have volunteered for service. Pastors have joined the military chaplaincy to serve as pastors to the men and women in uniform. Methodists have agreed in believing that faith in Christ applies to actions on social questions.

The second group bearing the Methodist name in America was the Methodist Protestant Church, separated from the Methodist Episcopal Church in 1830 by a dispute over the power of the bishops and the lack of lay representation at the Annual Conference. Exact details are not available on when the first Methodist Protestants came to Iowa, but it was in the 1830s. More information is given in another chapter.

The first Methodists in America concentrated their attention on English-speaking settlers, and neglected the German-speaking people in Pennsylvania, Maryland, and Virginia. That neglect allowed the formation of the United Brethren in Christ and the Evangelical Association under the leadership of Philip Otterbein, Martin Boehm, and Jacob Albright. In 1837 John Burns came into Iowa as the state's first minister of the United Brethren in Christ.[3]

Philip Otterbein

Martin Boehm

Jacob Albright

The Evangelical Association, formed under the leadership of Jacob Albright to serve German-speaking people, came to Iowa eight years after the United Brethren in Christ. The story of the growth, division, and re-uniting of the Evangelical Church is told more fully later.

In the early days the Methodist Episcopal Church concentrated its efforts on reaching the English-speaking people, leaving the many German settlers to the United Brethren and the Evangelical Association. However, in later years Methodism broadened its vision, and began to serve other Americans who preferred to worship God in their mother tongue.

Eventually American Methodists were to organize conferences for Spanish, Japanese, German, Swedish, Norwegian, and Native Americans. These various language conferences did not reach all Iowa, but four (including two German) have worked in the state.

In 1864 both the Northwest German and the Southwest German conferences began in Iowa. Almost from the beginning, these conferences did most work in German, but its use diminished as the younger generation no longer learned German. Frequently two Methodist Episcopal churches were located in the same town, one known as the "German" church and the other as the "English" church. In 1924 the St. Louis German Conference was dissolved. A large part of it merged with the Iowa and Des Moines conferences and gave up its separate ethnic identity. Likewise in 1933 the Chicago Northwest Conference was dissolved, with its churches and pastors joining contiguous English-speaking conferences and the German heritage being shared by all.

The Swedish Northwest Conference began its work in Iowa in 1876 and continued until 1942, when it was absorbed into the English-speaking conferences. Its churches no longer have services in the Swedish language, but many Swedish names remain on the membership rolls, and the older members remember the days when they could worship in the language of their parents.

The Norwegian and Danish conference began in Iowa in 1890, and continued until 1940, when separate churches using the Norwegian language were no longer needed.

The United Methodist Church has more black members in the United States than any other predominantly white, Protestant church in America. Iowa has always had black members in predominantly white congregations, and some of them have played prominent roles in the history of their congregations. In addition, four separate black congregations, placed in the Central Jurisdiction at the time of the 1939 merger, are now in the Iowa Conference.

Through the years circuits and conferences have re-drawn their boundaries. Styles of worship and church buildings have changed. In the early days members opposed ornate furnishings and musical instruments in the church. Now Methodists are proud of their beautiful buildings and fine organs.

Barton Randle is said to have exclaimed, forty years after his work in Dubuque,

> Well done! To collect money, build a splendid log meeting house and pay for it, hold a two days' meeting in it, and receive twelve members, all in about four weeks. Who can beat that in Iowa now? We shall see. O, it was the Lord's doing, let Him have the glory. Amen.[4]

The modern Methodists might not consider that log cabin a "splendid" meeting house compared to present-day churches. The early people who were called "shouting Methodists" have descendants who are quite sedate.

Each generation has been confronted by new problems and sought solutions. If H. G. Wells' time machine could bring Barton Randle, Tom Kirkpatrick, and Bennett Mitchell to visit an Iowa church on Sunday morning, or an annual conference session, they would be amazed, maybe shocked.

The United Methodist Church and its antecedent bodies have led in movements for inter-church cooperation and toward church union. In the coming pages, we will trace the development of the United Methodist section of the Church Universal.

Footnotes

1. *1970 Journal, Iowa Annual Conference of the United Methodist Church* (Iowa Annual Conference) p. 356.
2. *The Book of Discipline,* The United Methodist Church 1972 (Nashville, Tennessee: The United Methodist Publishing House, 1972) p. 39.
3. *1970 Journal Iowa Annual Conference of the United Methodist Church* (Iowa Annual Conference) p. 358.
4. Edmund H. Waring, *History of the Iowa Annual Conference of the Methodist Episcopal Church* (n.p. n.d.) p. 18.

Tilt-top table designed to hold John Wesley's Bible when he preached in private homes between 1740 and 1780. Given to Iowa United Methodists by Estella Boot of Iowa City, whose grandmother—Hanna Gale—bought it at a sale in England. Displayed at Iowa UMC Headquarters

—Dick Cook Photo

2
Iowa Beginnings

Few white people lived in Iowa before the first settlement in 1833. Julien Dubuque settled at the spot bearing his name today, but other French Canadian fur traders left almost no traces in the state. On the first day of June, 1833, the Indians' title to Black Hawk Purchase lands expired, and white men did not wait until morning to enter the new land. However, no legal government existed in the new territory, and as late as 1785, Congress still forbade anyone to enter such lands until they were surveyed and offered for sale. The circuit riders' first congregations were made up of squatters on land not included in any organized territory. That was a small matter, which did not bother the early settlers or the preachers.

As a part of the United States, these lands had been attached first to the Territory of Indiana, then to the Territory of Louisiana, later to the Territory of Missouri. After Missouri was admitted into the union in 1821, Iowa land was left without government until 1834. In 1833 Iowa was truly the "Far West." In 1834, Iowa was made part of the Michigan Territory; in 1836, part of the Wisconsin Territory. The Territory of Iowa was established on June 12, 1838.

The Methodist Episcopal Church

To understand the connection between the Missouri Conference of the Methodist Episcopal Church and Iowa Methodism, one must realize that parts of Missouri were settled long before the first white settlers built their cabins in what is now Iowa. Missouri became a territory in 1812, and in 1821, under the Missouri Compromise, entered the Union as a slave state. That was twelve years before white settlers, other than Julien Dubuque, attempted to make their homes in Iowa. The Missouri Conference of the M.E. Church was organized by Bishop McKendree in 1816, including Missouri, Arkansas, Illinois, and western Indiana.

The Illinois Conference was organized eight years later, comprising those parts of the Missouri Conference in Illinois and western Indiana. As a result, the presiding elders in northeast Missouri thought all territory west of the Mississippi was their domain, while Peter Cartwright claimed those parts of Iowa lying across the river from his district in Illinois.

Cartwright sent his cousin, Barton Cartwright, to Flint Hills (now Burlington) to preach and establish classes, and sent Barton Randle to Dubuque. At approximately the same time, the Missourians extended their

Barton Randle

Barton H. Cartwright

circuits into southern Iowa. A member of the Missouri Conference, John H. Ruble, age 24, followed Barton Cartwright to Burlington, but he made his headquarters at Mt. Pleasant. Ruble was married to Miss Diana Bowen in Burlington in February, 1836. He died of influenza April 14, 1836, and is buried in the old cemetery in Mt. Pleasant—the first Methodist Episcopal preacher to be married in Iowa and to die there.

When Ruble was appointed to the Burlington circuit, an indignant Peter Cartwright said that Missouri was poaching in his territory. The first Methodist preachers actually to enter Iowa were from Illinois, but the Missourians were close behind. The General Conference of 1836 placed the Black Hawk Purchase in the Illinois Conference before there could be more argument. The southern part of the purchase was placed in the Quincy District with Peter Cartwright as presiding elder. The northern part was placed in the new Chicago District of the Illinois Conference with John Sinclair as presiding elder.

Dr. William Ross

The early Iowa settlers did not conform to any one pattern, but were molded by many influences. Some were border ruffians, while others were devout Christians setting up their family altars and endeavoring to live a Christian life. Many of the settlers, such as Dr. William Ross of Burlington, were well trained in Methodist class and prayer meetings in their previous homes. They were eager to organize the church in the wilderness.

Among the lead miners coming to Galena, Illinois, were Cornish Methodists from England, looking for work. They brought their Methodism with them, and the Illinois Conference had maintained a mission for them at Galena since 1829. Thus Illinois was ready to reach across the river into Iowa when settlers came.

At the 1833 session of the Illinois Conference Barton Randle and John T. Mitchell were appointed jointly to the Galena and Dubuque Mission, which, for the first time, included territory on both sides of the river. Upon leaving the site of the conference at William Padfield's at Union Grove near Lebanon, Illinois, they traveled to their assignment in the company of their presiding elder, John Sinclair.

Reaching Galena on October 25, 1833, Sinclair preached two Sabbaths and held the first quarterly meeting of the conference year. At this meeting it was agreed that Mitchell should make his headquarters at Galena and Randle was to settle at Dubuque.

This matter arranged, Randle set an appointment for services in the new town. He preached his first sermon in Iowa the evening of November 6, 1833, in the tavern of Jesse M. Harrison, on the site of the present Julien Motor Inn. Mitchell preached there the next day.

Some have claimed these were the first Christian sermons preached in Dubuque, or in the territory. However, the first Protestant preaching in the state was probably by Rev. Aratus Kent, a missionary of the American Missionary Society, who preached as early as August, 1833, at the house of a Mrs. Allen, before the town was laid out. A Catholic priest had also visited, celebrated the Mass, and preached to Catholics in the vicinity.[1]

Controversy exists as to which Iowa church can claim priority, Dubuque or Burlington, and good arguments are offered on each side. Randle, as mentioned, preached his first sermon in Dubuque on November 6, 1833. The first Methodist class at Dubuque was organized by Randle on May 18, 1834, and the first log church building was erected there under his leadership in June, 1834.[2]

The bringing of Methodism to the vicinity of Flint Hills (now Burlington) has been credited to Dr. William R. Ross. He wrote to Peter Cartwright, then presiding elder of the Quincy District, asking that a preacher be sent to the new settlement. On March 23, 1834, Peter Cartwright appointed Barton Cartwright to that place. He promptly left for Flint Hills and reported to the cabin of Dr. Ross.

Dr. Ross says, "Barton Cartwright brought over in March a team of oxen, and broke prairie for me and others during the week, and would preach for us on Sundays, in Burlington and out at Avery's, west of Bur-

Dubuque Log Church Marker

lington."[3] Barton Cartwright wrote of his work saying, "I immediately formed a class of six persons, with Dr. Ross as leader, which I believe to be the first class formed in Iowa."[4]

It appears that Randle preached in Dubuque first, but thanks to Dr. Ross, the first class actually was organized in Burlington. The strength of Methodism was based not only on the zeal of its preachers, but on its organization, which held its converts together and cultivated the Christian life. However, pioneer circuit riders sometimes had more enthusiasm for their preaching than for organization and keeping records.

The boundaries of the early conferences were not clearly defined. Missouri claimed all territory west of the Mississippi River. Accordingly, men were sent from Missouri to supply the early settlers along the Des Moines and Skunk rivers. The first of these preachers was Learner B. Statler whose circuit extended up the Des Moines River to Keosauqua and north to the Skunk River. From there he went down the river to the Flint Hills (now Burlington).

On May 30, 1835, Andrew Monroe, who was known as the "patriarch of Missouri Methodism" held a quarterly meeting at Burlington. At that time he was presiding elder of the St. Louis District, Missouri Conference. It is noted that 18 persons united with the church in Burlington.

Waring's *History of the Iowa Annual Conference of the M.E. Church* tells of another minister around Burlington at an early date. The Rev. J. M. Jamison, a member of the Missouri Conference, stated that he was assigned in September, 1833, to the Palmyra Circuit, Missouri, which extended as far

DUBUQUE, 1834

Subscription List for Dubuque Log Church

FIRST CHURCH IN IOWA

north as Tulley on the Mississippi. In December he extended the circuit to the Des Moines and up that river to a point about fifty miles from its mouth. In the spring of 1834 he crossed the Des Moines and preached in the Half Breed Reservation, now in the state of Iowa.

Jamison thought he preached the first Methodist sermon in Iowa, but he was mistaken. However, if he extended his circuit fifty miles above the mouth of the river in December, 1833, he must have preached in Iowa sometime late that year. In any case, we have no trace of any class organized in Iowa by Jamison.[5]

The Mississippi River was both a highway and a barrier in those days, so Iowa had a unique situation. Settlers were pouring into Iowa and the Methodist preachers worked tirelessly, forming classes as soon as possible after each new settlement was formed. By 1839 the population had increased so that the Illinois Conference was divided. The northern part of Illinois and Iowa became the Rock River Conference. Iowa was further divided into the Iowa District and the Dubuque District.

Settlement continued until by 1844 it seemed expedient to form an Iowa Conference of the Methodist Episcopal Church. The first conference session was held in a little brick church in Iowa City under the leadership of Bishop Thomas A. Morris.

Bishop Morris

Bishop Morris opened the first session by reading the fifth chapter of First Peter with its admonition to the workers. Next he read the list of the charter members, and proceeded with the business. The first statistical report counted 5,431 white members, 12 colored, and 61 local preachers. The preaching in those days was not all done by ordained conference members. The local preachers played a very important part in building the pioneer church. They earned their living by other occupations, and preached nearby on Sundays. This made it possible to have regular preaching services while the circuit rider was elsewhere.

The early Methodist congregations met regularly in various places. As an example, the Methodist congregation in Keosauqua, organized in

November, 1836, met first in the Purdom cabin near the river, just above the present town. The church continued to meet there for about eleven years, during which Keosauqua was incorporated and Iowa became a state.

From the Purdom cabin the class moved into town and used a large upstairs room of the new stone and brick Pearson house. In 1984 the house is still standing. After about a year the preaching services were held in the courthouse, class and prayer meetings in the homes of members. When a church building was started, the construction went slowly and was not completed until 1850.

Many pioneer congregations met in homes and in country schoolhouses for some time, until a church building was erected. As communities changed, some neighborhoods never constructed a church building.

Church buildings were often used for secular purposes. For example, the first four sessions of the legislature of the Territory of Iowa met in Old Zion Church in Burlington. This spot on the west side of Third Street between Columbia and Washington is now a parking lot. The original log church at Dubuque, located where the Julien Motor Inn now stands, was used as a schoolhouse during the week.

Old Zion

SKETCHED BY DONOVAN E. TEMPLE FROM A PHOTOGRAPH.

Interesting as historic buildings were and are, profiles of "the Lord's horsemen" are more revealing. In his *Makers of Iowa Methodism* Aaron Haines describes Henry Summers, the pioneer presiding elder who oversaw the work of Barton Randle in Iowa. He quotes an unnamed writer who remembered Summers as a man "of medium height, strong and sinewy frame; in appearance, prepossessing; in disposition, social; in intellectual ability, above the average. His emotions were easily kindled, and his preaching abounded with unction. Over one hundred conversions have been known to follow his preaching at a single quarterly meeting."[6]

Brother Summers was undoubtedly an effective preacher in his day, with the congregations to whom he preached, but this writer wonders what became of all those converts. The church was growing with amazing speed in those days, but one can only wonder at a hundred conversions at one frontier quarterly conference!

At the Conference of 1848 Landon Taylor was reassigned to the Dubuque Circuit for a second year. Many years later he wrote, "And now came a new experience. I found it much easier to get the people converted than it was to have them 'stay converted,' and thus I labored hard to maintain the ground that I had gained. But the Lord was with us, and gave us during the second a very pleasant year."[7]

It is not easy to describe in detail the progress of Methodism in a fast-growing community. The situation was continually changing due to the shifting population, and not all preachers were careful about keeping records. Many records of individual churches have been lost when local officials failed to recognize their importance. On the whole, the story was one of continuous growth even though the arrangement of the circuits was an ever-changing picture.

Methodism is ubiquitous in Iowa because the circuit riders followed settlers everywhere, to preach the gospel and organize classes. The Methodist system of circuits insured that each local society would be served by a preacher and a long break between pastors would be avoided. In pioneer days the lay class leader fulfilled many of the pastoral functions now the responsibility of the minister. The circuit-riding Methodist preacher was an administrator and evangelist.

Under the conditions of isolation and loneliness of pioneer times, the quarterly conference, meeting four times a year, was of great interest to everyone. These meetings were held in schoolhouses and private cabins. S. N. Fellows says that "usually the class leaders, stewards, trustees, and local preachers with their families, not having seen each other for three months, came from the remote parts of the circuit to attend the meeting, which was of social interest and of spiritual life and fire unknown today."[8]

The presiding elder usually commenced the services with a sermon at two o'clock Saturday afternoon. As most of those present were the official members and their families, the sermon would be adapted to their needs. Following the sermon came the business of the quarterly conference. On Saturday evening, the circuit preacher would preach.

Sunday was the big day when many came from far and near. It began with a Love Feast at nine o'clock in the morning, with testimonials, confessions, thanksgiving, and praise. This was followed by the "big" sermon by the presiding elder, and by the holy sacrament. The Sunday evening service was a time for victory and gathering of souls. One author has written a description:

A sermon to the unsaved was usually preached, followed by an exhortation and an appeal to sinners to yield and be saved. The terrors of the laws, the glories of heaven, the horrors of hell, the future judgment, the infinite love of

God, the dying love of Jesus on Calvary, were portrayed in tender and sometimes in terrible imagery, and many were gloriously saved.[9]

The population of Iowa grew swiftly during the first twenty-five years. The 1840 census showed 43,000; 1850, 192,000; and 1860, 675,000. It soon became expedient to divide the conferences. In 1853, the United Brethren in Christ divided into two conferences: the Iowa and the Des Moines. In 1856 the Methodist Episcopal Church divided into the Iowa and the Upper Iowa Conferences. In 1858 the Methodist Protestant Church divided into a North Iowa and an Iowa Conference.

The Methodist Protestant Church

The exact date when the Methodist Protestant Church first came into Iowa is unknown. The Methodist Protestant split coincided with the time of migration into Iowa. It had resulted from conflict over issues which seemed more important back East than on the frontier. When a new Methodist circuit rider arrived, no one asked whether he was M.E. or M.P. Rather he was accepted or rejected as a Methodist preacher. With much of the work in both churches being done by laymen, they neither knew nor cared much about the differences.

The first known Methodist Protestant preacher in Iowa was Oliver Atwood, who was active in Muscatine County. As a licensed exhorter in the Illinois Annual Conference, he was left without appointment in 1837. That summer he began farming in Iowa and holding preaching services in his home. In September Atwood's career ended when he was killed by Sauk Indians in reprisal for the murder, by a frontier ruffian, of a brother of Chief Poweshiek.

Methodist work in that vicinity died temporarily. It is ironic that the man killed would have been the Indians' friend, while the ruffian would have scorned the preacher almost as much as he did the Indian.

As far as can be determined, the first organized Class of the M.P. Church was formed in English River Township of Iowa County in 1841 by William Patterson, perhaps the outstanding early leader of the denomination in the state. Records indicate the first Class Meeting was held May third. Because of the sparse population, however, this first class was absorbed by the M.E. Church in the winter of 1842-43.

Iowa City was the site of the most ambitious project of early days. Although the Methodist Protestant Church never became large in Iowa, its influence has been considerable among many southeast Iowa Methodist laymen who were never inside an M.P. Church. They may have been scarcely aware of its existence, but its effect has been like the yeast in the loaf, leavening the whole. The United Methodist Church bears the marks of the M.P. Church, and its heritage has been maintained.

The United Brethren in Christ

The United Brethren in Christ followed the frontier westward as did the other branches of what is now The United Methodist Church. The United

Brethren, like the Evangelical Association, began to serve the German-speaking people in Maryland and Pennsylvania. But as time went by, and a younger generation came along, the German language yielded to English. By the time the church entered Iowa most German services had been dropped though the German background was not forgotten.

This group traces its beginning to a Class organized near Burlington in 1835 by Barton G. Cartwright, the same Methodist who preached the first Methodist sermon in Flint Hills (now Burlington), mentioned earlier. A Methodist preacher organized the class, but it later affiliated with the United Brethren. The differences may not have seemed important, or perhaps something appealing in the United Brethren fellowship attracted those people.

In 1837 John Burns came to Iowa in search of a mission field, as the first minister of the U. B. denomination. The same year, Christian Troup of the Wabash Conference came to Iowa, becoming a prominent minister and presiding elder. In 1841, Ira B. Ryan, a layman and later a minister, formed the first Class, meeting in the home of Father Edgington.

In 1842 F. R. S. Byrd formed a Class in Henry County. The first Quarterly Conference was held at Yankee Grove (Lisbon) in Linn County. On August 14, 1845, the Iowa Conference of the United Brethren in Christ was organized, with Bishop John Russell presiding at the home of William Thompson in Louisa County.

Bishop John Russell

The Evangelical Association

The Evangelical Association made its entry into Iowa from Illinois, as had the Methodist Episcopal and Methodist Protestant Churches. John Hoffert, a missionary, was first to push westward, but poor health limited his ability to accomplish much.

In 1843 J. G. Miller began preaching in the neighboring Iowa Territory while serving the Rock River Circuit of the Ohio Conference, which included Illinois at the time. He was in a two-man circuit, enabling him to make several trips into Iowa. Since it cost fifty cents to cross the Mississippi by ferry, he was sometimes pressed for funds. On one occasion he had to sell his personal copy of *Thomas-a' Kempis* for passage. Upon his return to Illinois a fellow traveler, who had heard him preach in Iowa, gave him his fare to cross the river.[10] Also in 1843, Charles G. Koch, later editor of *Der Christliche Botschafter,* preached in Bloomington (now Muscatine), and traveled as far northwest as Linn County.

When the Illinois Conference, which included Illinois, Wisconsin, and Iowa was organized, Iowa was connected to the Galena Mission in Illinois—the same pattern followed by the Methodist Episcopals about ten years earlier. The Galena Mission at that time included fourteen preaching places in three states.

J. G. Miller was stationed on this circuit, and by November, 1844, he reported finding German hospitality in Dubuque and in Sherrill's Mound, a settlement about ten miles further north. He indicated four preaching services at Sherrill's Mound, reading the Disciplinary rules, and organizing a Society with seventeen charter members. Miller said this was the first Society west of the Mississippi and "the furtherest frontier of Germans within Indian territory."[11]

In 1845, Matthias Hauert was sent to the newly organized Class, which had become a mission. Despite poor health which forced his early return, he did much to build up the tiny Society and organize new classes.

In one way Hauert's story is typical of frontier preachers of all denominations. Life was hard and many, unable to endure the hardships, had to leave the traveling ministry after a short time. The famous Peter Cartwright of the Methodist Episcopal Church spent more than fifty years on the Illinois frontier, but he was not typical. Few had his physical stamina.

Jacob J. Esher followed Hauert and served the pastoral limit two years. During Esher's first summer Bishop John Seybert crossed the Mississippi to make the first episcopal visit to Iowa.

Early German settlers coming from Pennsylvania, Ohio, and Illinois usually established themselves in colonies, much as they had in other states. One such group came from Dauphin County in Pennsylvania and settled near Grandview in Louisa County in 1852. They organized a class of twenty-two members with George Gipple elected Class Leader and Joseph Martin, Exhorter. The Class erected the first Evangelical Church building in Iowa, dedicated on November 27, 1857. The second building was erected at Independence in 1858, the third at Greencastle in 1859.

By 1854, growth encouraged separation into two parts. The area around Dubuque was named "the Dubuque Mission" and the rest of the area was called "the Cedar River Circuit." Prior to 1856 these circuits belonged to the Peoria District but were attached to the Freeport District when it was organized.[13]

Iowa had three centers of operation in 1856, but the pioneer preacher was never satisfied with a single preaching place. Each center probably included at least a half-dozen school houses or homes as preaching places. "New preaching places'' and ''extend the borders'' were common phrases in those days.[14]

The mission work in Iowa became a separate district in 1857. William Kolb was elected the first presiding elder in Iowa. With the annual appointments, two young men—J. W. Mohr and Rudolph Dubs—were assigned as junior preachers at Cedar River and Dubuque. The only railroad in the state ended at Iowa City, making horse-and-buggy the usual mode of travel. Roads were bad; bridges were few; and many streams had to be forded. Because of his aggressive program of soul-winning and good administration despite these conditions, Dubs was later elected to the episcopacy.

During the twelfth session of the General Conference meeting at Naperville, Illinois on October 5, 1859, the Iowa Conference was authorized. This new conference comprised the Iowa District of the Illinois Conference, the Minnesota District of the Wisconsin Conference, and the mission fields of Kansas, Nebraska, and Missouri.

Bishop W. W. Orwig

The first session of the new conference was held May 29, 1861 at Grandview, with Bishop W. W. Orwig presiding over 32 preachers. They elected S. Dickover presiding elder of the Iowa District, composed of churches in Iowa and Minnesota. Levi Eberhardt was elected presiding elder of the Kansas District, including Fort Des Moines and Greencastle in Iowa, and the Nebraska and Kansas Missions. Because of illness, Eberhardt resigned the office and M. J. Miller was elected to take his place. The Iowa Conference of the Evanglelical Association was on its way.

Footnotes

1. Waring, Edmund H., *History of the Iowa Annual Conference of the Methodist Episcopal Church* (Iowa Conference published 1910) p. 15.
2. Ibid., p. 20.
3. Ibid., p. 25.
4. Ibid., p. 25.

5. Ibid., p. 26.
6. Haines, Aaron W., *The Makers of Iowa Methodism* (Cincinnati: Jennings & Pye, 1900) p. 25.
7. Taylor, Landon, *The Battlefield Reviewed* (Chicago: McCabe, 1881) p. 92.
8. Fellows, Stephen Norris, *History of the Upper Iowa Conference* (Cedar Rapids: Laurance Press, 1907) p. 23.
9. Ibid., p. 24.
10. Deaver, Leonard E., "The Evangelical Church in Iowa", *Proceedings. . . . The Historical Society, North Central Jurisdiction United Methodist Church, 1975,* p. 85.
11. Ibid., p. 85.
12. Ibid., pp. 86-87.
13. Ibid., p. 87.
14. Ibid., p. 87.

3

The Methodist Episcopal Church in South Iowa

The differences between northern Iowa and southern Iowa must not be exaggerated, but they are real, and have influenced Iowa Methodist history. They provide a reason for dividing the story of the Methodist Episcopal Church into separate chapters.

With the conference session of 1856, a new beginning is marked in the Methodist Episcopal Church in Iowa. Or rather, it could be called the "end of the beginning." The M.E. Church had been active in Iowa for 23 years, growing with the population, organizing congregations in each new community formed, and spreading westward across the state. By 1855, it became apparent that the conference should be divided, forming two. In that year a Committee on Conference Division reported:

> The committee on conference boundary, having consulted thereon, report the following lines of division, vis:
> Beginning at Davenport on the Mississippi River, thence by railroad to Iowa City, thence up the Iowa River to the corner of Iowa, Benton, Tama, and Poweshiek Counties, thence west to the Missouri River, leaving Davenport and Iowa City in the Northern Conference.
> David Dickinson, Sec'y   H. W. Reed, Chairman[1]

The recommended changes were approved by the 1856 General Conference, and Iowa was divided into the Iowa Conference and the Upper Iowa Conference. In spite of the changes taking place during the following hundred years, North and South Iowa remained separate until 1969. Following union with the Evangelical United Brethren Church, they were reunited into a new Iowa Conference.

A study of the development of Methodism in Iowa is therefore divided into two parts, North Iowa and South Iowa. Many differences have been noted between the two sections of the state. One might consider first the styles of agriculture caused by the differing topography and soil types. Twenty thousand years ago approximately the northern half of the state was covered by the Nebraskan glacier. It leveled the landscape and left the till, providing the basis for the rich, black soil which has enabled Iowa farmers to produce bumper crops of corn and soybeans.

The southern part of the state is hillier, better suited to different farming methods. A study of a soil map of the state provides insight. Most rivers and smaller streams flow from north to south or southeast, making more bridges necessary. This made it more difficult and expensive to build roads in the southern part of the state.

The earlier settlers of South Iowa formed smaller communities geographically than those in North Iowa, resulting in more small churches. In one locality of Van Buren County, the pioneers built two churches within sight of each other, on locations inaccessible to each other during many weeks of the year. Douds had a church on the north side of the Des Moines River and Leando had its church on the south side. The two rival communities were separated by the river until a steel bridge was built in 1897. After that, merging the two congregations was a slow process. Each congregation had developed its own traditions and loyalties. Following the floods of June, 1947, and later that year a fire, which destroyed the building in Douds, the congregations were united.

In the mid-nineteenth century, settlers poured into Iowa from the east. There were two mainstreams of migration. The southern stream came down the Ohio River from Virginia and Kentucky to St. Louis, then up the Mississippi to Keokuk to enter the state. Rapids on the Mississippi between Keokuk and Ft. Madison interfered with traffic going further up the river. As a result, main migration routes into the state were up the Des Moines River and along a wagon road between the Des Moines and Skunk River basin from Keokuk to Des Moines. Many of these settlers came from families who had been in America for two or more generations.

The second mainstream was from New England and New York, through the Great Lakes, and across from Lake Michigan to northern Iowa. Many of these settlers came directly to Iowa from Europe, bringing different viewpoints and slightly different dialects. Because of the topography, developing towns were farther apart and larger. Except in Northeast Iowa, there were few very small churches.

As railroads and better highways were built, they ran east and west, rather than north and south. A railroad had been built from Davenport to Iowa City by 1856. The Chicago, Burlington, and Quincy Railroad started building their lines westward from Burlington in 1855. They reached Ottumwa by 1859.

After the Civil War, the railway network was extended westward with feverish speed. The need to reach California and the West Coast by rail served as a pretext for congressional aid for building railroads. An act of Congress, May 15, 1859, to encourage building, made a gift of alternate sections of land six miles on each side of the right of way, for each prospective road. In January, 1867, the railroad which was later to be known as the Northwestern reached Council Bluffs from Clinton.

The Mississippi & Missouri Railroad, later known as the Chicago and Rock Island, reached Council Bluffs from Davenport in 1869. Also in 1869 the Chicago, Burlington, and Quincy Line reached the Missouri at a point opposite Plattsmouth. In 1870, it ran a spur north to Council Bluffs, thus crossing the state from Burlington. Other roads were built across the state by 1870, making it easier to cross the state from east to west than the much shorter distance north and south.

Communication ties divided Iowa until the day when the automobile and telephone became common and one could travel easily in all directions. Even then, the first paved roads across the state were constructed from Illinois to Nebraska rather than from Missouri to Minnesota.

For many years the two sections of the church followed parallel and cooperating paths. They sent fraternal delegates to each other's conference sessions. There were similarities in the resolutions passed regarding social issues, indicating regular communication. Individual ministers often transferred from one conference to another. An Iowa Methodist State Convention was held in Iowa City July 11-13, 1871.

Consider first the growth of the M.E. Church in South Iowa. As mentioned earlier, Iowa was originally a part of the Illinois Conference. Preachers were assigned appointments across the Mississippi River in Iowa for ten years before the Iowa Conference was formed in 1844.

In 1839 Bishop Morris formed the Iowa circuits into a new Iowa District. Henry Summers was presiding elder, with nine pastoral appointments, in a district without bridges and almost without roads. It extended from the Turkey River on the north to the Missouri line on the south, and from the Mississippi River on the east to the last settler's cabin on the west. One can read of this work in detail in Edmund Waring's *History of the Iowa Conference of the Methodist Episcopal Church.*[2] Waring lists the names of the preachers assigned to this district and names of many of the preaching places. As one reads the story, it is easy to understand why many preachers were physically and economically unable to stay with the work.

In spite of the difficulties on the frontiers, as population increased, the M.E. Church grew. In 1840 the Illinois Conference was divided and the Iowa Territory was made part of the Rock River Conference. At the 1840 session of the Rock River Conference, the Iowa District was divided into the Dubuque and Burlington Districts, with Bartholomew Weed as presiding elder of the Dubuque District and Henry Summers as presiding elder of the Burlington District. The territory included in the Dubuque District fell into the area of the Upper Iowa Conference in 1856.

The Burlington District was divided in 1843, and the Des Moines District was formed. In 1844 the Iowa Conference was formed with three districts. H. W. Reed was presiding elder of the Dubuque District, B. Weed of the Burlington District, and Milton Jamison of the Des Moines District. It is interesting to note that even though four of the nine appointments were along the Des Moines River, none of them were in the territory of the present (1984) Des Moines District.

One of the well-known men of the early days was G. W. Teas, better remembered for an amusing aberration in his early career than for the many later years of faithful service. Teas entered the ministry and served in Arkansas and Missouri before coming to Iowa. He turned to the law and opened an office in Burlington. When Iowa was taken into the Michigan

Territory, he was a candidate for election to the Territorial Council, but lost. Blaming his Methodist friends for his defeat, he withdrew from the church, placing a notice on his office door which read,

Let all men know from shore to shore,
That G. W. Teas is a Methodist no more.

Not long afterward, at a revival, Teas reconsidered and rejoined the church. At this point someone wrote:

Let all men know from California to Maine,
That G. W. Teas is a Methodist again.

In 1849 he was re-admitted and served very acceptably as an itinerant preacher in the Iowa Conference.[3]

The primary goal of the conference was evangelism. S. N. Fellows, in his *History of the Upper Iowa Conference,* states:

The aim of the Conference was to carry the gospel to every newly formed frontier settlement, however remote, and thus to establish Methodism in the forefront of advancing civilization. For this purpose they crossed vast intervening prairies without a road, a tree, or an inhabitant.[4]

The preachers were not assigned to a single location; rather they were sent to a circuit which might cover several counties. James F. Hestwood writes:

In 1854 I was received on trial in the Iowa Conference and sent to Millersburg, which took part of Johnson, Iowa, Keokuk, and Washington Counties. With the help of a few friends, I built a log cabin in which to live.[5]

The camp meeting was a colorful part of the religious life on the frontier. People were lonely, and most work was drudgery. Neighbors saw each other only on special occasions. The camp meeting was one occasion when people could travel, sometimes many miles, to renew old acquaintances and make new ones. They brought camping equipment and provisions, prepared to stay eight or ten days. Camp meeting preaching services were held morning, afternoon, and evening. Religious emotion was high, with sudden and spectacular conversions common.

Camp meetings came in for considerable criticism, and not all came to praise the Lord. Rowdies sometimes tried to break up camp meetings. In 1832 while Peter Cartwright was presiding elder of the Sangamon District, a group attempted to break up a meeting with various disturbances, including violence. Before the meetings were over, an uneducated preacher who knew his people succeeded in reaching them by a sermon. He closed by saying, ''I have faith to believe that God will convert every one of you that will come and kneel at the place of prayer.'' Cartwright reported:

There was a general rush for the altar, and many of our persecutors, and those who had interrupted and disturbed us in the forepart of the meeting, came and fell on their knees, and cried aloud for mercy; and it is certainly beyond my power to describe the scene; but more than fifty souls were converted to God that day and night. Our meeting continued for several days and about ninety professed to obtain the pardon of their sins, most of whom joined the Church, and great good was accomplished, although we waded through tribulation to accomplish it.[6]

When people came together for a religious "revival," it sometimes became an occasion for extremes of emotional display. The excesses often evoked ridicule. In the words of Peter Cartwright,

Just in the midst of our controversies on the subject of the powerful exercises among the people under preaching, a new exercise broke out among us, called the "jerks," which was overwhelming in its effects upon the bodies and minds of the people. No matter whether they were saints or sinners, they would be taken under a warm song or sermon, and seized with a convulsive jerking all over, which they could not by any possibility avoid, and the more they resisted the more they jerked. If they would not strive against it and pray in good earnest, the jerking would usually abate. I have seen more than five hundred persons jerking at one time in my large congregations. Most usually persons taken with the jerks, to obtain relief, as they said, would rise up and dance. Some would run, but could not get away. Some would resist; on such the jerks were generally very severe.[7]

People attended camp meetings for many reasons, but when they got there, they heard the gospel message preached, and many were converted.

During the nineteenth century the camp meetings were an important source for new converts, and the spiritual level of the Methodist people was raised. The whole community felt the impact, and the moral tone of society was greatly elevated. After the end of the nineteenth century the camp meetings lost their influence. Those held were changed, with little resemblance to the earlier ones.

As settlers continued to move into the state, the center of population moved westward. On January 3, 1839, Governor Robert Lucas proposed to the Territorial Assembly that three commissioners be selected to choose a site in Johnson County for a new Territorial Capitol. In December, 1841, the territorial government moved to a clearing along the Iowa River, even though the new stone capitol building (now known as "the Old Capitol") was not yet finished.

With the Territorial Capital being established in Iowa City, Bishop Morris wanted Methodism to establish a firm base there. In 1841 the Rev. G. B. Bowman was transferred from the Missouri Conference and assigned to the Iowa City mission. The bishop hoped he could gather a strong congregation and build a good brick church near the capitol. The church was built, and in 1844 the first session of the Iowa Conference was held in it. At that session Iowa City reported 324 members.

By 1844, when the Iowa Conference was organized, Methodism was firmly established in Iowa life. Old Zion had been used as a territorial capitol building in Burlington and a good brick church had been built in Iowa City. The circuit riders had been everywhere, and Methodist Classes were meeting in most communities.

At the same time that the Iowa Conference was formed, Iowa Wesleyan College came into being. A series of efforts had been made to organize a school in Mt. Pleasant. On February 17, 1842, the territorial legislature approved a bill authorizing the formation of a "Literary Institute" in Mt. Pleasant. On March 8, 1843, ten of the sixteen incorporators met with ten other citizens of Mt. Pleasant and made plans. The Mt. Pleasant Collegiate Institute was incorporated on February 15, 1844. The name was changed to Iowa Wesleyan University in 1855, and to Iowa Wesleyan College in 1912. The history of the college parallels that of the Iowa Conference.

Questions which arose among Methodists during the latter half of the nineteenth century may seem strange to modern United Methodists, but they illustrate the seriousness with which issues were faced. Use of musical instruments and membership in secret societies were such issues.

Fine clothes, jewelry, and musical instruments were looked upon as signs of worldliness, which could lead people from God. The early circuit rider could not carry an organ with him, and was inclined to be suspicious of such innovations when they became possible.

During the pastorate of O. C. Shelton at Agency in 1854, the first church building, a 24 x 36 structure, was erected. Not long afterward a controversy arose over the installation of a small reed organ. One group was very much opposed to the idea. They were sure that the devil would be let loose. Others prevailed, and the "wooden music" instrument was installed.

Michael See, who served in the conference from 1845 to 1885, had a circuit near Iowa City, with only one church building. See came to the church after an absence and was horrified to find a small reed organ in the sanctuary.

He promptly rolled it out to the wood shed and chopped it up with an ax. When people came to the church that evening, the service was opened by the "lining out" of the hymns[8] as usual. Nothing was said about the organ. The one who had installed the organ must have had a guilty conscience, but a modern pastor wonders what was said among the people after the forceful circuit rider was gone.

Opposition to musical instruments continued as late as 1900 where conflict surfaced in local congregations when an organ was proposed. Some members left the M.E. Church to join other denominations which were "less worldly." However, some of those who left now have great-grandchildren singing in United Methodist choirs, accompanied by electronic organs.

One would not expect a secret society, such as the Masonic Lodge or the Odd Fellows, to have a place in Methodist history, although lodges have been in Iowa since the beginning. Opposition to Masonry was an issue in the early days. The Anti-Masonic movement influenced American life the first part of the nineteenth century, including an Anti-Masonic political party in American elections from 1827 to 1836. In 1831, a national convention was held, nominating a candidate for president.

Some Dubuque lead miners who were Methodists were said to be members of a Masonic lodge at Galena, Illinois. Territorial Governor Lucas, a Methodist, was one of the organizers of the first lodge formed at Burlington. The Grand Lodge of Iowa was organized the same year as the Iowa Conference.

Anti-Masonry had declined as a political movement by the time the Iowa Conference of the M.E. Church was formed, but differences of opinion regarding Masonry still existed. In 1845, at the second session of the Iowa Conference a resolution was passed stating:

> Resolved: That it is the opinion of this Conference that it is inexpedient for our ministers to connect themselves with Masonic Lodges and similar institutions and that we respectfully request those members of this Conference who are now connected with Masonry to discontinue their attendance on the lodges.[9]

The Anti-Masonic resolution approved in 1845 did not settle the matter, for it was discussed again in 1846, 1848, 1849, and 1850. Finally, in 1850, a resolution passed unanimously, rescinding all previous resolutions, and stating "that we will bury our mutual differences on these questions in forgetfulness, and by mutual forbearance show the ungodly world how Christians of different opinions agree in brotherly kindness, and in loving one another."[10]

The period between 1844 and 1856 was a time of rapid growth for the church. The statistical report of the first session of the Iowa Conference reported 5,431 white and 12 colored members, and 61 local preachers. The last session of the conference before the division in 1855 showed 19,363 members and 298 local preachers, an increase of nearly four times. After division in 1856, the southern conference still reported 15,889 and 209 local preachers, a number much greater than when the Iowa Conference was first formed.

In the early years, the passing of the character of the preachers was not a mere formality; any preacher could, and sometimes did, bring charges against a brother. The requirement that each man be of blameless character was not taken lightly, but great care was taken to assure the accused a fair hearing. The first preacher expelled from the Iowa Conference (1848) was charged with gross immorality. At the same session a question was raised regarding two men who had joined secret societies, disregarding the resolution of 1845. Both men were passed, which indicated that the Anti-Masonic movement was losing.

The Iowa Conference 1856-1932

THE END OF THE BEGINNING 1856-1900

The sessions of the Iowa Conference have been numbered from the 1844 session held in Iowa City. The 1856 session of the Upper Iowa Conference was the first of that conference, while the 1856 session of the southern section of the divided conference, which kept the name "Iowa Conference," was called the 13th. Thus the 1984 session of the Iowa Conference of the

United Methodist Church was numbered the 141st. From 1856 to 1860 the history of the Iowa Conference includes only the southern half of the state. From 1860 to 1932, the story of the Iowa Conference is that of Methodism in Southeastern Iowa.

In 1856 the Iowa Conference was divided into nine districts, and 82 pastoral charges. With their presiding elders the districts were:

Keokuk District, M. Miller
Burlington District, J. H. Power
Muscatine District, E. W. Twining
Mt. Pleasant District, J. McDowell
Albia District, J. Q. Hammond
Oskaloosa District, E. Simpson
Ft. Des Moines District, J. B. Hardy
Chariton District, P. F. Ingalls
Council Bluffs District, M. Guyles[11]

By 1856 the Methodist Episcopal Church was firmly established in Iowa. The Iowa Conference had been founded and had grown to the point that it needed to be divided into two, Iowa and Upper Iowa. Four years later the (new) Iowa Conference was divided. At that time the western part of the conference was set apart to form the Western Iowa Conference.

In 1857 the Swede mission in Iowa was attached to the Peoria Conference for better control of the work. The Swedish M.E. Churches played a part in Iowa Methodism until the Central-Northwest Conference (Swede) was dissolved in 1942 and its churches and ministers absorbed into the contiguous English-speaking conferences.

E. H. Waring notes in his *History of the Iowa Conference* that the decade of the 50s was a time of "wonderful development" in the conference. During that time one hundred sixty-eight preachers were received on trial, fifty came in by transfer, twenty-two were readmitted, and eighty-one were received into full connection. Twenty-six were dismissed by location; twenty-four by transfer; sixty-one by division of the conference; seven by death. The net gain was one hundred twenty-two.[12]

An example of Methodist development in a pioneer situation is Brooklyn, in Poweshiek County. Brooklyn was plotted as a town in 1855. In 1846 the Iowa Conference organized a mission, called the Bear Creek Mission, which was designed to cover the country stretching west from Iowa City.

One of the appointments of the mission was at Talbott's Grove, near the present site of Brooklyn. In 1862 the circuit had twelve appointments, which extended from near Iowa City to a point ten miles northwest of Brooklyn, and south to Williamsburg. In 1864 the lower part was removed, and Brooklyn became the head of a new circuit. About 1866 Brooklyn was made a station church with one hundred ninety-five members. In 1909 it had three hundred fifty-three.[13] In 1981 Brooklyn reported 433 members.

The period between 1860 and 1869 was stressful for the church, as for the nation. The western part of the conference was separated to form the new Western Iowa Conference in 1860. This took away thirty-six ministerial members of the conference and six probationers, leaving the old conference eighty-seven members and seventeen probationers.

The 1860 session of the conference met under the stress of the presidential campaign in which Lincoln was elected. Before the next session, the country was divided by the Civil War, which left its mark on American history.

When the Iowa Conference met in Burlington in 1861, it declared that the war was waged by southern states for the destruction of civil and religious liberty and the perpetuation of human slavery. The conference resolved that "the present government of the United States should be sustained by every citizen, at any expense of men or money, in prosecuting the war to a favorable issue."[14]

The war caused a financial depression affecting church life. In 1861 the stewards reported a total deficiency of $10,208.59 in preachers' support. The book agent reported about 40% had been paid on his bills. Collections received for the conference claimants produced only 15½% of the amount needed.

Many Methodists were among the thousands who marched away to war. The life of every community was disrupted. A decrease in total membership of 2,361 was noted. Total receipts for ministerial support were only 74% of the claims. Many of the best workers among the laity were in the army, leaving those at home weakened and discouraged.[15]

Ever since 1860 a boundary dispute had troubled the Iowa Conference and the Western Iowa Conference. The Western Iowa Conference objected to the border line drawn along the Des Moines River from the Red Rocks northwest to the northern edge of the conference. They claimed that it should have gone on straight north, leaving Des Moines in the western conference.

The 1864 General Conference corrected the north-south line separating the conferences, continuing it north to the Minnesota border, and putting the whole western half of the state into a new Des Moines Conference. The same General Conference also established both the Southwest German Conference and the Northwest German Conference, taking the two German Districts from Upper Iowa and placing them in the new German Conference.

In 1865, with the war ended, the conference was ready to go forward. In compliance with the action of the General Conference, a Conference Centenary Society was formed to observe properly the centenary of American Methodism in 1866. A part of the plan was to call for a thank-offering from the churches, to help support the educational and benevolent work of the church.[16] The statistical reports show a total of $40,358.69 raised in two years. The conference also adopted a report endorsing lay representation to General Conference.

The General Methodist Extension Society was formed in 1865 to help weak societies secure places of worship for themselves. Population in Iowa was growing rapidly, and congregations were formed to meet growth needs of new members. However, some divisions occurred which seem hard to justify after an interval of one hundred years.

In Oskaloosa some agitation was present from 1856 on, but division did not happen until 1868. Two churches operated under the names of First Church and Simpson Chapel, until they reunited in 1894. The Fairfield Church was also divided, into two churches known as Church Street and Harmony. In 1876 the two were reunited.[17]

During and after the war a number of black people came north and settled in Oskaloosa. At first they worshiped with the other Methodists, but in 1868 secured a frame church building for themselves under the name of Wesley Chapel. The 1870 JOURNAL lists forty-seven full members and one probationary member. Eleven black people who came up the Mississippi River joined Ebenezer M.E. Church in Burlington February 25, 1866. They remained active in the church until they decided that they could do better in the A.M.E. Church, and transferred their membership.

Lay representation at conference had long been a point of controversy among Methodists. This was an important issue in the conflict leading to the formation of the Methodist Protestant Church in 1835. The M.E. Church took a significant step in 1871, which helped prepare for the eventual reunion with the M.P. Church seventy years later. In that year a lay electoral conference assembled for the first time. Dr. I. A. Hammer and the Hon. James Harlan were elected as lay delegates from the Iowa Conference.

The conference in Iowa undertook an ambitious project in 1871, holding an "Iowa Methodist State Convention" in Iowa City July 11-13. It was not a legislative body with power to act, but rather an inspirational meeting of both lay and ministerial church leaders.

Papers were presented with histories of the three conferences in the state and of the German work in Iowa. Those present took a look at the various educational institutions in Iowa, and shared dreams of future progress. No record can be found of the number of ministers attending, but 70 laymen represented all of the conferences and the German effort in the state.

The 1877 Annual Conference approved a resolution forbidding preachers to vote for political candidates who opposed prohibition of the sale and manufacture of ardent spirits, including wine and beer. The conference apparently believed the correct stand on this one issue outweighed any other qualifications for office.

To most ministers and congregations the decade of 1880-90 seemed a stable period, during which lay membership increased by 3,052, with a net gain of 23 ministers. One historian who was there refers to the conference of 1882 as one that was "taken up with little else than the ordinary business, and was a pleasant and profitable one."[18]

However, developments which were to have long-range effects were taking place. In 1883 the Conference Auxiliary to the Women's Home Missionary Society was organized. In 1889 a Conference Board of Deaconesses was established. Roads and railroads had been built in Iowa. Many communities in Southeast Iowa had reached their greatest population. Some farmers used four-horse teams pulling two-bottom plows, and farms grew larger. Van Buren County reached its peak population in the census of 1890. It became possible for most young people to obtain a high school education.

All of these trends had influence on the Methodist Episcopal Church. In the earlier days the Methodist preacher was primarily an evangelist. During the 1890s the annual revival meeting was still an important event in every community, but the preacher was also becoming a pastor. It was still customary for preachers to move every year or two, but a few stayed on one charge for a longer period.

The economic conditions in the country were not good, and raising finances was not easy. When new churches were built, they represented sacrifices by the people. Preachers did not always receive their salaries in full. Christian people had organized more churches than could be supported, in some communities. A few churches were closed, with memberships transferred.

THE IOWA CONFERENCE 1900-1932

The "turn of the century" is an artificial distinction dividing one period of time from another. It is also a psychological landmark. The Spanish American War had not lasted long, but it marked a change in attitudes toward the rest of the world. The United States had overseas territories—Puerto Rico and the Philippines—and had assumed a protectorate over Cuba. The political climate made it possible and expedient to help Panama in its break away from Colombia.

The United States was united, North and South, as it had not been before. Within the church, men began to look back and examine the progress of the last two-thirds of the century. Ministers were inspired to begin work on conference histories, which were published before the new century was very old: Aaron W. Haines, *The Makers of Iowa Methodism,* 1900; Bennett Mitchell, *History of the Northwest Iowa Conference,* 1904; S. N. Fellows, *History of the Upper Iowa Conference,* 1907; Edmund Waring, *History of the Iowa Annual Conference,* 1910; and E. W. Heinke et al, *Geschichte der Nordwest Deutschen Konferenz,* 1913; E. C. Magaret et al, *Jubiläumsbuch der St. Louis Deutschen Konferenz,* 1909.

The first decade of the 20th century, like the last of the 19th, was a period of many changes. The rule limiting the number of times that a preacher could be reassigned to one charge was dropped in 1900, making it possible for a minister to remain indefinitely in one community. Neither preachers nor congregations were quick to take advantage of the change.

During most of the 19th century presiding elders' reports were full of glowing accounts of the founding of new churches. Around 1900 the situation changed. The state was settled, and churches had been established in nearly every community. The Methodist Episcopal Church became more a "church" and a little less an evangelistic movement. It is not known whether the change represented progress or a decline in fervor, but the church continued membership growth and influence.

With almost every church able to have services each Sunday, less need was felt for the class meeting. W. G. Thorn, Muscatine District presiding elder reported in 1906:

. . . . the love feast in many places has grown aged, decrepit, and too often fails to make an appearance. Her aged and honored sister, the class meeting, also clothed with memories of respected and vital energy, has grown very infirm in many places, and too often fails to make an appearance amid the busy throng of current activities. Too much alive to be buried, and too much dead to be counted among the aggressive forces of the current church.[19]

The decline of the Class Meeting was not always acknowledged even while it was occurring. Brother Thorn wrote his gloomy report of the class meeting in 1906, but in 1907 the presiding elder of the Oskaloosa District reported:

The class meeting is still living actively among us and exists with more or less power in nearly every charge. We listened in one Quarterly Conference recently to 15 written reports from Class Leaders that would delight this conference if they could be repeated here.[20]

That same year (1907) the Burlington District presiding elder reported: "The class meetings are not generally maintained."[21]

Early in this century the Epworth League and the Sunday School played a significant role in the life of the younger people. It might be said that these replaced the Class Meeting and the Love Feast. As pastoral terms lengthened, it became more and more common for traveling evangelists to conduct revival meetings and move on, leaving the task of consolidating the results to the resident pastor. Discussing the loss of enthusiasm, a presiding elder wrote:

What is the remedy? Special evangelists? Possibly, sometimes. But it is my conviction that far too often the work of the special evangelist is merely a performance in which there is enough pious enthusiasm to gloss over the performance to make it temporarily palatable while it is going on, but when the evangelist is gone the gloss of enthusiasm fades and the awful relapse or collapse is left for the unfortunate pastor to wrestle with.[22]

(Some changes occur in the church which are not important in themselves, but which should be mentioned. After the General Conference of 1908, the title of the presiding elder was changed to district superintendent.)

Coal mining was an important industry in southern Iowa for many years, and many of the miners were Methodists. When the mines were "worked out," the miners moved away. As early as 1901, the conference appointed a committee to dispose of two abandoned churches in the Oskaloosa District at Carbonado and Muchakinock, both mining towns south of Oskaloosa. Many members of the Muchakinock church became members of the Buxton church in Monroe County when richer mines were opened. Now Buxton is only a memory.

In 1909 the district boundaries were changed, leaving the Iowa Conference with four districts instead of five. The Ottumwa District Superintendent wrote of his district in 1910:

The western part of this newly organized district is composed of a string of coal mining camps, 70 miles long, running zigzag from the northwest to the southeast, representing a population of 16,000 people, two-thirds of whom are English-speaking. In these camps we have seventeen churches, composed nearly altogether of this excellent, but transient class, while adjacent to these camps are numerous small churches composed more or less of miners.[23]

These people presented a challenge to the M.E. Church. Miners' wages were low and they could not do much to support the church, but churches were organized and served their communities. Later, when the mines closed and most of the miners moved, churches were left with too few members. The members remaining had strong loyalties to their almost abandoned churches, and resisted efforts to combine congregations. Eventually the Iowa-Des Moines Conference would struggle with this problem.

Writers of history tend to devote attention to dramatic events that make headlines, but much of life is made up of prosaic affairs. The "presiding elders' " reports until 1908 and the district superintendents' reports until 1917 give much attention to new church buildings, new parsonages, and improvements on old ones. Revival meetings were held in most churches every year. Changes in the church were not always recognized immediately. One might mourn because the class meeting and the prayer meeting were losing ground. Another might rejoice because the Sunday School and the Epworth League were gaining.

The first Wesley Foundation was organized on the campus of the University of Illinois October 13, 1913, but the four Iowa Conferences were supporting a pastor for students at the Universtiy of Iowa before then. The 1913 session of the Iowa Conference voted to ask each district to contribute $100 toward the support of a campus pastor.

The year 1916 marked the end of an era in the life of the Methodist Episcopal Church. As Iowa farmers had prospered since 1900, preachers' salaries had increased. Sunday School attendance was growing. Most leaders were looking ahead, expecting a still better future. Few believed that events in Europe could have much effect on Iowa.

But things were not the same after the United States entered the First World War on April 6, 1917. From 1917 to 1945 there was a rather steady decline in average Sunday School attendance in American Protestant churches. During the same years most denominations lost more ministers through death and retirement than they received by young men's response to a call. William H. Perdew, Superintendent of the Ottumwa District, wrote in September, 1917: ". . . the enlisting in various branches of the National Service of many of our young men from colleges and high schools—preachers in the making—threatens our future supply of ministers. . . ."[24]

Brother Perdew was something of a prophet, for many young men did not return to school after the war. Iowa Methodism was most supportive of the war. The 1917 committee report on "The State of the Church and the Country" said:

> We urge our preachers to make their pulpits echo and reëcho with a patriotism so constructive as to counteract the destructive influence of hypocritical pacifists, unthinking pro-Germans, and anarchistic agitators who shall find in Methodism a foe unrelenting and irresistible.[25]

The church did not always rise above the war hysteria, but a few kept their poise. In 1918 E. J. Shook, district superintendent of the Burlington District, reported:

> Our pastors have been faithful, and with few exceptions have held special meetings. We are sorry to have to report only a few conversions. Other matters have so absorbed the attention of the people that it has been impossible to rally them for revival work.[26]

The 1918 list of appointments reported five army chaplains and seven members enlisted in the army. Pastoral records indicate that two of the "enlisted" were actually army chaplains.

At the beginning of the 1918-1919 conference year the country was still at war. The influenza epidemic killed 500,000 people in the United States. All of the churches in the Burlington District were under quarantine from three to five weeks. In the Oskaloosa District some churches were closed for thirteen consecutive Sundays, and others were closed for as many as three different periods between the first of October and the first of April.[27]

Despite the problems in 1918, the Methodist Episcopal Church launched an ambitious evangelistic and missionary campaign commemorating the centennial of the Methodist missionary movement. The goals were to win a million persons for Christ by June 1, 1920, and raise a vast sum for worldwide mission projects. The fourth quarterly conference in each charge named a Centennial Council in preparation for the coming emphasis.

The Annual Conference launched the campaign on September 6, 1918. The Centenary was given the "right of way" during the 1918-1919 conference year. Appeals were made in each charge for cash pledges to be paid over five years. It is surprising that the program was so successful in the midst of the influenza epidemic and the war. For the most part, pledges were paid in spite of the slump in farm produce prices beginning in 1920.

The return to peace-time conditions did not come easily for Iowa farmers. Prices for farm products had been kept high during the war. This led to a wave of speculation on farm land. On May 31, 1920, it was announced that the guaranteed price on wheat was being withdrawn, and supports for other crops soon went the same way. Loans to European countries were stopped at the same time. "Most cruel of all, the farmer found that prices and wages in other parts of the economy were holding up while the prices he received were going down."[23]

Many farmers soon realized that their farms could not produce enough to pay the interest on their mortgages and taxes. The talk of American prosperity during the 1920s did not apply to farmers. Farm prosperity did not return until the beginning of the Second World War. Any cash contributions to the church represented a real sacrifice. Dr. Wm. Perdew of the Ottumwa District wrote in 1921:

Owing to economic conditions prevailing the latter half of the year, many of God's people on this district have endured a test of faith in the matter of financial support of the church. In the face of falling markets, money shortage, and unemployment they have not withheld from the church but have stood heroically by with their person and their purses to sustain the Financial Morale of the Kingdom.[29]

At the same time there was a change in attitude toward public amusements. The Burlington district superintendent wrote in 1921, "There has been a frightful letting down of standards. Who better than the Methodists can call this country back to holy living?"[30]

During the war the churches of the St. Louis German Conference had been forbidden to use the German language in their services, and after the war most of them continued using English. With the abandonment of German, they no longer had much reason for maintaining a separate organization. In 1925 the St. Louis German Conference was dissolved. Its preachers and congregations were absorbed into the contiguous English language conferences. The church and its pastor in Muscatine were taken into the Chicago Northwest (German), but the others within its boundaries were taken into the Iowa Conference. The preachers Iowa received were H. W. Brandt, G. E. Heidel, M. H. Kruse, A. F. Ludwig, and G. A. Schmidt.

Upon the death of Dr. George L. Minear, superintendent of the Muscatine District, during the conference year of 1924-1925, the four districts were re-divided into three. They were the Burlington, Ottumwa, and Oskaloosa districts.

The period of the 1920s was a hard time for Methodist preachers. Too many churches waited to make an effort to raise cash to pay the bills until near the end of the conference year, which was in September. As of the first of August, each church still owed the preacher a large part of his salary, and he owed the grocer. When times were hard, or the preacher was not popular, it was difficult to collect money for the church. He might go to conference without some of his salary, leaving unpaid bills behind him. A second financial problem which began to appear at this time was the cost of maintaining an automobile. Each dollar spent on a car making pastoral calls was one dollar less for his family.

By the end of the decade it was becoming apparent that the church could do its work better, under the new conditions, if it were organized into a larger administrative unit. Plans were made for a merger with the Des Moines Conference. The new conference was to have boundaries similar to those of the old Iowa Conference before 1860. The last session of the Iowa Conference was held in Muscatine, September 9 to 13, 1931. The first session of the Iowa-Des Moines Conference was held in Grace Church, Des Moines September 20-26, 1932.

Western Iowa Conference 1860-64

One cannot commence the history of the Western Iowa Conference with 1860, when the conference was set aside from the Iowa Conference. Rather we must tell the story of the movement of settlers into the territory which was later to become the Western Iowa Conference, and then Des Moines Conference. When the first Methodists entered Southwest Iowa, Methodism was already firmly established west of the Mississippi River, and the Iowa Conference had been formed. The movement westward was a continuation of what had already been going on.

The Western Iowa Conference had a short and hard life, consisting of the war years of 1860 to 1864. Yet one could say those four years were actually the first four years of the Des Moines Conference, which had a long and successful history. Later sessions of the Des Moines Conference were numbered from the first session of the Western Iowa Conference in 1860. The 1865 session, held in Indianola with Bishop Matthew Simpson presiding, was counted as the sixth session of the Des Moines Conference.

Settlements within the bounds of the Iowa Conference continued expanding westward after the state had been divided into two conferences in 1856, the Iowa and the Upper Iowa. By 1859 there were enough members in the western half of the state that the Iowa Conference petitioned General Conference for authority to divide again. This was done, but the line was not drawn where the Western Conference wanted it to be, causing controversy until 1864.

The 1859 session of the Iowa Conference asked that the dividing line be drawn from the southeast corner of Wayne County, due north to the line of the Upper Iowa Conference, leaving Knoxville on the west side of the line, and Monroe, Newton, and Greencastle on the east. However, all five of the delegates elected to General Conference were serving appointments in the eastern part of the state.[31]

The next year (1860) General Conference ordered the division but changed the boundary line, starting the line at the corner of Wayne County and running north to the Des Moines River at the Red Rocks in Marion County, and then up the river to the southern line of Boone County. This change deprived the new Western Iowa Conference of portions of Marion, Jasper, and Polk Counties which contained several prosperous parishes in the longest settled part of the new conference. The brethren of the West were incensed![32]

Even without the change of boundaries, the new conference would have had problems. It was composed of two narrow strips of settled territory, on the east and on the west, separated by about one hundred miles of sparsely settled prairie. Railroads did not cross the state at that time, and few roads existed. During the four years of its life the conference showed only minor changes. There was little increase in membership, as both public and private interest was absorbed by the Civil War between the states. Little energy was left for evangelism. The first session of the new conference was held in Indianola with Bishop E. S. Janes presiding and Rev. E. M. H. Fleming as secretary.

It seems to us, in the 1980s, that population moved slowly across the state, but there was good land near established communities to be settled first. A Methodist local preacher, William Rector, settled in Fremont County about 1847, and preached wherever he could find an audience.[33] Methodist preachers also came occasionally from Missouri.[34]

The Western Iowa Conference was not just a prelude to the formation of the Des Moines Conference. It was a continuation of the western expansion of the white settlers starting in 1833 and lasting until the state was entirely settled.

The Civil War years saw expansion slowed to a crawl. The building of railroads to the west stopped until after the war, and the conference saw approximately 500 of her sons in the Union Army. Methodism was spreading westward, and Western Iowa Conference did not lose members during those agonizing years—a testimony to its vitality. After the war, the railroads were built on across the state, and the church resumed its growth.

The first preacher to be assigned to Southwest Iowa from the Iowa Conference was Rev. William Simpson. He came to Kanesville (now Council Bluffs) in 1850 in search of some stolen horses. Kanesville had been founded by the Mormons on their way to Utah. It served as the final staging area for their migration west. With the 1849 gold rush to California and the Oregon colonization movement, it became an outfitting point for many emigrant parties. Here assembled all the flotsam and jetsam of vice, crime, and godlessness from the whole upper Missouri Valley.[35]

Simpson was disturbed by the moral conditions existing there, and reported what he had seen when he went to Annual Conference that fall. He was appointed to the Council Bluffs Mission, which covered the area from St. Joseph, Missouri to Sioux City, Iowa. On the Council Bluffs work Simpson established several Methodist societies, including one in Kanesville.

Simpson was not welcome in Kanesville, which was dominated by Mormons. He preached a sermon on one occasion comparing the Mormons to the frogs of Revelation 16:13-14. Following that sermon the Mormon leader, Orson Hyde, sent word to Simpson indicating he had received a "revelation" that Simpson would suffer an early death. Simpson informed Hyde that he would be held personally responsible if anything tragic happened. Nothing did.

Another story is told of the death of Simpson's infant daughter. His Mormon neighbors refused to give any help, so Simpson had to build a coffin, dig the grave, and bury her himself.[36]

Growth was rapid the first decade in Southwest Iowa. In 1852 the conference formed a Council Bluffs District with three fields—Kanesville, Page and Taylor, and Sidney. In 1859 it had grown to twelve fields and a membership of 1,310. Six buildings had been constructed.[37]

The Western Iowa Conference in 1860 can be described as an interlude between what had gone before and what was to follow. During this time the school which later became Simpson College was established in Indianola. An advertisement appears in the Western Iowa Conference Minutes of 1860 for the first term of the Indianola Male and Female Seminary (Simpson's forerunner), beginning September 24, 1860. Tuition for the thirteen-week term was from $3.00 to $8.00, depending on branches studied. Board cost $1.50 to $2.00 per week.

The Western Iowa Conference ended with the formation of the Des Moines Conference August 31, 1864. At that time the Western Iowa Conference was merged with the western half of the Upper Iowa Conference to form a new and larger conference.

The Des Moines Conference 1864-1932

1864-1872

The Des Moines Conference of the Methodist Episcopal Church, formed in 1864, was actually a continuation of the Western Iowa Conference of 1860, with significant changes of boundaries. The former Western Iowa Conference was merged with the western half of the Upper Iowa Conference, making a new conference. It included approximately the western half of the state of Iowa, and was given a new name—the Des Moines Conference. The first session of the new conference was convened on August 31, 1864 with Bishop Edmund S. Janes presiding. At the time of organization it had six districts: Des Moines, Chariton, Council Bluffs, Lewis, Sioux City, and Fort Dodge; 67 preachers, 58 charges, and 7,293 members.

The eastern line of the conference in 1864 began at the southeast corner of Wayne County and ran directly north to the southern line of Marshall County, west to the southeast corner of Story County, then north to the Minnesota border. This territory included six strong parishes, in the northeast corner of the Des Moines District, which the western Iowa Conference members believed should have been included in the Western Iowa Conference in 1860.

In 1872 the northern half of the conference was separated from the rest and became, with the addition of the Dakota Territory, the Northwest Iowa Conference. This left the Des Moines Conference comprising the southwest quarter of the state, which was essentially the same as the old Western Iowa Conference except that by 1872 it had more people, more towns, and more roads.

Sixty years later (1932) the Des Moines Conference merged with the Iowa Conference, which at that time consisted of the southeast quarter of the state, to form the Iowa-Des Moines Conference covering the south half of the state. In its last year the Des Moines Conference had 320 churches, and 67,662 members.

One might question whether developments in Northwest Iowa between 1864 and 1872 should be discussed as a part of Des Moines Conference History or Northwest Iowa Conference History. As Mitchell starts his History of Northwest Iowa Conference with 1872, and Harvey includes that era in writing of the Des Moines Conference, it is better to follow the same pattern.[38]

Northwest Iowa had a varied background. The first white man to settle where Sioux City now is was Theophile Bruguier, a French Canadian fur trader, who built his cabin near the mouth of the Big Sioux River in 1849. Before that he had been up and down the Missouri River trading with the Sioux Indians and the American Fur Company of St. Louis. Other settlers found it convenient to settle near his trading post. The community grew, made up of Indians, French, and Americans who came across Iowa and up the river. The first Methodist class was organized with four members in 1855, in what was a very new community.

Many of the pioneer preachers followed the advancing settlers up the Des Moines River from Fort Des Moines into Northwest Iowa. In 1852 the Rev. H. J. Burleigh held a three-day meeting in the hospital tent at Fort Dodge. Fort Dodge was able to erect a frame church in 1857. Many other circuits in that area and westward were formed in the 1850s. The areas east of the Des Moines River line were organized from the East. Further details can be found in R. E. Harvey's article in the *Annals of Iowa*.[39]

However, records are scant for most of the early churches. Many of the local church records were not saved because later generations did not understand their importance. Often when a circuit was divided, the records of activities in one county were in the same book with those of another, and the writers of local church history never found the original records of their own church. Sometimes local church officers have kept church records in their own homes, and many such records have disappeared.

During the 1850s and 1860s the settlers in Northwest Iowa were few and scattered. The Ida Grove Methodist Episcopal Church with ten charter members, and Battle Creek, also on the Maple River in Ida County, were organized in 1869 as part of the Mapleton Mission by the pastor, eighteen-year-old L. H. Woodworth.

Preaching services were held at Sac City in Sac County and at Sergeant Bluff in Woodbury County by William Black in 1855, and services were held from 1856 at Lake City in Calhoun County. Buena Vista County cast only fifteen votes when it was organized in 1858 and had a population of fifty-seven in 1860. Yet there was a Methodist class organized in 1859 at Sioux Rapids. The Storm Lake church was enrolled October 4, 1868 on the Chamberlain farm at the west end of the lake by Rev. Thomas Whitely, a local preacher. Whitely, assisted by another local preacher, supplied a circuit reaching south to Ida Grove, west to Cherokee, and north to Peterson.[40]

In the fall of 1858 Little Sioux Mission was established, extending from Spirit Lake to Cherokee. C. S. Wright, the pastor, was paid $40 mission stipend and $27 from his congregations, for the year.[41] In 1864 the O'Brien work was put into the Smithland Circuit, and Rev. Seymour Snyder covered an area of seven counties reaching into Minnesota.[42]

Northwest Iowa was slow to develop both in population and church life because of its physical isolation from the settled part of the country. The only river road was the Missouri River, which was closed to travel from November to April each year. Along its lower course many dangers were due to the pro and anti-slavery Kansas controversy, later to the Civil War.

The overland route was almost as difficult, crossing a hundred miles of flat land west of the Des Moines River. This area was largely treeless and had many ponds and sluggish streams, hazardous country to traverse before the ponds were drained and the farmland tiled. Winter blizzards were a fact of life. Fear of wide-ranging prairie fires in late spring and early fall was justified. This country was not thickly settled until after railroad construction and extensive drainage projects.

The eight years that the Des Moines Conference included the entire western half of the state was a period of dramatic change and growth. The Civil War was over, and public attention turned to other matters. Four trunk railways crossed the state during those years, with another not far behind. All of them had feeder lines north and south, with depots and stockyards every few miles. Towns grew up around these stations, replacing many of the pioneer community centers.

The circuit riders of the Methodist Episcopal Church, with their flexible organization, quickly took advantage of the situation, organizing churches in each of these new communities. A proportionate number of the recent settlers had been Methodists in their old homes, and promptly joined the Methodist Church in their new location. Many who had belonged to other denominations previously, not finding their own church in the new territory, joined the one that was already established. They brought much that was good with them.

The Methodist Church, receiving these new members by transfer, gained much more than numbers. It developed a breadth of viewpoint, and became even more representative as an American Protestant church than it had been before.

The church had not been making progress during the war years when Southwest Iowa was in the Western Iowa Conference, but with the end of the war the situation changed. The same General Conference that created the Des Moines Conference also raised the time limit for a preacher to serve one appointment to three years. Hindsight indicates this was a positive step, but the conference was slow to take advantage of this new flexibility. Many preachers continued to move each year.

When the Des Moines Conference was formed in 1864, it contained fifty-eight charges. In 1865 there were sixty-four; in 1866, seventy-four; in 1867, seventy-seven; in 1868, ninety-four; in 1869, one hundred thirteen; in 1870, one hundred twenty-nine; and one hundred fifty-three in 1871. This was a period of steady growth.

One of the interesting movements of this period in Iowa Methodism was the attempt to establish "seminaries" in several communities, an effort to provide education beyond the common schools. Many of these efforts failed. Some never really got off the ground. Others provided educational opportunities until the need disappeared, with the development of public "high schools" all over the state.

Epworth Seminary in the Upper Iowa Conference was organized in 1857 and continued for more than half a century. Indianola Male and Female

Seminary was able to move ahead, changing its name first to Indianola Seminary, and later to Des Moines Conference Seminary. In 1866 the school was raised to college rank and became Simpson Centenary College.

During those eight years (1864-1872) many devoted preachers labored without much recognition, doing the Lord's work—as they understood it and as they were able. Their names cannot all be listed in a book of this length.

1872-1900

1872 marked a new period in the life of the Des Moines Conference. That year it was divided, and the northern half became the Northwest Iowa Conference. This left a smaller conference with good transportation facilities east and west. The new conference was crossed by the Burlington, Rock Island, and Northwestern railroads, and was soon to have the Milwaukee. All four of these lines had feeder lines reaching north and south.

Along the eastern edge of the conference, the Des Moines Valley Line ended dependence on the unreliable Des Moines River traffic. Now even the most remote community was within a day's distance of transportation facilities. Extreme isolation was over.

General Conference had lay representation for the first time in 1872. The newly-limited conference contained twenty-seven full counties and halves of three others, comprising two-sevenths of the state's area. There were 108 parishes, with the largest number of the members in rural communities. The district reports the first year did not mention any extensive revivals, but 918 conversions were reported from Sunday School attendants. The churches were alive spiritually.

On the third day of the 1872 Des Moines Conference word was received of the death of the Rev. Peter Cartwright at his home in Illinois. Cartwright had never been a member of an Iowa conference, but he was the presiding elder who assigned the first preachers to Iowa appointments. Cartwright had been ordained by, and first appointed by, Francis Asbury, American Methodism's first bishop. With Cartwright's death, the M.E. Church lost a strong personal link with its early beginnings. The name of Peter Cartwright is written large in the records and the legends of early midwestern Methodism. To understand fully the church's history at that period a person of the late twentieth century should read his *Autobiography*.

Another highlight of the 1872 General Conference was the recognition of the Women's Foreign Missionary Society. That year the Des Moines Conference women contributed $49.75. The next year, when they were first allotted space in the statistical tables, they gave three and one-half times as much. The amount contributed increased every year until 1900 when the total was $8,947.

The Women's Home Missionary Society was accredited in 1880, but was not organized in the Des Moines Conference until 1883. Their first reported contributions in 1884 totaled only $20, but it was a start. Their 1900 contribution was $1,193. The inclusion of the Deaconess Movement in their agenda in 1893 gave them added prestige. First Church Des Moines employed a deaconess as a parish worker in 1892. The Deaconess Home Association was quickly organized, and in 1896 the Bidwell Deaconess Home in Des Moines.

During this period the interdenominational and international Women's Christian Temperance Union was enlisting large numbers of Methodist women. It did much to keep Methodist people aware of the liquor problem and to keep the M.E. Church in the forefront of the "battle against booze." The W.C.T.U. was never an official Methodist organization, but it was close.

Before 1872 most of the evangelistic work was accomplished by pastors and presiding elders on their rounds, assisted by local preachers. Sometimes, but not often, neighboring pastors would help each other, like farmers at harvest time. Camp meetings brought in many new converts and provided social life besides. Gradually a class of specialists with particular skills for conducting revival meetings developed. Sometimes they took a "supernumerary" relationship to the conference and devoted themselves principally to revival work as employed by different churches.

Most of these men were available as supply preachers in emergency situations caused by death or illness, when requested by the presiding elder. As time went on, these men were replaced by those who were engaged solely in conducting revival meetings, leaving the results of the meetings to be cared for by the pastors after the evangelist was gone. Some of these were conscientious men who served faithfully, while others sought personal publicity, become a liability rather than a help. Some flew off on a tangent, emphasizing a particular phase of Christian experience, and stirring up unnecessary controversies. Some were very intolerant of anyone who disagreed with their personal interpretations. One writer has commented, "That the cause of Christ prospered despite this abuse of the liberty of conscience is the best proof of its divine origin vouchsafed to the present age."[43]

During this period many new churches were built. Most of the pioneer chapels were enlarged or replaced by more pretentious buildings. Probably none of the 1872 parsonages were still in use in 1900. The life in the parsonage was becoming somewhat less spartan.

The city of Des Moines was growing. By 1866 the original Fifth Street Church had become crowded. This caused a number of members, living on the northwest outskirts of the city, to form a new congregation on Seventh Street, named the Centenary M.E. Church. This church continued for fifteen years until the parent congregation, crowded out of its Fifth Street location by encroaching business, also moved north and west. The two congregations merged and formed First M.E. Church at Ninth and Pleasant Streets.

An interesting tale comes from Council Bluffs where the Methodist people outgrew their primitive chapel, and secured the site of the old Ocean Wave Saloon on Broadway. These Methodists, proud of replacing a notorious vice resort on a conspicuous corner, built Broadway Church.

The coming of the railroads and the building of new towns called for new

Council Bluffs Broadway M. E. Church

churches. This led to considerable denominational pride. A presiding elder's report boasted that in a given year his preachers delivered a dozen "first" sermons in new towns along the railroad lines. Another reported registering five new churches each year of his term. One said that while other Protestant denominations were building fifteen churches in his territory, he was leaving twenty-four more Methodist sanctuaries than he found.[44]

The changing scene in rural communities led to problems later. When new towns came into being, an old village center two or three miles away would often die, the village church was left with an abandoned building, and a few individuals unable to admit it was dead and refusing to attend any other church.

During these years Simpson College was struggling with many problems and becoming more firmly established. Without high schools in its area, much of the student body was enrolled in grammar and preparatory classes.

Efforts were made without success to move the college to Des Moines. The most serious attempt was presented to the All Iowa Methodist Convention in 1881. It would have established an Iowa Methodist University in Des

Moines with the other Methodist colleges reduced to seminary level, as feeders. The proposal was defeated, but was brought up again in a different form in 1888 when Highland Park College was founded.[45] During this time Simpson's most famous student, George Washington Carver, came north and attended the school.

The care of retired or disabled ministers, their widows and orphans, received little attention before 1872. The reason may have been that there were so few of them. The Preacher's Aid Society, incorporated in 1872, was a death benefit association which functioned well for over twenty years, paying $500 to each family of a deceased member.

Later in the 19th century the increasing number of retired ministers and widows rendered funds inadequate. In 1900 one individual received $250 for the first time, while several others received only $25. Ministers who made strong efforts to raise funds for other causes did not press for a more adequate pension system. Perhaps they feared it would appear selfish to be looking after their own. R. E. Harvey discusses the development of a pension system in the Des Moines Conference at considerable length in his history.[46]

Before 1872 little or no effort had been made to provide a church program for particular age groups. Near the end of the century the Epworth League came into being. The various young people's societies were formed into one organization, and received denomination-wide recognition by the General Conference of 1892. Leagues were organized in every pastoral charge. Often they became the only Sunday night service of any kind, taking the place of the class and prayer meetings.

Ministerial discipline is an unpleasant but necessary procedure for a church whose congregations have little choice of pastors and even less opportunity to check their qualifications. The denominational promise of "ministers, blameless in life and conversation" necessitates a system of oversight to eliminate any moral misfits. As the presiding bishop would call the roll at annual conference, the required inquiry was, "Is there anything against him?" If the answer came, "There are complaints against Brother _____," disciplinary action had to be instituted.

The procedures took form, depending upon the nature of the complaint. If the minister was charged with "maladministration," i.e. errors of judgment or blunders in management, he might be referred to his presiding elder for investigation, and for a report next year. In that case the matter was usually ironed out and nothing more came of it.

In more serious cases, an investigating committee was appointed to determine whether there were sufficient facts to justify a trial. If so, the accused was tried before a "Select Number," which was a panel of ministers of good judgment who exercised the judicial powers of the conference. If their decision was for acquittal, it was final. If for conviction, it could be appealed to the entire conference.

Thirty-nine cases of ministerial discipline were considered between 1873 and 1900 in the Des Moines Conference. Several of these cases were regarded as of little importance. They were dismissed without trial. Of the ministers brought to trial under church law, twelve were acquitted; four withdrew under charges; and fourteen were convicted. Of those convicted, eight were expelled, and six were suspended from the ministry for one year.[47] It is probably true that some guilty men were permitted to withdraw and thus avoid exposure.

One of the characteristics of old-time Methodism was frequent moves of pastors. Every preacher was assigned to a new charge every year. During the four-year life of the Western Iowa Conference a preacher could be reassigned for a second year, but not for a third.

The limit was raised to three years in 1864, and in 1888 to five years. In 1900 the limit for pastoral tenure was removed, but the term for presiding elders was left at six years. Despite the change permitting longer pastorates, few took advantage of the new rule. It is not clear whether churches were looking for the ideal preacher, or preachers were looking for the ideal appointment. The custom of frequent moves was stronger than the rules.

Various reasons are cited for retaining short-term pastorates. Many laymen believed the system set up by the church founders had worked well and should be retained. The practice also fostered a craving for novelty on the part of both laymen and ministers. One minister described how this was voiced to him by a parishioner, "who wanted the ministers moved at least annually, so as to afford him the pleasure of hearing the greatest possible number of them."[48]

To some ministers the grass is always greener on the other side of the fence, and they welcome a move. Young ministers who have made blunders on one charge hope to prove themselves in a new place. In 1931, the last list of appointments for the Des Moines Conference indicated an average appointment of only slightly more than two years and two months.

1900-1932

The history of the M.E. Church and the other bodies joining to make the United Methodist Church of today is kaleidoscopic. The beginning of the new century marked a milestone which may have been more psychological than material, but it was there.

After the 1900 General Conference laymen of the M.E. Church took an increased role in the running of the church. In early times, however, the class leader had been a key person holding the local class together between visits of the traveling preacher or circuit rider.

Laymen had built churches, established schools, taught Sunday School classes, and paid the bills. After 1900 they were given a more significant role in conference affairs. In his history of the Des Moines Conference R. E. Harvey calls this last period a time of "broadened laymen activity."

Each annual conference was entitled to the same number of ministerial and lay delegates to the General Conference. The lay delegates were elected by a Lay Electoral Conference which met at the same time and place as the regular Annual Conference made up of ministers only. The laymen of the

Des Moines Conference were slow to show much interest in the work of the conference, but they gradually learned to assume more responsibility.

The granting of female eligibility to Lay Conference membership did not bring immediate results, but the right led to increasing demand for recognition of women preachers. Women had been gaining access to Methodist pulpits as evangelists and as temperance lecturers for some time. Deaconesses were used as assistant and mission pastors, and it was difficult to see why they should not be licensed as "local preachers."

In 1920 the licensing of female local preachers was authorized, and immediately a few were assigned to supply charges. In 1924 they were granted ordination to local orders, and later on, the status of "accepted supply pastors." Not until 1956 were women preachers given the same rights to conference membership as men.

One of the more significant advances of the first decade of the 20th century was the establishment of the Iowa Methodist Hospital in Des Moines. The hospital received financial support from all parts of the state. The institution opened its doors on January 16, 1901. Eight months later it was reported that 329 patients had been treated, one-fourth of them charity cases.

A home for retired ministers was purchased in Indianola and named "The Francis Home." In 1912 it housed twenty-four guests with room for more. However, its affairs later fell into such condition that the 1914 conference ordered it sold and the earnings from the proceeds used for relief of especially destitute cases among the claimants.

New church legislation in 1908 established for the first time a pension system based on years of service, regardless of individual financial circumstances. To assure funds for this, an apportionment was made part of the parish salary budget in each church, along with the claims of district superintendents and bishops. The size of the assessment was fixed as a certain percentage of the pastor's salary. As salaries went up, so did pension funds.

For a decade the new plan failed to provide enough for an adequate pension, because the conference was reluctant to vote an adequate apportionment. The conference feared a heavier assessment might provoke lay opposition, and the entire salary budget might suffer as a result. In 1916, when the apportionment was raised to 12%, there was no complaint from the laymen. The 1916 General Conference cut the men's pensions by 10% so that the widows' pensions could be raised to 75% of the deceased husbands' pensions. In 1927 the Des Moines Conference extended pension rights to "supply pastors" and their dependents who had given fifteen or more years' service.

The 20th century so far has been a time of continuous change in farming practices. It has become possible for one farm family to cultivate more and more land, leading to migration elsewhere. Farm population has decreased. Open-country and village churches have closed. Iowa's rapid population growth ended with the 1900 census. 1910 actually showed a slight decrease.

The increases since then are in the cities and towns, not in the country.

District superintendents have come to conference, no longer boasting about new churches started, but instead having to ask for permission to dispose of abandoned church buildings. In 1900 the Des Moines Conference reported 448 church buildings, and only 320 in 1931, the last year of the conference before merging with the Iowa Conference to form the Iowa-Des Moines. However, this loss in church buildings does not represent a corresponding decline in church membership. "In 1901, there were 50,326; 1911, 54,384; 1921, 69,513; 1931, 76,100."[49]

The Iowa-Des Moines Conference 1932-1957

The Iowa-Des Moines Conference of the Methodist Episcopal Church was formed in 1932 by the merger of the Iowa and Des Moines Conferences. By that time one could cross the state easily by train, or by automobile on newly paved highways. Automobiles were in common use and were causing many changes in church programs.

To most, it seemed desirable to merge the two southern Iowa conferences into one stronger conference. Differences were ironed out and the union took place. The conferences which had been rivals since 1860 were together again. The influences of distance, which had made it necessary to divide Iowa into four conferences, were now working to make reunion desirable.

Quoting the superintendent of the Clarinda District in 1930, "I am happy to report that two sets of tire chains have sufficed for my use for the entire year. The previous requirement was six sets per year. This is the first fruit of the new paved highway system."[50]

In 1930 the Des Moines Conference voted 108 for and 31 against the merger, while the Iowa Conference had only one dissenting vote. Accordingly, the Joint Commission, made up of representatives of the two annual conferences, memorialized the 1932 General Conference to take the necessary action to unite the conferences. On September 20, 1932 the new conference met for the first time, in Grace Church, Des Moines.

The Iowa-Des Moines Conference began at the end of ten years of hard times for Iowa agriculture. Through the first decade of the new conference America was experiencing the Great Depression, which affected all segments of society. During the years between 1923 and 1932, preceding the conference merger, preachers' salaries declined 30%.

One of the readjustments made in 1932 was to redraw district boundaries, reducing to six districts instead of eight. While this may have saved some overhead expense, it did not save enough to allow churches to pay ministers' salaries in full.

The 1932 *Journal* reported salaries short $85,799. Because of economic conditions churches lowered preachers' salaries more than $93,000, hoping that they could meet the lower goal. Yet in 1933 there was another shortage of $86,392. Only eight of the fifty pastors in the Ottumwa District received their salary in full. In 1934, times were some better. Fourteen out of the fifty received full salaries.

The Chicago-Northwest Conference (German) was dissolved in 1933. Its churches and preachers were received into the contiguous English-language conferences. Iowa-Des Moines received the Cedar Street Church in Muscatine with its pastor, W. H. Schwiering; also one retired man, Herman Schiert.

During the hard times of the 1920s and 1930s, when most women did not work outside the home, the women of the churches did much to raise funds through bazaars and church suppers. The district superintendents' report for 1935 states:

> The work of the women of our conference deserves special mention. But for them many of the churches would now be closed. Large sums of money have been raised by them and turned over to the church budget. In many cases they have taken over the work of repairing the property and have paid the entire expense budget of such repairing.[51]

A Christian Youth Camp for Junior High Boys was established at Lake Ahquabi by W. M. Doughty in 1938. This provided a valuable experience for a number of boys each summer. The program quickly became co-educational. Similar work was soon established all over the state.

In 1939 American Methodism took a long step forward. The Methodist Episcopal Church, the Methodist Episcopal Church South, and the Methodist Protestant Church were merged into one church, *The Methodist Church*.

Some of the changes accompanying the merger were very significant. Realigning some pastoral charges made for more efficient use of ministerial man-power. With a shortage of ministers, this was important. With the Methodist Protestants, the Iowa-Des Moines Conference received its first woman ministerial member, Mrs. Pearl Spurlock. There were no M.E. Church South congregations in Iowa at this time, but several preachers from border states became available for transfer into Iowa, as congregations merged in communities having two branches of Methodism in the same town.

The biggest change apparent to the average lay church member was the reorganization of the women's organizations, conforming to the pattern which had been working very well in the southern church. The Ladies' Aid, the Women's Foreign Missionary Society, and the Women's Home Missionary Society were merged into one organization—the Women's Society of Christian Service—and eventually eliminated the jealousies between rival organizations in the same local church.

A second important change in the new church was the admission of laymen into the Annual Conference on an equal basis with ministers. Laymen now had a greatly strengthened voice in the life of their church. They were slow to accept the opportunities made available, but the change came. The Methodist Protestant Church had been weak in numbers, but their influence was significant. Their rule giving laymen more voice in church affairs made The Methodist Church a more democratic organization.

The church had gone through economic hard times for twenty years. Buildings had not been maintained, and churches had accumulated debts. By 1939 times were getting somewhat better. The district superintendents' report stated: "This year has been a notable one in improvements of property, almost universally, with the restoration of God's temples." Also, "It has been a notable year for debt-paying."

The superintendents had hoped to name the churches that had made significant payments on their debts that year, but there were too many to be listed. 188 churches had paid a total of $124,142 on property and improvements or reducing debts in the one year.[52]

For many years, Iowa towns had been growing larger. Each local church had wanted to become a "station church," not sharing their pastor with another church. But by 1940 the church was beginning to recognize the annual conference as distinctly rural. Even though Iowa was no longer in the horse-and-buggy days, many people on farms were unwilling to drive to larger towns for church.

The Methodist Church had to plan to strengthen small town and open-country churches. In 1950 the Town and Country Commission reported on special work in several localities: Burton Bastuscheck on Van Buren County; Lloyd Latta on Clark County; Cecil Wyant on Appanoose County; and Gene Carter on the Warren County group.[53]

The conference of 1941—the last before World War II participation—reported noteworthy developments. The Annual Conference had always met in the fall, after school had started. This caused hardship for preachers' children who entered school in September, not knowing whether they would be in the same school in October. When they moved, they were off to a late start in the new school, often with different textbooks and curricula. The first June conference met in 1941, receiving reports from a nine-month church "year's" work. Preachers' children were no longer penalized by a church calendar.

The Conference Women's Society of Christian Service held their organization meeting in Des Moines October 2, 1940. Soon almost every church had a W.S.C.S.

In 1942 the Central Northwest Conference (Swedish) was dissolved and its pastors and churches transferred into the contiguous English conferences. South Iowa received three pastors and five churches: Elmer Blomquist of West Hill in Burlington; Robert Dahl of Union Park Church in Des Moines; Ol. E. Olson of Boxholm; and two churches left to be supplied—New Sweden and Hiteman.

Many ministers served in the military chaplaincy, leaving the conference with fewer preachers. By conference time 1942, eight were already in the chaplaincy. In 1944 fifteen men were gone, and thus not available to be assigned to churches at home. In 1945 eighteen were in the chaplaincy.

The 1944 General Conference launched a four-year program looking toward the time when the war would end. Preaching the "stewardship of all of life," the *Crusade for Christ* undertook to raise $25,000,000 for

"Reconstruction and Relief" in war-torn countries. An appeal was made to young people to give their lives to full-time Christian service.

The "Church School Advance," as part of the *Crusade for Christ*, sought to restore an interest in the Sunday School. The 1946 district superintendents' report stated:

> For almost a quarter of a century this territory has recorded a decline in average church school attendance. It is high time for us to face the problem, seek its solution, and sell once more to Methodist people one of the greatest institutions for training people in the local church.[54]

During the four years of the *Crusade,* average Sunday School attendance in the Iowa Area increased 12%.

A fourth part of the program was evangelistic, striving to increase interest in the church as a *Crusade for Christ*. The crusade was a success at all points. Not only did Sunday School attendance begin to grow, but many young men who later became leaders in the conference entered the ministry. Church attendance improved, and during the four years the churches reported $560,717 raised toward the Iowa-Des Moines Conference's share of the national goal.

In the remaining years of the Iowa-Des Moines Conference church property was improved, preachers' salaries were increased year by year, and Sunday attendance continued to grow. The district superintendents' report in 1947 observed that, "This has been a great year to be alive and serve."[55]

Various needed projects were started in the period immediately after the war. A corporation was formed in 1946 to study the possibility of establishing a conference home for retired people and receiving gifts toward that end. In 1947 the purchase of "Wesley Acres" at 3520 Grand Avenue in Des Moines was announced.

After the war there was more response to the need for better care of open-country and village churches. In 1947 Gene Carter was appointed head of the Warren County Group Ministry, leading a team of Simpson College students serving small churches in that county. At the same time, the first tentative steps were taken to form a "Centerville Larger Parish" in Appanoose County. Later it was called the "Appanoose County Larger Parish."

Prior to the war, there had been a long period when too few young men had entered the ministry to replace those retiring. As a result, by 1944 the median age of all men in the effective relationship was 45.14 years. The superintendents' report said, ". . . we shall face the combined loss by retirement and death of more than 100 members in the next seventeen years." The report added, "The whole situation faces us with an immediate and insistent demand for a steady and positive emphasis upon the recruitment for the ministry."[56]

After the war many capable young men entered the conference. By 1957, when the name of the conference was changed to the "South Iowa Conference," a change toward a younger conference was noted.

For years the conferences in Iowa had held a joint Summer School of Theology for "accepted supply" pastors and for those taking the "Course of Study" looking toward conference membership. Beginning in 1944, the supply preachers taking the Course of Study did so by correspondence through Southern Methodist University. That allowed the Boards of Ministerial Training of the Iowa conferences to develop a new program of continuing education for all ministers in the state—the Pastors' School. The first was held at Clear Lake as a statewide project with W. M. Scheuermann as dean.[57]

In 1949 the Pastors' School was changed to a mid-winter event, meeting in Des Moines. Since then it has been an annual event using the facilities of Simpson College in Indianola.

The Methodist Episcopal Church did not accept women as members of the conference, though it did receive and ordain women as "accepted supply" pastors. These women served faithfully as pastors of local churches, though they were denied a vote at annual conference.

The 1939 merger with the Methodist Protestant Church brought Mrs. Pearl Spurlock as a member of the conference. She retired in 1948. No more women could be admitted until, in 1956, the General Conference added a new paragraph #303 which stated, "Women are included in all provisions of the *Discipline* referring to the ministry." Miss Nancy Nichols was admitted into the Iowa-Des Moines Conference on trial in 1956, as the first woman member of the conference under the new rules.

During the period following the Second World War a trend toward more cooperation between the north and south Iowa conferences eventually led to the reorganization of the state into one conference. The joint Pastors' School enabled preachers from all over the state to become acquainted with one another. The fact that Iowa had a resident bishop facilitated transfers between the conferences. In 1954 the Des Moines Area held a state-wide "Spiritual Life Mission." Preachers from northern Iowa led meetings in southern Iowa churches February 20-26 with 231 churches participating. March 6-12 southern Iowa preachers traveled to northern Iowa for similar services.

The name of the conference was changed to South Iowa in 1958, conforming to a recommendation by the North Central Jurisdiction that annual conference names should more accurately identify their geographical locations. For the eleven years leading up to the merger with the Evangelical United Brethren Church the conference in South Iowa was known by the new name.

South Iowa Conference 1958-1969

Several events and trends occurring during the years 1958-1969 made that period a time of transition for the South Iowa Conference. One of the first changes was not recognized as being important at the time. Before 1958 there had been no systematic rotation among members of the various conference committees. In some cases the same persons served on a board or committee for long periods, while others who might have been interested in serving had no opportunity. An amendment to the conference Rules of Order was adopted in 1958, limiting tenure on any conference committee, board, or commission to four years, or to two consecutive terms, whichever was longer. This meant that no one elected in 1958 or before was eligible to be re-elected in 1964.

The change was not much noticed when approved, but it attracted attention in 1964 when it necessitated a big turnover in committee personnel. Some conference members had to relinquish long-cherished positions. Many new faces appeared on committees that year. Since that time, committees may have been no more efficient, but they have been more representative. In 1969 a further restriction was made that "No person may be a member of more than one annual conference agency."[58]

Prior to 1960 the local church apportionments for the support of the district superintendents, the bishop, and the retired members had been expressed as a percentage of the local pastor's salary. Some people from small churches complained that this placed an unfair burden on them, and asked that the apportionments be based solely on membership. Representatives of larger churches feared that such a plan would be unfair to them.

An Apportionment Study Committee was appointed, which reported to the Annual Conference in 1958 recommending that, effective in 1960, a "Grade Figure Plan" would be adopted. Each charge would be assigned a decimal part of the total sum needed. This figure was based on three items —membership, pastor's salary, and other current expenses—which together should indicate the charge's ability to pay.

The new system was not perfect, but seemed as fair an arrangement as could be devised. The plan has been continued, in principle. Some minor adjustments have been made.

By 1958 it was becoming obvious that Iowa was in a period of marked change, and that the church should study its needs and carefully plan ahead. An Area Planning Committee recommended that Bishop Ensley be authorized to appoint an "Area Strategy Committee" to study the overall strategy of the Methodist Church in the Iowa Area during the years ahead.[59] This was done, and the committee made up of representatives of both North and South Iowa Conferences began work July 21, 1958. The committee presented a preliminary report to the annual conferences in 1959, summarizing the changes occurring in Iowa, and making some recommendations. A special session of each of the Iowa conferences was held in the fall to receive the final report and to make specific plans for the years ahead.

The special session of the South Iowa Conference met November twelfth and heard the full report. It was recommended that in 1960 the conference be divided into seven districts instead of six, so that they could more effectively supervise the work of the churches based on:

a) Affinity of needs and interests
b) Number of churches to be supervised
c) Future growth or decrease in population

d) Economic resources and economic or cultural centers
e) Strategic centers of Methodist importance
f) Load of supply charges and circuits[60]

Plans were initiated for the construction of an Area Headquarters building to be erected jointly by the two Iowa conferences. Other needs were considered, and plans were made for a Ten Year Capital Funds Program.

The Ten Year Program was designed to raise a total of $2,200,000 to be applied toward certain needs in the life of the church. They were:

1. Area Headquarters Building	$250,000
2. South Iowa Methodist Homes	500,000
3. Establishing new churches	250,000
4. Colleges	
a. Iowa Wesleyan College	300,000
b. Simpson College	300,000
5. Pension Fund	500,000
6. Camps	100,000

The plan was to ask each charge to increase its giving for benevolences enough to provide $220,000 each year over the regular benevolence budget, the increase to be applied on the Ten Year Program. The total conference budget was to be met first. Only the excess went toward the capital funds goal. If every church met its goal each year (established by the new "grade figure"), the total goal would be reached in ten years.

But the plan immediately met difficulties. The program was not well understood over the conference at first. Growth in giving was slow. Using the grade figure, some large churches which had been accustomed to give generously for benevolences were asked for no increase at all, as they had already been giving their share. Many smaller churches were asked to double their benevolence giving immediately without fully understanding the new program. The program was to be financed by the increased giving from churches which had not been giving before. It was hoped they would gladly meet the challenge of the goal assigned them under the grade figure.

At the end of eight years it was found that the total giving had increased each year, and more churches reached their goal every year than the year before. Yet the total was still far short of the amount needed. The sum remaining unpaid at the time of the merger into one conference was to be apportioned among the churches which had formerly been in the South Iowa Conference, each year until paid.

When the conferences merged into one in 1969, a paragraph was inserted into the Rules of Order stating, "All financial campaigns, unless the Annual Conference orders otherwise, shall be submitted to one full year of education, before the direct solicitation shall begin."[61]

The special sessions of the annual conferences which met in the fall of 1959 asked Bishop Ensley to appoint an Area Headquarters Building Committee. The committee was to locate a suitable site and develop plans for a

New District Alignment

```
CRAWFORD    CARROLL   GREENE   BOONE   STORY
                      Boone District

HARRISON  SHELBY  AUDUBON  GUTHRIE  DALLAS  POLK
                                              JASPER  POWESHIEK  IOWA  JOHNSON
                                                 Newton District
                                                                          MUSCATINE
POTTAWATTAMIE     CASS          MADISON  WARREN
                          ADAIR  Des Moines    MARION  MAHASKA  KEOKUK  WASHINGTON
Council Bluffs District          District                                  LOUISA

MILLS  MONTGOMERY  ADAMS  UNION  CLARKE  LUCAS  MONROE  WAPELLO  JEFFERSON   Burlington
              Creston District            Ottumwa District                  District
                                                                       HENRY   DES MOINES
FREMONT  PAGE  TAYLOR  RINGGOLD  DECATUR  WAYNE  APPANOOSE  DAVIS  VAN BUREN
                                                                         LEE
```

Map of South Iowa Conference

building to house the bishop's headquarters and other services adequately. The proposed expenditure was not to exceed $500,000.

By 1964 the planning committee had learned that the desired building would cost more than expected, but the added cost would not be beyond what could be financed. Under the leadership of Bishop Ensley and Layman Harry Young of Oelwein the building was completed. Bishop Ensley was transferred to Ohio West Area before the new building was finished, but he was able to return and participate in the opening consecration service held April 21, 1965. The United Methodist Church in Iowa has an attractive, practical, and visible headquarters building, conveniently located in the central part of the state.

The most dramatic series of events in the 1960s was the abolition of the Central Jurisdiction (the racially segregated jurisdiction) of The Methodist Church. The 1960 General Conference established rules for transferring its churches and conferences into contiguous conferences and eventually abolishing the Central Jurisdiction.

On June 21, 1964, the South Iowa Conference received two churches from the Lexington Conference of the Central Jurisdiction. They were Burns, Des Moines in the Des Moines District and New Hope, Ft. Madison in the Burlington District. The pastors were Kenneth McNeil and J. F. Johnson, an Approved Supply.

Abolition of the Central Jurisdiction meant that in July, 1964, a black bishop would be assigned to one of the predominantly white areas in the North Central Jurisdiction. The Committee on Episcopacy, responsible for assigning the bishops, had to decide which episcopal area should have the honor of being the first to break segregation within the church.

At the suggestion of the Iowa representatives on the committee, newly-elected Bishop James S. Thomas was assigned to the Iowa Area and installed as leader of Iowa Methodism on September 29, 1964. Bishop Thomas and his family were warmly received in Iowa, and were welcomed back for successive four-year terms in 1968 and 1972. Because the law of the church at that time limited the tenure of a bishop to twelve consecutive years, Iowa had to give up a popular bishop in 1976 when Bishop Thomas was transferred to Eastern Ohio.

During the years between the arrival of Bishop Thomas in Iowa and the merger with the Evangelical United Brethren Church two new programs were important to the people immediately involved. The first was the establishment of an "Area Counseling Service" for ministers and their families. The pastor often needs a pastor himself, and the counselor sometimes needs a counselor.

Accordingly, in 1966 an "Iowa Area Committee on Pastoral Care and Counseling" was appointed: first, to provide counseling and referral service for ministers and their immediate families; second, to help ministers become more proficient counselors; and third, to be alert to other counseling needs of persons. The records of all counseling sessions were to be strictly confidential.[62]

The next year the secretary reported that 49 Methodist ministers, 9 Methodist ministers' wives, and 59 non-Methodist ministers sought personal counseling help during the year.[63] The service was meeting a need.

Iowa Wesleyan College completed the new J. Raymond Chadwick Library on the campus in Mt. Pleasant in 1968, and included a historical archival room on the second floor. For the first time the conference had an adequate and permanent place to store archival material, where it could be shelved and studied. Previous storage space had been makeshift and temporary in other campus buildings.

The Methodist Church, the United Brethren in Christ, and the Evangelical Church had been following parallel paths from their beginnings. Many conversations concerning union had been held across the years. In 1946 the Evangelical Church and the United Brethren Church had merged, forming the Evangelical United Brethren Church. The logical next step was to develop a plan of union with The Methodist Church.

The union took place, and the first General Conference of the new United Methodist Church was held in Dallas, Texas April 22-May 5, 1968. In 1969 the three conferences in Iowa, two formerly Methodist and one formerly E.U.B., merged into one Iowa Conference of the United Methodist Church. Before the 1968 General Conference, there were already thirteen Methodist-E.U.B. "yoked fields" in operation within the bounds of the South Iowa Conference.[64]

Footnotes

1. S. N. Fellows, *History of the Upper Iowa Conference* (Cedar Rapids, Ia.: Laurance Press Co., 1907) p. 72.
2. Edmund Waring, *History of the Iowa Annual Conference of the Methodist Episcopal Church* (n.p., 1909) p. 92.
3. Ibid., p. 39.
4. S. N. Fellows, ibid., p. 31.
5. Ibid., p. 33.
6. Peter Cartwright, *Autobiography of Peter Cartwright* (Cincinnati: Cranston and Curts, 1856) p. 324.
7. Ibid., p. 48.
8. Russell G. Nye, *Pioneering on Iowa Prairies* (n.p., 1960) p. 149.
   "Lining out" hymns was a method used to lead congregational singing when only the preacher had a hymn book. He would read a line at a time, and the congregation would sing each line after him.
9. *Iowa Conference Journal* 1845, p. 29.
10. *Iowa Conference Journal* 1850, p. 135.
11. *Iowa Conference Journal* 1956, pp. 92-93.
12. Waring, ibid., p. 159.
13. Ibid., p. 161.
14. Ibid., p. 166.
15. Ibid., p. 167.
16. Ibid., p. 170.
17. Ibid., pp. 174-175.
18. Ibid., p. 182.
19. *Iowa Conference Journal* 1906, p. 276.
20. *Iowa Conference Journal* 1907, p. 408.
21. Ibid., p. 397.
22. *Iowa Conference Journal* 1910, p. 275.
23. Ibid., p. 272.
24. *Iowa Conference Journal* 1917, p. 203.
25. *Iowa Conference Journal* 1918, p. 214.
26. Ibid., p. 339.
27. *Iowa Conference Journal* 1919, p. 485.
28. Leland L. Sage, *A History of Iowa* (Ames: Iowa State University Press, 1974) p. 254.
29. *Iowa Conference Journal* 1921, p. 194.
30. Ibid., p. 185.
31. R. E. Harvey, "Reopening a Closed Chapter," *Annals of Iowa,* Vol. XXV, p. 298.
32. Ibid., Vol. XXVII, p. 45.
33. Dale A. Schoening, *Going on to Perfection* (Sioux City: Morningside College, 1980) p. 3.
34. Ibid., p. 3.
35. Harvey, ibid., XXV, p. 204.
36. Waring, ibid., p. 149.
37. Schoening, ibid., p. 4.
38. Bennett Mitchell, *History of the Northwest Iowa Conference* (Sioux City: Perkins Bros., 1904)
    Harvey, ibid., Vols. XXV-XXVII-XXIX.
39. Harvey, ibid., Vol. XXVII pp. 119-150.
40. Harvey, ibid., Vol. XXVII p. 126.
41. Ibid.
42. Ibid.
43. Harvey, ibid., Vol. XXVIII, pp. 301-302.
44. Ibid., p. 303.
45. Ibid., p. 305.
46. Ibid., p. 309.
47. Ibid., pp. 313-314.

48. Harvey, ibid. Vol. XXIX, p. 198.
49. Ibid., p. 220.
50. *Des Moines Conference Journal* 1930, p. 292.
51. *Iowa-Des Moines Conference Journal* 1935, p. 587.
52. *Iowa-Des Moines Conference Journal* 1939, p. 619.
53. *Iowa-Des Moines Conference Journal* 1950, p. 31.
54. *Iowa-Des Moines Conference Journal* 1946, p. 61.
55. *Iowa-Des Moines Conference Journal* 1947, p. 59.
56. *Iowa-Des Moines Conference Journal* 1944, p. 40.
57. Ibid., p. 60.
58. *Iowa Annual Conference Journal* 1969, p. 206.
59. *South Iowa Conference Journal* 1958, p. 143.
60. *South Iowa Conference Journal* 1960, p. 55.
61. *Iowa Annual Conference Journal* 1969, p. 210.
62. *South Iowa Conference Journal* 1966, p. 118.
63. *South Iowa Conference Journal* 1967, p. 200.
64. *South Iowa Conference Journal* 1968, p. 149.

4

The Methodist Episcopal Church in North Iowa

The Upper Iowa Conference

The story of Methodism in North Iowa properly begins with the flow of immigrants over the Allegheny Mountains, years before any English-speaking people had seen Iowa. Settlers kept crowding westward into the wilderness, often before the Indians had been induced to relinquish title. Where the settlers went, the Methodist preachers followed.

Among the first white men to appear in North Iowa were Methodist Episcopal, Methodist Protestant, Evangelical, and United Brethren preachers. They preached to any who would listen, then organized their converts into classes.

The Methodist Episcopal Church in North Iowa began in 1833, when the Illinois Conference assigned Barton H. Randle and John T. Mitchell to the Galena and Dubuque Mission. As settlers moved into the territory, new circuits were formed. The Iowa Conference was organized on June 14, 1844. By 1856, as population grew, it seemed best to divide the conference, and Upper Iowa Conference came into being.

During the winter of 1833-34 Randle established several appointments near Dubuque. Early in the spring of 1834 he undertook erecting the first Methodist meeting house in Iowa. The subscription paper describes it as "a hewn log house, 20 by 26 feet in the clear, one story ten feet high, upper and lower floors; to be pointed with lime and sand; and batten door; four twenty light and one twelve light windows, cost estimated for completing in good style, $255.00."[1]

Work commenced on the new chapel, June 23, 1834, and was completed July 25. Randle wrote of the experience, "Well done! to collect money, build a splendid meeting house and pay for it, hold a two days meeting and receive twelve members, all in four weeks! Oh! it was the Lord's doing, let Him have the glory. Amen."[2] At least one of the contributors is believed to have been a slave. Also one of the twelve original members of the first Dubuque society was listed as "Mrs. Charlotte Morgan (colored)."

The first quarterly conference of the "Dubuque Circuit" was held in the new log church on the 14th of November, 1835 with Alfred Brunson, presiding elder. Brunson's district included all of Northern Illinois as well as

**Map of Upper Iowa
Conference**

the northern part of the work in Iowa. The Methodist Episcopal work around Flint Hills (later Burlington) and in Southern Iowa was at that time in the Quincy District of the Illinois Conference with Peter Cartwright, presiding elder.

In 1839 Bishop Thomas Morris, presiding over the Illinois Conference, formed an Iowa district with Henry Summers as presiding elder. Of the nine circuits in the new district, four were in territory later to be a part of the Upper Iowa Conference.

The 1840 General Conference divided the Illinois Conference into the Wisconsin, Rock River, and Illinois Conferences, with the Iowa circuits in the Rock River Conference. The first session of the new conference found the Iowa District had grown considerably. It was divided into two, the Burlington and Dubuque districts. The Dubuque District comprised territory later in the Upper Iowa Conference, and had six appointments in 1840.

1856-1864

The last year Iowa was part of the Rock River Conference—1843—the Dubuque District had grown to ten appointments. The story of the period between 1844, when the Iowa Conference was formed, and 1856, when it was divided, was one of constant growth and adventure. Reports were full of first services for many communities now well known in Iowa United Methodism.

By 1855 Iowa Conference membership had grown from thirty-six to one-hundred-fifty. Church membership grew from 5,431 to 22,690. Presiding elders' districts had increased from three to thirteen. The conference extended over three-fourths of the state. The only means of travel was by horse-drawn vehicle or horseback. The conference had become unwieldy, and a division was needed.

In 1856 the Upper Iowa Conference was formed. The line dividing the conferences started at Davenport and followed the railroad to Iowa City, up the Iowa River to the southern line of Benton and Marshall Counties, then due west to the Missouri River. Davenport and Iowa City were placed in the Upper Iowa Conference while other towns along the railroad were retained in the Iowa Conference.[3]

The first session of the Upper Iowa Conference was held in Maquoketa, August 27 to September 1, 1856, with Bishop Edmund S. Janes presiding. The first list of appointments had seven districts. With their presiding elders they were:

Davenport District, J. C. Ayres
Dubuque District, H. W. Reed
Upper Iowa District, H. S. Bronson
Iowa City District, Andrew Coleman
Marshall District, J. M. Rankin
Janesville District, James T. Coleman
Sioux City District, Landon Taylor

The Sioux City District consisted of approximately the northwest one-fourth of the state. Sparsely inhabited, it had only three appointments in 1856. Eight years later it became a part of the Des Moines Conference, and in 1872 became the Northwest Iowa Conference.

In addition to the seven districts named above two German Methodist Episcopal districts were attached to the Upper Iowa Conference in 1856, but much of their work was in Wisconsin and Minnesota. In 1864 those two districts were included in the Northwest German Conference. When the Chicago Northwest Conference was dissolved in 1933, the German M.E. churches located in Northern Iowa again became part of the Upper Iowa and Northwest Iowa Conferences.

In his *History of the Upper Iowa Conference*, S. N. Fellows made comments about the original members of the Upper Iowa Conference which could be applied to the other conferences making up United Methodism as well. He described the conference as being a band of organized evangelists, each having an assigned field of work called a circuit, supervised by a district evangelist called a presiding elder. The Methodist itinerant preachers lacked scholastic training, but they were well qualified for their work. They knew how to preach Christ. They understood people living in pioneer conditions and could apply the truths of the Bible to their needs. Appointments from the bishop were accepted without question as coming from God.[4]

The life of the preacher and his family was one of hardship and privation. The preacher suffered hardship willingly while traveling his circuit, but to have his wife and children exposed was too much in many cases. Many of the men were forced to leave the ministry and turn to secular occupations to support their families. Fellows wrote in 1906 that during the first twenty-five years of the Upper Iowa Conference, five times as many were forced to leave the conference by location, in proportion to membership, as in the second twenty-five years.

Upper Iowa Conference tried to support three educational institutions almost from the beginning. They were Cornell College at Mt. Vernon, Fayette Seminary in Fayette (which soon became Upper Iowa University) and Epworth Seminary in Dubuque County.

Cornell College opened in 1853 as Iowa Conference Seminary. It prospered, and in 1855 was re-incorporated with the name changed to Cornell College. Cornell has an excellent scholastic reputation and continues as one of the five colleges supported by the Iowa Conference of the United Methodist Church.

Fayette Seminary was opened in September, 1857. During the first year its program was expanded and its name changed to Upper Iowa University. The school was formally accepted by the Upper Iowa Conference in 1858. The relationship continued until 1928.

Epworth Seminary in Dubuque County opened in 1857. The opening of other schools was also considered. To the 20th century historian, it seems that the Iowa conferences were overly ambitious in creating educational institutions. Stephen Norris Fellows, writing in 1907, commented,

> To properly appreciate the above policy to secure more schools of higher grade, it should be remembered that at that time there was no provision in law for high schools or colleges to be supported by the state. It was generally believed that education by the state would and should be limited to elementary or common schools, and that all educational institutions of higher and highest grade should be under private and denominational control. Such had been the policy of the eastern states and it was expected that such would be the policy of the new western states. Besides, it was further believed that seminaries or schools of secondary grade would be easily and forever self-supporting, and even remunerative, after suitable buildings and grounds were provided.[5]

To understand the early history of the Upper Iowa Conference one must remember it was formed at a time when the country was in political turmoil leading to civil war. Emotions ran high and debate over slavery could not be settled by reason. "The people of the time could not know that the country was on a collision course, and that the events of 1856 to 1860 would later be spoken of as 'the prelude to war.' '''[6] This tension overshadowed much that was happening, and when the war came, it captivated the public mind. As a result the work of the churches suffered.

The Civil War years were traumatic for Methodists in Upper Iowa, as for the rest of the country. S. N. Fellows, who was preaching in Northeast Iowa during those years recalled,

> Businesses were well nigh paralyzed, farms were worked and conducted largely by women, schools were greatly depleted and in some cases closed, churches were torn and distracted and congregations scattered.[7]

Fellows wrote that the preachers also suffered financially during the war.

> The cost of living was greatly advanced; the greenback dollar in which their salary was estimated became depreciated until worth only forty cents in gold, and the aggregate deficit in preachers' salaries for a single year was over eighteen thousand dollars.[8]

With the end of the Civil War, life gradually returned to normal. Lives had to be reorganized, and neglected work resumed. The 1864 General Conference merged the western half of Upper Iowa Conference with the Western Iowa Conference and formed the Des Moines Conference.

1864-1900

Along with the post-war building of railroads and the movement of settlers westward, the new conference prospered. After eight years it was divided, with the northern half of the Des Moines Conference made into the Northwest Iowa Conference.

Boundary lines between conferences, as between nations, sometimes create conflict. During the years that Iowa was being settled conditions were never stable. Conference boundaries in Iowa were changed in 1856, 1860, 1864, and 1872. Each time the change was made to accommodate population growth. After 1872 when the Northwest Iowa Conference was formed, the lines separating the four conferences remained unchanged until the Iowa and the Des Moines Conference merged in 1932. However, not everyone was satisfied with things as they were.

About 1870 some members of the Iowa Conference (Southeast Iowa) became dissatisfied, believing that the line should be moved farther north, making the southern conference stronger because larger. Petitions from the Iowa Conference requesting a change in the boundary line were sent to General Conference in 1872, 1880, 1900, and 1904.

However, Upper Iowa Conference members were satisfied with the line, and Iowa failed to make a convincing case for change. The line remained unchanged until it was removed by the merger of all Iowa conferences in 1969. S. N. Fellows tells more about the controversy in his *History of the Upper Iowa Conference.*[9]

A great many Bohemian (Czech) people settled in northeastern Iowa and made a genuine contribution to American life. Many lost contact with the

Catholic Church upon coming to America and could be reached only by the Protestant churches. The Presbyterians reached some in Cedar Rapids, and the young people of St. Paul's Methodist Episcopal Church in Cedar Rapids started a Bohemian Mission in 1890.

1900-1920

By 1905 the Bohemian work of the Methodist Episcopal Church had spread to Belle Plaine and Elberson. The church in Cedar Rapids had grown to 65 full members, 6 probationers, 30 adherents, 2 Sunday Schools, and 130 scholars.[10] Services were not conducted in Czech after World War I, and John Huss Church in Cedar Rapids merged with Asbury in 1957. A new generation had become Americanized. People of Bohemian background are to be found in many United Methodist Churches of Northeast Iowa today.

The first decade of the 20th century was, in Upper Iowa, a time of consolidation. A church had been established in nearly every community, but in too many places, small towns had become overchurched. Competing denominations each tried to maintain a church without enough people in the community. Churches had been built as each small town dreamed of becoming a metropolis. Reorganization has been an ongoing process ever since.

Open-country churches had been built to serve the community, but farms became larger as early as 1900. As travel improved many farm families preferred to drive a short distance to the nearby village church, and open-country churches often lost out. A district superintendent wrote in 1908, "That we are failing to meet the conditions now prevailing in the rural districts is a confession we are compelled to make."[11] That problem has continually troubled district superintendents.

The payment of pastors' salaries was a problem confronting the church for many years, even when economic conditions were relatively good. Churches frequently failed to make plans for finance until the last month of the church year. Money placed in the collection plate on Sunday mornings was applied toward current bills, and the preacher received some of his salary from time to time. However, many bills, including the pastor's overdue salary remained unpaid until the last month of the year. Then a drive was made to "pay the preacher."

If he were personally unpopular, or the crops had been poor, that was not easily done. A preacher who owed debts around the community for six months each year could never be of maximum effectiveness, even though he did succeed in paying all of them by the time he left for Annual Conference.

The presiding elder of the Cedar Falls District wrote in 1905, "Pastors' claims have been the object of special solicitude. Lax business methods are the rule on the charges."[12] The Davenport district superintendent wrote in 1908, "Pastors' claims have been met better than in years. An increasing number of charges are adopting the latest methods of church financing."[13] (The title of the presiding elder was changed to district superintendent in 1908, but the responsibilities remained the same.)

In 1909 the superintendent of the Cedar Falls District stated that a majority of the official boards planned to meet all of their financial obligations, including the pastor's salary, monthly, and that "we should not be satisfied until every charge does this." He also stated: "The careless and haphazard method of some charges is a shame and a disgrace."[14]

In the early 1900s the superintendents' reports speak often of the need for more systematic business methods in the area of church finance. However, they usually also report improvements of the church property and the payment of old debts. The church was truly moving ahead in its management of material things.

Before 1912 new converts were enrolled as "preparatory members" for six months. At the end of that time they were either received into "full membership" or dropped from the rolls. After 1912, the term "preparatory member" was applied to all baptized children. These children were to be received into full membership upon reaching a proper age and upon having been adequately trained. The earlier six-months probation period disappeared.

The first steps leading to the establishment of the Wesley Foundation in the state colleges were taken in 1910. At that time the Iowa State Commission was formed with representation from each of the four conferences of the Methodist Episcopal Church.

The first meeting of the Commission was held in Grace M.E. Church in Des Moines on February 18, 1911. An adjourned meeting resumed later in the Des Moines Y.M.C.A. building on August 9, 1911. At that time some organizational changes were made. A recommendation was offered that "an All-Iowa Methodist Convention be held at such time as shall be deemed advisable."[15]

The Commission's most significant action was to request that each district superintendent add $100 to his district's apportionment for domestic missions. This sum was to be forwarded as soon as possible to the Commission Treasurer for the sole purpose of supporting university pastors in the state educational institutions at Ames and Iowa City. That program has been important in the life of students at Iowa schools. In 1912 L. F. Townsend was appointed pastor to the students at Iowa City and William Hintz to the students at Ames.

With the approval of the Iowa Conferences, the Inter-Conference Commission called an Iowa State Convention, held February 13 and 14, 1912. It was well attended. The chief subjects presented and discussed were: The Rural Church, The Church and Labor, Iowa's Educational Problems, Interdenominational Comity, and The Liquor Traffic. Plans were made looking toward the formation of an "Inter-Church Federation of the State of Iowa."

The Methodist Deaconess Movement opened its first institution within the bounds of the Upper Iowa Conference in March, 1914—The Hillcrest Deaconess Home and Baby Fold at Dubuque. This institution has continued its work, with modifications, since that time. For many years it was primarily a home and a home-finding institution for orphaned children. Its successor is now known as "Hillcrest Family Service."

The First World War disrupted the work of the church in Northeast Iowa. In 1915, while the United States was not yet directly involved, the Upper Iowa Conference spoke with care. The "State of the Church" report included the following:

> To our brethren in the countries now in the turmoil of war, we extend our heartfelt sympathy and earnestly pray that the scourge may pass, and that they may be kept for service when peace shall come.[16]

Two years later, after the country was actually in the war, a "Committee on War Situation" gave a lengthy report which said, in part,

> We call upon our pastors to express and cultivate the sentiment of patriotism, to display in every church in our conference the "Stars and Stripes," that all our worship may be under the shadow of our flag.[17]

The churches of Northeast Iowa tried to keep their programs going. In his annual report to conference R. F. Hurlburt, Superintendent of the Davenport District, summed up many of the problems caused by the war as seen in his district:

> Our church people are all so absorbed in the war issue that it seems to be increasingly difficult to interest them in any larger program of activities for the local church. The war occupies the world horizon and the most of our Methodist constituency can see nothing and talk of nothing, unless it is somehow bound up with the problem of the winning of the war. Most earnest effort has been made in evangelistic services by many of our pastors during the last year. But results have been meager when compared with the energy expended. Our Sunday Schools and Epworth Leagues are feeling most seriously the loss of the young men, who have gone to the front and of the young women who have gone into war work. In the interests of fuel conservation, the uniting of churches in a number of towns for the winter months has resulted in the saving of fuel, but it has greatly crippled the Methodist work along denominational lines. By the imperial forces of circumstances, church services, especially the Sunday night services, have frequently been transformed into war meetings. There are not enough days in the weekly calendar to keep Liberty Loan rallies away from Prayer Meeting nights. Red Cross work continues to interfere with the largest usefulness of the Ladies' Aid Society. So heavy are the drafts made upon us for the support of the Liberty Loan, the Red Cross work, and the Army Y.M.C.A. work, that our benevolences suffer in spite of the oft-repeated scriptural admonition: These ought ye to have done and not to leave the other undone.[18]

The 1918 Conference Journal lists two pastors who left their appointments to enlist as soldiers in the army. Two are listed as serving in the army as chaplains, and four served with the military as Y.M.C.A. workers. When the 1918 Conference Journal was printed, the list of pastors and pastors' sons in war service was prepared a little hastily, and some "pastors' sons" were listed as "pastors." There may be other mistakes. It is clear that the war had a tremendous impact on the life of the church.

Across America from 1917 to 1945 Sunday School average attendance steadily declined. Most denominations lost more ministers through death and retirement than the number received as replacements. Many young men who were in college in 1917 preparing for the ministry left for the army and did not return to school when the war was over. This trend was not recognized at first because it was gradual. By the 1930s the shortage of pastors was obvious. Reversal of the trend did not come until 1945.

The last year of World War I and the years immediately following were a period of difficulties and changes. The 1918 influenza epidemic was a disastrous blow to the morale of every community. Many churches were closed for a time in an effort to inhibit the spread of the disease. One cannot be sure whether closing of the churches on Sundays saved anyone from the flu, but it was certainly a damper on the spiritual life of the congregation, and hindered church finances.

1920-1948

The one positive influence in the life of Methodism the last year of the war and immediately following was the Centenary Movement. The hundredth anniversary of the formation of the Methodist Missionary Society, which later became the Board of Missions, was observed by both the Methodist Episcopal Church and the Methodist Episcopal Church South. Plans were made for aggressive evangelistic efforts and fund-raising to expand missionary projects. This happened to coincide with the end of the war in Europe, and people were optimistic when they made their pledges.

Most districts over-pledged their apportionment, and church members made heroic efforts to pay their five-year pledges even when prices for farm products took a dramatic plunge. The superintendent of the Davenport District reported in 1922:

> No one could or did foresee at the time of the Centenary campaign the terrible change that has since come in the financial condition of the country, with its almost disastrous effect on every department of the church and business world.[19]

The period between 1920 and the Methodist merger in 1939 was trying for Iowa Methodists and their pastors. In the first place, the country faced an emotional slump after the war. Public interest had been directed to the war, leaving the church in second place in many minds. The Centenary Movement had helped stem the tide of indifference, but economic and social alterations in the rural communities of Iowa—new farming methods, school consolidation, road improvement—actually weakened the open-country church.

During the war the government had maintained an artificially high price for wheat, and farmers had prospered. After the war, when the price controls were removed, farm produce prices dropped sharply, yet costs farmers had to pay did not decline in the same degree. Land values became inflated, and when the slump came in 1920, many farmers found themselves unable to meet payments. Church budgets suffered, too, when economic conditions made it difficult to meet the absolute minimum expenses of the farm.

The period during and after the First World War was a trying time for church colleges, with all facing serious financial problems. The situation was particularly critical in the Upper Iowa Conference, as the Conference was attempting to support two colleges.

The 1927 session of the Conference authorized a financial campaign for $1.2 million for the two Conference colleges—Upper Iowa University and Cornell College—the campaign to be conducted "not earlier than May, 1929." An executive committee was approved by the Conference to promote the campaign. Because of emergencies arising at both colleges, this committee advanced the date to the fall of 1928.

Early in February the official boards of a number of the stronger churches in the conference passed resolutions urging the economic necessity of making the campaign for one conference college rather than for two. In response to the requests of the laymen and of bi-district conferences held in Mt. Vernon and in Fayette, an Educational Council was convened at Waterloo on March 6, 1928, consisting of "members of the upper Iowa Conference, supply pastors, members or alternates of the Lay Electoral Conference, with five members at large in each district, appointed by the respective district superintendents, with the Bishop of the Area presiding."[20]

The Council reached the conclusion that it was not possible to support two colleges in the Conference. They believed it was preferable to merge the colleges, rather than risk losing them both. As as a result, it was resolved that the colleges should be merged under the name "Cornell-Upper Iowa College," located in Mt. Vernon. Immediately after the Council meeting which recommended the merger, a protest meeting was held in Fayette. The Upper Iowa trustees rejected the proposal by a two-thirds vote.

Since it appeared impossible to conduct a successful financial campaign to support two colleges, and Upper Iowa University refused to accept the proposed merger, Upper Iowa University was released from its relationship with the Upper Iowa Conference.

The campaign was conducted successfully for Cornell College alone. Upper Iowa went its own way as an independent college in Fayette. It appeared to many, at the time, that Upper Iowa University was doomed to fail for lack of support, but more than fifty years later, Upper Iowa College is still serving the area.[21]

Epworth Seminary was changed to a boys' military academy in 1923. Free public high schools had taken the place of the seminaries. In 1926 Colonel Brown, who had headed the military academy for three years, arranged with the board of directors to assume private ownership of the institution. It was no longer Methodist-connected. The military academy continued until 1928.[22]

Rural population was shifting during the 1920s and 1930s, threatening the small country churches. In an earlier time one preacher could serve a multi-point circuit, preaching morning, afternoon, and evening. Later people became unwilling to attend the afternoon service. Improved transportation made it possible to attend social affairs on Sunday afternoons and evenings. Numerous small churches died, and not all members of the congregations transferred to town churches.

The district superintendents' reports during the 1920s lacked the exuberant optimism of an earlier day when the state was being settled and each year the presiding elder boasted of members added to the rolls and new church buildings erected. The 1920s and 1930s were a time of retrenchment. Dead wood was being pruned from the rolls, and churches abandoned.

The agricultural depression had not been foreseen. Most churches made real sacrifices to pay pledges for the Centenary Movement, but when that was done, benevolent giving fell off, and Methodism's over-all missionary program had to be re-thought.

At the 1931 session of the Upper Iowa Conference the World Service Council recommended ". . . that we remind our people that unless the present situation in World Service can be met by October 31st, 250 foreign missionaries will be brought home and 1,000 men and women employed by the boards operating in America will be released."[23]

The local churches also found it hard to pay the preacher's salary. At the beginning of the year, the church would set goals which it proved unable to reach. In 1931, for example, an over-all shortage of four percent on pastors' salaries was noted. This kind of situation continued until the 1940s.

Between the two World Wars Methodists of Upper Iowa were struggling to create a Christian atmosphere in their communities. At first rejoicing in the nation's adoption of the Prohibition Amendment they had championed, many were disappointed by its ultimate repeal. Convinced of the "Protestant work ethic's" soundness, they met economic depression with triumphant courage and perseverance. Gradually developing a more mature social conscience, they were supporting Clear Lake Conference Campground and its Epworth League Institute, White Cross offerings for Hospitals, and Hillcrest Baby Fold.

The background of an important addition to the Upper Iowa Conference in the 1930s points up the significance of language in church history. Methodism had been strong among German-speaking people in the United States for years. Back in 1864 the German churches located in northern Iowa had been assigned to the Northwest German Conference. From that time on they had followed a parallel path beside their English-speaking brethren. Eventually as the younger generation did not use German in church, reasons for remaining separate no longer existed.

In 1933 the Chicago Northwest Conference (German) was dissolved and its churches and preachers merged into the contiguous English conference. On October 1, 1933, Upper Iowa received thirteen charges and 1,677 church members. The active ministers received were W. F. Belling, Charles City; A. H. Meyer, Colesburg; B. A. Wendlandt, Dubuque; H. E. Hilmer, Flood Creek; W. L. Feller, Giard; J. J. Hoffman, Gladbrook; J. L. Menzer, St. Charles; Theodore Staiger, Sherrill; A. C. Prust, Wood; Herman Nedtwig, Ridgeway; G. H. Kohler, Mason City. Besides the active ministers, Upper

Iowa received four retired men: George C. Clausen, Albert F. Damerow, Herman J. Leomker, and August Panzlau. Six widows of ministers were assigned to the conference: Anna Hartke, Hanna Hertel, Elizabeth Kruger, Caroline Spicker, Emma Thiel.[24]

American Methodism had been divided between South and North for the entire life of the Upper Iowa Conference. During the period under examination a growing movement led toward a re-unification in the church. Finally, in 1939, the three largest groups of Methodists—The Methodist Episcopal Church, The Methodist Episcopal Church South, and The Methodist Protestant Church—were merged into one, The Methodist Church. This had less effect in Upper Iowa than in South Iowa, as there were no southern churches there and few Methodist Protestants. The Upper Iowa Conference received one church, Rhodes, with 110 members and one pastor, Rev. C. R. Green, from the Methodist Protestant Church. Rev. Green retired in 1940 with forty-three years' service.

The change most felt in each local church was the uniting of the Ladies' Aids, the Woman's Foreign Missionary Societies, and the Woman's Home Missionary Societies into the Woman's Society of Christian Service.

The dissolution of the Central Northwest Conference (Swedish) in 1942, and of the Norwegian-Danish Conference in 1943, added no churches or preachers to the Upper Iowa Conference.

The departure of young ministers to the military in World War II made worse the shortage of preachers which already existed. At conference time, 1944, six members of the Upper Iowa Conference were in the military chaplaincy, increasing to eleven by 1945.

During the closing years of World War II the Methodist Church launched the Crusade for Christ which is discussed in Chapter Three. The Crusade was successful in Upper Iowa, as in the rest of the country. Financial goals were reached, Sunday School attendance increased, and young men answered the call to ministry.

The 1948 session of the conference was the last. In 1949 the Northwest Iowa Conference and the Upper Iowa Conference merged into one—the North Iowa Conference.

Northwest Iowa Conference

Frontier preaching and class meetings were on the scene in Northwest Iowa about the middle of the 19th century. A history of the First Methodist Church of Sioux City records the first class organized in 1855 by the Rev. William Black, assigned there by the Iowa Conference meeting in Mt. Pleasant. However, this is not confirmed in the conference minutes: the 1855 session met in Keokuk; the 1856 session met in Mt. Pleasant. The first session of the Upper Iowa Conference meeting in 1856 assigned Landon Taylor to Sioux City and as presiding elder of the Sioux City District.

It appears that Methodist activity started earlier, and it may very well have been led by Black. The local church history may be correct except as to the location of the 1855 conference session. The 1856 session of the Upper

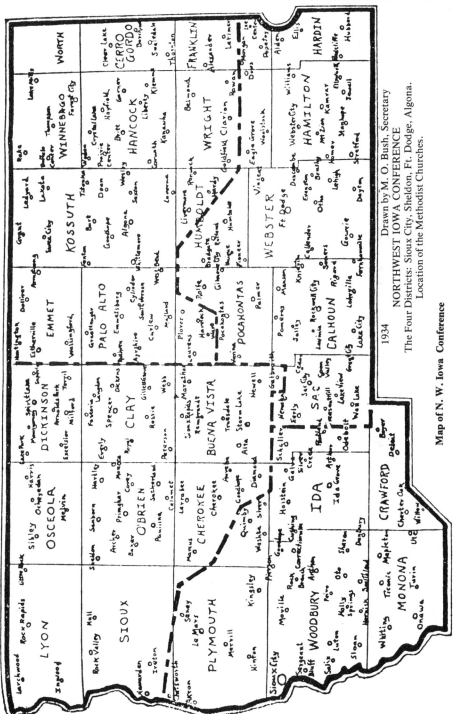

Drawn by M. O. Bush, Secretary
NORTHWEST IOWA CONFERENCE
The Four Districts: Sioux City, Sheldon, Ft. Dodge, Algona.
Location of the Methodist Churches.

1934

Map of N. W. Iowa Conference

Iowa conference made the following appointments in what was later to become the Northwest Iowa Conference:

Sioux City District, Landon Taylor, presiding elder
Sioux City and Sargeant's Bluff (sic), Landon Taylor
Smithland, Ashland, and Belvidere, D. J. Havens Sac, Carroll, and Crawford, W. Black[25]

The Northwest Iowa Conference was set off from the Des Moines Conference by the General Conference meeting in May of 1872. It comprised the northern half of the Des Moines Conference and the Dakota Territory. On September 18 of the same year it convened for the first time at Fort Dodge, with Bishop Edward G. Andrews presiding.

In his history of the Northwest Iowa Conference Bennett Mitchell commented that Bishop Andrews'

". . . administration was painstaking, thorough, and efficient. He was just entering his episcopate, and was without any of that imperialism that sometimes creeps unconsciously into the lives of some of our good bishops who have, perhaps, been too long in the office."[26]

The new Northwest Iowa Conference had three districts of 52 charges, 23 charter members, and 3,392 lay members. At the first roll call it was announced that G. M. Binks had withdrawn from the church and had gone into the ministry of the Congregational Church. New members were admitted into the conference that year, several coming by transfer from other conferences.

1872-1900

Commenting on the new conference, Bennett Mitchell wrote:

When our Conference was organized the country was in its early bud. It took not, however, a seer's vision to see the full bloom and the glorious fruitage that was to follow. Even the most prosy person could not look upon it without seeing in the near future flourishing cities, towns and villages, productive farms, fruitful orchards, fields of waving corn, and herds of cattle upon a thousand hills. One only needed to put the ear to the ground to hear the coming tramp of the many thousands that now rejoice in the goodly heritage.[27]

The second session of the Northwest Iowa Conference met at Yankton, South Dakota September 25, 1873 with Bishop Bowman presiding. Twenty-two answered roll call. Mitchell reported the work of the conference was largely routine, but then told of the formation of the Dakota mission, which was of great future importance.

He also reported one amusing incident which illustrates the way old-country politics influenced life in America. The anti-English bias of the Irish is well-known, but the feeling of first-generation Norwegians toward Swedes has also had its influence on American church affairs.

On the occasion Mitchell mentions, the conference had appointed a Norwegian, Brother Arveson, to examine a Swede, Brother Moor, on his progress in the course of study. The report was not altogether flattering.

Bennett Mitchell

No sooner had it been made than Brother Moor sprang to his feet and said in his broken language: "Yes, Mr. President, Brother Arveson examined me, and I examined Brother Arveson. Sometimes Brother Arveson beat me and sometimes I beat Brother Arveson." Then, in the midst of a roar of laughter, Brother Moor was advanced to the class of the second year.[28]

Living the Christian life is not always easy when people are trying to live down past memories. The problem with which Brothers Arveson and Moor were struggling seemed funny to the English-speaking preachers, but it was serious to the Scandinavians. Arveson and Moor were to be commended for the way in which they were able to handle the situation.

Regarding the 1873 conference Bennett Mitchell reports that the average preacher's salary for the year was $383. The year before the average salary had been a little over $400. The church fell down in this matter, but the benevolent collections grew a little, and the membership of the church increased 161, while the preachers increased in number from 23 to 33.[29]

A dollar was worth far more in those days than it is now. Automobiles, which we regard as necessities, were unheard of. Life was so organized that a man could walk or use a horse in circumstances where the automobile is now needed. Mitchell states:

The preacher in those days who had one whole suit of clothes was well furnished; and if by reason of some accident a rent was made in a garment, or if some one garment had been worn until it needed a patch, the deft fingers of our wives and mothers could readily make the necessary repairs. I knew one preacher, Brother Terrill, who went without shoes most of the Summer, and sometimes preached when his feet were bare. Let it not be said that these were thriftless fellows. I resent the insinuation. It is slander. These men stayed by and did their work, almost without pay, while the nicer fellows left their needy flocks and went in search of better salaries.[30]

Mitchell's published story of the Northwest Iowa Conference becomes a little tedious at times, as he gives copious details regarding the doings of each session of the annual conference. He tells us who was admitted, who located, who was transferred in or out, and adds many personal comments about the appearance and personality of each man. A large number of men took the supernumerary relationship, or retired, only to be readmitted a few years later.

Without verifying each instance, one suspects preachers had to drop out to earn money for accumulating bills. Each year some transferred to another conference where the grass seemed greener, or it might be easier to support a family. Some men withdrew from the Methodist Church to enter the Congregational Church, where they could have a settled ministry. Many heroic preachers died young, in the midst of hardships.

The fifth session of the conference met in 1876 at LeMars with forty preachers answering the roll call, nearly doubled in four years. The population of the territory was growing rapidly, and the preachers were all evangelists. The chief goal was to win persons to Christ, although other matters of Christian concern were not neglected.

From 1880 to 1900 all but one year shows an increase in church members. In twenty years the total membership more than tripled. New churches and parsonages were built during this period of optimism.

However, roads were poor and travel arduous. Histories tell interesting stories of the troubles encountered, particularly in the springtime. Bennett Mitchell recounts one occasion when B. W. Cole and his presiding elder were traveling up the Little Sioux River south of Correctionville. Both team and buggy became mired in a wet place between the loess hills and the river. The two preachers had to get out into the mud, unhitch the team, pull one mule at a time out of the mud, and then the buggy. The preachers went to church in Correctionville that evening dressed in mud-stained clothes because they had no others.[32] The loess soil of western Iowa, when wet, has an unusually sticky consistency. Real dedication was needed to move around the circuits in mud season.

An effort was made to establish a conference college at Algona in Kossuth County in 1878. The college failed in two years, leaving the way clear for the development of Morningside College later on, in a better location. When the Algona school failed, the Northwest Iowa Conference joined with Upper Iowa in sponsoring Cornell College at Mt. Vernon. Four members of Northwest Iowa took their places on the Board of Trustees of Cornell. However, the dream of establishing a Methodist college in the northwestern part of the state was not abandoned—merely postponed.

In 1889 the conference approved a commission to consider a possible conference seminary. No bids were received, but an independent group of men obtained a charter for a school in the Morningside section of Sioux City, to be known as the University of the Northwest. The 1891 conference voted to endorse the new college. Although it was never under the control of the conference, enough cooperation existed to make it appear a conference failure when the school failed financially.

The conference of 1894 appointed a commission with authority to

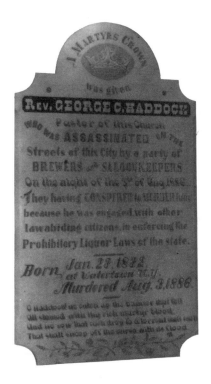

George Haddock Memorial Tablet at First Methodist Church, Sioux City.

establish a college in Morningside or elsewhere. Morningside College was incorporated December 5, 1894. The campus and buildings that had been known as the University of the Northwest were purchased for $25,250.[33] Morningside College opened September 11, 1895, with 196 students enrolled. In 1914 Charles City College, an institution of the Northwest German Conference, was merged with Morningside.

A tragic event in 1886 was the assassination of the Rev. George C. Haddock on a Sioux City street. It is believed men hired by some saloon keepers killed Haddock to stop his efforts to have the state temperance laws enforced in Sioux City. This murder provided a temperance movement martyr, inspiring the campaign for prohibition of the liquor traffic in Iowa.

1900-1920

As has been mentioned in other chapters, Methodists in Iowa experienced numerous changes coming into the 20th century. By 1900 the settled territory was served by a network of railroads. The United States Post Office first introduced Rural Free Delivery in 1896. The service was quickly extended across the country. It was now possible for small-town and farm families to subscribe to a daily newspaper, which tended to broaden their interests.

The most outstanding program marking the turn of the century in the Methodist Episcopal Church was the Twentieth Century Movement. It had national goals of saving two million souls and raising a twenty-million-dollar "thank offering" in three years for various purposes. Each conference made plans and set goals.

A committee of seventeen was appointed in 1899 to direct the movement in northwestern Iowa. In 1900 the committee reported that $54,927.92 was raised, most of which went to Morningside College. Bennett Mitchell commented, "To me it seemed that the movement in our conference was embarrassed a little by too much machinery. This hindered somewhat the spontaneity and freedom necessary to best results."[34] But the goals were reached.

Many changes came so gradually that they were hardly noticed until accomplished. In 1900 the rule limiting the number of consecutive years that a preacher could serve one appointment was dropped, but the change came gradually in practice. Most churches continued having a new preacher every two or three years. Some historic Methodist practices such as Class Meetings were being phased out. People no longer felt the need of them. The 1902 report on "The State of the Church" begins by saying, "We regret that many of our members do not have a lively interest in some of the means of grace, especially prayer and class meetings."[35]

Home missions and camps were organized within the conference early in the new century. Shesler Home in Sioux City was incorporated on March 20, 1900 and has served Siouxland since that time. At first it was a home for deaconesses, but for many years it has been a home for working girls. Also in the first decade of the century Helping Hand Mission and Wall Street Mission, both in Sioux City, were getting started and laying firm foundations for later work.

Near the end of the same decade a "work" was started among the Bohemian people of Fort Dodge. In 1909 fourteen members were reported, and in 1911 J. F. Zavodsky was assigned for the third year. The Bohemian work disappeared from the list of appointments in 1919.

The Methodist Camp at the northeast end of West Lake Okoboji began in 1915 as a Sheldon District project. The Camp Meeting, later called the Bible Conference, has met every August for sixty-nine years, and is a continuing part of church life in Northwest Iowa. Northwest Iowa's first Epworth League Institute was held in 1918, introducing in the conference a movement which influenced many youth.

During the war years approximately one thousand black people moved to Sioux City, and more were expected. After consultation with the Board of Home Missions and representative black people, the previously closed Haddock Memorial Church was reopened. The Reverend Dudley Smith of the Central Missouri Conference (Colored) was assigned as pastor.[36] This work continued until 1923.

World War I greatly affected the work of the church in Northwest Iowa. Five preachers served as military chaplains, ten went to work for the Y.M.C.A., and seven served in the military.[37] A decline in Sunday School attendance and in the number of young men entering the ministry began during this period, lasting until 1945.

It is interesting to note that in the midst of wartime turmoil a committee on "The State of the Church" wrote a two-page report (1918) citing the growth of "formalism" as the church's chief problem.[38] Read in the 1980s, the analysis seems inadequate.

With a quite different concern D. A. McBurney wrote in 1919 of his six years on the Sheldon District. McBurney was an optimist and always looked for the best, despite a big membership loss in the western end of the district. The loss had been steady as Dutch people belonging to the Reformed Church moved into the area. But McBurney commented,

> Thank God we are not giving way to the enemy. Our competition is a friendly Christian organization that with steady strides moves on, gaining ground with the passing of every real estate agent, and holding what it gains. I refer to Holland people, with their ardent loyalty and devotion.[39]

The best publicized activity of 1918-1923 was the Centenary Movement, a church-wide movement to expand the world-wide mission of the Methodist Episcopal Church. The membership of every church was canvassed for five-year pledges to finance the program. This campaign was carried out during post-war optimism accompanied by a boom in land prices. Each district more than met its pledge goal in the Northwest Iowa Conference. All that remained to be done was to collect the pledges.

During the war American farmers were urged to produce more and more. A popular slogan was "Wheat will win the war." Crop prices went up, leading to speculation on farm land. Farms changed hands at inflated prices. When the slump in the prices of farm produce came in 1921, farming communities found themselves burdened by an impossible debt.

In his report for 1922, H. E. Hutchinson, Superintendent of the Sheldon District, wrote of difficulties in collecting the pledges:

> Part of this is due to the fact that the railroad strike has made it an absolute impossibility to sell grain in some of the towns. Most of it is due to the effects of the land speculation of a few years ago that have made debts far beyond any possibility of payment. . . . This means that many farms are carrying a higher amount of debt for interest than can be produced by the crop. This makes no provision for taxes or living.[40]

However, F. B. Nixon of the Ida Grove District wrote, "Centenary interests have been faithfully looked after. . . . Men have given sacrificially and even borrowed money to pay their pledges."[41]

The decade of the 1920s had some bright spots to relieve its frustrations. In 1922 Northwest Iowa Conference celebrated a "Semi-Centennial" to commemorate fifty years of growth and service. People looked hopefully toward the future.

But the 1930s brought depressing times for the church, as for all aspects of life. The previous decade had been discouraging for the farmers, but with

bank closings the situation became more difficult. In 1932 the Superintendent of the Algona District, W. H. Lease, wrote in his sixth annual report,

> Economically, these years have become increasingly difficult. Nineteen banks
> closed in Algona District our first year and have been going with monotonous
> regularity until now there are very few remaining that are not new or reorgan-
> ized banks.[42]

That same year Herbert Clegg, Superintendent of the Fort Dodge
District, reported, "In my last round of conferences, there were thirty-nine
places where references were made to money being tied up in closed banks
or by the waiver plan."[43]

The German language churches lost their reason for remaining separate
during the war, when the last of them turned to the English language. Many
older people still preferred worship in German, but younger ones tended to
turn to a nearby English-language church. In 1933 the Chicago Northwest
Conference was dissolved. Its churches and preachers were absorbed into
the contiguous English conferences.

The Northwest Iowa Conference received four pastoral charges: Dows-
Morgan, LeMars, Odebolt-Richland, and Varina; four members in effec-
tive relation—G. H. Wessel, S. C. Steinbrenner, W. J. Loeck, and F. W.
Schneider; two members in retired relations—F. O. Barz and Frederick
Schaub; and two widows of members—Katharina Feller and Minnie Klaus.
Schneider was Vice President of Morningside College and S. C. Stein-
brenner a professor at Morningside.[44]

In 1939 the Northwest Iowa Conference of "The Methodist Episcopal
Church" became the Northwest Iowa Conference of "The Methodist
Church." Since no Methodist Protestant churches were within the con-
ference, there were no resultant changes in charges. The "Lay Delegate" to
conference became a "Lay Member" with a vote. Each church elected a
"Lay Leader." The three women's organizations were merged into the
"Woman's Society of Christian Service," which absorbed the responsibili-
ties of all three.

The churches of the Norwegian-Danish Conference within Northwest
Iowa Conference territory were taken into the contiguous English conference in 1940 as the German conference had been seven years earlier.
C. H. Pettersen and A. R. Nygaard were received into the N. W. Iowa Conference. (Other parts of the Norwegian-Danish Conference were not dissolved until 1943.)

The Central Northwest Conference (Swedish) was dissolved in 1942. The
churches and pastors were transferred into the contiguous English conferences. Northwest Iowa received Richard Johnson and the Harcourt
church, Curt Noren, an accepted supply, with the Sheldahl church, and
Godtfred S. Bruland with the Stratford church. Bruland was transferred to
Dallas in the South Iowa Conference.

The early 1940s were dominated by World War II with resulting displace-
ments. The 1943 list of appointments named eleven ministers in the military

chaplaincy and thus not available for appointment to churches. In 1944 there were thirteen chaplains from the N. W. Iowa Conference. By 1946 most of them had returned to civilian life, with four chaplains continuing on active duty.

The North Iowa Conference was formed in 1949 by the merger of Upper Iowa and Northwest Iowa. The histories of the two conferences were continued in the life of the new, larger conference.

The North Iowa Conference

On June 22, 1949 the Upper Iowa and the Northwest Iowa Conferences merged to form the North Iowa Conference of The Methodist Church. The Upper Iowa Conference had consisted of the northeastern part of the state since 1864, and earlier all of northern Iowa. The Northwest Iowa Conference had included the northwestern part of the state since 1872. (Until 1885 it had also included Dakota Territory.)

The first session of the North Iowa Conference of the Methodist Church was held at St. Paul's Methodist Church in Cedar Rapids June 21-26, 1949. On Tuesday, June 21st the two conferences met separately to complete any unfinished business. Then each adjourned, to reconvene the next morning as a merged conference.

The new conference had 454 ministers and 135,000 laity. No changes were made in the district lines, leaving the new conference with the same eight districts as had made up the two old conferences. The districts and their superintendents were: Algona, F. W. Ortmeyer; Cedar Rapids, F. F. Travis; Davenport, H. M. Grant; Dubuque, H. H. Dill; Fort Dodge, C. J. Semans; Sheldon, A. F. Schuldt; Sioux City, H. W. Farnham; Waterloo, C. S. Hempstead. Details regarding the merger are recorded in the 1949 *Journal of the North Iowa Conference.*

Many important actions did not make headlines, and do not appear in this book, but contributed to the twenty-year existence of the North Iowa Conference. Conference committees met, passed resolutions, and led the thinking of Methodist pastors and people. Some resolutions were not taken seriously by very many, but they represented the efforts of Christian people seeking to deal with the world's problems through the agency of The Methodist Church.

Meanwhile the daily life of the church went on. Families worshiped God and participated in church activities. Pastors comforted the sick and the suffering. Churches were built, and young people entered the ministry.

During the two-decade life of the North Iowa Conference membership increased more than 11.6% even though purging of membership rolls removed names of people who had ended all contacts with the home church. The increase may seem small when compared with the dramatic gains reported a hundred years earlier. But this increase came in a period when the state was already settled. Young people were migrating to the West and the Southwest in search of economic opportunities. Yet the church at home was still growing. Average Sunday School attendance in North Iowa increased 15.6% during the post-war "baby boom" years.

In the fall of the 1950-51 conference year the two Iowa conferences joined a state-wide "Des Moines Area Evangelistic Advance." South Iowa sent guest pastors to lead evangelistic meetings in cooperating churches of North Iowa, and vice versa. Faithful members were inspired, inactive members became active, and unchurched persons were visited. Charles Hempstead wrote in the District Superintendents' Composite Report:

> Possibly the outstanding endeavor of the year was the part we played in the Area Evangelistic Mission in December. Under the leadership of Bishop Brashares and Eugene Golay, 215 guest pastors came from surrounding conferences to lead the laymen of 248 churches in making 16,286 interviews, to secure 6,545 commitments. The total attendance at the various preaching services during the ten days was 104,758.[45]

A similar series of meetings was held again in 1954 with comparable results.

After ten years the conference discovered it could be administered with one less district. The 1960 conference re-drew district lines. Some district names and most boundaries were changed. The former Algona and Davenport districts disappeared. A Mason City District was created, and the Waterloo District absorbed much of the former Cedar Rapids District. The Cedar Rapids name now covered much of the Davenport District.

A strength of Methodism is its ability to plan and cooperate on programs beyond the local church. An "Area Planning Committee" was established in 1958 by the North and South Iowa Conferences to study the needs of the state and to make plans to meet those needs. The committee members from North Iowa were: ministers, L. D. Havighurst, Fred Miller, and Jackson Burns; district superintendents, H. D. Temple and C. S. Hempstead; lay members, Mrs. R. E. McGowen, Charles D. Bell, and H. C. Weaver.

A need was seen for a quadrennial emphasis on spiritual renewal with three phases. 1961-62 was designated a year of Bible Study; 1962-63 a Year of Evangelism; 1963-64 a year of Membership Cultivation and Spiritual Renewal.[46]

The Methodist churches of the state studied the Book of Romans during 1961-62 under the guidance of Bishop Gerald Ensley. The bishop met first at the Y.M.C.A. in Des Moines with a group of pastors—one from each sub-district in the state—to study the book together. These sub-district leaders in turn met with the other pastors in their respective sub-districts, and passed the training on to them.

The lay people were introduced to the Romans study at Churchmanship Institutes held in each district in the state, at which the bishop spoke on "The Importance of Bible Study." Then 281 pastors held study groups in their churches. The district superintendents' report at the next session of the annual conference stated:

As was to be expected, the results seemed to be most favorable in those churches in which the pastor worked the hardest and had the greatest enthusiasm for study. The general impression was one of deep appreciation for such a study and an enthusiastic request that a similar study be planned for next year.[47]

Conference programs often succeed to the extent that they are supported by pastors. An important reason for the success of the 1961-62 program was the enthusiasm with which it was accepted by the pastors and their congregations.

A memorable series of events of the 1960s was the abolition of the Central Jurisdiction (the racially segregated jurisdiction) of The Methodist Church. The 1960 General Conference made rules for transferring Central Jurisdiction churches into appropriate conferences and for the eventual abolition of the racially segregated jurisdiction.

The Central West Conference (black) merged with the Lexington Conference (black) on June 21, 1964. On July 9th that summer the churches and pastors of the Lexington Conference were transferred into the contiguous white conferences. North Iowa received two churches and their pastors: Morrow Memorial Church, Marshalltown, with pastor, Beverly William Wynn, and Union Memorial Church, Mason City, with Orville Blanks, a part-time accepted supply pastor. The conference also received one retired member, Jordan Ray, who died September 4, 1964. The abolition of the Central Jurisdiction gave the North Central Jurisdiction the newly elected Bishop James Thomas, who was assigned to the Iowa Area.

The formation of the United Methodist Church at Dallas, Texas in 1968 by the merger of The Evangelical United Brethren Church and The Methodist Church set the stage for further changes in Iowa. In 1969 the three Iowa conferences merged into one: the former Iowa Conference of the E.U.B. Church and the North and South Iowa Conferences of the former Methodist Church came together in one new Iowa Conference of the United Methodist Church.

Footnotes

1. S. N. Fellows, *History of the Upper Iowa Conference* (Cedar Rapids, Ia.: Laurance Press Co., 1907) p. 12.
2. Ibid., p. 12.
3. Ibid., p. 39.
4. Ibid., pp. 44-45.
5. Ibid., p. 55.
6. Leland L. Sage, *A History of Iowa* (Ames: Iowa State University Press, 1974) p. 140.
7. Fellows, ibid., p. 81.
8. Fellows, ibid., p. 83.
9. Fellows, ibid., pp. 72-80.
10. *Upper Iowa Conference Journal* 1905 p. 199.
11. *Upper Iowa Conference Journal* 1908 p. 39.
12. *Upper Iowa Conference Journal* 1905 p. 170.
13. *Upper Iowa Conference Journal* 1908 p. 42.
14. *Upper Iowa Conference Journal* 1909 p. 173.

15. *Upper Iowa Conference Journal* 1911 p. 451.
16. *Upper Iowa Conference Journal* 1915 p. 509.
17. *Upper Iowa Conference Journal* 1917 p. 265.
18. *Upper Iowa Conference Journal* 1918 p. 396.
19. *Upper Iowa Conference Journal* 1922 p. 376.
20. *Upper Iowa Conference Journal* 1928 pp. 58-59.
21. *Upper Iowa Conference Journal* 1928 pp. 58-68.
22. *Upper Iowa Conference Journal* 1926 p. 396.
23. *Upper Iowa Conference Journal* 1931 p. 616.
24. *Upper Iowa Conference Journal* 1934 pp. 395-396.
25. Fellows, ibid., p. 48.
26. Bennett Mitchell, *History of the Northwest Iowa Conference* (Sioux City: Perkins Bros. Company, 1904) p. 78.
27. Ibid., p. 7.
28. Ibid., p. 26.
29. Ibid., p. 30.
30. Ibid., p. 30.
31. Ibid., p. 53.
32. Ibid., p. 78.
33. Ibid., pp. 209-210.
34. Ibid., p. 259.
35. *Northwest Iowa Conference Journal* 1902 p. 195.
36. *Northwest Iowa Conference Journal* 1919 p. 558.
37. *Northwest Iowa Conference Journal* 1918 p. 373.
38. *Northwest Iowa Conference Journal* 1918 pp. 416-417.
39. *Northwest Iowa Conference Journal* 1919 p. 551.
40. *Northwest Iowa Conference Journal* 1922 p. 313.
41. *Northwest Iowa Conference Journal* 1922 p. 315.
42. *Northwest Iowa Conference Journal* 1932 p. 39.
43. *Northwest Iowa Conference Journal* 1932 p. 41.
44. *Northwest Iowa Conference Journal* 1933 p. 112.
45. *North Iowa Conference Journal* 1951 p. 700.
46. *North Iowa Conference Journal* 1961 pp. 102-103.
47. *North Iowa Conference Journal* 1962 p. 104.

5

The Methodist Protestant Church in Iowa

The division in American Methodism over the question of slavery in 1844, which led to the formation of the Methodist Episcopal Church South, is well known. But there was an earlier split over matters of church government which also had great significance. We cannot afford to forget the contributions of the Methodist Protestant Church to United Methodism.

The Methodist Protestant Church was a major branch of Methodism which joined with the Methodist Episcopal Church and the Methodist Episcopal Church South to form The Methodist Church in May, 1939. It was one of the threads woven into the fabric of United Methodism, and although the "M.P.s" were not numerous in Iowa, their influence has been more important than their numbers would indicate. Their story tells us something of Iowa of the nineteenth and early twentieth centuries. Their spirit of democracy and their essential conservatism have each made their mark on the United Methodist Church in Iowa.

The Methodist Protestant Church was organized in Baltimore, Maryland in 1830 as a result of dissatisfaction with the power of the episcopacy and the lack of lay representation in the conferences of the Methodist Episcopal Church.[1] Through the years the larger branches of Methodism made changes, one by one, which lessened the authority of the bishops and which gave laymen representation at annual and general conferences. As a result, most of the issues which had caused the division were resolved in favor of the Methodist Protestant view. Thus when the 1939 union came, a member of the Methodist Protestant Church could say, "The Methodist Episcopals have all come over to our side, and so we kindly consent to take them in."[2]

BEGINNINGS OF THE M.P. CHURCH

The authority of the leaders appointed by John Wesley was not seriously questioned in America. The itinerant system was very well adapted to the frontier situation in the new nation. The power to send the preachers to their circuits was entirely in the hands of the bishop. However, this complete power of the bishop in the American church, and the lack of lay representation, together with some minor issues, were sources of dissension within the church in the colonies from the beginning.

In 1792 James O'Kelley led a group out of the Methodist Episcopal Church, when the Annual Conference rejected a motion which would have allowed the preachers to appeal their appointments. "O'Kelley's Schism" was one of several small groups which later united to form the Disciples of

Christ. This schism did not finally settle the matter; the question lay dormant for about thirty years.[3]

At the close of the 1820 General Conference, William S. Stockton, a layman of Trenton, New Jersey began publishing a magazine—*The Wesleyan Repository*—which advocated lay representation at conference, election instead of appointment of presiding elders, and abolition of the episcopal office. This journal became the voice of the reformers.

In the 1824 General Conference, a resolution calling for an elective presiding eldership was rejected by a 63-61 vote. The issue of lay representation had also been discussed during the previous quadrennium, but memorials on this issue were referred to a committee headed by Nathan Bangs, who opposed lay representation. The memorials were rather curtly dismissed by the committee, and the committee report was approved by another 63-61 vote. Passions had run high, and during the next quadrennium several annual conferences passed resolutions intended to repress the reformers. Under these resolutions some dozen ministers were expelled from their conferences.

In November of 1827, six months before the 1828 General Conference, the reformers met under the name of "The Associated Methodist Reformers" and prepared a memorial to the General Conference. When the General Conference met, the reformers were defeated at every turn. Their memorials were not even considered.

After their defeat at General Conference, the reformers had to choose whether to remain within an ecclesiastical organization that they did not like, or to withdraw and organize a new church more to their liking. Many of those who had joined the reformers were regarded as "progressive" Methodists. Among those who chose to remain in the Methodist Episcopal Church were Peter Cartwright, Freeborn Garretson, and David Ostrander. Men such as Nicholas Snethen, Dennis Dorsey, and William Stockton—among the best preachers and laymen in American Methodism—joined the reformers and left the Methodist Episcopal Church.

After the 1828 General Conference adjourned, the Associated Methodist Reformers met again, formed a provisional organization, and appointed committees on Constitution, Discipline, Hymnody, and other topics. The provisional organization was made permanent in November, 1830, by the adoption of a constitution and the choice of a name, The Methodist Protestant Church. Just how many members were lost to the Methodist Episcopal Church because of the split is not known, as the M.E. Church was growing so fast during this period. The growth was certainly slowed for a time. However, it is probable that about one in seven or 50,000 members and over 200 ministers, joined the new M.P. Church.[4]

The reformers who founded the Methodist Protestant Church were not anxious to change more than was necessary to correct what they considered to be injustices. They regarded themselves as having been expelled, rather than as having seceded. Little was changed except the episcopacy and certain aspects of church government which were considered undemocratic.

The General Rules and the Articles of Religion were retained unchanged, and there was little change in the ritual. The office of bishop was abolished, the office of presiding elder was made elective, and pastoral appointments were made by committee. Laymen were given equal representation with ministers. Appointments could be appealed.[5]

A new American denomination which was to take its place in the religious life of America for 109 years had come into being. Later the Methodist Protestant heritage was to manifest itself in the new church it helped to form by merging with the Methodist Episcopal Church and the Methodist Episcopal Church South.

> Soon after the division, the controversies died down, the *Mutual Rights* suspended publication. The Methodist Episcopal Church, as soon as the reformers were no longer in their midst, quit attacking them.[6]

M.P. BEGINNINGS IN IOWA

From its beginning the Methodist Protestant Church was strong in the northern states east of the Mississippi River. From this base it moved westward across the nation with the frontier. It was never as large as the M.E. Church, the Baptists, or the Presbyterians, but it was there as a part of growing America. The conflict which had led to the division was of little significance on the frontier, and most pioneers had not heard of the controversy or the split. A Methodist was a Methodist. Since there were not many ordained ministers on the frontier, the work was carried on, for the most part, by laymen. These laymen had little interest in the quarrels of their eastern brethren.

The exact date when Methodist Protestant work actually started in Iowa is hard to determine. There may have been some M.P. work in Iowa earlier by laymen, but the first known Methodist Protestant preacher in Iowa was Oliver Atwood. He was a licensed exhorter in the Illinois Annual Conference of the Methodist Protestant Church. He was left without appointment in 1837, and moved to Iowa in the summer of that year. He began farming and did some work among his neighbors in Muscatine County, holding preaching services in his home. In September he was killed by the Sauk Indians in reprisal for the murder of a brother of Chief Poweshiek by a frontier ruffian. Methodist work in that vicinity died for the time being.

Early history is sometimes based on local legends which are not easily verified. The town of Winchester in Van Buren County boasted a Methodist Protestant Church from its founding. The town was platted February 29, 1840. The church met in the homes of its members as it did not have a building for some time. The congregation reported regularly to the Illinois Conference even though it did not have a regularly appointed minister in those early years. Despite its lack of a building, it retained an important place in Iowa Methodist Protestant History for several decades. Several early meetings of the Iowa Conference of the M.P. Church were held in Winchester. Winchester is now only a memory. However, in the opinion of some, the spirit of Methodist Protestantism lingers on in Van Buren County United Methodism.

As far as can be determined, the first class of the M.P. Church was organized in English River Township of Iowa County in 1841 by William Patterson, perhaps the outstanding leader of the church in Iowa in the early days. The first class meeting was recorded on May third of that year. Patterson later left the work in the hands of Joseph Hamilton, a physician who held a deacon's license. With the scarce population on the frontier in those days, this class was absorbed into the Methodist Episcopal Society in the community during the winter of 1842-43. Other societies and classes were formed in frontier communities along the Mississippi River and its tributaries, but none of them continued for any great length of time.

Iowa City was the site of one of the earliest and most ambitious projects attempted by the Methodist Protestant Church in Iowa. Burlington had been capital of the Iowa Territory from its formation in 1838 until the designation of Iowa City as capital in 1841. The new legislature meeting for the first time in Iowa City had offered (on April 24, 1841) a quarter block to each church that would erect a building upon it for religious or educational purposes. On May fourth, following the passing of this piece of legislation, Rev. John Libby, a Methodist Protestant minister, organized a Methodist Protestant society.[7]

The next day a lot was obtained and construction of a two-story brick building was begun. At the time, the building had the distinction of being the only brick building, the only two-story building, and the only church in the town. Governor Robert Lucas was the principal speaker at the laying of the cornerstone on May thirteenth.

As was often the case in early times, the church was used for most of the large public gatherings in the new capital city for several years. The territorial legislature met there from 1842 to 1844, just as it had met earlier in Old Zion, a Methodist Episcopal Church in Burlington. It also housed various educational enterprises. The first public school in Iowa City and the academic department of Iowa City College also met there. It was the earliest home of the Iowa School for the Blind, which later located at Vinton, Iowa.[8]

One of the founders of the church, William B. Snyder, launched the first religious periodical printed in Iowa—*The Iowa City Colporteur*—in 1841. Because there were not enough interested people in the area to support such a periodical, it died after six issues had appeared.

William Snyder and his brother, Thomas, had been among the leaders of the reform movement in Cincinnati, before coming to Iowa City to set up a dry-goods store. They brought their interest in reform with them, and without their help the church could not have been built. They contributed over two-thirds of the cost of the structure in the form of a loan amounting to $1,200. This debt, in the end, led to the death of the church.

The congregation at Iowa City reported only twenty-three members in 1842, and was not strong enough to support its ambitious programs, or to

Nicholas Snethen

maintain the building that had been erected. The minister, Rev. Libby, received only $43.81 of a proposed salary of $250. He found it necessary to preach at the Iowa City Univeralist Church in order to remain financially solvent. We have no record of what the M.P. people thought about their pastor preaching at the Universalist Church in addition to theirs.

Despite the small congregation's financial problems, they were willing to begin a larger and more ambitious project the following year. John Libby was moved, and William K. Talbott was appointed to the Iowa City field. Iowa City lacked a school, and to meet the need Rev. Talbott opened a common school with himself as teacher. With the encouragement of the Snyder brothers, a preparatory department was added, and then a "college."

Attached to the college was a theological department to assist young men preparing for the ministry. To those of us living in the 1980s this whole project appears a little preposterous, but it was entered into with all seriousness. And if Nicholas Snethen, the first president, had lived longer, there might have been a favorable outcome.

Dr. Nicholas Snethen had become a Methodist minister in 1791 at the age of twenty-two. He was one of those who went with the reformers at the time of the break, and had become one of the great men in the M.P. Church. Now at the age of seventy-five, he accepted the offer of the presidency of the new school which was to bear his name.

He came to Iowa City during October, 1844, and while there acted as chaplain at the opening session of the first state constitutional convention. Soon after his acceptance of the presidency of the new college he attended the session of the Illinois Annual Conference of the M.P. Church, and there secured an endorsement for the school. A system of subscriptions was set up, a set of rules for the administration of the seminary was outlined, and objectives were defined.

Dr. Snethen promised to assume his duties as soon as a class of six students was assembled. He returned to his Cincinnati home to write some one hundred lectures, select textbooks, and make other preparations. In March the class was ready and he set out for Iowa City. On the way he stopped to visit his sister and son in Princeton, Indiana. While there he contracted pneumonia, and died May 30, 1845.[9]

Dr. Snethen's death was a blow to the seminary. However, it should be noted that in a town of 1,000 inhabitants, six academies had sprung up, and all of them folded. Rev. Talbott kept Snethen Seminary open for one year at his own expense. Then, together with faculty members from the other institutions, he founded Iowa City University, which met at first in the Methodist Protestant Church building. This university is said to have been the precursor of the State University of Iowa.

Not only the Snethen Seminary failed, but the church at Iowa City disappeared from the records of the Illinois Annual Conference. The membership had declined to ten in 1845, and the church did not ask for a minister. In 1846 the Iowa City society was not represented at the first session of the Iowa Annual Conference of the Methodist Protestant Church. When the Iowa City building was lost because of failure to pay the debt, the Methodist Episcopal Church took over both the building and the debt. The legal transaction occurred under a cloud, and the issue was not finally settled until 1879 when the M.P. Church gave up its claim for a settlement of $300.[10]

The failure of optimistic plans in Iowa City is not surprising when the numerical weakness of the M.P. Church in Iowa at that time is considered. Only one minister (Rev. Talbott) was regularly appointed in the territory. There were only two other circuits in the state, with only six groups organized as churches. Both of these circuits were served by laymen. Only 235 members in the whole territory were reported to the Illinois Annual Conference in 1845, the last year the record of the Iowa churches was included in the statistics of that conference. The next year the Iowa Annual Conference was formed with the following present: William Patterson, George Pierson, Oliver Kellog, Alexander Caldwell, Preston Friend, and Henry Nesmith. The last two named were lay representatives.

The first session was called to order by William Collins of the Illinois Annual Conference, sent to aid in the organization of the new Iowa Conference. He was elected an honorary member of the new conference and served on most of the important committees. He also served as a mediator in an unsuccessful effort to straighten out the affairs of the Iowa City church and seminary. Evidently work had been done in some fields during the previous year, as three circuits made reports to the conference, with salaries for the coming year to total $1,020.

The permanent organization of the conference made William Patterson president for the following year. Appointments were made the day preceding adjournment so that dissatisfied brethren would have time to appeal. However, there were no appeals. The 1846 model of Methodist preachers must have been more easily satisfied than those of later times.

Rules were drawn up defining a mission, a circuit, and a station. Missions were fields of work having less than forty members. A circuit had forty members or more, and a church was designated a station when it came to have sixty members. The missions were not subject to the constitution and discipline of the Methodist Protestant Church, but circuits and stations were.[11] Three circuits and two missions were recognized at the first annual conference. The first session had set up an organization which could coordinate future work in the state even though its constituency was small and scattered over a largely unsettled region.

1847-1858

The year 1847 was not one of great progress in the M.P. Church in Iowa. Snethen Seminary was finally "denied," which brought that project to a close at last. One new field of work was added, the Fort Des Moines Mission. Only two hundred persons were living at that time in the six-county area around Fort Des Moines, and only seventeen of them were connected with the M.P. Church. Both church and business developers were planning with an eye to future growth.

Lack of ministerial support proved to be a serious problem. Of the $1,020 promised for salaries, only $269 had been paid. Four of the ministers found it necessary to locate that year. Only one new minister was admitted to the itinerancy.[13]

The year 1848 was better. The population of the state was growing swiftly and was reflected in the increase of membership of the church. 146 members were added, and six new ministers were added to the itinerancy. The Committee on Boundaries set up three new fields of work.[14] The salary situation improved, with the ministers receiving sixty percent of their promised salaries. A call was made for funds to redeem the Iowa City church.

The Iowa Annual Conference identified itself with the interests of the American Sunday School Union in 1849, and urged its churches to take part in that organization's program. Five new charges were formed that year. Fifteen ministers were on the roll, and all of the charges were assigned ministers. Two delegates were named to represent the Iowa Conference at the General Conference which was to meet the following year.

The failure of the Snethen Seminary in Iowa City had not destroyed the optimism of the Iowa Annual Conference. In 1854 the conference accepted the offer of a building in Ashland, Wapello County, for a seminary. The seminary opened on July 10, 1854, with Rev. Lewis Dwight, formerly an instructor at Asbury College (a Methodist Episcopal institution in Greencastle, Indiana), as principal and sole instructor. The conference assumed the building debt of $1,288. The institution flourished for two years, but the principal absconded with the funds in 1857 and left the conference with a debt of $1,800. That was the end of Ashland Seminary.[15]

During the next several years the issue which occupied the Annual Conference in Iowa, as well as the whole Methodist Protestant Church was slavery and the Civil War. Those things which were not directly concerned with the war effort got little attention.

In 1853 a resolution had been proposed for dividing the conference geographically, to make the seat of the conference more readily accessible. The Des Moines River was suggested as dividing line because the river was often out of its banks at conference time in the spring. No action was taken until

1858, when the conference was divided into the North Iowa Conference and the Iowa Conference. Both conferences belonged to the northern convention of the church, and the division seems to have been largely a matter of geographical expediency. Friendly relationships and cooperation between the conferences were the rule until their reunion in 1875.[15]

THE NORTH IOWA ANNUAL CONFERENCE

When the two conferences met in 1858 they were within "shouting distance" of each other. Most of the time at the first sessions was taken up by organization. The North Iowa Conference chose William Patterson to be its president. He was the same man who had been first president of the Iowa Conference when it was founded and its outstanding leader in the intervening years.

Discussion concerning union with other non-episcopal Methodist bodies took place in 1859. Rev. Daniel Cartwright, a former Methodist Episcopal minister who had been among the pioneers bringing Methodism to Iowa, urged the union with the Wesleyan Methodists. Like his brother, Barton Cartwright (the first M.E. preacher at Burlington), he had been a pioneer of that era. He had withdrawn to join the Wesleyan Methodist Church during the slavery controversy, and later joined the Methodist Protestant Church (1866).[16]

It is interesting to note that in the 1859 session of the North Iowa Conference the anti-tobacco people finally had their first triumph. A resolution was passed requesting that "gentlemen are hereby requested to abstain from the use of tobacco in the conference room."[17] The question of ministerial use of tobacco does not die easily. The North Iowa resolution was the first anti-tobacco resolution passed by any group, religious or secular, in the state of Iowa.[18]

A General Convention of delegates from the Northern and Western Conferences of the Methodist Protestant Church, which met at Springfield, Ohio in November, 1858, set up an anti-slavery voice for the M.P. Church known as the *Western Methodist*. This was considered necessary because the pro-slavery elements had controlled the General Conference session and the Methodist Protestant press at Baltimore. The North Iowa Conference approved the action establishing the *Western Methodist*, and every conference member was assessed twenty-five cents to help finance the project.

The Minnesota Annual Conference of the M.P. Church sent representatives to the North Iowa Annual Conference, and upon their request they were "loaned" the two northern tiers of counties to give them a boost. At the same session the North Iowa Conference refused an invitation to participate in the founding of a school of higher education. Evidently they remembered the Snethen Seminary and the Ashland Seminary.

The 1859 conference passed a resolution instructing the lay delegates to raise funds to buy a horse for Rev. Patterson for his use in carrying out his administrative duties. Before the conference adjourned, the horse was purchased. By the end of the year Rev. Patterson had died and his work for the church in Iowa ended. His death marked the close of an era following which the conference became a much more democratic organization.

The rapid population growth in the north central and northwest parts of the state gave the conference a real opportunity for evangelism, and they did their best. In two years the number of circuits in North Iowa had increased to twenty-one, and the membership to 984, a gain of over 300 members.

The North Iowa Conference of the M.P. Church was preoccupied by the Civil War from 1861 until 1865, as was all of the nation. The resolutions passed dealt with slavery and rebellion. Several ministers left to join the Union Army; the *1862 Journal of the North Iowa Conference* lists four of the twenty-three members in military service.[19] Others left later, but the exact number is unknown. The 1861 Annual Conference in North Iowa had passed a resolution calling slavery unholy and tyrannical, and the conference resolved to pray for the success of the Union arms.

The Republican nature of the Iowa frontier showed in the North Iowa Conference of 1864, which passed a resolution urging the nation not to "change horses in midstream." The secretary of the conference, Rev. R. B. Groff, presented a resolution "welcoming all traitors with bloody hands to hospitable graves." It passed by acclamation.

Some interesting sidelights in the 1862 *Journal* indicate that times have not changed as much as we sometimes think. A resolution was presented by laymen urging the resumption of house-to-house visitation by the ministers. The laymen thought that some ministers had become lax in that area. Another resolution was offered by Nicholas Rosenberger, a layman who had two sons training for the ministry at Adrian College in Michigan. His resolution called for ministers to "love one another, and treat one another in a brotherly manner, never speaking an unfavorable word in a brother's absence."[20] Since no one dared vote against it, it passed unanimously.

There has always been a tendency for Methodist ministers to enjoy conference and not to keep their noses to the grindstone. In 1863 the conference was meeting in a schoolhouse about two miles north of Toledo. Some ministers asked to have the conference moved to town. Most of the laymen voted against it, and the motion lost.[21]

Theological education was a controversial matter in the mid-nineteenth century in the Iowa M.P. Church. A committee on "The Wants of the Church" reported to the 1864 conference and spoke against theological education because such education tended "to limit and cramp the mind." Nicholas Rosenberger spoke against the report, but it was adopted.

The same conference declared that tobacco was injurious, "especially to a minister." The secretary noted that the resolution passed "after a noisy discussion." Such secretarial interpolations reveal much about the opinions of the members of the annual conference.[22]

A movement for an organic union of all non-episcopal Methodists took shape during the Civil War years. The movement began in 1859 with overtures from the Wesleyan Methodist Church and led to an agreement to combine forces, which was done in 1866. Besides the M.P.s, the union involved the Free Methodists, the Independent Methodists, and the Wesleyan Methodists. The merger was never completed and did not have much effect in Iowa. It did result in the Methodist Protestant Church's being renamed as simply "The Methodist Church" until 1877. In that year the northern and southern divisions of the church (caused by the disputes over slavery) reunited under the old name of "The Methodist Protestant Church."[23]

The 1868 North Iowa Annual Conference set up a school for pastors, which was to meet in December. This effort ended in complete failure, and the next session of the conference stated that it would never again undertake such an endeavor.[24] Never is a long time, and seventy years later former members of the Methodist Protestant Church gave whole-hearted cooperation to the Iowa Area Pastors' School after they had become a part of The Methodist Church.

Concern was growing for missions, both home and foreign. One of the chief problems of this period was the church's failure to establish itself in the cities of Iowa. However, no great advances in this area were made, and until the 1939 merger, the Methodist Protestant Church in Iowa was almost entirely a rural church.

The failure to establish churches in the larger towns was not for lack of trying. In 1876 an effort was made to establish a church in Osage, but a few years later the Osage church was dropped from the records. The Home Extension Board tried to establish a church in Des Moines in 1880. This church endured for a while, but by 1900 the membership had dropped to fifty, and in 1904 the property was sold.[25] Another attempt was made in Ottumwa, and it looked promising for a number of years. However, in 1906 the congregation had declined until it was deemed necessary to merge with a small Congregational church. This federated church eventually disappeared.

Two urban projects were slightly more successful. A church started in Keokuk is still in existence and in 1976 reported 197 members. A church was organized in the industrial section of Newton in 1932.

Baptism, a thorny question on the frontier, was discussed on the floor of the 1868 annual conference. The problem of Quakers who wanted to transfer into the Methodist Church apparently prompted a resolution asking that water baptism not be required for reception into the church. A counter-resolution, asking that only immersion be recognized, was also brought to the floor. Neither resolution passed, and the issue was indefinitely postponed.[26]

Opposition to the episcopacy reached its peak during the period around 1870. A resolution deploring the "dictatorship of the episcopacy" passed almost unanimously. The Methodist Protestant Church was beginning to lose members to the Methodist Episcopal Church, and a resolution lamented "proselytizing" by that body.[27] Perhaps it was to be expected that a denomination made up of small, scattered, rural congregations would lose members to the similar body whenever a family moved to a town away from the home community. Proselyting may be too strong a term, but it is certainly how things appeared to the Methodist Protestant congregations.

Various problems held the attention of the M.P. Conference between 1868 and the merger of the two Iowa conferences in 1875. The 1869 Annual Conference reversed a previous position, taken in 1864, and by a narrow margin adopted a report favoring theological education. A resolution for reunification with the Methodist Protestant Church in the South was passed.

The problem of working with an interdenominational organization such as the American Sunday School Union stimulated feelings favoring a denominational Sunday School. The Annual Conference of 1872 reaffirmed a resolution adopted in 1869 favoring formal education, but urged that more attention be devoted to training in the doctrine of the Holy Spirit. During this period stress was placed on the importance of the Holy Spirit in Christian experience. Camp meetings had become an accepted part of the work of the Methodist Episcopal Church and were adopted in 1872 by the Methodist Protestant Church in Iowa.

We get one clue to the theological stance of the Methodist Protestant Church in Iowa by the adoption in 1872 of a resolution recommending that the denomination seek representation in the Evangelical Alliance, a conservative group formed to forward the interests of evangelical Christians.

The two Iowa M.P. conferences met separately in 1874 for the last time. In 1875, since the reasons for remaining two separate conferences (e.g. distance, transportation) no longer applied, an action of the General Conference brought the two back together again.

THE IOWA ANNUAL CONFERENCE

When the conferences reunited, there were over 3,500 members in the state and two-thirds of them were in the Iowa Conference. It is worth noting that this is as many members as the conference had at any time until the merger with North Missouri in 1916. To say that the church began to decline at this time would be inaccurate because, by 1900, the church still reported 3,551 members, actually a percentage gain. The rural areas in which the Methodist Protestant Church was strongest comprised an area of declining population. While the population declined thirty percent, the M.P. Church held its own. This could be called an era of consolidation.[28]

Two years after the reunification of the two Iowa conferences, the northern and southern wings of the Methodist Protestant Church were united nationally (1877). This did not have much effect on the church in Iowa except to restore the older name, The Methodist Protestant Church.

One can speculate about reasons why the M.P. Church ceased to grow in this period. Possibly the main reason was that the factors which had brought the Methodist Protestant Church into existence some fifty years ago no longer applied. Laymen were represented at the Methodist Episcopal conferences, and the power of the bishop had been altered. Methodist

Protestants began to look forward to eventual union with the Methodist Episcopal Church.[29]

A memorial from the Iowa Conference in 1880 to the General Conference of the Methodist Protestant Church called for the adoption of the Methodist Episcopal hymnal with the Methodist Protestant imprint on the title page, rather than the preparation of a distinctively denominational hymn book. The transfer of ministers between the Methodist Protestant and the Methodist Episcopal conferences in Iowa became commonplace. This created a problem for the M.P. Church as the M.E. salaries were generally larger.[30]

During the last quarter of the nineteenth century considerable attention was given to the advancement of ministerial education and some consideration to improving relationships with the Methodist Episcopal Church. Women had been accepted into the ministry of the Methodist Protestant Church. Mrs. Pauline Martindale was received by the Iowa Conference in 1872 and became the only woman minister in the state. Women ministers were definitely encouraged in 1896, and two were admitted. When merger came in 1939, Mrs. Pearl Spurlock, whose husband was also a minister, became the only woman conference member in The Methodist Church in Iowa.

Ohio Church
(Iowa County)

THE TWENTIETH CENTURY

From 1900 on, the Methodist Protestant Church in Iowa either lost members or failed to gain. Several factors were behind this loss. One was that proposals for union with other groups created a spirit of uncertainty, which resulted in a stagnation of efforts.

Another important factor was the growth of the Nazarene Church. The Methodist Protestant Church was more conservative than the Methodist Episcopal Church, but less so than the Nazarenes. The Methodist Protestant Church was small and unable to match the evangelistic fervor of the Nazarenes. The Nazarenes attracted some of the more conservative of the Methodist Protestants at the same time some of the more liberal ones were joining the Methodist Episcopals.

One problem which affected the M.P. Church in Iowa was that leaders in the Iowa Conference did not always see eye-to-eye with the national leaders. This led to dissatisfaction with the church as a whole, which did not help efforts to grow.

A sizeable loss of church extension funds became a source of dissension in the M.P. Church in Iowa. The Board of Church Extension had, without adequate authority, loaned funds to Kansas City University, a school sponsored by all conferences of the M.P. Church west of the Mississippi. The venture failed, and all the funds were lost.

Union with the United Brethren was seriously discussed, and in both 1908 and 1911 the conference came near to agreeing upon merger proposals. This merger was especially appealing to those who feared the loss of identity in the event of a merger with the larger Methodist Episcopal Church.

The most encouraging development in the later years of the M.P. Church was the rise of the Christian Endeavor, an interdenominational youth movement. This became a dynamic group in Iowa and attracted many young people.

The North Missiouri Conference of the Methodist Protestant Church was experiencing many of the same problems as the Iowa Conference. In 1915 they asked the Iowa Conference to consider merger. The merger was approved at the 1916 General Conference, and in August, 1916, the first session of the Iowa-Missouri Conference was held in the Ohio church in Iowa County.[31]

Developments during the First World War and following led to further decline in the Methodist Protestant Church. The farm deflation of the early 1920s and the resulting decrease in rural population brought about a corresponding loss in church membership. The Iowa-Missouri Annual Conference lost about thirty percent of its members, and never recovered. The farm depression and the growing mobility of the farmer using an automobile both contributed to the trend toward fewer and larger churches. As the Methodist Protestant Church had predominantly country churches, it felt the loss more than did other denominations. The number of circuits declined from forty in 1918 to twenty-four in 1939, and the number of churches diminished almost every year.

The last ten years of the Methodist Protestant Church were taken up with negotiations for a national Methodist union. The Commission on Union reported in 1936 a plan for the union of the Methodist Protestant Church, the Methodist Episcopal Church, and the Methodist Episcopal Church South, to form a new church: The Methodist Church. The General Conference approved, and referred the matter to the annual conferences for their action. After two-thirds of the annual conferences approved the proposal, the president of the General Conference declared that it had been duly adopted by the Methodist Protestant denomination.

The proposal for union came before the Iowa-Missouri Conference on August 17, 1936. After a long and earnest discussion, it carried by a vote of 25-17. The Iowa-Missouri Conference was one of only five in which the "nay" vote represented a substantial minority. In all of the other conferences the merger was overwhelmingly accepted. By the time of the 1938 annual conferences, all three of the denominations concerned had approved, and the call was issued for a uniting conference to be held in Kansas City in April, 1939.

The Iowa-Missouri Conference of 1939 met in New London just long enough to complete any unfinished business and to declare itself a part of the Iowa-Des Moines Conference of The Methodist Church. The churches in Missouri were given to the North Missouri Annual Conference of The Methodist Church. Two churches—Rhodes and Spring Grove—went, by reason of geography, into the Upper Iowa Conference. The Rev. C. R. Green went with the Upper Iowa Conference for the same reason.

For many of the Iowa Methodist Protestants the merger was not easy to accept. Their representatives had opposed the merger on the floor of General Conference, and their Annual Conference had passed resolutions opposing the merger movement. Years of rivalry had split Methodism in Iowa, and this was not readily forgotten. The agitation over "modernism" and "fundamentalism" did not help. However, the movement toward merger went on, and most became resigned to the fact that merger had come.

Most of the ministers joined The Methodist Church—some willingly and some reluctantly. Four ministers did not see how they could, with a clear conscience, become members of The Methodist Church. Two of them became Free Methodists, one became a Congregationalist, and one began serving community churches. The laymen were not unanimous in their support either. Five local churches refused to go along with the merger, and declared themselves community churches.

What was, until 1939, The Methodist Protestant Church in Iowa has had a significant influence on the life of Iowa and on what is now The United Methodist Church. It has been a conservative influence in many ways, but it has also led the way toward more democracy in the church. From the Methodist Protestants the church got the office of "Lay Leader" and the equal representation of clergy and laymen at the Annual Conference. United Methodism has benefited from their contributions.

Footnotes

1. *Encyclopedia of World Methodism,* Vol. II, pp. 1578-9 (Nashville, The Methodist Publishing House, 1974).
2. R. E. Harvey, "Hail and Farewell," *The Annals of Iowa* XXIV October, 1942, p. 188.
3. More detail in Jim Morris, *A History of the Methodist Protestant Church in Iowa,* a B.D. Thesis in the Drake University Library, 1966.
4. Morris, ibid., pp. 12-13.
5. Ibid., p. 14.
6. Ibid., p. 15.
7. Rev. John Libby, a Methodist Protestant minister, a representative to the territory from the Bureau of Indian Affairs, was instrumental in the passing of this piece of legislation. See Morris, ibid., pp. 21-22.
8. R. E. Harvey, ibid., p. 62.
9. "Snethen, Nicholas," *Dictionary of American Biography* (New York: Charles Scribner's Sons, 1946) XVII, p. 382.
10. Harvey, ibid., p. 65.
11. *Journal of the Iowa Annual Conference of the Methodist Protestant Church,* 1846, n.p.
12. Ibid.
13. Ibid.
14. *Journal of the Iowa Annual Conference of the Methodist Protestant Church,* 1847, n.p.
15. W. H. Betz, *100 Years of the Methodist Protestant Church in Iowa,* Unpublished manuscript in the Iowa Conference Archives in Mt. Pleasant, Iowa, p. 25.
16. Harvey, ibid., footnote on p. 172.
17. *Journal of the North Iowa Annual Conference of the Methodist Protestant Church,* 1859, n.p.
18. Morris, ibid., p. 47.
19. *Journal of the North Iowa Annual Conference of the Methodist Protestant Church,* 1862, n.p.
20. *Journal of the North Iowa Annual Conference of the Methodist Protestant Church,* 1862, n.p.
21. Morris, ibid., p. .
22. *Journal of the North Iowa Annual Conference of the Methodist Protestant Church,* 1864, n.p.
23. Harvey, ibid., pp. 176-177.
24. *Journal of the North Iowa Annual Conference of the Methodist Protestant Church,* 1868, n.p.
25. Morris, ibid., p. 67.
26. *Journal of the North Iowa Annual Conference* ibid.
27. *Journal of the North Iowa Annual Conference of the Methodist Protestant Church,* 1869, n.p.
28. Morris, ibid., p. 64.
29. Ibid., p. 65.
30. Ibid., p. 66.
31. Minutes of the Iowa-Missouri Annual Conference of the Methodist Protestant Church, 1916, p. 5.

6

The United Brethren in Christ

Note: The data in this chapter was collected by the Reverend Robert Mac-Canon and included in a paper he presented to the 1975 annual meeting of the North Central Jurisdiction's Archives and History Commission, held on the campus of Westmar College in LeMars.

In the introduction to this book the modern United Methodist Church was compared to a tapestry woven from many varying threads. One of those threads is the church known as The United Brethren in Christ. No story of Iowa United Methodism could be complete without a study of its work.

The United Brethren in Christ came into being early in the nineteenth century as a part of the spiritual quickening of America late in the eighteenth and early in the nineteenth centuries. During this period the Methodist Episcopal Church was spreading westward with the frontier, extending its influence wherever English-speaking pioneers settled. At the same time, essentially the same movement was making its way among the German-speaking people of Pennsylvania, Maryland, and Virginia. As a part of this religious activity, both the United Brethren in Christ and the Evangelical Association arose.

These movements among the Germans and the Methodist Episcopal Church interacted. Philip William Otterbein, a patriarch of the United Brethren, and Francis Asbury, the first bishop of the Methodist Episcopal Church, were close friends and influenced one another. Philip Otterbein was one of those present at the Christmas Conference when the Methodist Episcopal Church was formed. He participated in the consecration of Francis Asbury as the first bishop of the new church.

The church of the United Brethren in Christ was organized originally among the German-speaking people in Maryland, Pennsylvania, and Virginia around 1800, and moved westward following the people from those areas. Later, as times changed and a younger generation came along, it stopped using the German language, but never forgot its German roots.

Philip William Otterbein (1726-1813) is credited with having provided leadership in the formation of the United Brethren in Christ. He was trained in the German Reformed tradition and was sponsored in America by the German Reformed Church. He was called to the Lancaster, Pennsylvania congregation in 1752. He soon gathered around himself a group of lay persons who contributed to a spiritual awakening among the Germans in the Middle Atlantic states.

About 1767 Otterbein attended a "great meeting" held on the farm of Isaac Long in Lancaster County, Pennsylvania, and heard a German Mennonite, Martin Boehm (1725-1812), share his faith. Otterbein is reported to have rushed forward following the meeting, to embrace Boehm and exclaim, "Wir sind Brüder" (We are brethren!). These men became friends who worked together over the years, becoming the human founders of the United Brethren in Christ.

In 1789 at Otterbein's parsonage in Baltimore a conference was held. It gave a simple organization to a fellowship which had been holding conferences from time to time since 1774. On September 25, 1800, a formal organization was created at a two-day conference which met at the home of Frederick Kemp, a mile west of Frederick, Maryland. At that time Otterbein and Boehm were elected bishops. A name—The United Brethren in Christ—was adopted, and other business transacted. From that time on, annual conferences were held.

Both Otterbein and Boehm soon withdrew from active responsibilities because of their age and declining health. Two of their followers—Christian Newcomer and George Adams Geeting—became leaders and carried on their work.

The movement followed the frontier. On August 13, 1810, Newcomer called a conference in the home of Michael Kreider in Ross County, Ohio. There, a second conference was organized. With the formation of the Western Conference, later called the Miami Conference, problems of communication between the two groups developed. To meet this situation, the western group requested a delegated conference with their brethren farther east. This became the first General Conference, and met at Mount Pleasant, Pennsylvania, June 6, 1815. At that time a *Discipline* and *Confession of Faith* were approved, and a form of church government was instituted.

A second General Conference was held at Mount Pleasant on June 2, 1817. It improved the *Discipline*, elected two bishops, formed a third Annual Conference, and arranged for quadrennial sessions of the General Conference. The English language quickly replaced the German. By the time Iowa was settled, it was almost entirely an English-language church.

During the nineteenth century certain controversies disturbed the serenity of the church. One of the more irritating of the questions was that of secret societies, more particularly Freemasons. Sentiment was not unanimous either for or against lodges. The 1841 constitution had forbidden members to belong to secret societies, but the issue would not stay down. It came up almost quadrennially, and the vote against the prohibitory rule grew stronger.

Two additional questions provided occasion for long, and at times dull, debates. They were lay representation in the conferences of the church, and pro rata representation of the conferences at General Conference. By 1873, when a majority favored the changes, the center of the debate had shifted to the constitution itself.

Could the constitution be changed? And if it could be, by whom and how? The 1885 General Conference appointed a Church Commission of twenty-seven members to prepare an amended form of the constitution and *Confession of Faith* which should be presented to the membership of the denomination for ratification or rejection. In November, 1888, the referendum was taken with the following results:

51,970 for the amended *Confession of Faith;* 3,310 against
50,685 for the amended Constitution; 3,659 against
48,825 for lay delegation in Gen. Conference; 5,634 against
49,994 for section on secret societies; 7,289 against

The General Conference of 1889 received the report of the ballot and adopted all the work of the Church Commission, whereupon the opponents of revision, holding themselves to be the continuing body, gathered and organized a separate denomination. A minority led by Bishop Milton Wright, father of Orville and Wilbur Wright of aviation fame, walked out to form the new group, United Brethren in Christ (Old Constitution).

This one split in the church must be mentioned, not only because it is a part of the United Brethren history, but because it affected a number of local churches in northeastern Iowa. They withdrew from the majority group and became a part of the new church (Old Constitution). A few of them still function.

Over the years the church engaged in conversations with other bodies relative to organic church union. Some of these negotiations were with the following:

Methodist Episcopal—1809-17
Evangelical Association—1813-17
Methodist Protestants—1829-33
Wesleyan Methodists—1855
Methodist Protestants and Congregationalists—1902-09
Methodist Protestants—1909-17
Evangelical Synod of North America) 1926-30
Reformed Church in the United States)
The Evangelical Church—1933-46

The last listed was the only one which actually led to union.

The Iowa Conference of the United Brethren traces its beginning in Iowa to the last half of the 1830s and the first half of the 1840s. The wanderings of the early circuit riders on the frontier were not always carefully recorded, but about 1836 John Burns began filling appointments in Lee County. He is considered the first minister of the United Brethren in Iowa. He was followed by F. R. S. Byrd, who formed a class in Henry County in 1842. This church is still functioning and is known as the Cottonwood Church.

Bishop Henry Kumler Jr. and John Denham visited Iowa in 1844 at the direction of the Wabash Conference. They held what is referred to as the Iowa branch of the Wabash Conference on May 19, 1844, at Columbus City, and transacted conference business. The 1845 session of the General Conference authorized the formation of an Iowa Conference.

Bishop Kumler

Bishop John Russell and his wife made the long trip to Iowa in a carriage to organize the conference. In many wide stretches of Iowa at that time nothing could be seen but sky and the tall prairie grass. While en route the Russells lost their way. Bishop Russell went ahead on foot, parting the grass with his hands in order to see, and lifting his hat on his cane so that Mrs. Russell could follow him, driving the carriage.

The Iowa Conference was regularly organized, holding its first session in the farm home of William Thompson in Louisa County on August 14, 1845. Although this conference validated all actions of the 1844 conference, sessions have been numbered from the 1845 conference.

The Iowa Conference grew rapidly despite poor roads and difficult travel. By 1849 it had twenty-five preachers, eight circuits, forty-five classes, and 519 members.

Thompson Farm House

Robert MacCanon names three streams of migration of United Brethren people into Iowa, which affected the makeup of the church here: Northern, Middle, and Later Streams. The first, or Northern Stream, entered Northeast Iowa in the summer of 1851, having left Indiana in June of that year. These pioneers traveled by ox-drawn wagon train across Illinois to Prairie du Chien, Wisconsin. They crossed the Mississippi by ferry into Iowa, landing at McGregor, continuing to Winneshiek County, and settling on farms in Broomfield Township near Castalia.

Many others later traveled this same route and established churches in Castalia, Postville, McGregor, Lansing, and Goshen. Eventually they reached out to Fayette, West Union, Sumner, Murphy, and Finnell, which is near Sumner. Some went on west to Dumont, Mason City, Washington Chapel near Cedar Falls, Waterloo, Stilson, Bristow, Hudson, Webster City, Lundgren, and other places.

For almost every church established and built, there were five or six "classes" that met in homes or schoolhouses. Efforts were made by American Bicentennial Committees in 1976 to list all of the churches in each county, but they met with difficulties in the case of Methodist, United Brethren, and Evangelical classes. Many of them met in homes, and having left no buildings were hard to trace. The strength of these denominations was in a fellowship of Christian people rather than in a church building.

The second stream of migration of the United Brethren people can be called the Middle Stream, to distinguish it from the Northern Stream and the Later Stream, which came into southern Iowa. The Middle Stream included primarily Pennsylvania Dutch people, dominated by Pennsylvania Dutch customs and language.

Christian Troup was the first United Brethren minister to serve in Yankee Grove near Lisbon. General Conference was held there in 1881. In 1847 Rev. Christian Hershey brought sixty-one people from Pennsylvania to Lisbon in Linn County. They traveled down the Ohio River by flatboat, up the Mississippi to Bloomington near what is now Muscatine, and then overland to Lisbon. The route of migration stretched on westward through Cedar Rapids, Tama, Toledo, Marshalltown, Garwin, Badger Hill (Gladbrook), Ames, Webster City, Ventura, Moville, Adaville, and into Dakota Territory.

Many strong United Methodist Churches across Central Iowa trace their lineage to those United Brethren Churches of the Middle Stream of migration. The oldest continuously functioning former United Brethren Church west of the Mississippi is the Cottonwood Church near Wayland, Muscatine District. Three General Conferences of the church met in churches or the college which got their start as part of this Middle Stream. They were: Western College in 1865; Lisbon in 1881; Toledo in 1897.

The Later Stream was primarily post-Civil War and came mostly from Ohio and Indiana. It was at least one generation removed from the Pennsylvania source before migrating to Iowa. First homes were in lean-tos or in wagons until a log house was built. These United Brethren first met in

Cottonwood Church
Congregation 100th Anniversary
1942

schoolhouses and homes for worship, as did the other "Streams." Not many preachers accompanied these Later Stream people.

The people who came to South Central and Southwest Iowa were intent on evangelism and conducted hundreds of revival meetings. The meetings were very successful and the results impressive. However, these Later Stream immigrants were not skillful at organization, and not many churches were established. Most of their converts joined or helped establish Methodist Episcopal Churches. Over the years this uniting development turned out to be a bond that helped in the union of the three Iowa Conferences of the United Methodist Church.

Three United Brethren bishops served in Iowa before being elected to that office. C. B. Kephart was president of Western College for thirteen years. A. B. Statton was ordained in the Iowa Conference and served the Olin Circuit at one time. C. J. Kephart served several charges in Iowa and was president of Leander Clark College three years.

Just ten years after the first regular session of the Iowa Conference it was decided to form a college. In 1856 Western College was chartered and located eight miles south of Cedar Rapids in Linn County. The site for the college was influenced by the gift of land and cash gifts exceeding $6,000. It was hoped that the college would attract a town around itself, but that did not happen. Also the proposed railroad from Cedar Rapids to Iowa City never developed. The school always struggled against difficulties, mostly financial.

Classes began January 1, 1857, in a new brick building with three teachers, President Samuel Weaver, and thirty-eight students. There was never enough money to meet the school's needs. The Civil War crippled the school when a high percentage of the men students went into the volunteer army. President Weaver resigned in 1864.

Many preachers and lay persons opposed the college. It finally became necessary to relocate. Toledo in Tama County, with an offer of $20,000, was chosen as the new site for the college, to be known as Leander Clark College. It opened in 1881.

The college provided leadership for Iowa for many years, but its history is a story of financial problems. The supportive church membership was too small. In 1917 the college was merged with Coe College, a Presbyterian school in Cedar Rapids.

During the 1840s and 1850s the population of Iowa was growing so fast that official census reports were out of date before they were published. The population in 1860 was more than fifteen times as great as it had been in 1840. The membership of the church was increasing the same way. In 1853 the General Conference divided the state into two conferences, with the Iowa River as the dividing line. The northern conference kept the name— the Iowa Conference. The southern part was called the Des Moines Conference.

As growth continued, the General Conference of 1861 divided the Iowa Conference again—into the Iowa Conference and the North Iowa Conference. At the same time the Des Moines Conference was divided into the East and West Des Moines Conferences. Thus for a while, Iowa had four United Brethren Conferences.

The Civil War slowed the progress of the church in Iowa. The Iowa and North Iowa Conferences did not realize the expected growth. As a result, General Conference authorized the reunion of these two conferences. The merger was effected in 1874.

After the Civil War many new railroads were constructed, roads were improved, and travel became easier. Between 1870 and 1889 the East Des Moines Conference lost membership. By 1889 it seemed wise to unite East Des Moines Conference with the Iowa Conference. The combined membership in 1890 was 5,884.

After 1889, West Des Moines Conference was named the Des Moines Conference. It took in Des Moines and all of the western part of the state. This arrangement was satisfactory until 1909 when the two Iowa Conferences merged into one Iowa State Conference. In 1908 the Des Moines Conference had reported 5,094 members.

During the years of Iowa's rapid population growth one of the church's main concerns was evangelism. The preachers were evangelists. Revival meetings were held every year. Camp meetings for evangelistic purposes were inseparable from the early history of the United Brethren in Iowa. However, the time came when the state was no longer experiencing a large influx of new inhabitants. Growth in church membership slowed to a halt. 1917 was the high-water mark in membership for the United Brethren Church in Iowa, when the Conference Minutes reported 11,636 members and 159 churches.

Following 1917 several things happened. The coal mines closed in southern Iowa, which cost the United Brethren Church in membership, just as it cost the Methodist Episcopal Church. The United Brethren Church was largely composed of small-town and country people, and the decline in the size and number of farm families also hurt the church. A tendency to hang onto open-country churches too long was another negative factor. The change in the farming community hurt the Methodist Protestant Church at the same period.

Another trend affected the life of all of the churches. That was the decline in church attendance for more than twenty-five years following 1917. During those years the various churches of America suffered a loss in attendance and in the number of candidates for the ministry. This was especially hard on the smallest churches, which were marginal at best.

A consensus developed that the work of the church could be done more efficiently by joining forces with a sister denomination of similar background and beliefs: The Evangelical Church. The significant contributions which the United Brethren in Christ had made, and could continue to make, would best be accomplished by merger. The story of the United Brethren in Christ after 1946 is included in the history of a new denomination, The Evangelical United Brethren Church.

7

The Evangelical Church in Iowa

Leonard E. Deaver

Note: This chapter was presented as a paper at the 1975 annual meeting of the North Central Jurisdiction's Archives and History Commission, held on the campus of Westmar College in LeMars.

It was with the ministry of the Evangelical Church in Illinois that Iowa first received the young missionaries of the Evangelical Church. "John Hoffert, the missionary, was pushing farther westward, and extending the field of operations across the Mississippi River into Iowa. The prospects were very favorable, but on the account of Hoffert's rather feeble health, not much could be accomplished at that time."[1]

In 1843, J. G. Miller began preaching in the Iowa Territory, while he was riding the Rock River Circuit, a part of the Ohio Conference in Illinois. He was the second man on this circuit and made several trips into Iowa as a result. It cost fifty cents to cross the mighty Mississippi River by ferry, and on one of his trips, being limited in funds, he was forced to sell his personal copy of *Thomas-a-Kempis* for passage. Upon his return to Illinois, a fellow traveler who had attended one of his meetings in Iowa gave him his fare to recross the river.

Also in 1843, Charles G. Koch, later editor of *Der Christliche Botschafter*, and one of the progressive leaders of the church, visited Iowa, preaching in Bloomington, now known as Muscatine, and traveled as far west as Linn County.

With the formal organization of the Illinois Conference, which consisted of Illinois, Iowa and Wisconsin, the Iowa missionary endeavors were connected with the Galena Mission in Illinois. This was a circuit embracing fourteen preaching places in Illinois, Wisconsin, and Iowa. J. G. Miller was stationed on this circuit, and "by November 1844, he reported having found German hospitality in Dubuque, and in a settlement about ten miles to the north of there called Sherrill's Mound. At the latter place he reported having preached four times, read the Disciplinary Rules, and organized a society with seventeen charter members. This Miller pronounced, 'the first Society west of the Mississippi,' and 'the furtherest frontier of Germans within Indian Territory.' 'O Lord,' he continued, 'be their protector.' "[2] In June the next year a movement toward building a church at Sherrill's Mound was inaugurated, but it came to naught.

With the settlements in the territory so widely scattered and the fact that Iowa had not yet been admitted to statehood, this truly was a pioneer mission. In 1845, Matthias Hauert was sent as pastor to the newly organized class, which had been made a mission, but ill health necessitated his early return. Although Hauert was a sick man he did much to build up the tiny society and organize new classes so that the name was changed from Dubuque to the Iowa Mission.[3]

Jacob J. Esher, an energetic junior preacher in the ministry, followed Hauert, and served for two years—the pastoral limit—with marked success. During Esher's first summer there Bishop John Seybert crossed the Mississippi and paid the first episcopal visit to this growing frontier area.

Conrad Epply, a former miller from Cedarville, Illinois, followed Esher and served the mission for one year. The records for the succeeding year show that the circuit was "to be supplied," which meant that the presiding elder of the district would try to find some man to come and serve as the pastor during the year. This seemingly did happen although no records are given by the historians of the church. However, the record of the progress of the program indicates evidence of the work being carried on continuously.

Bishop Seybert

The early settlers, being German people from Pennsylvania, Ohio, and Illinois, established themselves in Iowa much as in other states—usually in colonies. One of the earliest of these German colonies in Iowa was a group of settlers who came from Dauphin County in Pennsylvania and migrated to the area of Grandview in Louisa County, in 1852. These folks were greatly encouraged to settle in this area by Bishop John Seybert, and to organize a class with the understanding that he would send them a minister.

In September they organized a class composed of the following members: George Gipple and wife Mary, and children J. Samuel, Margaret, George W., and Mary; Solomon Wagner and wife, Susanna; Jacob Snyder and wife, Catharine; Jos. Martin and wife, Mary; James Shartzer and wife, Eliza; John Snyder and wife, Susanna. Also three European Germans: F. Beik, George Hahn, and Chas. Wabnitz, with their wives.[4]

George Gipple and Jos. Martin, both of whom were farmers, were elected

Grandview Evangelical Church

Class Leader and Exhorter, respectively. To this class and society goes the honor of the erection of the first church building of the Evangelical Church in Iowa, dedicated on November 27, 1857. The second church building was erected at Independence in 1858, and the third followed at Greencastle one year later.

In 1854 the work in Iowa had become so extensive that it was deemed best to separate it into two parts. The territory adjacent to Dubuque was called the "Dubuque Mission" and the remaining area was called the "Cedar River Circuit." Until 1856, these points had belonged to the Peoria District of the Illinois Conference, but when the Freeport District was organized in 1856, these points were attached to it. At this time there were only three centers of operation in Iowa. However, the pioneer preacher was never content with merely one preaching place. Therefore each center probably had at least half a dozen schoolhouses or homes as preaching places, and the circuit rider was busy hunting for another place where he might preach the Gospel of Jesus Christ to new people. "New preaching places" and "extend the borders" were common phrases in those days.[5]

The mission work in the state had reached such proportions by 1857 that it was made into a separate district with a presiding elder in charge. Wm. Kolb was elected the first presiding elder of the Iowa District, which was composed of the following circuits: Grandview, North Bend Mission, Cedar River and Dubuque. It is interesting to note that the Evangelical Church elected its presiding elders by a vote of the ministers and laymen in attendance at the Annual Conference session. At the session of the Illinois Conference meeting in Washington, Illinois in 1857 permission was given to acquire lots for mission churches in Maquoketa and Independence, Iowa.[6]

Meanwhile petitions for preachers for Iowa appeared in abundance. Some of these appeals came from west of Muscatine, midway between the Mississippi and the Des Moines Rivers, some from the fertile prairies one hundred miles west of Dubuque, some from the vicinity of Des Moines. Abraham Eberhardt, living about eighteen miles west of Cedar Rapids wrote: "I intend to put up an index board to show travelers where to turn off the road to come to our house, and if any Evangelical preacher should make it suit to give us a call, we would be very happy." Earnest and fruitful efforts were made to meet these appeals.[7]

With the appointments in 1857 two young men—J. W. Mohr and Rudolph Dubs—were stationed as junior preachers at Cedar River and Dubuque respectively. Both young ministers preached with their older colleagues at many points that had been without a preaching service up to that time. Mohr in his movements found an entrance into the territory around the city of Waterloo. In Independence he purchased the lot as authorized by the Annual Conference, and opened the avenue for the second Evangelical Church building in Iowa. Other preaching places were opened at Belle Plaine, Toledo, Webster and Marshalltown.

J. Schaefele, the senior pastor with Mohr, stopping to water his thirsty horse in Waterloo, learned that many Germans were in the village, but that there was no German-speaking preacher. He then sent his "assistant" in, and in such a casual manner the Evangelical Church has its beginnings in that community.[8]

"It was 'hard work,' " was Mohr's comment on the ministry which he performed. He was compelled to ford rivers that were often swollen by rains. There being only one railroad in the state and that terminating at Iowa City, the usual mode of travel was by horse and buggy.

Rudolph Dubs had not been idle while serving on the Dubuque Circuit. He had been finding new preaching places, and after serving on the circuit for one year, he was transferred to the Marion Circuit, where he was instrumental in establishing much of the work in the vicinity of Cedar Rapids and Marion. For many years the Evangelical Church was the only church represented in the vicinity of Alburnett and Cedar Point. Dubs was also instrumental in overseeing the building of the church at Independence. Through his aggressive program of soul winning and effective administration, he later was elected to the episcopacy.

Muscatine, Waterloo, and Des Moines Missions were established by the Conference in 1858. In the far western part of the state J. F. Schreiber was appointed by the Illinois Conference as Missionary to Nebraska. He began his ministry at Council Bluffs and by the end of the year had secured a number of preaching places, most of them in the neighborhood of Council Bluffs.

During the twelfth session of the General Conference, meeting at Naperville, Illinois on October 5, 1859, the organization of the Iowa Conference was authorized. It was composed of the Iowa District of the Illinois Conference, the Minnesota District of the Wisconsin Conference, and the Mission Fields of Kansas, Nebraska, and Missouri.

The first session of this newly organized conference was held May 29, 1861, at Grandview with Bishop W. W. Orwig presiding. There were thirty-two preachers in Iowa at that time. They elected S. Dickover presiding elder of the Iowa District and Levi Eberhardt presiding elder of the Kansas District. The Iowa District was composed of churches in Minnesota and Iowa. The Kansas District was composed of fields in Iowa: Fort Des Moines and Greencastle, and the Nebraska and Kansas Missions.

Because of illness Levi Eberhardt resigned his office, and at the Conference session in Grandview M. J. Miller was elected to succeed him. Miller in his report to the Missionary Society, which met at Baltimore, Maryland on November 14, said the following concerning his work on the district which contained part of Iowa:

> The Council Bluffs Mission is a very extensive field of labor, and bids fair for the future, but we should have two men there. This mission extends from Council Bluffs north to Dakota Territory. I spent two Sabbaths with H. Kleinsorge on the mission, and was up north to Sioux City with him, where we held a quarterly meeting and had a precious visit. But brethren, I tell you, this is an almost endless district. I traveled early and late from Monday morning, the 18th, till Monday evening the 26th, in the following week to get home, a distance of 330 miles. This trip takes me through six or seven Indian reservations, and unsettled prairies of from ten to twenty miles in length and width, where there is not a single house to be seen, and were it not for frequent springs and rivulets along the dim and wearisome tracks, both man and beast would pine away before reaching a settlement. I made 720 miles in the round trip and must make this distance as often as I go to Council Bluffs.
>
> I met with entertainment wherever I came. One night, however, I was entertained all alone, out on the open prairie. A piece of dry bread and three eggs, which I had with me, served for supper and my buggy cushions and great coat for my bed, down in the grass by the side of my buggy. I had far better time of it than in many of the small smothering cabins along the road, where bugs and fleas are your night long associates.
>
> On Council Bluffs Mission the Lord gathered a little flock of faithful souls and the prospects are good. H. Kleinsorge is well and labors very diligently on this mission. He travels frequently from forty to forty-five miles a day, and is content with a piece of dry bread for his dinner on the open prairie.[9]

In 1862, with the conference session again opening at Grandview, Bishop J. Long presiding, the conference announced that new missions had been established at Fort Dodge and Decorah.

It was during the session of the General Conference at Buffalo, New York in 1863 that Kansas was separated from the Iowa Conference and made into a separate conference. With the loss of the Kansas District, the Iowa Conference was reorganized into three districts, namely Des Moines, Dubuque, and St. Paul. Five years later the Minnesota Conference was organized, and when the Iowa Conference was reshaped, Cedar Rapids became the third district.

As more people moved westward, the conference gave more time and attention to the organization of more mission fields in Nebraska. In 1870 the Nebraska mission became a district of the conference with E. J. Schultz as the presiding elder. With further expansion throughout the state, missionaries journeyed into the northern and western parts of Iowa, and with

Melbourne Church, Merrill— Mother Evangelical Church of Northwest Iowa

their coming to these new pioneer settlements, missions were established. Among the new missions in 1874 were Stanton, Aurora, Sioux City, Humboldt, Grand Junction, Magnolia, Seneca, Nora Springs, and Boone. The Ackley District was added to the Conference in 1874 to serve this northwestern area of the state.

The use of the English language was introduced into Iowa Conference circles in the early development of the Conference with the coming of J. W. McKesson, a missionary from the Pittsburg Conference. He arrived in McDonough County, Illinois on June 28, 1853, and began to preach immediately in both Illinois and Iowa. J. W. Mohr had preached in English in the "fifties" and others had followed in his footsteps. Because of these men there were a number of English appointments in the Iowa Conference. However, the main thrust of the Conference was still with the German language. However, the best interests of the Evangelical Church in Iowa suggested the wisdom of the organization of the English appointments into an annual conference, and the General Conference was urged to make provision toward this end.

Resolutions recommending the division of the Iowa Conference by the next General Conference were adopted by the Annual Conference meeting in Belle Plaine, April 15, 1875. The General Conference meeting in Philadelphia in 1875 received the Iowa Conference resolution favorably and authorized the organization of the Des Moines Conference to be composed of all the English fields of the state.

The first session of the newly created Des Moines Conference met at Blairstown, Iowa on April 13, 1876, with Bishop Rudolph Dubs as chair-

man. This was an important event, for it marked the beginning of exclusively English conferences in the Evangelical Church. Iowa enjoys the credit for
this achievement of Americanism in the Evangelical Church. Two districts
were formed: Des Moines and Cedar Rapids, with D. H. Kooker and C. W.
Anthony the presiding elders, respectively. The Iowa Conference (German
speaking) met at Merrill in the same year, and the Dubuque, Ackley, and
Nebraska Districts constituted the organization.

With both conferences working for the expansion of the church in the
state, the result was a widespread expansion of the Evangelical Church.
Before, the language question had been a handicap in entering many of the
newer communities. Now each group was working industriously, that it
might bring a new church into its own conference.

The Story City Mission had its beginnings with the coming of B. H.
Neibel, a young itinerant preacher of the Des Moines Conference. He tells
of entering the community south of Story City. Most of the people had been
reared in infidel homes; none of them professed in believing anything. The
Sabbath was spent in horse-racing, ball-playing, gambling, and drinking.
The young people seemed to be outstripping their elders in lawlessness and
wickedness. At length it became too bad for them, and one man, the father
of several children, turned to Neibel and asked him to come to the country
schoolhouse and conduct church services.

The first Sunday was rainy. Only the man who had given the invitation
appeared, but Neibel was undaunted by the size of his "congregation" and
went ahead and preached. The man—not a Christian—was converted, and
with his conversion and the story of Neibel's bravery in preaching to him
alone became a first class advertisement. In two weeks the little country
schoolhouse was full. It was taken up as a regular appointment. During the
succeeding months a revival meeting was held and a class was formed.

The Afton District was formed by the Des Moines Conference in 1878. Its
territory extended into Nebraska, where English work was organized. Even
after the formation of the Nebraska Conference in 1880, the English missions retained their membership in the Des Moines Conference. However,
in the year following the Nebraska churches formed the Platte River Conference, which became the second exclusively English Conference in the
denomination.

The ministry of the Evangelical Church was nicely established within the
borders of the State of Iowa, and it flourished encouragingly and without
interruption until 1894 when an unfortunate rupture occurred in the church.
The denomination had held true to its course in point of doctrine and polity
without serious interruption up to this time, although here and there along
the way points of difference arose. These differences resulted in the leaving
of the Conference and the Evangelical Church by individual ministers who
sought greater freedom elsewhere.

In the middle of the nineteenth century a rather pronounced emphasis on
the doctrine of entire sanctification proved to be an ominous indication of
serious difficulty. However, the lines held steady, and at no time has there

been a serious breach within the denominational circles on the basis of doctrine.

In the early "eighties" of the nineteenth century, disturbances arose concerning what some regarded as an undue centralization of authority in the episcopacy and in the field of general administration. In the year 1894 at Naperville, Illinois a representative group of ministers and laymen, who disapproved of certain procedures by the General Conference in handling of internal problems, convened in special session and organized independently under the name of the United Evangelical Church. They elected Rudolph Dubs, William Stanford, and C. S. Haman as bishops of the new church.

In this new organization the same doctrinal position was maintained as in the mother organization. Greater rights were given to the laity, property rights were in a somewhat larger sense vested in the local congregations, and tenure of office for bishops and presiding elders was limited to two four-year terms or a period of eight years. Other adjustments, many of which were later incorporated in the Evangelical Association as well, and finally in the merged denomination, were inaugurated by this new organization. However, we do well to keep in mind that both denominations maintained a very definite insistence on the importance of sound orthodoxy, the seeking and attaining of a godly life for the individual believer. The same evangelistic fervor and missionary zeal animated both groups. The newly organized United Evangelical Church was composed of a membership of 61,120, with 415 itinerant and 226 local preachers.

The Mother Church, or Evangelical Association, retained the strength of 110,095 members and 982 itinerant ministers in 1894. The disturbance in the denomination had its repercussions in Iowa. The Iowa Conference suffered the loss of approximately twelve ministers who for a period of time affiliated with the Des Moines Conference, which in large part went with the newly organized United Evangelical Church. Later—in 1899—these ministers, formerly of the Iowa Conference, were organized into a separate conference known as the Northwestern Conference of the United Evangelical Church. This newly organized conference carried on work with the congregations that had left the Iowa Conference of the Evangelical Association. The group also took over the work in such congregations of Minnesota, North and South Dakota which were alienated from the Association. The Northwestern Conference of the United Evangelical Church continued its work until 1922. A small salient of men and churches (approximately ten of the former) of the Des Moines Conference remained with the mother organization and in 1912 were merged with the Iowa Conference.

This unfortunate chapter in the life of this denomination was brought to a happy termination in 1922 by the merger of the two divisions into the Evangelical Church. In 1927 the Iowa Conference and the Des Moines Conference held their respective sessions in Cedar Falls, where they were merged by authorization of the General Conference meeting in Williamsport, Pennsylvania in 1926. They were merged into the Iowa Conference of the Evangelical Church, which embraced all the work of this communion in Iowa, and which, according to the Conference Journal of 1946 (prior to the merger with the Church of the United Brethren in Christ) had a membership of 12,165 with eighty-nine congregations and ninety-seven itinerant elders. The conference was composed of three districts: Cedar Falls, Des Moines and Fort Dodge, with official headquarters at Cedar Falls.

The Evangelical Church stressed evangelism from its very inception, being born in the midst of a revival. The zeal of the early pioneer preachers led them to heroic sacrifices, incident to the hardships of those days. These evangelistic efforts culminated in special gatherings at focal points where camp meetings, tent meetings, and bush meetings were held for extended periods.

Some of the oustanding camp-meeting centers were at Waterloo, Waverly, Center Point, Anita, Merrill, and near North Liberty. They found their ultimate successor in what is known as the Assembly Center of the denomination located in Riverview Park, Cedar Falls, where there is a Tabernacle which will seat approximately 1,500 persons, Missionary Hall, which accommodates 300 persons, and a children's building with a small chapel holding 100 folk. The dining hall seats 300. A retreat center is open the year around. Other accommodations are ninety-eight cabins.

The Conference used this park for its camping program, which was helpful for youth as well as adults. In 1945 the Conference began a camping program for Junior High youth that was very successful, with an enrollment of 310 for the first camp. The Woman's Missionary Society held its annual branch meeting here in August in conjunction with the Annual Assembly. The Assembly also included a study program for the ministers, taught by various seminary professors, the evening being used for an evangelistic service with a number of altar calls and full-time commitment calls extended. It was in this way that young people responded for full-time Christian service as missionaries and ministers.

The Evangelical Church believed from its beginning in a well trained ministry, and at a surprisingly early date established its first educational institution in Greensburg, Ohio (1855). Various other institutions were established at points both east and west, from coast to coast.

The early ministers of the Middle West mostly received their education at what was known first as Plainfield College, Plainfield, Illinois—later known as Northwestern College in its re-location at Naperville, Illinois, and still later renamed North Central College. On this same campus Union Biblical Institute—the first theological institution—was established, later known as Evangelical Theological Seminary. Most of the Iowa pastors were graduates of this fine seminary.

In the state of Iowa the first educational enterprise was launched at Blairstown in 1867 by the Iowa Conference. Professor W. J. Hahn, formerly president of the Greensburg, Ohio Seminary, was its president. The school was called Blairstown Seminary and had two courses, a classical course of four years and a teachers' course of three years. After being in operation thirteen terms the seminary was unable to overcome many difficulties with which it had to contend, and was forced to suspend operations.[10]

Not until 1900 were further efforts made along this line. At that time the church acquired the property of the LeMars Normal School, which was named Western Union College. This name was chosen in recognition of the fact that a number of conferences in adjoining states cooperated in this venture. Dr. H. H. Thoren was elected the first president; Dr. Denton E. Thomas succeeded him and was the acting president for several years. Dr. C. C. Poling, father of the distinguished Dr. Daniel Poling of Christian Endeavor fame, succeeded Dr. Thomas. Others who have headed the school were Dr. C. A. Mock, Dr. D. O. Kime, Dr. H. H. Kalas, Dr. Laurence C. Smith. (Dr. John F. Courter and Dr. Arthur W. Richardson have followed since this was written.)

Following the merger of the Evangelical Church with the Church of the United Brethren in Christ, the college changed its name to Westmar College. The name of Western Union was becoming a burden with the growth of the telegraph company. Many folks linked it, and thought in terms of its training young persons for that company!

The Evangelical Church in Iowa has all through the years maintained a lively interest in philanthropic work and humanitarian services. It established one of the first homes for retired persons in Iowa and in the Midwest —the Western Old People's Home (1912) in Cedar Falls. Superintendents of the home were A. L. Hauser, Dr. W. C. Lang, Dr. H. J. Faust, Dr. Ward B. Tarr, Dr. J. Ivan LaFavre, and Donald Iles.

The missionary spirit in the congregations in Iowa has been evidenced by very generous giving for home and foreign missions and also by the fact that a large company of young men and women have represented the church in Iowa in denominational mission fields of Africa, China, and Japan as well as in the Kentucky Mountain mission work known as Red Bird Mission. This latter work was begun by an Iowa pastor and those helping him were natives of the state of Iowa. Among the congregations that not only gave substantial financial support for missions but also sent their sons and daughters was Hubbard.

Some of the outstanding men of the Des Moines Conference were J. H. Yaggy, C. W. Anthony, E. F. Mell, J. F. Yerger, J. E. Stauffacher, D. H. Kooker, Charles Pickford, E. B. Utt, A. A. Couser, J. G. Walz, and S. N. Ramige, all of whom served as presiding elders (later known as district superintendents). Dr. Jacob Auracher served as district superintendent and later as treasurer of Western Union College. Dr. B. H. Neibel served successively as a pastor, district superintendent, field agent of Western Union College, and corresponding secretary of the denomination's Missionary Society. Charles H. Stauffacher was advanced from the pastorate to the district superintendency, then to the position of field secretary of the Missionary Society, and from there elevated to the office of Bishop.

Bishop Stauffacher was appointed to serve the episcopal area in which Iowa was included, living in Kansas City. It was a joy and privilege to have a native son as episcopal leader. He used his influence and knowledge to bring the merger of the Evangelical and United Brethren Churches in Iowa together.

The following men were leaders in the Iowa Conference and served in the capacity of district superintendents: S. Dickover, M. J. Miller, Rudolph Dubs, H. Langeschulte, J. Buzzard, H. J. Bowman, E. J. Schultz, J. Henn, E. Nolte, Jacob Knoche, M. Gruener, C. C. Fundt (also served as the superintendent of the denomination's Flat Rock, Ohio orphanage, which was supported by the Iowa Conference), L. W. Bock, J. H. Engel, G. L. Bergeman, Dr. J. A. Haehlen, Dr. R. H. Aurand, and I. L. Baumgartner. B. R. Wiener, a successful pastor, was elected field secretary of the denomination's Missionary Society and later Secretary of Evangelism. Dr. O. M. Yaggy, who served important pulpits in the Conference, rendered conspicuous service in the field of Christian Education, both in the ranks of his own denomination and in the wider interdenominational circles. In the Northwestern Conference outstanding men were: F. Belzer, William Jonas, E. Mueller, F. A. Frase, D. C. Hauk, W. F. Brecker, and Thomas Koch. They, too, served as efficient district superintendents.

Footnotes

1. S. P. Spreng, *The Life and Labors of John Seybert* (Cleveland, Ohio: Lauer and Matthill, 1888) p. 232.
2. Paul H. Eller, *History of Evangelical Missions* (Harrisburg, Pennsylvania: The Evangelical Press, 1942) p. 68.
3. F. R. Blakly, *The Evangelical Association as a Factor in the Development of the West* (Thesis for M. A. Degree, Northwestern University, 1914) p. 36.
4. A. Stapleton, *Annals of the Evangelical Association of North America* (Harrisburg, Pennsylvania: Publishing House of the United Evangelical Church, 1900) p. 335.
5. F. R. Blakly, op. cit., p. 38.
6. J. G. Schwab and Dr. H. H. Thoren, *The History of the Illinois Conference of the Evangelical Church* (Harrisburg, Pennsylvania: The Evangelical Press, 1937) p. 37.
7. Paul H. Eller, op. cit., p. 69.
8. Paul H. Eller, op. cit., p. 70.
9. A. Stapleton, op. cit., p. 334.
10. A. Stapleton, op. cit. p. 200.

Bibliography

Raymond W. Albright, *"History of the Evangelical Church."* Published by the Evangelical Press, Harrisburg, Pennsylvania, 1942.

F. R. Blakely, *"The Evangelical Association as a Factor in the Development of the West."* A thesis written in partial fulfilment of the requirements for the Degree of Master of Arts, Dept. of History, College of Liberal Arts, Northwestern University, 1914.

Paul H. Eller, *"History of the Evangelical Missions."* Published by the Evangelical Press, Harrisburg, Pennsylvania, 1942.

B. H. Neibel and Rudolph Dubs, *"Evangelical Missions."* Published by the Home and Foreign Missionary Society of the United Evangelical Church, 1919.

J. G. Schwab and Dr. H. H. Thorne, *"History of the Illinois Conference of the Evangelical Church, 1837-1937."* Published by the Evangelical Press, Harrisburg, Pennsylvania, 1942.

S. P. Spreng, *"The Life of Seybert."* Published for the Evangelical Association by Lauer and Mattill Agents, Cleveland, Ohio, 1888.

S. P. Spreng, *"History of the Evangelical Church."* Published by the Publishing House of the Evangelical Church, Harrisburg, Pennsylvania, 1927.

A. Stapleton, *"Annals of the Evangelical Association of North America."* Publishing House of the United Evangelical Church, Harrisburg, Pennsylvania, 1896.

A. Stapleton, *"Flashlights of Evangelical History."* Published by the Author (1908).

Albert H. Utzinger, *"History of the Minnesota Conference of the Evangelical Association, 1856-1922."* Published by the Evangelical Press, Cleveland, Ohio, 1922.

Other Sources: Dr. J. A. Haehlen, who gave me very valuable information that was impossible to obtain in written form, otherwise and who aided in the correction of my manuscript in regards to historical data in my book, *"One Hundred Years With Evangelicals in Iowa."* Published by the Iowa Conference of the Evangelical Church, 1944. Printed by the Olson Press, Story City.

Periodicals

Der Christliche Botschafter (1846-1866)—Translations of Iowa Historical material by H. C. Schulter and E. Nolte, Iowa Conference Historical Library.

The Evangelical Messenger, S. P. Spreng, *"Leaves From a Pioneer-Itinerants Note Book."* June 4, 11, 18, 25, 1932.

The Seminary Review, Vol. XXXI, 1944.

Un-Published Materials

L. W. Bock, *Camp Meetings in the Iowa Conference.* Iowa Conference Historical Library.

Mrs. C. A. Arihood, *History of the Evangelical Church in Grandview.* Iowa Historical (Conference) Library.

Daniel B. Byers, *The Personal Diary of Daniel B. Byers.* Original in Evangelical Theological Seminary Library, Naperville, Illinois, copy of Iowa Material, Iowa Conference Historical Library.

William Kolb, *An Auto-biography*, Iowa Conference Historical Library.

Jacob Schaefele, *Diary of Jacob Schaefele,* Iowa Conference Historical Library.

J. Keiper, *Diary of J. Keiper on Grandview, 1858-1861.* Translation by E. Nolte, Iowa Conference Historical Library.

Personal Interview

H. C. Schulter, Member of the Iowa Conference Historical Committee.

8

The Evangelical United Brethren Church 1946-1968

Note: The data in this chapter was collected by Dr. Alferd E. Wilken and included in a paper he presented to the 1975 annual meeting of the North Central Jurisdiction's Archives and History Commission, held on the campus of Westmar College in LeMars.

The Evangelical United Brethren Church was formed in 1946 with the merger of the Evangelical Church and the United Brethren in Christ. At that time there were approximately 750,000 members in North America. Most of them were in the northern states and Canada. Iowa had 22,903 members in 164 organized congregations, with 158 itinerant ministers, active and retired.

The heritage of the Evangelical United Brethren Church was in the histories of the Evangelical Church and the United Brethren. Each of these denominations had been organized early in the nineteenth century among the German-speaking Americans in the same areas of Pennsylvania, Maryland, and Virginia. No great difference between them would have been noticeable to an outsider. They both had been influenced by the same movements which had given birth to the Methodist Episcopal Church and the Methodist Protestant Church. It was only natural that the two groups should eventually merge, but that event did not take place for more than a century. The names and the traditions of both the Evangelical Church and the United Brethren were kept in the merger, made effective at a special General Conference session held in Johnstown, Pennsylvania on November 16, 1946.

The two annual conferences in Iowa did not merge immediately, but continued as two separate conferences of the same church for five years. They were designated as the Iowa Conference (EV) and the Iowa Conference (UB) of the Evangelical United Brethren Church. However, planning was started at once, anticipating the merger that was to come later.

The first session of the Iowa Conference (EV) was held at Cedar Falls May 7-11, 1947, six months after the General Conference in Johnstown. The United Brethren Conference had traditionally met in the fall. Thus the first session of the Iowa Conference (UB) following the denominational union was ten months after the meeting of the general conference. It met in Chariton, Iowa September 17-21, 1947. Each conference sent fraternal delegates to the sessions of the other. Each conference named a seven-member committee on Church Union, which would plan with the other.

The annual Summer Assembly, at which attendance had long been required for all EV pastors, became a joint venture in 1947. As the ministers and their families lived on the campgrounds at Riverside Park while participating in the week's program, they had a good opportunity to become acquainted and to share in the common life as Evangelical United Brethren.

In 1948 Dr. W. B. Tarr, a Conference superintendent, said in part:

> We believe that our Evangelical United Brethren Church has a place in the realm of denominations. We must cooperate where it is workable to do together what we cannot do alone. Our church is no longer a small church in statistical terms. We rank thirteenth in the total picture of American churches. We are a church that believes in the Word and Work of God among men. We were born as an answer to prayer on the part of a few early pioneers; we still must know the effect of prayer upon our work and progress. There is a field for our endeavors both in America and abroad. Our church now encircles the earth. There are 3,500 licensed men serving 5,000 churches. We are not easily convinced that there are too many preachers for the job; if so, then moral and spiritual levels have lowered because of too many men rather than not enough. We need to catch the spirit of the ultimate triumph of righteousness in the earth and gird ourselves for a full fledged battle against the inroads of sin, as found in immorality, the liquor evil, the false philosophy of military strength, broken homes, degrading literature, and most of all, the shallow and insincere concepts of Christianity which are held by countless people around us.[1]

The local church organizations were not changed much by the merger, as few communities had both Evangelical and United Brethren Churches. After the conferences were merged, it became possible to arrange more practical parish boundaries, by assigning neighboring churches to one pastor, thus eliminating unnecessary travel.

The two conferences maintained their old relationships to the General Church Institutions. The UB conference still helped support York College at York, Nebraska, Otterbein Home at Lebanon, Ohio, and Bonebrake Seminary at Dayton, Ohio. The EV conference continued its relationship with Westmar College in LeMars, Iowa; Evangelical Theological Seminary in Naperville, Illinois; Western Home in Cedar Falls, Iowa, and Flat Rock Children's Home in Flat Rock, Ohio.

Different bishops presided over the two conferences for the first five years. Bishop V. O. Weidler presided over the UB Conference in 1947, 1948, 1949, and 1950. In 1950 the conference changed from a fall to a spring conference, meeting on May 9-12, and making that year cover an eight-month period. Bishop Weidler died in the fall of 1950. Bishop D. T. Gregory of Pittsburgh, Pennsylvania presided over the closing session of the UB conference which met at the St. Andrew's Church, 31st and Iola Streets in Des Moines, May 1-2, 1951.

Bishop C. H. Stauffacher presided over each of the four sessions of the EV conference. The closing session met May 1-2, 1951, in the First Evan-

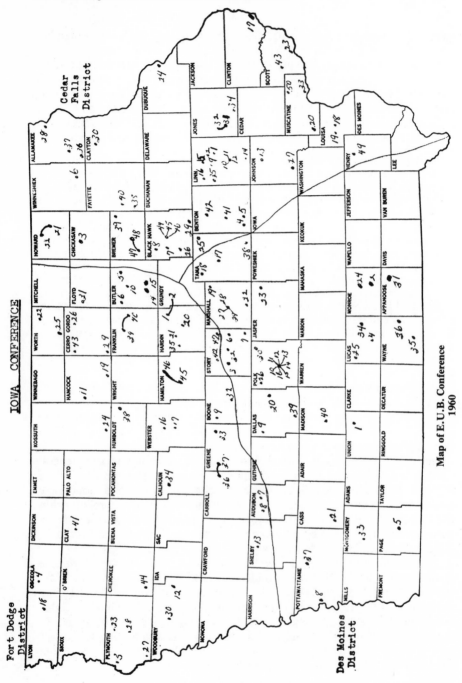

Map of E.U.B. Conference
1960

H.   Map Of Iowa Conference

(Numbers indicate the churches in each district)

1. CEDAR FALLS DISTRICT

1. Alburnett
2. Alburnett, Lafayette
3. Alta Vista
4. Belle Plaine
5. Blairstown
6. Castalia
7. Cedar Falls, First
8. Cedar Falls, Washington Chapel
9. Cedar Rapids, Buffalo
10. Cedar Rapids, Faith
11. Cedar Rapids, Salem
12. Cedar Rapids, Sharon
13. Cedar Rapids, Shueyville
14. Cedar Rapids, Union
15. Center Point, Alice
16. Center Point, Union
17. Clinton
18. Columbus Jct. Cairo
19. Columbus Jct. Spring Run
20. Cranston
21. Cresco, First
22. Cresco, Zion
23. Davenport
24. Dubuque
25. Dysart
26. Hudson
27. Iowa City, Sharon
28. Lansing
29. La Porte City
30. Monona
31. Morley
32. Morley, Forest Chapel
33. Muscatine
34. Olin
35. Palo, Lincoln
36. Postville
37. Postville, Forest Mills
38. Sumner, Murphy
39. Sumner, Salem
40. Sumner, Union
41. Van Horne
42. Vinton
43. Walcott
44. Waterloo, Calvary
45. Waterloo, First
46. Waterloo, Graves
47. Waverly, First
48. Waverly, Warren
49. Wayland
50. Wilton

2. DES MOINES DISTRICT

1. Afton, Beulah
2. Albia
3. Ames
4. Chariton
5. Clarinda, Rose Hill
6. Collins
7. Colo
8. Council Bluffs
9. Dawson
10. Des Moines, Christ
11. Des Moines, First
12. Des Moines, Marquisville
13. Des Moines, Miller
14. Des Moines, St. Andrews
15. Des Moines, Sheridan Park
16. Des Moines, Staves
17. Garwin
18. Gladbrook
19. Gladbrook, Chapel
20. Granger
21. Griswold, Noble
22. Laurel
23. Laurel, Hickory Grove
24. Lovilia
25. Lucas, Norwood
26. Madrid, Hopkins Grove
27. Marshalltown, Bethany
28. Marshalltown, First
29. Marshalltown, Grace
30. Maxwell, Loring
31. Moravia
32. Nevada
33. Discontinued
34. Russell, Bethel
35. Sewal
36. Seymour
37. Silver Creek (Hancock address)
38. Toledo
39. Van Meter
40. Winterset, Oak Grove

3. FORT DODGE DISTRICT

1. Ackley
2. Pleasant Valley
3. Adaville
4. Allendorf
5. Discontinued
6. Aredale
7. Audubon, Mt. Zion
8. Audubon, Ross
9. Boxholm
10. Bristow
11. Britt, Stilson
12. Correctionville
13. Defiance
14. Dumont, Bethany
15. Dumont, Salem
16. Fort Dodge
17. Lundgren
18. George
19. Goodell
20. Hubbard
21. Hubbard, Evergreen
22. Kensett, Bolan
23. LeMars
24. LuVerne
25. Manly
26. Mason City
27. Merrill, Melbourne
28. Merrill, Stanton
29. Meservey
30. Moville
31. Nora Springs
32. Ogden
33. Paton
34. Pomeroy
35. Radcliffe
36. Ralston
37. Maple Grove
38. Renwick
39. Sheffield
40. West Fork
41. Spencer
42. Story City
43. Ventura
44. Washta, Meadow Star
45. Webster City
46. Mulberry Center
47. Zearing

gelical United Brethren Church located at 12th and Des Moines Streets, in Des Moines.

In a footnote at the end of this chapter are given statistics taken from the Conference Minutes for the years 1946 (the year of denominational union), 1967 (the year of the union of the two Iowa conferences), 1967 (the last year prior to the union of the EUB and Methodist denominations), and as of December, 1974, for those ministers and congregations which had been Evangelical United Brethren.[2] Membership had declined during those years, but at the same time attendance at worship services had increased.

At the uniting session in 1951 the conference was divided into three districts, with the conference superintendents living at Des Moines, Fort Dodge, and Cedar Falls. Ward B. Tarr, John A. Dowd, and Reuben H. Aurand were elected as superintendents, and served in their respective districts. The General Conference assigned the Iowa Conference to the Southwestern Area, with Bishop C. H. Stauffacher of Kansas City as the presiding bishop.[3]

Bishop Stauffacher

The respective conferences had established relationships with certain institutions, which were maintained by the uniting conference. The changes were that they now became related to the entire denomination, and were not limited for support to the conferences in which they were located. The Evangelical United Brethren Church now had two colleges west of the Mississippi River—Westmar at LeMars, and York College at York, Nebraska—and three retirement homes, Western Home in Cedar Falls, Iowa, Friendly Acres at Newton, Kansas, and another in California.

The first two congregations to unite were located in Sumner, in Bremer County. The second were two open-country congregations west of Washta in Cherokee County, which united to form the Meadow Star congregation.

During the years other congregations of the two denominations merged. Also, between 1951 and 1968, thirty-five congregations of the two groups were discontinued for reasons not related to the merger. Farms were becoming larger, farm families smaller, and roads better. Rural Iowa was changing.

A long and enriching relationship existed between the Iowa Evangelical United Brethren people and York College during the years that it was related to the denomination. Following the loss of the main building by fire in 1951, the trustees voted to discontinue York College and transfer its assets to Westmar College in LeMars. This was a traumatic experience for the alumni and friends of York College, but the faculty, students, library books, and other assets brought to Westmar made it a stronger institution.

Before the Evangelical United Brethren union in 1946 each of the two denominations had considered merger with the Methodist Episcopal Church, as well as other possible unions. However, the union in 1946 led to the postponement of such discussions until that merger was fully accomplished. In the 1960s the talks could be resumed.

A Plan and Basis of Union for merger with The Methodist Church was prepared. In 1966 the General Conference of The Methodist Church and the General Conference of the E.U.B. Church met concurrently in Chicago. They each approved the plan and the necessary enabling legislation, then recommended it to the annual conferences of the two denominations for ratification.

The 1967 session of the Iowa Annual Conference of the Evangelical United Brethren Church was historic. The session met in Trinity Church at Fort Dodge on May 2. At the 8:30 a.m. session the Resolution on the Union of the Methodist Church and the Evangelical United Brethren Church was presented for vote. Each member of the conference, both ministerial and lay, was asked to stand and vote yea or nay. The vote was "yea" 151; "nay" 36; abstaining 1. An enabling resolution was approved, establishing a Commission on Conference Union of the Iowa Annual Conference of the E.U.B. Church with the North Iowa Conference and the South Iowa Conference of The Methodist Church.

The Plan of Union was approved by the necessary majority of the three annual conferences in 1967. As soon as the union had the approval of the conferences, the Commission on Conference Union began meeting under the leadership of Bishop Paul Milhouse and Bishop James S. Thomas. The

Bishop Milhouse

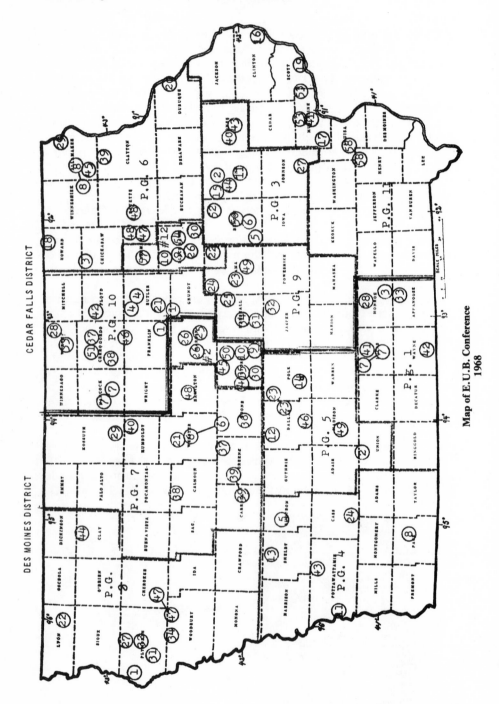

Map of E.U.B. Conference 1968

I. LOCATION OF CHURCHES

Pleasant Valley: 3 miles north and 1½ miles east of Wellsburg

2. Alburnett: 2 blocks west and 1 block north of bank
1. Ackley: State and Second Streets
    Alburnett, Lafayette: ¼ mile east and 1 mile north of Lafayette
    Alice: 6 miles east of the north edge of Center Point
3. Alta Vista: 2 blocks south of Main business intersection
4. Aredale: East of business district on Main St. (White frame church)
    Bristow: 1 block west of school in east part of town
5. Belle Plaine: 7th Ave. and 10th St.
6. Blairstown: 1 block south and ½ block west of bank
7. Britt, Stilson: 7 miles southwest of Britt, or 3½ miles south of Hutchins
    Goodell: 1 block east of school on Hiway 69
8. Castalia: West edge of Castalia
    Forest Mills: 10 mi. N.E. of Postville on Hwy. 51, ½ mi. S.
9. Cedar Falls, First: West 9th and Clay Sts.
10. Cedar Falls, Washington Chapel: 4 miles north of Cedar Falls on Hwy. 218, 1 mi. W.
11. Cedar Rapids
    Faith: 1000 30th St. N.E.
    Buffalo: 2 miles west of Hiawatha, from cemetery corner
    Salem: 1st Ave. at 3rd St. S.W.
    Sharon: 18th Ave. at 9th St. S.W.
    Shueyville: From Cedar Rapids, 6 miles S. of Hawkeye Downs Fair Grounds on Hwy. 218, then E. at Swisher Corner 1 mi.
    Union: S.E. of Cedar Rapids, 2 mi. E. of Hwy. 218 on Hwy. 30 and 1 block north
15. Center Point, Zion: 1 block W. of Main St.; 2 blocks N. of school
16. Clinton: 1605-13th Avenue North
17. Cranston: 3rd Ave. and Main St. (Only church in town)
18. Cresco: 5 mi. N. of Cresco, ½ mi. W., 2 mi. N., 2½ mi. W.
19. Davenport: 3322 W. Lonbard Ave.
20. Dubuque: Jackson and 25th Sts.
21 Dumont, Bethany: 4 blocks west of City park
    Salem: 1 block east of business district, North to school grounds
22. Dysart: Across street from school
23. Garwin: 2 blocks north of park on Central Avenue
24. Gladbrook: Johnson and Gould Sts.
25. Gladbrook, Chapel: 3 miles west and 4 mi. S. of Gladbrook
26. Hudson: On Hwy. 63 at corner of 3rd and Washington
27. Iowa City, Sharon: 4 mi. S.W. of Iowa City on Hwy. 1, 4 mi. S. to Sharon Center, 1 S., ½ E.
28. Kensett, Bolan: East from Kensett on County Hwy. 4 mi., 1 mi. N., and ¼ mi. East
29. Lansing: Opposite the Public school
30 LaPorte City: 600 Third & Walnut St.
31. Laurel: 1 block W. of Hwy. 14
32. Laurel, Hickory Grove: 4½ mi. S., 4½ mi. E., ½ mi. S. of Laurel
33. Manly: Broadway and Walnut St. or 1 block south of school
34. Marshalltown:
    Bethany: West State and 7th Sts.
    First: 201 Anson, or 2 blocks east of Hwy. 14
    Grace: E. State and 5th Ave.
37. Mason City: 14th and Adams Ave. N.W.
38. Meservey: North end of Main St., across from school
39. Monona: Corner of Egbert and Depue Sts.
40. Morley: Opposite the public school
    Forest Chapel: 5 Mi. north of Morley. ½ mi. W.
41. Muscatine: Mulberry Ave. and 6th St.
42. Nora Springs: Across street from town water tower
43. Olin: 2 blocks N, and 2 blocks W. of business district
44. Palo, Lincoln: 3 mi. S. of Palo on Hwy. 74, 2 mi. W.
45. Postville: 2 blocks N., 1 block E. of large Lutheran Church
46. Sheffield: E. Borst and 3rd Sts. 1 block east of High School
    West Fork: 6 mi. E. of Sheffield, then 3 mi. S. on road to Hansel
47. Sumner, Murphy: 2¼ mi. W. of Westgate on Hwy. 295, ¼ mi. N.
48. Sumner, Salem: 2nd St. and Chicago Ave.
    Union: 4 mi. E. of Sumner on Hwy. 93, 2 mi. S.
49. Toledo: East High and Church Sts.
50. Van Horne: 2 blocks N. of Hwy. 109, next to school
51. Ventura: On main Hwy. N. from school
52. Vinton: E. 4th St. and 3rd Ave.
53. Walcott: On Hwy. 228 in N. edge of town
    Wilton: 1 mi. W. of Wilton Jct. on Hwy. 6, then 1½ mi. S. on Hwy. 38
54. Waterloo:
    Calvary: E. 4th and Newell St.
    Graves: W. 4th St. at Allen
    First: Kimball and Byron (Turn S. off W. 4th St. onto Kimball)
57. Waverly: 2nd St. and 3rd Ave. N.W.
    Warren: 3 mi. E. of Waverly on Hwy. 3, 2 mi. N.
58. Wayland: 3 mi. W. of Wayland. (Called Cottonwood Church)
    Spring Run: 12 mi. W. of Wapello, 1 mi. N. on Columbus City Rd.

1968 session of the Iowa Conference—the first session as United Methodists —met in Nevada, Iowa May 13-16 with Bishop Milhouse presiding. On the afternoon of May 13th Dr. John A. Dowd presented the report from the Commission on Conference Union. The resolution was approved 139 to 21. The same resolution was approved later by the North and South Iowa Conferences.

The Plan and Basis of Union of the three Iowa Conferences was approved by the North Central Jurisdictional Conference of the United Methodist Church which met in Peoria, Illinois July 24-28, 1968. This plan provided that the three conferences in Iowa continue separately until June of 1969, when they would merge into one.

The three conferences met simultaneously in special session October 31-November 1, 1968, at the First United Methodist Church in Des Moines. They met separately, and each conference took care of items of business peculiar to itself. Dr. A. E. Wilken presided over the Iowa Conference; Bishop Thomas over the North Iowa Conference; and Dr. F. E. Miller over the South Iowa Conference. On Friday, November first, the three conferences met as one to adopt the Plan of Union of the new Iowa Conference which had already been approved by each of the conferences meeting separately.

The Evangelical United Brethren Church had played an important role in the life of evangelical Christianity in Iowa, and though its name is relegated to history, its spirit and devotion carry on as an integral part of United Methodism.

Footnotes

1. A. E. Wilken, "The Evangelical United Brethren Church in Iowa 1946-1968," *Proceedings of the Annual Meeting*, the Historical Society, North Central Jurisdiction, United Methodist Church, 1975, pp. 101.
2. Wilken, ibid., p. 105.

	1946	
	Ev.	U.B.
Itinerant Ministers	97	61
As pastors	52	31
As Conf. Supts.	3	1
Special Assignment	11	8
Retired	31	21
Organized Congregations	89	75
Total Membership	12,165	10,738
Average Attendance	6,670	3,706

	1951	
	Ev.	U.B.
Itinerant Ministers	89	62
As pastors	59	30
As Conf. Supts.	2	1
Special Assignment	8	8
Retired	20	23

Organized Congregations	88	72
Total Membership	12,717	10,030
Average Attendance	6,859	3,699
	6-1-67	12-74
	E.U.B.	E.U.B.
Itinerant Ministers	129	102
As pastors	75	56
As Conf. Supts.	2	1
Special Assignment	17	15
Retired	35	30
Organized Congregations	134	104
Total Membership	22,094	
Average Attendance	12,856	

3. Wilken, ibid., p. 105.

9

Iowa Conference—
The United Methodist Church

This chapter on the new Iowa Conference of the United Methodist Church is being written at a time when much of the story is too late to be news, yet too early to be history. It is too soon to evaluate the many changes adequately. The writer has been too close to the events to be altogether objective.

When the United Methodist Church was formed by the 1968 merger of the Evangelical United Brethren with The Methodist Church, the leadership of the two groups tried to consummate the union in such a way as to gain strength, keeping all that was best in both traditions without losing the warm fellowship of the smaller conferences. If the E.U.B. group had been merely blended into the contiguous Methodist conferences, much would have been lost through the separation of old friends placed in different con-

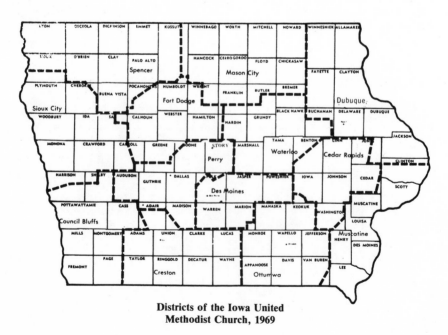

**Districts of the Iowa United
Methodist Church, 1969**

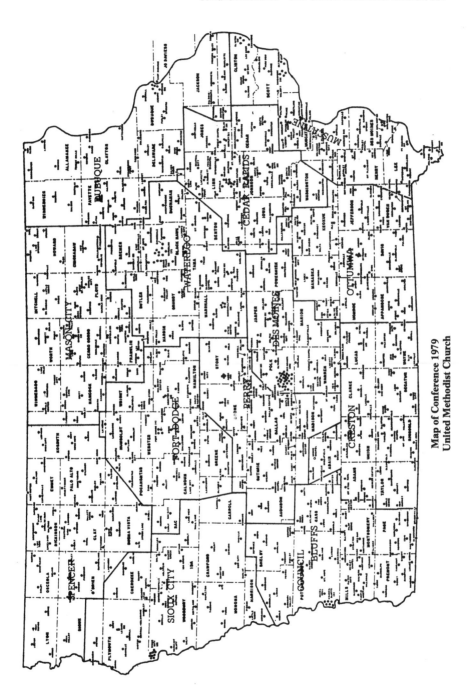

Map of Conference 1979
United Methodist Church

ferences. The former Methodists living in communities where there had been no E.U.B. churches needed to be made aware of the changes, some of which were vital to the success of the union.

Many preachers in the two Methodist conferences (North and South Iowa) had been urging for several years that the time had come to reunite all of the Methodists in the state into one conference. Communication had improved to such a point that anyone in Iowa could easily pick up a telephone and talk to another member anywhere in the state. Paved highways and fast cars had made travel easy. Unified planning could be more effective on a state-wide basis, as had been shown by inter-conference programs in the 1950s. The voice of the church could be heard more clearly when it spoke statewide. Accordingly all three conferences—Evangelical United Brethren, North Iowa, and South Iowa Methodist—voted to unite.

The first session of the Iowa Conference of the United Methodist Church was held in Veterans' Auditorium at Des Moines June 8-12, 1969. The conference divided itself into thirteen districts (1) Cedar Rapids, (2) Council Bluffs, (3) Creston, (4) Des Moines, (5) Dubuque, (6) Fort Dodge, (7) Mason City, (8) Muscatine, (9) Ottumwa, (10) Perry, (11) Sioux City, (12) Spencer, and (13) Waterloo Districts.

A very careful study had been made to see that the new districts' boundaries corresponded with natural divisions. It took into consideration the trading areas of principal cities, the highways, and other factors. In most cases the work was well done, but the districts on the eastern and western borders of the state presented special problems. In the Council Bluffs, Sioux City, Dubuque, and Muscatine Districts the state boundaries split the natural sociological and trade areas. For example, "Siouxland" includes part of Iowa, Nebraska, and South Dakota.

The new conference had 309,205 members divided among 585 pastoral charges. There were 483 pastors in full connection, available to be assigned to charges. The rest of the charges were served by probationary members, 25 associate members, and "local pastors." The number of supply pastors was nothing new, as Methodism has always utilized many "Local Preachers," ordained and unordained, in the smaller churches. However, with the merger, changes were made in the rules regulating the preachers' appointments and nomenclature.

Ministerial Categories

Formerly, local preachers, either full or part-time, could qualify for ordination as deacons and elders by taking the "Course of Study." Many faithful men and women were ordained local elders and rendered diligent service as full-time local pastors. They served even though they could not vote at annual conference regarding the programs which they implemented.

In the new church the local preachers serving as "supplies" were given a new title—local pastor, which was more descriptive of their actual responsibilities in the church. A local pastor can become an associate member of the conference when he or she has (1) served four years as a full-time local pastor; (2) completed the four-year ministerial course of study, in addition to the license to preach and introductory studies; (3) completed a minimum of sixty semester hours toward the Bachelor of Arts degree, or in an equivalent curriculum; (4) been recommended by the District Committee on the Ministry and the Board of Ministry; (5) declared his or her willingness to accept continuing full-time appointment; and (6) furnished a certificate of good health.

The new associate members had to meet more requirements than the former "accepted supplies," but they had more status and also a vote at conference. They could be ordained deacon upon completion of the course of study, but could no longer be ordained elder. The order of deacon was no longer merely a stepping-stone toward become an elder. For persons completing seminary and becoming conference members, it was still a stepping-stone, but for associate members it had a new dignity all its own.

Rules for the reception of candidates into probationary and full membership were also revised. To be admitted as a probationary member, one must have completed one-fourth of the requirements for a Bachelor of Divinity degree. To be ordained deacon, he or she must have been received as a probationary member of the conference or as an associate member. Under the new rules an associate member had to study more to qualify than before. Previously a local preacher was ordained as local deacon upon completing two years of the course of study, even though he/she might have no expectancy of becoming a conference member. Now he/she must complete the whole course before being ordained deacon.

Under the new rules a probationary member could be received into full membership after graduation with a Bachelor of Divinity degree from an approved school of theology, ordination as deacon, and two years' full-time service under the supervision of a district superintendent. To be ordained elder, one must have been received as a full member of the conference. This was new. There was now a close correlation between conference membership and ordination, which had not existed before.

All churches have been slow to admit women into the ministry on a par with men, but the United Methodist Church has moved gradually in that direction. The Methodist Episcopal Church refused to grant a woman a local preacher's license until 1920. In that year the Des Moines Conference appointed Alta Nichols to Ellston as a supply. She continued to serve as a full-time pastor, being ordained deacon in 1928 and elder in 1930. Others followed in her steps.

With the merger of the Methodist Episcopal Church and the Methodist Protestants in 1939, the Iowa-Des Moines Conference acquired its first woman member of the conference in the person of Mrs. Pearl Spurlock. No more were received into conference membership until 1956 when Nancy Nichols was admitted on trial. Since the formation of the United Methodist Church in 1968, women members have been received at an increasing rate.

During the life of the Iowa Conference, it has been led by four different bishops. When the United Methodist Church was formed, Bishop James

Bishop Thomas

Thomas had already been the leader of Iowa Methodists for four years. He had been assigned to Iowa in 1964. He continued in Iowa for two more four-year terms. In his address to the Iowa Annual Conference June 15, 1970, he stated:

> During the last eighteen months, we have reorganized and merged our three annual conferences; we have organized the program council; we have changed our district boundaries; we have extended new ministries; we have organized district councils; we have purchased a new Area Residence; we have become one people.

When the disciplinary limitation on episcopal terms required that he move in 1976, Bishop Thomas was assigned to the East Ohio Area. In the Iowa Area he was followed by Bishop Lance Webb, who came from Central Illinois and remained until his mandatory retirement in 1980. Bishop Wayne Clymer was transferred from the Minnesota Area to Iowa in 1980, and served until his retirement in 1984.

Bishop Webb

Bishop Clymer

Bishop Job

Bishop Rueben P. Job followed Bishop Clymer in the Iowa Area. A native of North Dakota, he was graduated from Westmar College and Evangelical Theological Seminary. He had a variety of pastoral experiences. At the time of his election as bishop he was world editor of the *Upper Room*.

The Iowa Conference of The United Methodist Church has been active in many spheres of Christian life. A few of them are mentioned here.

Continuing Education

A part of the work of a minister in any denomination has always been to maintain a program of personal study and growth. The early circuit rider carried a Bible, a hymn book, and a *Discipline* in his saddle bags, and he studied them—but that was not all. He was in touch with all sorts of people in a period of rapid growth. He grew with his people. Now it has become necessary to grow faster just to keep up. It has become essential to have a more *planned* program of continuing education.

A Continuing Education Committee of the Board of Ordained Ministry prepared a working paper for presentation to the 1980 session of the annual conference in an attempt to define minimum standards for pastors in the area of continuing education. This paper stated that Continuing Education gains its justification from the obvious fact that professional expertise is not simply a plateau to be achieved, or once gained, a static commodity throughout one's career. It went on to say that "The rationale for continuing education is predicated on the assumption that one should grow in the context of his or her profession."

The committee recommended a program calling on each minister to earn at least three C.E.U.s (Continuing Education Units) a year, as a measure of study and growth. A C.E.U. is defined as ten contact hours of participation. The annual Pastors' School was to be the foundational continuing education experience which would provide two units.

The program of continuing education was designed to provide a helpful plan for study that begins at the close of formal training and ends at the termination of the career.

Bishop Job and Cabinet 1985-1986

(Left to right in front): Stanley Kennedy, Council Bluffs, Dean of the Cabinet; Merlin Ackerson, Spencer; Joan Hoover, Dubuque; Bishop Rueben Job; Nancy Allen, Ottumwa; Lester Moore, Muscatine. In back from the left: Keith Scott, Mason City; Weldon Whitenack, Des Moines; Rollin Oswald, Cedar Rapids; Carroll Usher, Waterloo; William Cotton, Creston; Bonifacio Mequi, Fort Dodge; and Richard Pearson, Sioux City.

Automobile Expense

A problem faced by the Bishop and his cabinet when making appointments was trying to estimate the actual out-of-pocket expense paid by each pastor traveling about his parish and to nearby hospitals. It might appear in the treasurers' report in the conference minutes that two pastors were receiving equal salaries, when in fact the amounts might be quite different.

The expense of maintaining an automobile came out of the preacher's own funds, and the cost was not uniform. A two or three-point charge always involved more driving than a station charge. The distance and number of hospitals used by the community also made a difference. The more pastoral calls made by a pastor, the less money he had for his family's needs.

Beginning in 1983 in the Iowa Conference, each minister kept a record of necessary travel and presented a voucher to the local church treasurer monthly, to be reimbursed for the miles driven. The salary was the minister's own, and became a more accurate measure of the pastoral support provided by the charge.

Summer Renewal Institute

One of the activities which had meant much to the Evangelical United Brethren people before the 1968 merger was the annual Summer Assembly, held each year at Riverview Park in Cedar Falls. It had originally been called a "camp meeting." Attendance was required at Summer Assembly. It was a time when all of the ministers and their families came together for a week of fellowship and inspiration. They all had an opportunity to become acquainted with one another in a way that is impossible in the much larger Iowa Conference of the United Methodist Church.

Many ministerial families own cabins on the grounds. Since merger, the assembly has been continued in a somewhat different form. The 90th session was held July 24-29, 1983, under the name of the "Summer Renewal Institute." Bishop Wayne Clymer preached at the opening worship service.

Okoboji Bible Conference

Bishop Clymer also preached at the Okoboji Bible Conference in 1983. The Northwest Iowa Conference of the Methodist Episcopal Church had had a camp on the northeast side of West Okoboji Lake, rather similar to the E.U.B. campground at Cedar Falls in some respects. It had been established in 1915 as a Sheldon District project. The Camp Meeting, later called Bible Conference, has continued as an annual event since that time.

Many ministers of the Northwest Iowa Conference built their own cabins, which were used to house youth camps and institutes most of the summer, except when they were wanted for family vacations. Some have now been "winterized" and are being used as retirement homes by older ministers, who formerly spent much time there with youth groups. The Bible Conference continues to be an important event in the life of Northwest Iowa United Methodists.

Conferences on the Holy Spirit

The first of a series of biennial "Conferences on the Holy Spirit" sponsored by the Iowa Conference and the United Methodist Renewal Services Fellowship (UMRSF) was held in Veterans Auditorium at Des Moines in September, 1974. The conference attracted 4,000 persons of various denominations, although the majority of them were Methodists. Thirty workshops on different topics were conducted as part of the program.

Additional conferences on the Holy Spirit were held in Des Moines in 1976, 1978, 1980, and 1982. The one in 1976 attracted 3,000 participants; in 1978, 6,000. The conference in 1980 drew only 1,200 persons, but in 1982, 2,000 were in attendance.

The "Charismatic Movement"—an emphasis on the influence of the Holy Spirit in the Christian experience—became prominent in American church life in the 1970s. This movement is not well understood by those who are not participants in it. When charismatics try to explain their experiences to outsiders, it often sounds like jargon to them. The Holiness Movement of the 1800s had tended to be divisive and led to the creation of new "holiness" churches. The modern charismatics have made a consistent effort to keep the movement within the main-line churches, giving them a much-needed spiritual growth. It is much more than speaking in tongues or praying with one's arms in the air. It is a vital movement in the church among people who take their religion seriously.

A Dynamic Church

The denominations which have merged to make up the United Methodist Church have always had a few members from races other than "white," but they have been an easily overlooked minority. The fourteen years of the Iowa Conference have been a time of transition. The spirit that abolished the Central Jurisdiction also opened the doors and welcomed people of diverse languages and races into the church. By 1983 the Iowa Conference had four Korean churches, and a work among Hispanic people in Des Moines and Muscatine. In 1983 the first black woman minister was assigned to a church of the conference. The Rev. Louise Spears was assigned to Keosauqua in the Ottumwa District.

The new Iowa Conference has been a dynamic conference in a changing world. The church has initiated or continued programs designed to meet the needs of the community. Some of the best known are the Wesley Foundations, Wall Street Mission and Goodwill Industries, Hawthorn Hill, Hillcrest Family Services, urban ministries, hospitals, colleges, and retirement homes.

In 1984 the Iowa Conference of the United Methodist Church had 247,496 members in 576 pastoral charges with 906 local churches. These were served by 438 pastors and district superintendents, 55 probationary members, 38 associate members, 24 full-time local pastors, and numerous part-time local pastors. The United Methodist Church is a large denomination in Iowa and has wide influence, but the membership decline since 1969 has prompted a program to recapture its evangelistic zeal.

10

Ethnic Churches

Up to this point, reference to the Methodist Episcopal Church organization in Iowa has meant only the English-speaking congregations. Most migrants coming into Iowa have spoken English, at least as a second language. The United States has long been called a "melting pot" where persons from many nations have come together and become one people, each group making its own contribution to the whole. The same has been true of United Methodism as it developed in Iowa. Germans, Swedes, Norwegians, Danes, Czechs, Hispanics, and Koreans have all come to Iowa to work, and have worshiped in Methodist churches using their native languages. After a period of years, younger generations have all but forgotten the old languages, and the congregations have become integral parts of the United Methodist Church.

GERMAN METHODISTS

The largest and most influential of these groups was German. The Evangelical Brotherhood and the United Brethren in Christ brought evangelical Christianity to the German-speaking people in Maryland, Pennsylvania, and Virginia. In the early days Bishop Francis Asbury insisted on confining the work of the Methodist Episcopal Church to the English language, although he worked in close cooperation with Philip Otterbein of the United Brethren, who preached in German.

The United Brethren had already changed to the use of English by the time they first came into Iowa. The Evangelicals continued using both English and German for many years after entering Iowa.

The story of the spread of the Methodist Episcopal Church among the German immigrants in the Ohio and Mississippi River valleys properly begins with the conversion of William Nast (Wilhelm Nast) on January 11, 1835. Nast (1807-1899) was born in Stuttgart, Germany. He studied in Blauberg Seminary preparing for the Lutheran ministry, in keeping with a family tradition. At the age of eighteen he transferred to the University of Tübingen. After two years he withdrew because of weakened faith and mental doubts. While in a restless state of mind, at the age of twenty-one, he came to America. Almost from his arrival, Nast found himself in contact with the Methodists.

In the spring of 1834, while teaching German and Hebrew at Kenyon College in Gambier, Ohio, he had the religious experience which he had been

William Nast

seeking, at a Methodist revival meeting. He was immediately convinced that his life work was in the Methodist Episcopal Church.

Within two weeks after his "aldersgate experience" he received his exhorter's license, and in July he was granted a local preacher's license. Nast was admitted on trial into the Ohio Annual Conference on September 15, 1835, and was appointed as missionary to the German-speaking people in and around Cincinnati.

The German work moved slowly at first, but it soon gained momentum. In 1838 Nast was appointed editor of a German-language publication yet to be named. Nast devoted himself to the new "Christliche Apologete" (*The Christian Apologist*) and to the mission. He held the position as editor for fifty-three years, traveling far and wide promoting the *Apologist* and preaching. By the end of 1840 there were nine regular missionaries in the Ohio field.

One of the great names among the German Methodists in the West was Ludwig Jacoby (1813-1874). Jacoby as the fifth of six children in a pious Jewish family in Alt-Strelitz, Mechlenberg. He was converted to Christianity in Leipzig, and was baptized in the Lutheran Church. He arrived in America in 1838 and became acquainted with the Methodists of Cincinnati in 1839. On the Monday night before Christmas that year he joined the Methodist Episcopal Church.

Jacoby's first appointment as a Methodist preacher was to the German immigrants at St. Louis, Missouri in 1841. He did not receive a welcome from the Germans at first, but in spite of a hostile reception, his efforts produced a Methodist society. A year after his arrival he dedicated a new church building. By the end of the second conference year his society had two hundred members.

Work among the Germans expanded rapidly, and by 1845 eleven circuit riders were covering the territory now included in the states of Missouri, Illinois, and Iowa. In 1845 the territory was organized into a German-speaking district attached to the Missouri Conference, with Jacoby as the first

Ludwig Jacoby

Sigourney Bethel, early German M. E. Church

presiding elder. With the north-south division of the Methodist Episcopal Church in 1845, the Germans, who were loyal to the North because of their opposition to slavery, were transferred to the Illinois Conference and became the Quincy District. It is interesting to note that Jacoby wrote to the 1846 session of the Iowa Conference, reporting on the work he had done among the Germans living within the bounds of that conference.

Quincy, September 1st, 1846

To the President and Members of the Iowa Annual Conference in Session at Bloomington

Dear Brethren:

I believe it is my duty to give you a report of the German Missions of my district, which lie in the bounds of your conference.

1. Dubuque Mission is now in existence for about two years; but there had been done very little and the principal reason was, because the missionary had

to visit Galena and the neighborhood, and often in the winter, when the work commenced, he had to be absent again for some weeks, because he was hindered to return in reason of the ice of the river. We hope, however, that, if the Bishop would find it suitable, there will be missionaries enough to attend to this mission better than ever before.

2. Bloomington Mission has been commenced since New Year. The Lord blessed the labors of our missionary; he has about eighteen members and a church built about 9 miles from Bloomington. It is a very large field of labor, for many Germans are scattered around in the neighborhood of Bloomington, Iowa City and Davenport.

3. Iowa Mission situated in Keokuk, Washington and Jefferson counties. This mission has been commenced two years ago, and is in a flourishing condition. We had a camp meeting in Iowa, and the Lord blessed us in a powerful way.

4. Burlington Mission—This is the only place where we could not get a start. The principal difficulty is, we have no suitable place of worship; but I hope the Lord will break the ice, and bring sinners to repentance and faith. It is, as you all know, one of the principal places in Iowa; and we should persevere, until the Lord opens us a door.

5. Palmyra Mission—The neighborhood of Farmington belongs to this mission. The Lord has blessed the work there, and two small classes have been commenced. We had one protracted meeting in July; the fruit of it was about eleven conversions, amongst them two Catholics.

Now, my brethren, we recommend this part of God's vineyard to your especial patronage. You travel amongst the Germans; you could encourage them to come to hear us; you could assist our missionaries in their many difficulties and trials; and especially send your fervent prayers for us to heaven. But I have to lay one thing more before you. Since last year a German publishing fund has commenced to be raised. Certainly you have experienced the worth of our publications, and you would not wish to be without them. Now only remember the Germans; as well preachers as members are without them. Will you not help us in collecting funds for that great and worthy enterprise, to have our publications translated and printed? Certainly you will.

May the blessing of the Lord be with you is the prayer of your brother in Christ.

Ludwig S. Jacoby,
Presiding Elder of German Quincy District[1]

The work among German-speaking Methodists grew rapidly until by 1860 there were eighteen German districts attached to eight different English-speaking conferences. The Galena District with nine appointments and the Minnesota District with thirteen appointments were attached to the Upper Iowa Conference. Each district had some churches within Upper Iowa territory. The Burlington District (German) of the Rock River Conference had some churches within the Iowa Conference territory.

The arrangements whereby German districts were placed in English conferences was not satisfactory. Paul F. Douglass wrote in his *The Story of German Methodism*:

The German Mission had all kinds of peculiar problems which did not concern the English-speaking brethren and which they did not understand. Many of the German itinerants had such a meager command of English that they could not even follow the proceedings of the Annual Conference. Despite these facts, the Germans had been so warmly received by the English brethren, presiding elders, and bishops in the Annual Conferences that many of them were reluctant to sever the bonds of brotherhood which united them. They feared a religious isolation behind a language barrier.[2]

In 1864 the German districts were formed into four German conferences: the East German Conference, the Central German Conference, the Northwest German Conference, and the Southwest German Conference. The churches located in the northern part of Iowa were in the Northwest German Conference, and the churches in Southwest Iowa were in the Burlington District of the Southwest German Conference. When the St. Louis German Conference was separated from the Southwestern Conference in 1884, the Iowa churches were still in the Burlington District of the St. Louis German Conference.

By 1872 the German work in northern Illinois and southeastern Wisconsin had grown until it seemed desirable to divide that area from the Northwest Conference and form a separate Chicago German Conference in northeastern Illinois and southeastern Wisconsin. This did not make much difference to the German districts in Iowa; they continued their work as before. In 1924 the two conferences reunited. German congregations in Iowa were spread across the state in many communities from east to west. A 1913 *History of the Northwest German Conference* listed charges (arbeitfeld) in Colesburg, Decorah, Dubuque, Giard, Lansing, Sherrill, Tomah, Yellow Creek, Alden and Dows, Burt and Fenton, Charles City, Denison, Flood Creek, Fort Dodge, Garner, Gladbrook, Klemme, LeMars, Mason City, Odebolt, Reinbeck, Rudd, St. Charles, Sioux City, Spencer, Storm Lake, and Varina.[3]

The St. Louis German Conference published a twenty-fifth anniversary history in 1909 which gave short accounts of appointments in Bridgewater and Lewis, Central Avenue Burlington, St. Paul's First Church Burlington, Council Bluffs, Davenport, Des Moines, Harper, Keokuk, Mt. Pleasant, Muscatine, Victor, Wapello, West Burlington, and Pine Mills.[4]

Most of the appointments listed included more than one preaching place. One cannot determine the exact number of German congregations which have existed in Iowa at different times, or how many present congregations can trace their beginnings to German roots.

German Methodism made an impressive contribution to the Methodist Episcopal Church in various ways. The pioneer German preachers were first in many frontier communities where German immigrants settled. Many of the churches they organized are important to the current life of the Iowa Conference of the United Methodist Church. In his *Story of German Methodism* Paul Douglass has written,

Methodism touched a chord in the pietistic German nature almost as naturally as the eagle takes to the skies. Within the German-speaking branch of the Methodist Episcopal Church the ardor and simplicity of Methodism burned as deeply and continued longer than in any other section of the denomination.[5]

During the best years of the German conferences there was a flow of members from them into the English-speaking churches. The Germans were loyal Methodists, and when a family moved to a new community, they would seek out the local English-speaking Methodist Church. Zwingli F. Meyer wrote of the Germans, ". . . German Methodism during its century of existence, transferred to the Mother Church three out of every four members received."[6]

German Methodism played a significant part in the building of the church in the United States, but the time came for it to be absorbed into the larger English-speaking church. The German church had been losing preachers and laity to the "English" churches from the beginning. A decline in the number of immigrants eventually had its effect. The First World War forced the church to give up the use of the German language for the period of the war. After the war, churches which had already been giving up the use of German for the Sunday School and young people's work were not inclined to resume its use. The young people were turning to the English language, and German Methodism had become an older people's church. Candidates for the ministry with German ancestry were attending "English" seminaries and joining "English" conferences.

In 1924 the St. Louis German Conference merged with the contiguous conferences, which in Iowa meant the Iowa and the Des Moines Conferences. One congregation in Davenport joined the Chicago Northwest German Conference. At that same time, the Chicago German Conference rejoined the Northwest German Conference. This was a temporary adaptation, as in 1933 the Chicago Northwest German Conference also merged with the contiguous English conferences. The German Methodists had made their mark on the Methodist Episcopal Church in Iowa, and that church was much richer because of their contributions.

SWEDISH METHODISTS

The Scandinavian immigrants who became Methodists had felt the same economic and political pressures for migration that were found in other European countries during the nineteenth century. However, the pressures in Scandinavia were more economic than political, as contrasted with the chiefly political pressures in Germany.

In communities where the immigrant Scandinavians settled there was no Lutheran state church (as there had been in their homelands), but a warm welcome in Methodism. Like other immigrants, the Swedes, the Norwegians, and the Danes found it easier to worship in their mother tongue. Like the Germans, they formed their own Methodist Episcopal churches.

The welcome received by the Scandinavian immigrants and seamen in New York Harbor is a thrilling story. Between 1840 and 1876, 200,000

Scandinavian immigrants arrived in New York, and additional thousands of Scandinavian sailors touched at the port. Methodist preachers held impromptu services on the ships and were received so cordially that in 1845 New York's *Asbury Society* bought an unseaworthy ship and berthed it at the foot of Carlisle Street on the North River. It was rechristened *John Wesley* but was more popularly known as *Bethel Ship Mission.*

Olaf Hedstrom was appointed pastor. He welcomed newcomers, gave them help and advice, and steered many of them to new homes in America. Many of the first Swedes and Norwegians who settled in Iowa came because of his advice. The influence of a Swedish preacher in New York Harbor had much to do with establishing the church here in Iowa![7]

The growth of the Methodist Episcopal Church among the Scandinavian people was somewhat delayed by the efforts of Americans to organize them into joint congregations. The Scandinavians seemed to have brought some of their old-country antagonisms to America with them. The Scandinavian work made its most outstanding progress after the Swedes and Norwegians were separated into different districts and conferences.

An attempt was made to organize a Scandinavian theological seminary, but the effort failed. Arlow Andersen, author of *The Salt of the Earth, a History of Norwegian Methodism in America*, states:

> If nothing came of the proposal for a Scandinavian seminary it was doubtless because feelings grounded in national issues in the European fatherlands precluded harmonious cooperation. As Haagensen explains it, Scandinavianism was a dream that was destined to fail short of fulfillment, whether in connection with a seminary, a publication, books, districts, or annual conferences.[8]

New Sweden Church

The first Swedish Methodist Church in Iowa was the New Sweden Methodist Episcopal Church northeast of Fairfield in Jefferson County. It was almost a direct outgrowth of the Bethel Ship Mission in New York. Several families left from the Kisa parish of the province of Ostergotland, Sweden in early May, 1845. They had several delays enroute, and came under the guidance of Pastor Hedstrom and the Bethel Ship Mission. Their church in Iowa was organized in 1850.[9] They were a part of a Swedish district until the Swedish Northwest Conference was organized in 1876.

The congregation grew as more Swedes moved into the community, but they eventually faced the same problem as have other open-country churches with the language question. The church probably reached its low mark between 1931 and 1937 when it was without a pastor and was inactive. The Swedish Northwest Conference was merged into the surrounding English conferences in 1942. In recent years the New Sweden congregation has been served by a capable and energetic, part-time lay pastor, Charles Sloca.

The dissolution of the Central Northwest (Swedish) Conference brought three pastors and five churches into the Iowa-Des Moines Conference, but none into Upper Iowa. Northwest Iowa received three churches and their pastors.

NORWEGIAN AND DANISH METHODISTS

The Norwegians and Danes have been associated amicably in American Methodism. Their languages are mutually intelligible, and they have had no old-country animosities to keep them apart.

A pietistic movement resembling the Wesleyan revival in England existed in the Norwegian state church under the leadership of Hans Nielsen Hauge. This was not directly related to Methodism, but it did create an atmosphere in which it was easy for Norwegian immigrants to turn to Methodism when they came to America.

Many of the Norwegian immigrants came to the Midwest. The first Norwegian Methodist class in America was probably the one organized in southern Wisconsin. Andersen states:

> The Fox River community witnessed the formation of the first Norwegian Methodist class, in which the members prayed and testified in their pioneer homes. After the organization of the Rock River Conference in 1840 they found themselves within its boundaries. When Solomon Denning began to ride the Milford circuit within the new conference in 1843, the Norwegian settlement was one of his appointments. Denning thereby became the first Methodist preacher to an organized body of Norwegians in America.[10]

Some of the Fox River group moved into Iowa and settled in Winneshiek County. Ole Peter Petersen preached his first sermon as pastor of Norwegian Methodists in Iowa in the cabin of Nelson Johnson in Washington Prairie, Winnesheik County, on November 10, 1851. A congregation was formed in the spring of 1852. Johnson's cabin was probably the first

Norwegian Methodist meeting-house west of the Mississippi. Later Ole Peter Petersen was the first Methodist missionary to Norway.

Arlow Andersen has listed three problems faced by the Norwegian-Danish work prior to and during the Civil War. First the prevailing suspicion of foreigners.

> With the swelling immigrant tide, especially of the Germans and Irish, American nativism bristled in the newspaper press and from the public platform. As European cultures came to be less appreciated, often openly denounced as dangerous to true Americanism, Scandinavians bore some of the stigma of alien birth and strange speech. Northern states were caught up in the super-patriotism of the Know Nothing movement and the "Order of the Star Spangled Banner."[11]

The second problem was the shortage of pastors, and the third was opposition from the Lutheran church.

As the second and third generations, who knew English better than Norwegian, came along, pressure to change languages began to appear. Andersen states that as early as 1890 the question of the advisability of turning to English was becoming acute.[12] In 1907 the Epworth League page in

Washington Prairie Church

the church periodical, *Talsmand*, was published in English for the first time.[13]

The Norwegian-Danish Conference was disbanded in September, 1940. Its churches and preachers were absorbed into the contiguous English conferences. By the time that the Norwegian-Danish Conference was dissolved, most of the churches and pastors in Iowa had already been transferred to English conferences. In 1940 two pastors—C. H. Pettersen and A. R. Nygaard—were transferred into the Northwest Iowa Conference.

BOHEMIAN METHODISTS

The people who migrated to America from various European countries were not conformists by nature. Otherwise they might have stayed at home. The Bohemian people (Czechs) who settled in and around Cedar Rapids were no exception. Many of them were in revolt against all churches and took pride in being Freethinkers. However, they were not overlooked by the churches. The Catholic Church took care in the assignment of priests, to be sure that there was someone who could speak Czech. The Jan Huss Memorial Presbyterian Church was established to serve Czech-speaking (Bohemian) people.

In 1890 the young people of St. Paul's Methodist Episcopal Church in Cedar Rapids founded a mission for Czech Protestants. A young man named Jan Tauchen, who had been a bank clerk in Chicago, volunteered to work as a missionary among the Czechs. After his death in 1895, the church was moved to the west side of the river, where most of the Bohemians lived at that time. Services were conducted in both Czech and English until after the pastorate of F. D. Chada, who was the last Czech-speaking pastor of the church.[14]

The Rev. John Moore was assigned to John Huss Methodist Church in 1957, and in 1958 the congregation was merged with Asbury Methodist Church. The first Czech Methodist Church in the world lives on as part of the Asbury congregation.

A short-lived effort was made to establish a Bohemian work in Fort Dodge, but not enough Czechs resided there to make a strong church. J. F. Zavodsky was assigned as supply pastor for three years. The Conference Minutes of 1914 lists it "to be supplied." The 1915 district superintendents' report states that the congregation had only occasional help from Cedar Rapids before that time. John Drahousal was appointed as the supply pastor. In 1916 he reported six members and forty-four enrolled in Sunday School. The pastor's salary was sixty dollars.

During the First World War it was not possible to have services in any language other than English. The 1919 Conference Minutes makes no mention of the Bohemian Mission.

People of Bohemian ancestry now customarily join English-speaking churches. There are many people of Bohemian descent in Iowa United Methodist Churches, but they are not segregated from other Methodists.

KOREAN CHURCHES

The newest of the ethnic groups to establish United Methodist churches in Iowa is the Korean. The first Korean preacher admitted into an Iowa conference was Howard Cho. He had come to Iowa Wesleyan College from Korea as a student in 1955. While there he joined The Methodist Church and heard his call to preach. Following graduation from Iowa Wesleyan he attended Garrett Theological Seminary (now Garrett-Evangelical). After finishing seminary study in 1962 he was admitted on trial in the South Iowa

Conference, and ordained deacon. He served two years at St. Charles and Patterson, which were at that time in the Des Moines District. After ordination as elder and reception into full membership in the conference, he transferred to the Central Autonomous Conference in Korea.

Korean Church

Ten years later (1957) Cho transferred back to the Iowa Conference, and was assigned to Fremont-Cedar-Kirksville in the Ottumwa District. While serving these small-town Iowa United Methodist Churches, he also flew weekly to Davenport to help establish a Korean congregation which was meeting in St. John's United Methodist Church.

The church in the "Quad cities" did well, and in 1983 was able to purchase a building of its own in Bettendorf. The Rev. Hong Ki Kim was transferred from the Seoul Annual Conference in June, 1983, and assigned to the Bettendorf church.

Meanwhile, a congregation of Korean Christians had been meeting in Des Moines since 1972. They met first in the Highland Park Christian Church and then in the Windsor Heights Lutheran Church. In 1978 they became a part of the Iowa Conference of the United Methodist Church, sharing the facilities of Christ United Methodist Church. Howard Cho was transferred from Fremont to Des Moines, and served both congregations, meeting in one building. He led them until 1980 when he became pastor of the Korean Emmanuel United Church in Toronto, Canada.

The Rev. Sang Kook Ro came from the North Dakota Conference of the United Methodist Church as Cho's replacement. In 1982 the Des Moines Korean congregation secured an unused dental-chair plant which could be renovated for church and education purposes. The new church was consecrated on December 19, 1982.

The Korean United Methodist Church in Ames began in the spring of 1980 with small groups of students meeting in private homes for Bible study. A committee was soon formed to study the possibility of establishing a church in Ames. While Korean residents of Ames had been attending services in the Des Moines Korean church, they felt a need for a church of their own in Ames.

In September, 1980, the new church held a constituting service at the Ames Collegiate United Methodist Church with thirty-nine members. The Rev. Sang Kook Ro moved from the Des Moines Korean church in June, 1982, to serve Boone's Marion Street United Methodist and the Ames Korean Church. The Rev. Mu-Young Kim came from the Seoul Annual Conference of the Korean Methodist Church to take his place in Des Moines.

The Ames church, located in a university town, has an opportunity to serve students who are away from home in a strange environment. About 85% of the Korean United Methodist Church members are students and faculty members. Some attend who have not been part of a Christian community previously.

A small group of Korean Christians, living in Iowa City and feeling the need for a community of believers of Korean background, met in the home of Elder Sung Woo Park on May 10, 1976. As a result of that meeting, twenty-one Korean Christians began worshiping at two o'clock each Sunday afternoon in the Union Memorial Chapel on the University of Iowa campus. At first Donyan Paik, a University of Iowa student, served as pastor. The congregation moved to St. Mark's United Methodist Church in October, 1977, and became officially a United Methodist Church on January 16, 1983, with Rev. Hyun Chan Bae as pastor. They continue to meet on Sunday afternoons in St. Mark's Church.

In Sioux City a small group of Koreans have been meeting in Grace United Methodist Church since March, 1980. Because there are not enough Korean people in the Sioux City area to form a church of their own, they are continuing as an outreach program of Grace Church. They celebrated their third birthday March 25, 1984.

BLACK METHODISTS

Black people were among the first settlers in Dubuque in 1833 and they were part of the first M.E. church established there. One, Mrs. Charlotte Morgan, was a member of the first Methodist society organized by Barton Randle on May 18, 1834. At least one black person—possibly a slave—contributed to the building fund for Dubuque's first log church. When the Iowa Conference was organized in 1844, the Dubuque station reported four "colored" members. In 1853, the last year that black members were reported separately, Dubuque reported a small gain of white members and the loss of one "colored" member.

After 1853 the black members became the invisible Methodists and there are no statistics to indicate how many black people belong to predominantly white congregations in Iowa. There have always been some.

During and after the Civil War ex-slaves came north looking for work and new homes. Eleven of them joined the Ebenezer M.E. Church (also called the Division Street Church) in Burlington on February 25, 1866. They

				Remarks
Margaret Lynch				
Mattie D. Middleton		Ann.		Dismissed by Letter
Cynthia Bowers	M			
Mary Fuller	s			Restored to full membership by rejection
Lorain Daniel	M	"	11	Feb. 23/68
Mary Winney	s		13	
Cornelia Winney	s	Discontinued		
Lucy Mines	"		13	
Mary McRea	M		15	
Emily Page	"		16	
Lavania Pollet	s			
Jane Brady	s	Removed to Oskaloosa	17	Dismissed by Letter
Alva Bowers	s		18	Feb. 24 1865
Lillie Morgan	M	Feb. 12th		
Mattie Alford	s			
Hattie Bradley	s	March 4th 1865		
Louisa Donaldson	M			
Emma Carter	Colored			
Sarah Johnson	Discontinued	"		These were all slaves but are now by the events of war all free
Martha Courtwright	"			
Sarah Harris Discontinued	"			
Walter Dixon	"	"		
Louisa Sandford	"	1866 Feb. 23,		
Pashena White	"			
Amy Courtwright	"	Feb. 1866		
Jack Dixon	"			
Mary Dixon	"			
Robt. Riesley				

DIVISION STREET CHURCH CLASS OF SLAVES, 1865 (FREED BY CIVIL WAR).
Originally Ebenezer M.E. Church—Burlington, Iowa 1854-1899

Burns Memorial Methodist Church

were active for a while but later withdrew to form an African Methodist Episcopal Church in that city. Ebenezer eventually merged with Old Zion to become First M.E. Church. Both First United Methodist and the A.M.E. Church are proud of their former relationship.

The first all-black M.E. Church organized in Iowa was Burns Memorial in Des Moines, which started its work in 1866. The first minister appointed to Burns began serving the congregation in 1867.[15] About that time a number of black people settled in Oskaloosa. At first they worshiped with the white Methodists, but in 1868 secured a frame church building for themselves under the name of Wesley Chapel. The 1870 Journal lists forty-seven full members.

During the years that mining was an important industry in South Iowa many black people came to Iowa to work in the mines. They were poor people and did not live long in a community. Changing employment opportunities made it difficult to maintain strong churches.

The 1892 General Conference placed the Negro congregations of Iowa, Nebraska, and Western Illinois in a separate district—the Iowa District— and attached it to the Iowa Conference. W. E. Wilson, the presiding elder, reported to the conference in 1894 and 1895, telling a story of struggling congregations with too few members to support a full-time pastor. The list of appointments in the 1895 Journal shows eleven charges, seven of which were left *to be supplied*.[16] In 1896 the General Conference transferred the Iowa District to the Central Missouri Conference (colored).

During World War I approximately one thousand black people moved to Sioux City, and more were expected. After consultation with the Board of

Home Missions and representative black people, the previously closed Haddock Memorial Church was reopened. The Reverend Dudley Smith of the Central Missouri Conference (colored) was transferred to the Northwest Iowa Conference and was assigned to Haddock Memorial as pastor.[17] This work continued until 1923.

The Iowa churches remained in the Central Missouri Conference until 1929, when Central Missouri merged with part of the Lincoln Conference to form the Central West Conference. That conference became part of the Central Jurisdiction with the denominational merger of the northern and southern churches in 1939.

When the Central Jurisdiction was dissolved in 1964, the separate racial conferences came to an end. On June 21, 1964, the Central West Conference merged with the Lexington Conference. Nineteen days later, on July 9th, the Lexington Conference was dissolved and its churches absorbed into the overlying white conferences. The two Iowa conferences received four churches and their pastors.

The South Iowa Conference received Burns Memorial in Des Moines and its pastor, K. C. McNeil, and New Hope in Fort Madison with its pastor, J. F. Johnson. North Iowa received Union Memorial in Mason City and its pastor, O. E. Blanks, and Morrow Memorial of Marshalltown with its pastor, B. W. Wynn. North Iowa also received one retired conference member, Jordan Ray, who lived only a few weeks following the transfer, dying on September 4, 1964. His obituary appears in the 1965 North Iowa Conference Journal.[18]

The last session of the Central Jurisdiction elected James S. Thomas to the office of bishop. With the dissolution of the Central Jurisdiction, he was assigned to North Central Jurisdiction and became Iowa's first black bishop. He served Iowa for twelve years (1964-1976), the disciplinary limit of tenure in a conference.

Union Memorial Church in Mason City had always had a close relationship with First Church in that city, so at the close of the Annual Conference session of the United Methodist Church in 1965, they merged.[19] New Hope and Santa Fe churches in Fort Madison were merged in 1969.

Since 1969 other black ministers have been transferred into the Iowa Conference of the United Methodist Church. In 1983 Rev. Louise Spears became Iowa's first black woman United Methodist minister, appointed to Keosauqua-Center Chapel-Bentonsport.

HISPANIC MINISTRIES

Spanish-speaking people have had a small but increasing part in the life of Iowa. The railroads used Mexican "extra gangs" in building and repairing the road-beds during the latter part of the nineteenth century and the first part of the twentieth, but the Methodists had almost no contact with them. Later Hispanic migratory labor was used on the truck farms in the Mississippi bottoms south of Muscatine. Again the Methodists were slow to establish contact because of the transitory nature of the work and the language barrier.

At the 1962 session of the South Iowa Conference S. R. Root, pastor of the Muscatine North Circuit, reported on the work of the Muscatine Migrant Council.[20] In 1963 he reported on the Migrant Ministry and presented C. R. Crews, pastor of the Muscatine South Circuit, as director of the ministry. This migrant ministry was a project of the State Migrant Committee of the Iowa Council of Churches and of the Roman Catholic Diocese of Davenport. It provided a day-care center and a school, as well as other services.

The work of the Migrant Ministry continued during the years that Crews was pastor of the South Circuit (1962-1970). Each year the South Iowa Conference Methodist Youth Fellowship sponsored a work camp to help with the program. Twenty-one youth and four adults participated in 1962, and similar numbers assisted in other years. The project was not large, but it did provide some service and a Summer School for the children of migrants. It also made persons all over the conference aware of a need.

Hispanic people have been among the residents of Des Moines through a

St. Paul's United Methodist, Muscatine

century or more, but Methodism has not been able to reach them effectively. In 1981 the Iowa Conference appointed Roberto Mariano to Des Moines in an effort to establish a Hispanic Mission there.[21] In 1982 Verne Lyon, a bilingual layman, was appointed temporary director[22] and Mariano was transferred to the church in Fayette.

About that same time the Central Illinois Conference was sponsoring a Hispanic ministry in the Quint Cities area, which includes Davenport and Bettendorf.[23]

At this writing the strongest Hispanic work among United Methodists is the Muscatine Hispanic Mission. In 1978 the Rev. Donald Campbell and Rev. Dora Campbell were appointed to the Otterbein-Park Avenue charge, also to start a mission to the Spanish-speaking people of the area. They opened a store-front mission and began their work. Because the project was slow to gather momentum, the charge was divided in 1981. Don Campbell was appointed to the Otterbein-Park Avenue charge, and Dora, a native of Mexico, was appointed to the Hispanic Mission, which formed St. Paul's United Methodist Church in July, 1984.

Footnotes

1. *Journal Iowa Annual Conference M.E. Church* 1846, pp. 45-46.
2. Paul F. Douglass, *The Story of German Methodism* (Cincinnati: The Methodist Book Concern, 1939) pp. 75-76.
3. E. C. Henke et al., *Geschichte der Nordwest Deutschen Konferenz* (Charles City, Iowa: By Conference, 1913).
4. E. C. Magaret et al., *Jubilaumsbuch der St. Louis Deutschen Konferenz* (Cincinnati: Jennings and Graham, 1909).
5. Douglass, ibid., p. 271.
6. Zwingli F. Meyer, *A Century of German Methodism 1835-1935 Part II* (Manuscript, Iowa Wesleyan Library) p. 50.
7. V. L. Nicholson, *Together,* "Old Bethel: The Ship That Was a Church," August 1961, pp. 31-32.
8. Arlow Andersen, *The Salt of the Earth, A History of Norwegian Methodism in America* (Nashville: Parthenon Press, 1962) p. 64.
9. Souvenir Booklet of New Sweden congregation at the time of their 90th anniversary, 1940.
10. Andersen, ibid., p. 18.
11. Andersen, ibid., p. 59.
12. Andersen, ibid., p. 163.
13. Andersen, ibid., p. 166.
14. Martha Eleanor Griffith, *Iowa Journal of History and Politics,* "The Czechs in Cedar Rapids," 42: 114-161, July, 1944.
15. *The United Methodist Hawkeye,* October, 1978, p. 1.
16. *Iowa Conference Journal M.E. Church* 1894, p. 195.
17. *Northwest Iowa Conference Journal M.E. Church,* 1919, p. 558.
18. *North Iowa Conference Journal, the Methodist Church,* 1965, p. 252.
19. *The Hawkeye Methodist,* July 14, 1965.
20. *South Iowa Conference Journal, The Methodist Church,* 1962, p. 68.
21. *The United Methodist Hawkeye,* September 1981, p. 10.
22. *Iowa Conference Journal United Methodist Church,* 1982, Vol. I, p. 56.
23. *The United Methodist Hawkeye,* October, 1981, p. 9.
24. *The United Methodist Hawkeye,* March, 1984, p. 12.

Note bene: Although there is a preference now for the term "black," the words "colored" and "Negro" are used where needed for historical accuracy.

11

Women's Contributions

Miriam Baker Nye

Today women serve in almost every capacity in United Methodist local churches of the Iowa Area, and in some major offices at district or conference levels. By comparison, the opportunities for women during the first century after United Methodist antecedent denominations began to arrive in the state were limited.

Jean Caffey Lyles declared in reviewing *Women in New Worlds* (Abingdon), "One section of the volume that should interest historians of all churches consists of five studies tracing the history of women's acquisition of leadership and rights in denominations that make up the Methodist tradition. (She refers to the Methodist Episcopal Church South, as well as to Methodist Protestant, Methodist Episcopal, Evangelical, and United Brethren in Christ Churches.) The stories parallel one another at several points, though the various traditions moved at different rates in according women full laity rights and eventually clergy rights. Often women gained influence in the church through separate 'women's work'—building financially powerful and effective women's missionary associations."[1]

Women's contributions to the United Methodist Church in Iowa are briefly treated in this chapter under the following headings: Women Ministers; Ministers' Wives; Deaconesses and Women Missionaries; Women's Organizations in the Church; Women as Lay Members of Annual Conference and General Conference.

Women Ministers

Jesus' reliance upon women's interest and efforts during his ministry and the scriptural references to women whose influence was significant among early Christians comprise a foundation for later generations' certainty that women could and should be active promoters of their faith.

Earl Kent Brown has pointed out, "In Mr. Wesley's Methodism—the Methodism of the eighteenth century—women became public speakers, class and band leaders; intimate advisors to the Wesley brothers and other male leaders; school founders and teachers; visitors to the sick, the prisoner, and the backslider; ministers' wives; leaders in female support-groups; itinerants; patrons; and models of the Christian life for male and female alike."[2]

However, prejudice against Methodist women's speaking or leading stiffened after John Wesley's death. Francis Asbury found in America many examples of what he called "heroines for Christ," but did not extend to women as many opportunities as had been allowed in England. He encouraged his young men preachers to remain single as they itinerated on the frontier.

According to Ruth Gallaher, "In Iowa, Methodist women were, from the beginning, co-workers with the men except in official positions. Women could be class leaders and Sunday School teachers, but not deacons or elders. They could pray, and sing, but they were not members of the official board. They could testify, but they could not preach."[3] Even so, Elizabeth Atkinson, a Primitive Methodist preacher licensed by the English Church, preached often at the Methodist Episcopal mission in Dubuque, as early as 1834.

Almost thirty years later (1872-73) Isabella Cornish Hartsough held revival meetings at various points on the Dubuque District (M.E.). In the spring of 1873 at the Quarterly Conference in Epworth the presiding elder, Elias Skinner, unbeknown to the Reverend Lewis Hartsough and his wife, recommended her for a local preacher's license, and the motion carried unanimously. She was thus the first woman granted a license to preach west of the Mississippi, and much in demand as an evangelist.

The United Brethren in Christ removed all distinctions as to the licensing and ordination of women at their General Conference in 1889. Almost one hundred women were ordained in the decade that followed. Most of these women did not serve as itinerating ministers, but as evangelists. Ordination of women continued in the United Brethren Church until 1946, the time of the merger with The Evangelical Church. After the Evangelical United Brethren Church was created, the ordination of females was for the most part "quietly abandoned."[4] Some older Iowans recall having a woman minister in their respective United Brethren Churches long ago. One of these is Rev. Marion Donat, who attended Center Grove United Brethren Church three miles north of Maynard and remembers Mrs. John (Alice) Neudigate as pastor, during his boyhood.

Since neither the Evangelical Association nor The Evangelical Church ordained women, there were no women ministers to list in Deaver's *One Hundred Years with Evangelicals in Iowa*. However the reading of memoirs reveals the activity of women such as Florence Yaggy Vandersall (1878-1969), the well-educated wife of Charles Hammer Vandersall. Florence had "long desired to preach the gospel as a missionary," and she assisted her husband as a woman preacher during his pastoral assignments in the Ohio Conference of the Evangelical Church. A district superintendent there "appointed her to assist with pastoral duties." In Iowa the Vandersalls served Waterloo Calvary, Cedar Rapids, Dumont, Harlan, Spencer, Silver Creek, Paton, and Alta Vista.

Mrs. Pauline Martindale, a Methodist Protestant, has been listed as the only woman minister in Iowa in 1872, received into the Iowa M.P. Conference. Rev. Pearl Moats Spurlock, who had been ordained elder of the

Methodist Protestant Church at Harmony, Missouri in 1931, was received as a member of the Iowa-Des Moines Conference of The Methodist Church when Methodist Protestants, the Methodist Episcopal Church, and the Methodist Episcopal Church South united in 1939. She and her husband had served appointments in Iowa at Ohio, Marne, Harmony, Iconium, and Malcom. After his retirement she served Malcom and the Ottumwa Circuit, retiring in 1948.

The General Conference of the Methodist Episcopal Church denied Anna Oliver ordination in 1880, and revoked licenses to preach already given other women. Almost a generation later, the 1916 General Conference was still refusing licensing and ordination to women.

A turning point came in 1920 when General Conference authorized granting of local preachers' licenses to women. A committee of seven was directed to report in four years concerning ordination. The ordination of women as (local) deacons and (local) elders was authorized at the 1924 session, but women still could not become annual conference members.

Margaret Rhine McBlain, born in a log cabin on a farm in Jasper County September 11, 1869, became the first woman in the Iowa Conference of the Methodist Episcopal Church to be ordained local deacon and local elder. While her husband Alexander was pastor at Wilton Junction, Mrs. McBlain served three and one-half years at the nearby Moscow M.E. Church, beginning in 1926. She was ordained local deacon in 1927 and local elder in 1929. Another local preacher, Mrs. Ethel O. McAninch, was elected and ordained local deacon in 1928.

Alta Nichols, Ida I. Roberts, and Mrs. Myrtle Wolfe were all serving as local preachers in the Indianola District of the Des Moines Conference (M.E.) in 1930. Alta Nichols was ordained (local) elder and Grace Anderson (local) deacon that year. Alta Nichols had served eight years as a local preacher before being ordained (local) deacon in 1928.

Rev. Nancy Nichols was the first woman received as a full member of the South Iowa Conference of The Methodist Church. After General Con-

Rev. Nancy Nichols

ference changed the rule, to admit women[5] who met the requirements, in 1956, she was a probationary member and deacon. She became a full member and elder in 1958.

By 1983 fifty women were serving as ministers of the United Methodist Church in Iowa, including sixteen full conference members, three associate members, eighteen probationers, seven local pastors, one part-time local pastor, one student pastor, and four from other denominations. In addition, nine women were serving as diaconal ministers.

Of thirteen ministerial delegates elected in 1983 to attend General Conference from Iowa in 1984 one was a woman—Joan Hoover. Two women clergy were among the thirteen ministerial delegates elected to attend Jurisdictional Conference—Nancy Allen and Martha Ward. Three others were Jurisdictional Conference Reserves—Tompsie Duecker, Nancy Nichols, and Dora Campbell.

On February 18, 1985, Bishop Rueben P. Job announced the appointment of the Iowa United Methodist Church's first women district superintendents—the Rev. Joan S. Hoover to be superintendent of the Dubuque District and the Rev. Nancy Allen to be superintendent of the Ottumwa District.

Rev. Joan Hoover   Rev. Nancy Allen

Minister's Wives

During the pioneer period in Iowa preachers were most often single men, free to travel. When a preacher married, religious commitment was the quality most sought in a mate. Women who accepted marriage proposals from itinerating preachers generally did so because they themselves wanted to serve God by encouraging the preacher-husband in his work.

When *The Itinerant Wife: Her Qualifications, Duties, and Rewards* was published in 1851, the author made it clear that the preacher's wife should circulate in society and cultivate friends in order to shape society's character and standards. She should be armed with "correct doctrine" so that she could answer questions, be a model in her devoted attendance at services, invite sinners to come to the Saviour, and promote growth in grace. But her work should never overshadow her husband's, and family obligations were to be her Number 1 priority.[6]

The preacher's wife, declared H. Eaton, needed common sense, evangelical but cheerful piety, acquaintance with literary and religious sources, and love of the itinerancy. Many of the wives were highly visible in evangelical roles. They also tended to be "producers," economically speaking, for they engaged in farming activities, sold milk, eggs, vegetables, and butter. Some ran schools or boarding houses.

In a later (1913) tribute entitled *The Pastor's Wife, The Other Half*, written in German for the Northwest German Conference of the Methodist Episcopal Church by E. W. Henke, and translated by Dr. Max Volkmann, we read:

> Not much has been said among the many sketches of life in this book (concerning the pastors' wives). Where is the report of their work in the study, their long, tortuous journeys, their eloquence in the pulpit, their activity among youth, their untiring pastoral visits, their difficult and oft with thanklessness rewarded efforts to gather moneys for the building of new churches and other matters? Who can describe the feeling of responsibility, the worry during the day, the tears by night, the words of comfort at the death bed and at the grave, their sorrows for souls? What is it concerning their joys, their gratitude for a word of recognition—appreciation—their bliss in revivals, their fortune in victory? That one must read between the lines.
>
> But listen! If all were told, only the half could be told. The other half would stand on the pages unwritten, which are not bound up in this book.
>
> The preacher is away from home quite often and for a long time, but the house remains warm. The children are being cared for, the parsonage is open to all who are in need, the sick are visited and comforted, hearts full of care find sympathy, the Sunday School class is being taught, the women's organizations find a steady support. The salary is small, but the preacher always finds ready an inviting meal; money is scarce, but his clothes are well cared for (without holes and spots) corresponding to his profession; he has a small salary, but he makes possible large expenses for the education of his children. And finally he is able to lay aside a penny for his old age. How is that possible? That is the other half of the parsonage, the preacher's wife. Yes, and in spite of all the fatigue and disappointments, in spite of all the criticisms and in spite of all the narrow-mindedness, the preacher is still able to make a friendly face. How come? Somebody once said, "That is grace in the heart." And so it is, but the preacher's wife has something to do with it, too. The good parson's wife is lively, pious, and satisfied; industrious, cautious, friendly, sympathetic, composed, self-denying, patient, and going without. . . .[7]

Brief "Memoirs" in annual conference journals record biographical facts of numerous pastors' wives who have made vital contributions to ministry. Parishioners who remember these women's personalities could no doubt add much interesting detail. Two representative women are mentioned here with the suggestion that readers turn also to the journals and to local histories for other sketches.

The lives and work of Mrs. Warner M. (Ida Binger) Hubbard and Mrs. Hal V. (Alta Klinefelter) Riggs spanned years from the 1880's to the 1970's. Alta Klinefelter was born in a log cabin on the home farm near Anamosa December 4, 1888. After her mother died when she was about two, Alta's father was "both father and mother" for nine years until he remarried. Alta met Hal Riggs when she was a student at Leander Clark College. They married in 1913. Besides rearing six children, Alta "entered into every realm of church work" as a co-worker with her husband. This included serving as a church officer, Sunday School teacher, youth sponsor, choir member, and leader in U.B. and E.U.B. women's organizations. She also helped raise and prepare large crops of vegetables, both for the family and for the meals needed by youth campers at Riverview each year. And she "janitored" the church when necessary!

Ida B. Hubbard   **Alta K. Riggs**

Another clergy wife, Ida Binger, was born in Tulare, South Dakota February 9, 1884. She attended Dakota Wesleyan University, and held degrees from Morningside College, Boston University, and Northwestern University. She and Warner Hubbard were married in 1915, and became parents of one daughter. Ida accomplished much in addition to her homemaking and her devoted service to the local churches where her husband was appointed. She was well known as an instructor at "observation" schools and "laboratory" schools for Christian educators from local churches, missionary education director for the Conference Women's Society of Christian Service, executive director of Christian education at Grace Methodist Church in Des Moines, and as a writer of curriculum materials and counseling editor for the Methodist Publishing House. She was a delegate to the White House Conference on Children and Youth.

Considering the accomplishments of clergy wives, it is interesting to note that by the 1940's, in the revised Methodist Church clergy pension system, a wife's labors on behalf of the church were valued at 70% of her husband's pension if she outlived him (based on the number of years served). Apparently it was understood that the minister's wife and her husband had worked as a team, though valued unequally.

Since the middle of this century, more and more clergy wives have pursued their own careers in varied fields. Some have managed to include a full schedule of church activities in their lives as well, but a number of congregations over the state have had to accustom themselves to ministers' wives who lack time for, or interest in, the work of the church.

Not surprisingly, some Iowa United Methodist clergy today have husbands, not wives. No doubt an interesting study could be made by a future historian, comparing the clergy husbands' concepts of their roles with the roles undertaken by clergy wives, past and present.

During recent years an increasing number of married couples, both of whom are ministers desiring appointments, have been serving in the Iowa area. In instances where they are assigned to separate charges, not much time or energy is left, after caring for one's own duties, to assume the role of "unofficial associate to the spouse" in his/her parish.

Women Missionaries and Deaconesses

A lengthy list of single women missionaries and missionaries' wives from Iowa have served with dedication in "foreign" and "home" mission endeavors of the United Methodist Church and antecedent denominations. Many were sent out by women's missionary organizations. Two examples were selected from among numerous accounts.

Anna Lawson (1860-1951) was "a lifelong missionary to India representing the Woman's Foreign Missionary Society of the M.E. Church."[8] A native Iowan and a graduate of Iowa Wesleyan University, she went to India in 1885 as the first missionary from the Des Moines branch of the society. "A skillful administrator and a beloved servant of the church," she worked effectively in orphanages, as a school principal, and in such projects

Anna E. Lawson

Rev. Janet Surdam & Rev. Luella Koether

as founding of the Landour Language School, serving over fifty years. According to a family tradition, Miss Lawson became engaged to a British army officer while in the mission field. Dutifully, she wrote home to Iowa, asking her father's permission to marry. He replied, "No. You have dedicated yourself to serving Christ as a missionary. You have 'put your hand to the plow' and must not look back."

Another outstanding record of missionary service by Iowa Area women is detailed in the book *Janella Journal*. The authors, T. Janet Surdam and Luella G. Koether, celebrated in 1979 forty years of "working together for the Lord." Luella also celebrated her Golden Jubilee of Christian Service (1931-1981).

Nurtured by her home church at Giard, Iowa, Luella went to China as a missionary in 1931. After a furlough in 1939, as she was returning to China, she met Janet—a young missionary from New York state—on shipboard.

The varied experiences of the two missionaries are well chronicled in their letters, collected in *Janella Journal*. Another effort from their pens, *Two Hundred Days*, tells of their arrest in Chungking on December 28, 1950, and their succeeding imprisonment.

People of North and South Iowa Conferences came to know Rev. Surdam and Rev. Koether (Associate Members of Conference) also through their pastorates at Riceville-McIntire (1955-62), Crystal Lake-Hayfield (1962-65), and Cumberland-Pine Grove (1968-74). Between the last two of these appointments they did further work as missionaries at the Henderson Settlement, Frakes, Kentucky (1965-68).

About to leave for China back in 1939, Janet Surdam had composed her song, "Bridges":

We're building bridges—you and I—
Bridges of Love from heart to heart.
Our Master Builder, the Lord Most High,
Bids us to build with care each part. . . .
(1st stanza)

But to build our bridges of brotherhood,
We must work from both ends,
Helping all people to be understood,
That we may all be friends. . . .

(3rd stanza)

Reflecting in 1981 upon her own and Luella Koether's missionary service, she contemplated also the recent condemnation of a span of the two-mile bridge across the Mississippi between McGregor-Marquette, Iowa and Prairie du Chien, Wisconsin after only six years' use.

She commented, "We know that God's plan is good, even as was the blueprint for the bridge. Perhaps some of our methods in missionary work in China were unsuitable, or the building materials we used inferior. Now we must work together at both ends, with the very best materials and methods available to bridge the chasm between the Chinese church and ours. But no bridge can be built without the full consent and cooperation of the people at both ends."[9]

Rev. Koether retired in 1972 while she and Rev. Surdam were at Cumberland-Pine Grove. Rev. Surdam was appointed to Giard 1974-78. Those who attended the retirement ceremony at the Iowa Annual Conference in 1978 paid rapt attention when she sang her impressive farewell.

**

German Methodism was the source of the American Deaconess Movement, which began in the 1880s in Chicago and eventually spread to various states, including Iowa. Bishop Matthew Simpson had observed the deaconess program in Germany. Iowan Annie Wittenmyer and Susan Fry of the Illinois Women's Foreign Missionary Society spoke at meetings around the nation to generate interest in the potential for deaconess institutions. Lucy Rider Meyer founded the Chicago Training School for City, Home, and Foreign Missions, where many deaconesses were prepared, some coming to serve in Iowa.

Annie Wittenmyer

Iowa State Historical Dept.

The Chicago Training School emphasized acquisition of skills and practical experience, particularly in the areas of Bible teaching and missions. Theology, social service, religious education, home economics, medicine, music, English, history, elocution, and accomplishments of women were also part of the curriculum. Women's responsibilities, not their rights, were stressed; likewise, service to the cause of Christ, not leadership of it.

Deaconesses hoped to transform cities. They raised questions concerning poverty, corruption, working conditions, unemployment, child labor, and alcohol problems. At a time when women were not allowed to vote, hold public office, or enter the ministry of the Methodist Episcopal Church, the office of Deaconess was authorized by the General Conference of the M.E. Church.

The 1888 *Discipline*, which first gave official status to Deaconesses, states in par. 207:

> The duties of the Deaconesses are to minister to the poor, visit the sick, pray with the dying, care for the orphan, seek the wandering, comfort the sorrowing, save the sinning, and, relinquishing wholly all other pursuits, devote themselves, in a general way, to such forms of Christian labor as may be suited to their abilities.

Some of the deaconesses were assistants to pastors. Others taught in children's homes (orphanages), worked with foreign groups in cities, nursed in hospitals, worked in retirement homes, visited in homes and institutions, distributed garments to the needy, aided travelers, conducted industrial schools, were active as evangelists.

Iowa produced its share of deaconesses. Minnie Claire Lockwood's life story is an example of their commitment. Minnie was born near Greene, Iowa, October 16, 1872. A lifelong member of the M.E. and The Methodist Church, she was graduated from Upper Iowa University in 1896, and taught in public schools. At the Boone, Iowa M.E. Church she became acquainted with a deaconess, and was so impressed that she decided to spend the rest of her years in full-time Christian work. She completed a two-year course at the Chicago Training School in 1902.

Miss Lockwood's next forty years were spent working in Chicago slums, serving as travelers' aid in Omaha, helping with special meetings in Nebraska, and serving as pastor's assistant in churches at Minneapolis, Minnesota, Aberdeen, South Dakota, and Yakima, Washington. As a retired deaconess she taught an adult Sunday School class, worked with youth, and led mission study classes in Alhambra, California. Living almost a century, she died in February, 1972.

When Col. Bidwell of Des Moines announced in 1896 that he would give his residence to the first organization that would carry on benevolent work, the four Conference Woman's Home Missionary Societies of Iowa organized a state W.H.M.S. Association (without precedent in the United States) and for a number of years helped to support the Bidwell Deaconess Home and Bible Training School. In 1900 the institution was known as The Iowa

Training School. It merged with the school at Kansas City in 1931, and the Des Moines property became Esther Hall, a home for working girls. (The successor to Esther Hall is Hawthorn Hill.)

Mrs. Johanna B. Shesler gave $2,000 on an annuity plan to purchase the first Deaconess Home in Sioux City. It was dedicated in 1901. When the first house was outgrown, a large 25-room building was constructed. The second Shesler Deaconess Home was dedicated debt-free in 1917, and is still in use in the 1980s at 1308 Nebraska Street as Shesler Hall, "a Christian home for girls away from home."

Shesler Hall

The first social service institution within bounds of the Upper Iowa Conference was founded March, 1914: The Hillcrest Deaconess Home and Baby Fold. At first primarily a home and home-finding institution for orphaned children, its successor is known as Hillcrest Family Services.

At Waterloo, Allen Memorial Hospital was one of several of the Evangelical Church's Deaconess Hospitals in the Midwest to see its income dried up during the Great Depression. After going into receivership, it was fully liquidated in 1944. Reorganized by the Allen Memorial Hospital Corporation, formed by a group of Lutherans from Waterloo and the surrounding area, it still operates under their management.

The Evangelical Church, the German Methodists, the Methodist Protestants, and the Methodist Episcopal Church all had deaconesses. Perhaps the reason why the United Brethren in Christ did not was that they removed distinctions as to licensing and ordaining women in 1889, thus opening to women the kind of vocational opportunities which women in other denominations yearned for and satisfied in deaconess work.

The Deaconess Movement was organized in the M.E. Church South in 1902, and in the Methodist Protestant Church in 1908. With the merger of the three branches of Methodism in 1939, all deaconess work was combined and placed within the framework of the Women's Division of Christian Service of the Board of Missions for administration.

Perusal of conference yearbooks furnishes glimpses of the Deaconess Movement continuing into mid-century and later. For example, Wall Street Mission and Helping Hand Mission deaconesses were presented at the 1941 Conference Women's Day by the North Iowa Deaconess Board. In January, 1951, Eva Damm was commissioned a deaconess at the Buck Hill Falls Board of Missions meeting, and came to serve First Methodist Church at Waterloo.

The 1964 South Iowa Conference reported three active full-time deaconesses: A. Katherine Bratton at Newton, Helen Aldrich and Mrs. Bernice Ziarko at Iowa National Esther Hall, Des Moines. The 1982 Journal of the Iowa Annual Conference listed one active deaconess, Beverly A. Reddick, staff consultant to the Conference Council on Ministries. Sixteen retired deaconesses related to the Iowa Conference were also listed, four living within bounds of this conference.

Women's Organizations in the Church

The evolution of women's organizations in the church during the last one hundred years is such a dramatic story that United Methodist Women portrayed it in a pageant at Veterans' Auditorium in Des Moines during the 1983 Iowa Annual Conference. Actually, they traced the beginnings back more than one hundred years to: the small mission group formed by women of Immanuel Evangelical Church in Philadelphia in 1839 (this early effort was discontinued because of a bishop's influence, but Evangelical women organized a Woman's Missionary Society in 1884); the Methodist Episcopal Women's Foreign Missionary Society (1869); the United Brethren Women's Missionary Association (1875); the Methodist Episcopal Women's Home Missionary Society (1880); the Methodist Protestant Woman's Foreign Missionary Society (1879); and the Methodist Protestant Woman's Home Missionary Society (1893).

All of the antecedent denominations which eventually flowed into the United Methodist Church had Ladies' Aid Societies, but since these were never organized on an annual conference level, published records are few. As early as 1768, in the old John Street Church, New York City, Methodist women organized to help with the church and parsonage.

Ladies' Aid Societies were first mentioned in the *Discipline of the Methodist Episcopal Church* in 1904. In 1911 the Methodist Book Concern published *The Ladies' Aid Manual*, with suggestions on how to organize and conduct a Ladies' Aid Society. "Opposing questionable means of raising money," the book offered plans designed to "contribute to the social, intellectual, and financial development of the church without incurring any just criticism."[10]

When the constituion of the Ladies Aid Society at the Cushing, Iowa M.E. Church was adopted in 1906, one unusual article stated that no gossiping would be allowed at any meeting, and any guilty member would be under penalty of a fine of twenty-five cents. Only one fine was reported. Dues were five cents per meeting. Women of the church sewed carpet rags at eight cents per pound, made soap to sell, and even husked corn to earn money with which they accomplished such improvements as a cistern and a foundation for the parsonage.

Ladies' Aids (some were called Women's Aids) generally saw to it that church and parsonage facilities were kept in repair. Frequently they managed to pay part of the minister's salary and bought Sunday School equipment and supplies.

By having bake sales, rummage sales, ice cream socials, bazaars, dinners and lunches of all kinds, and by tying comforters, quilting, compiling and selling cookbooks, and taking orders for flavorings, Ladies' Aids of Iowa often succeeded in saving their respective churches from financial disaster. Literally hundreds were saved.

Better yet, the Aids often took the lead in helping to stimulate the church's "growing edge." One example was a gift of $1,000 invested by the Ladies' Aid of First Evangelical Church, Cedar Falls, in the 1916 Riverview Park Camp Project.

In another instance, the Mount Vernon M.E. Ladies' Aid took two bold actions. They first voted to assume their church's pledge to pay $400 to the Clear Lake Epworth League Institute (an Upper Iowa Conference project) —$100 in annual installments beginning in 1928. In February of the same year, when Cornell College began a campaign for endowment, with "a burst of enthusiasm," they voted a subscription of $5,000, to be paid in five years. At the end of the first year, with "A Mile of Pennies" as the earning device rather than a bazaar, they had paid $1,000 on the college note and $100 to the institute fund.

Yet, as noted in Mount Vernon Methodist's Centennial Sketch of 1941, "The gain has not all been found in the treasurer's book (of the Ladies Aid) . . . for out of this cooperative effort have come comradeship, loyalty, and a sense of solidarity that pervades the life of the church."

Early in this century when Grace M.E. in Sioux City had no parsonage, the women of the Ladies' Aid bought part of E. C. Peters' cherry orchard for $1,500 as a building site. As Grace UMW historian, Mildred Gardner, wrote, "Plans and work were begun, but the men of the church realized they hadn't given their consent, and fearing the women would get the church in debt, managed to stop the work for a time. There is a story which says the banks would not loan any money to the women or to any (individual) woman without her husband's signature." The women went ahead and raised the money without the bank loan which they sought. Another version of the happening says that Mrs. Sniffen, President of the Aid Society, had the deed for the lot transferred to her own name, and work proceeded until the parsonage at 3811 Garretson Avenue was finished.

Since the era of the Woman's Society of Christian Service, which began in 1939, and on into the time of United Methodist Women, the division of "local activities" has carried much the same responsibility as the "aids" formerly undertook.

***

A brief study of "From These Roots," an historical chart of United Methodist Women, helps to convey a sense of the development through the years of the foreign missionary societies, home missionary societies, guilds, circles, and aids in the several denominations (see chart p. 166).

In most instances such organizations appeared in Iowa conferences within a short time after they came onto the national scene. The Women's Foreign Missionary Society (M.E.) had been organized in Boston, Massachusetts in 1869. In the fall of 1870 Miss Isabel Leonard presented this cause before the Upper Iowa Conference annual session. By 1888 it was estimated that one out of nine women in the Iowa M.E. churches was a member of the W.F.M.S.

Robert MacCanon records the 1878 organization of the Woman's Missionary Association in Iowa (U.B.) three years after its national beginning, with Mrs. Sarah J. Staves of Des Moines as founder.

Although the members of the Woman's Missionary Society of Kimball Avenue Evangelical Church in Waterloo had great enthusiasm in 1902-03, their pastor was unimpressed. He refused their request to have a report of the society's Quadrennial Convention read at a Sunday morning service.

Undaunted, the women continued to meet and pursue their missionary interests. In 1908 Mrs. Beuernfeind of the Kimball Ave. (Ev.) Woman's Missionary Society was elected general vice-president of the national organization. Reporting on the seventh annual convention in Cedar Falls, Mrs. Eichelberg addressed the members in English, and Mrs. Beuernfeind in German.

One senses the enthusiasm for missionary enterprise on reading an introduction by Samuel P. Spreng and William Horn to *Her Story—History of the Woman's Missionary Society of the Evangelical Association* by Mrs. H. Bennett:

> . . . not only an organization but a movement; not a mere machine but a living force in our Church. In the zenanas of India, the wretched hovels of China and Japan, the harems of Moslem lands and the crude huts of the Dark Continent, woman's deft fingers, gentle tact and loving grace have done pioneer work in carrying the Cross into the dark corners of the earth. Our Evangelical sisterhood . . . are not a whit behind their sisters of other churches in heeding this call to service.[11]

It cost $1 to be a member of the society annually, $10 to be a life member, $25 for an honorary member. Infants were listed on the Cradle Roll for 25¢.

In the view of some, the Woman's Foreign Missionary Society was "an accommodation to the system, the only way possible for women to work within the denomination and at the same time develop their vision and use their talents on behalf of the church."[12]

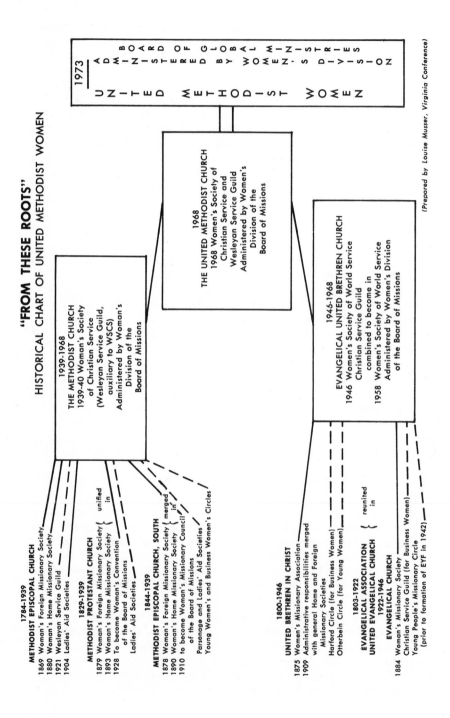

"FROM THESE ROOTS"
HISTORICAL CHART OF UNITED METHODIST WOMEN

1973
UNITED METHODIST WOMEN
AD INTERIM DIVISION OF MISSIONS, MEMBERS OF THE BOARD OF GLOBAL MINISTRIES, WOMEN'S DIVISION

1968
THE UNITED METHODIST CHURCH
1968 Women's Society of Christian Service and Wesleyan Service Guild Administered by Women's Division of the Board of Missions

1939-1968
THE METHODIST CHURCH
1939-40 Woman's Society of Christian Service (Wesleyan Service Guild, auxiliary to WSCS) Administered by Woman's Division of the Board of Missions

1945-1968
EVANGELICAL UNITED BRETHREN CHURCH
1946 Women's Society of World Service Christian Service Guild combined to become in 1958 Women's Society of World Service Administered by Women's Division of the Board of Missions

1784-1939
METHODIST EPISCOPAL CHURCH
1869 Woman's Foreign Missionary Society
1880 Woman's Home Missionary Society
1921 Wesleyan Service Guild
1904 Ladies' Aid Societies

1829-1939
METHODIST PROTESTANT CHURCH
1879 Woman's Foreign Missionary Society } unified
1893 Woman's Home Missionary Society } in
1928 To become Woman's Convention of the Board of Missions
Ladies' Aid Societies

1844-1939
METHODIST EPISCOPAL CHURCH, SOUTH
1878 Woman's Foreign Missionary Society } merged
1890 Woman's Home Missionary Society } in
1910 to become Woman's Missionary Council of the Board of Missions
Parsonage and Ladies' Aid Societies
Young Women's and Business Women's Circles

1800-1946
UNITED BRETHREN IN CHRIST
1875 Women's Missionary Association
1909 Administrative responsibilities merged with general Home and Foreign Missionary Societies
Harford Circle (for Business Women)
Otterbein Circle (for Young Women)

1803-1922
EVANGELICAL ASSOCIATION
UNITED EVANGELICAL CHURCH } reunited
1922-1946 } in
EVANGELICAL CHURCH
1884 Women's Missionary Society
Christian Service Guild (for Business Women)
Young People's Missionary Circle
(prior to formation of EYF in 1942)

(Prepared by Louise Musser, Virginia Conference)

The Woman's Home Missionary Society of the Upper Iowa Conference (M.E.) was organized in Cedar Rapids at the conference session held in September, 1882, just two years after the society was organized nationally. When the Northwest Iowa Conference W.H.M.S. was organized in 1883, the idea was still so new that some pastors would not permit an auxiliary to be organized on their charges.

The influence of the W.H.M.S. through the deaconess movement has been discussed earlier in this chapter. Projects of the W.H.M.S. in its early years included those in Louisiana, Alaska, Utah, and California. Young people's and children's groups organized by the local auxiliaries were Queen Esther Circles, Young Woman's Societies, Home Guards, and Mother's Jewels.

Women from a number of denominations led the temperance revival which erupted in the Woman's Crusade and later resulted in formation of the Woman's Christian Temperance Union. Iowa Methodist lay workers were among the actively involved, as they held prayer meetings in saloons, asked dealers to sign pledges that they would cease to sell liquor, and used petitions to help close saloons.

Activist Annie Wittenmyer warned against women's increasing drinking of alcoholic beverages, and called women's behavior into question, whereas much W.C.T.U. rhetoric tended to "secure woman on her pedestal." By the early 1890s Frances Willard made a sweeping statement: "I do not know a White Ribbon woman who is not a Prohibitionist, a woman suffragist, a purity worker, and an earnest sympathizer with the Labor Movement."[13]

A few women here and there across the state can remember the era when it was common for a local church to have two missionary societies and an "aid" competing with each other for members and support for projects. Very zealous women might belong to all three organizations, but many chose to give their loyalty more exclusively. In the interest of unifying women's contributions to the support of mission in the broader sense, new plans were eventually formulated.

Quoting the reflections of one church, "Until 1940 the ladies worked in somewhat overlapping groups: the Ladies Aid, Home Missionary Society, Foreign Missionary Society, etc., each group having its own officers, program, and budget. In 1940 all the (women's) groups in each church were united as the Woman's Society of Christian Service with a single budget."[14]

By having a Secretary of Foreign Work, a Secretary of Home Work, and a Secretary of Christian Social Relations and Local Church Activities, the Woman's Society of Christian Service established in 1939-40 provided for the essential aspects of the formerly overlapping groups to be maintained and developed.

As might be expected, there was some foot-dragging at the local level. Yet in numerous churches the transition was accomplished at a surprisingly rapid pace.

The composite report of the Northwest Iowa district superintendents in 1942 mentioned that the W.S.C.S. had had "an exceptionally fine year.

Having completed their reorganization, and adjusted themselves to the new order of things, most of our societies have been working with renewed enthusiasm. They have majored not only in missions but also in the support and upkeep of their churches. In addition to meeting their regular apportionments, the societies have generally responded well to the call for extra funds to support missionaries who have had to be moved and shifted because of war conditions. Would that every organization of the church were functioning as efficiently, well, and enthusiastically as our Women's Society!"[15]

A 1946 statement about the W.S.C.S. is also worth noting: "The growing enthusiasm for study has been manifested by the increase in the number of societies that have conducted approved study classes and those for Jurisdictional Recognition."[16]

The Christian Service Guild (originally Evangelical) was continued as the name for the business women's group after union of the United Brethren and Evangelical Churches was consummated nationally in 1946. United Brethren Churches had had Harford Circles for business women. The Women's Society of World Service combined with the Christian Service Guild in 1958 as the Women's Society of World Service administered by the Women's Division of the Board of Missions.

Mary Yaggy

Marjorie Kreager

E.U.B. and Methodist women united in the Women's Society of Christian Service in 1968. Four years later the Wesleyan Service Guild joined the W.S.C.S. in forming the present organization of United Methodist Women.

General Conference of 1972 had voted a "new inclusive women's organization" in the United Methodist Church. Each annual conference was allowed to proceed in its own way. The Iowa Conference voted a plan of procedure with locals organizing their units of United Methodist Women between January 1, 1973, and September 1 of that year, the districts and the conference to organize on September 15. This resulted in well over 900 local units with nearly 65,000 members in Iowa, "continuing with their missional emphasis supporting the total mission work of the church."

The first annual meeting of United Methodist Women of Iowa Conference, held at Ames in 1973, drew nearly 6,000 women from over the state. They pledged $525,000 for 1974.

In her address Mrs. William Yaggy, conference president, reminded the women, "We are in a period of 'transformation' from our present organization into a new organization that will be all inclusive. We are aware that there will be many questions, so we urge all women to study our Purpose, recognizing our commitment is to strengthen and participate in a creative, supportive fellowship that will expand our concept of mission through the Global Ministries of the church."

Mrs. Max (Marjorie) Kreager of Newton was installed as president of the Iowa Conference United Methodist Women September 15, 1973. Mrs. Donald (Doris) Riggs succeeded her in office 1976-1980. Mrs. Rosalie Brown served as president from 1980 until 1984, when Mrs. Leroy (Kathryn) Moore was elected.

Doris Riggs

Rosalie Brown

Kathryn Moore

"Called to Grow" was the theme emphasized at the 1983 Iowa Annual Conference where United Methodist Women focused attention on women's "one hundred years in mission." Each local unit was challenged to grow in breadth—a 10% increase in membership to be sought; to grow in depth—deepen understanding of God and express it in living, making use of studies in *Response* magazine; to grow in height—to be a light in the world, recapturing the sense of mission that foremothers had.

Iowa United Methodist Women are consistent leaders in mission giving, topping the nation by giving over $850,000 in 1982, and leading all conference UMW's with gifts totaling over $787,000 in 1983. They pledged $795,000 for 1984.

Schools of mission, retreats, and local study classes have proved to be effective methods of women's Christian education in recent years. Some may think it is still a rather modern idea to free a few days' time for attending. But an old *History of the Woman's Missionary Society* records, "We well remember with what conflicting emotions we were hustled off to our first convention. It did seem as if the home sky would fall if we were away three or four days, but it didn't. Husband and children assured us that they knew more about home-keeping than mother gave them credit for knowing and they did!"[17] Iowa's 1984 Schools of Mission for women, men, and youth over seventeen years of age were held July 9-12 and 12-15 at Iowa Wesleyan College, and drew 730 participants. Leroy and Kathryn Moore led the spiritual growth study. The general theme was "Visions of Peace—Actions of Faith."

In 1984 each local president of United Methodist Women in Iowa was sent a request from Rosalie Brown for a concise history of the local unit, to be placed in a Conference History Book of UMW in 1985. Instructions asked that units mention their roots—whether local unit was formerly EUB or Methodist, and in which former conference (e.g. North Iowa, South Iowa) it was located. When compiled, materials are to be placed in the conference archives.

Women of the Laity

Writing of "Women and the Nature of Ministry," Rosemary Keller noted that "one hundred years ago, four great movements of women were launched in the predecessor denominations of United Methodism—the Methodist Episcopal Church, the Methodist Episcopal Church South, the Methodist Protestant Church, the United Brethren in Christ, and the Evangelical Association. They represented the efforts for ordination of women and laity rights for females and the origins of women's missionary societies and of deaconess orders."[18]

As previously mentioned, the Church of the United Brethren in Christ took the lead in assuring laity rights to women at the same time clergy rights were opened to them, in 1889. Long before, from the time of their first General Conference in 1815, both women and men lay persons were eligible to vote for delegates to General Conference. (The delegates were ministerial, however.) From 1889 on, women delegates were elected to every successive General Conference of the United Brethren.

Mrs. Sarah J. Staves (from whom Staves Memorial United Methodist Church in Des Moines is named) was one of the first two women to sit in General Conference (1893). Twenty-four women were elected to the General Conference of 1905, twenty-two in 1909. But women seldom spoke in General Conference, and never chaired a committee through 1909. The Woman's Missionary Association of the United Brethren in Christ was largely responsible for securing new status and power for women in the period from 1872 until 1909.

The first layman in an Evangelical Association General Conference was seated in 1907. No women had this privilege until the 1940s when merger with the United Brethren appeared imminent.

Methodist Protestant women were "politically invisible" until 1878. In 1879 they founded their Woman's Foreign Missionary Association and began to make their own decisions and control their own funds. Eventually their self-reliance paid off in opportunities for leadership in the Methodist Protestant denomination.

Mrs. Pearl Moats Spurlock, the Methodist Protestant Annual Conference's clergy woman member, who was received as a member of the Iowa-Des Moines Conference of the Methodist Church at the time of union in 1939, had held many lay offices before entering the traveling ministry. These included the national level of the Woman's Home Missionary Society.

Early elections of women to be lay delegates to General Conference of the Methodist Episcopal Church resulted in frustration and disappointment. When the outstanding lay person Frances Willard of Illinois and four other women (including Mrs. Mary C. Ninde of Minnesota and Mrs. Angie F. Newman of Nebraska) were so elected in 1887, the 1888 "male dominated" General Conference refused to seat them.

Bishop Harmon of The Methodist Church observed, "Women have been given full laity rights . . . since early in the present (20th) century. Their admission to the conferences as lay persons followed the victory of lay representation in both Episcopal Methodisms. The struggle for full laity rights for women in the M.E. Church was concluded victoriously for them when the constitution of 1900 of that church was adopted. . . . Not until after union and in 1956 did the General Conference pass legislation declaring that 'women are included in all provisions of the *Discipline* referring to ministry.' . . . These rights were carried over into the United Methodist Church in 1968."[19]

In a Commission on Status and Role of Women report in the *Hawkeye*, it was noted that women comprised 55.7% of the laity membership of Iowa Annual Conference in 1983, men 44.3%. Yet in the first two days of the conference, laity responses in speeches on the conference floor were 51.2% by males, 44.3% by females.

Rev. Stan Kennedy, who had helped record the results of monitoring for

June Goldman

COSROW, remarked that "We need to do a better job of preparing people for annual conference membership. Too often the lay person a church sends is the one who is free to get away to go to Des Moines for a few days. They need some training."

Esther Kennedy, chairperson of COSROW, agrees concerning the need for training, but also feels that longer terms for lay members might help. She says women and men lay members "tend to be intimidated by the large numbers of people in the vast Veterans Memorial Auditorium, and it is tough to get up the nerve to head for a microphone."[20]

Of thirteen Iowa laity delegates elected in 1983 to attend General Conference in 1984, seven were women—K. June Goldman, Kathryn Moore, Mary W. Yaggy, Myrtle Felkner, Rosalie Brown, Marguerite C. Terrell, and Janet E. Stephenson. Five women—Jimmie Ruth Ellsworth, Martha S. Cline, Esther Kennedy, Arlene Carney, and Eloise Cranke—were among the thirteen laity delegates elected to attend Jurisdictional Conference, and six others were among Jurisdictional Conference Reserves—Kay Kerber, Margaret L. King, Naomi Christensen, Lucille Dellit, Elizabeth A. Ziebell, and Marjory J. Thompson.

Footnotes

1. Jean Caffey Lyles, Book Review, *United Methodist Reporter*, (Dallas: October 8, 1982).
2. Earl Kent Brown, *Women in New Worlds* edited by Hilah E. Thomas and Rosemary Skinner Keller (Nashville: Abingdon, 1981) p. 70.
3. Ruth Gallaher, *A Century of Methodism in Iowa* (Mount Vernon: Inter-Conference Commission, 1944) p. 15.
4. Keller, Rosemary, "Women and the Nature of Ministry," *Methodist History* Vol. XXII No. 2 (Madison, NJ: General Commission on Archives and History) p. 113.
5. *Discipline of the Methodist Church 1956.*
6. Hilah E. Thomas and Rosemary Skinner Keller, *Women in New Worlds* (Nashville: Abingdon, 1981) p. 146.
7. *The Northwest German Conference* (Die Nordwest Deutsche Konferenz der Bischoflichen Methodistenkirche) Editor E. W. Henke et al. (Charles City: 1913).
8. *Encyclopedia of World Methodism* (Nashville: United Methodist Publishing House, 1974) Vol. II p. 1398.

9. T. Janet Surdam and Luella G. Koether, *Janella Journal,* (Prairie Du Chien: Howe Printing, 1981) p. 399.
10. *Encyclopedia of World Methodism*, ibid., Vol. II p. 1366.
11. Mrs. H. Bennett, *Her Story—History of the Woman's Missionary Society of the Evangelical Association* (Cleveland: Mattill & Lamb, 1902).
12. Thomas and Keller, ibid., p. 248.
13. Ibid., p. 324.
14. *Reflections*, Grace United Methodist Church (Waterloo: 1976) p. 34.
15. *Northwest Iowa Conference Journal* 1942, pp. 394-395.
16. *Northwest Iowa Conference Journal* 1946, p. 455.
17. Mrs. H. Bennett, ibid., p. 67.
18. Keller, ibid., p. 107.
19. *Encyclopedia of World Methodism*, ibid., Vol. I p. 1400.
20. William Simbro, "Methodist Male Clergy Out-Talk Women: Analysis," *Des Moines Sunday Register*, February 20, 1983, p. 7-B.

Nota bene: As this book goes to press, word has been received of a new Iowa United Methodist resource pamphlet entitled "Commission on the Status and Role of Women June 1974-December 1984," a history by Beverly Everett.

12

Social Concerns

INTRODUCTION—THE "METHODIST ATTITUDE"

The United Methodist Church, and the antecedent bodies which united to make up the present church, have tended to be pietistic, but they have not been merely pietistic groups. They have also tended to be activistic in their concern about social and economic conditions which they have considered unjust. Many of the preachers have seen themselves as being in a line of succession with the Old Testament prophets, preaching righteousness. Occasionally a sort of moral arrogance has made some individuals unpopular.

One significant factor that must always be considered is that the members of the church are ideally "in the world, but not of the world." They strive to live by ideals but are always influenced by other forces in the community about them. The church member is taught to treat all men as brothers, but he lives in a community in which prejudices are often looked upon as being realism.

Every effort to correct social evils has been controversial for the simple reason that good men do not always agree either to the ends or the means. Often the "common sense view" is that some of the customs condemned by the preacher as evil are actually in the natural order of things. Church conferences have frequently passed resolutions that are only resolutions, nothing more.

As the church spread westward across America with the early settlers, the Methodist preachers were primarily evangelists, calling men to salvation, but they were also very much involved with the affairs of the here and now. They were concerned about the many special problems which confronted the frontiersman. Methodists tend to become social activists, working to remake society, both by persuasion and by political activity.

The 18th Amendment to the United States Constitution was adopted after years of agitation by Methodists, Baptists, and other concerned people. The repeal of national prohibition by the passage of the 21st Amendment in 1933 was considered by many Methodists to be a serious defeat for the Church.

Methodist activism has shown itself in the past by the support of labor unions, by support of the anti-slavery movement which led to the Civil War, and by support of the Civil War as a great moral crusade. The Methodist people have been divided in their attitudes toward military preparedness, but never indifferent. Most supported the Civil War as a "just war." More recently the pacifist movement has been strong among Methodists. Either way, Methodists have believed in applied religion.

In their roles as citizens individual Methodists have been deeply involved in partisan political campaigns. But they have seen an election campaign in terms of one issue only. For example, whenever temperance has been an issue, Methodist preachers have tended to support the dry candidate regardless of his other qualifications or lack. In recent years a better educated clergy have taken a more sophisticated view of their communities, a more rounded view of social problems, without losing any of the old-time zeal.

Slavery, Abolition, and Freedman's Aid

During the period preceding the Civil War, Methodist people were often divided in their thinking about human slavery. The influences leading to the Civil War were interpreted differently by southerners and northerners. The southerners saw the war as a war between sovereign states. The northerners saw it as a moral crusade to preserve the nation and abolish human slavery. Discussion of the economic causes of the war did not receive much attention until later.

At the same time, the division within the Methodist Episcopal Church was differently understood in the North and South. To the northerner, the basic question was human slavery, while to the southerner the question was the relationship between the bishops and the General Conference. Individual preachers and laymen in the church were influenced by many forces in addition to the voice from the pulpit or the resolutions passed at Annual Conference. A person reared in the South or in a border state might believe that slavery was a part of the normal order of things, which was to be accepted, while his neighbor who had come from New England might believe that it was a monstrous evil to be eradicated at all costs.

In the summer of 1833 when the first white settlers began to pour across the Mississippi River into the Iowa country, one of the most inflammatory problems confronting America was the question of slavery. The passions aroused by growing sentiment for or against slavery were setting the sections of the country against each other and leading toward Civil War. Even though Iowa was a frontier, it could not escape the effects of the controversy.

During the first decade of the settlement of Iowa, opinion became polarized. Many of the settlers arriving in the southern counties had come from southern states, and had brought their racial attitudes with them. The institution of slavery was condoned by many. Others had moved north because of their opposition to it.

Most of the migration into Iowa came from northern states, and these settlers looked forward to the admission of Iowa into the union as a free state. They were fearful of any influence which might open the territories west of the Mississippi to slavery. The Methodist Episcopal Church came into Iowa from northern Illinois in 1833 with the first settlers and brought with it a strong anti-slavery bias.

The circuit riders preached sermons against slavery and voted, at the sessions of the Annual Conference, for resolutions condemning it as opposed to the spirit of Christianity. During the ten years that elapsed between the first settlements in Iowa and the organization of the Iowa Conference of the Methodist Episcopal Church, the church and the nation were becoming increasingly divided in sentiment. The 1844 General Conference which authorized the formation of the Iowa Conference was the same conference at which the slavery conflict reached its climax and the church was divided.

The division of the church was not solely over the slavery question. To the southerners the issue was the authority of the bishops versus the General Conference. Besides, tension was growing over economic conflicts between the industrial North and the agrarian South. Political jealousies over states' rights muddied the waters even though they did not directly concern the church.

In the eyes of the northerners, slavery was the main issue that overshadowed all others. The Methodist Episcopal Church as a whole was divided in 1844 into two churches, northern and southern. The northern Methodists continued under the old name, "The Methodist Episcopal Church," while the southerners took the name, "The Methodist Episcopal Church, South." The division lasted long after the Civil War. The sectional churches were not reunited until 1939.

Iowa has been pictured as a free state in which slavery was never tolerated. However, that picture is not entirely correct. During the period of the settlement of America, the frontiersman did not pay much attention to the letter of the law. Pioneers held little respect for the lines drawn between Indian and White lands. Settlers felt few qualms when they crossed into Indian country to make their homes or to pasture their cattle. The settlers who crossed the Mississippi River in 1832 had to be removed by the army. They returned legally in 1833.

Settlers moving north temporarily did not consider it necessary to leave their slaves behind them in Missouri. The contractor who erected the government buildings for the Indian Agency in what became Wapello County (adjacent to the present town of Agency) brought two slave women with him to cook for the workers. An educated white man who chose to live on the frontier with his Indian wife, and lived for a time at the Agency, also had two slave women. Steamers coming up the Mississippi River from St. Louis often had slaves tending fires or working as deck hands. When the first Methodist Episcopal Church building was erected in Dubuque in 1834, three of the contributors were black and are reputed to have been slaves.[1]

A few slaves resided in Iowa during early days although it was not legal and public opinion was strongly against it. The census of 1840 reported 172 free Negroes in Iowa, a third of them in Dubuque County. In addition, despite the Missouri Compromise and a decision of the Iowa Supreme Court in the Ralph case, sixteen slaves were reported, all in Dubuque.[2] Perhaps it was the presence of those few slaves in what was supposed to have been free territory that helped to strengthen opinion against slavery in and out of the church.

During the early years of Iowa Methodism there was a strong consensus in opposition to slavery. The people making up the membership of the United

Methodist Church and its antecedent church bodies have often disagreed on theology and on the best solutions for social problems. However, most Methodists have agreed strongly on some stands. Methodists were convinced that slavery was wrong and should be ended. They were anxious to use their influence to end it.

Nowhere was anti-slavery sentiment so determined as in the pulpits. Between 1833 and the Civil War many sermons were preached pointing out the evil of buying and selling human beings as property. By the time that the war came, opinion was so crystallized that a pro-slavery preacher would have found himself in trouble in any Iowa M.E. Church.

Henry Clay Dean was one of those who felt uncomfortable in the ministry in Iowa because of his views. He came into the Iowa Conference in 1850 by transfer from the Pittsburg Conference, and was appointed to Keosauqua.[3] In 1856 he located at his own request,[4] i.e. he withdrew from the active ministry and maintained the status of Lay Preacher. One interpretation of Dean's opposition to abolitionism is that he was pro-slavery. Another is that he was strongly opposed to tendencies toward divisiveness. For a time during James Buchanan's administration he was chaplain of the United States Senate. After the war he resided in southern Iowa and practiced law.

By 1856 the atmosphere in the church was electric, and the conference expressed themselves in forceful resolutions. The Upper Iowa Conference passed the following:

> Resolved 1st, That slavery is opposed to the spirit of Christianity and the promulgation of the Gospel, as well as an aggravating sin against God.
>
> Resolved 2nd, That as ministers of Christ we will make every reasonable and consistent effort to maintain a healthy anti-slavery sentiment in our several congregations, in order to prevent the extension of slavery in our country, and to effect the extirpation of this great evil.[5]

Each year similar resolutions were passed. The same year that the Upper Iowa Conference passed the above resolution, the Iowa Conference, which included the southern half of the state, passed a resolution condemning slavery and published a minority report condemning it even more emphatically. The majority report had stated:

> 1. Resolved, That we will use all means, consistent with our high calling, to prevent the spread of American slavery.
> 2. That we will hereafter "Remember those that are in bonds, as being bound with them."
> 3. That we will set apart a day, (vis., The Sabbath between Christmas and New Year), as a day of solemn prayer to Almighty God for the emancipation of our degraded brethren in bonds in the Slave States.[6]

The writers of the minority report were not satisfied with the above, claiming it was too mild in tone. They reported:

1. Resolved, That, while we cheerfully submit to the "rules and regulations" of the Church, we cannot otherwise than feel dissatisfied with its temporizing policy, and hereby declare our uncompromising opposition to Slavery, with all its abominations and unrighteous gains, and will wage an unceasing warfare against it, till it shall forever be excluded from the pale of the Church.

2. That we believe the only remedy for this "great evil" to be "amputation" and that "conservation" in the Church, on the subject of chattelizing human beings is out of date and out of place. [7]

The same year that the above resolutions were passed, the United States Supreme Court issued the famous Dred Scott decision. Abolitionists all through the North were stirred up to a new level. At its next session, in 1857, the Upper Iowa Conference passed another resolution, condemning the Dred Scott decision.

When the division in the church took place, preachers in the South who opposed slavery found themselves in an uncomfortable position. It has been reported that several young men among the preachers moved to Iowa rather than remain with the southern church at the time of ecclesiastical split. One of them was Levin P. Dennis, who arrived in Iowa from Arkansas in 1844 and became one of the leading preachers in the Iowa Conference. [8]

Opposition to slavery was not just a matter of passing resolutions. One of the programs initiated early in the nineteenth century was embodied in the American Colonization Society. The society recognized that a large body of freed slaves in the United States would create a problem, so this group of idealistic people tried to encourage the freeing of slaves and returning them to their homeland in Africa.

The flaw in the program was the failure to recognize that the American Negro had become "Americanized" and had no homeland in Africa. Negroes were brought to America speaking different languages and representing differing tribes and traditions. After living in America they became a new people, speaking a different language from anything in Africa. Even if they could have been returned to the tribes from which their parents had come, they would still have been strangers in the community of their ancestors.

Beginning in 1821, small groups of freed slaves were taken to the coast of Africa, to the territory which has become Liberia. The descendants of the freed slaves constituted a minority of mostly urbanized people. During the period preceding the Civil War the movement received moral and some financial support of Iowa Methodists, and was promoted as the best solution for America's race problem. The same session of the Iowa Conference (1856) which passed the resolutions against slavery also approved the following resolution concerning the Colonization Society:

Report on Colonization—Your Committee on Colonization would respectfully submit the following:

In view of the degraded condition of nearly 200,000,000 of the Sable sons of Africa; also the oppressed condition of the Negro race in our own country, we would offer the following resolutions:

Resolved, 1. That we maintain the utmost confidence in the American Colonization Society, as an important instrumentality in elevating the aforesaid race.

Resolved, 2. That we recommend to the confidence and prayers of our people this important enterprise.

Resolved, 3. That each member of this Conference hereafter appointed to the regular work shall be required to preach on this subject at some convenient time during the coming Conference year.

Resolved, 4. That we recommend the continuance of Rev. Samuel Clark as agent for said Society.[9]

When the war came, the Union cause received the enthusiastic support of most Iowa Methodists. The pacifism which has become so vocal in the Methodist Church in the twentieth century was not apparent during the 1860s. Considerable sympathy for the southern cause could be found in some of the southern counties and in some areas along the Mississippi River, but it was seldom found among the Methodist clergy. The preachers and most of their congregations gave whole-hearted support to the Union cause.

While preachers at home were championing the war effort, others were entering the army as chaplains and accompanying their parishioners to the battle fronts. A long list of those who volunteered could be compiled. The list below is representative, but incomplete.

Michael Huston Hare was the only one of the chaplains who served all through the war. In 1862 he volunteered as chaplain of the 36th Regiment Iowa Volunteer Infantry, and stayed with them for the entire duration of their service. He was a prisoner on one occasion for four months before he was paroled. He was mustered out with the regiment when peace came, but was unable to return to his work in Iowa because of poor health. He died in 1868 of tuberculosis, acquired during his time in the army.

The last pastoral assignment of long-time preacher Isaac I. Stewart was as chaplain of the Keokuk Military Hospital, Keokuk, Iowa. He died on August 15, 1864, while serving there. Isaac P. Teter, who had been commissioned chaplain of the 7th Iowa Infantry and accompanied the regiment to the South until 1864, returned north, and took Stewart's place.

Samuel Hestwood was chaplain of the 40th Iowa Volunteer Infantry. After a year his health failed, and he was compelled to resign and return home. He never fully recovered.[10]

Dennis Murphy, one of the more colorful chaplains, was born in County Limerick, Ireland, June 24, 1833, and reared a Catholic. He was "converted" at a Methodist revival meeting in Ottumwa, Iowa in 1856. In 1858 he entered the ministry of the Methodist Episcopal Church. He was chosen as chaplain of the 19th Iowa Infantry in 1862, a position he held for two years.[11]

James W. Latham's service as chaplain of the First Iowa Cavalry was interrupted in 1862. A year later he returned as chaplain of the Third Iowa Cavalry and continued to the end of the war.[12]

Manasseh B. Wayman was admitted into the conference on trial in 1858. When the war came he went as chaplain of the 3rd Iowa Cavalry. He served for less than a year when he was forced to resign on account of poor health. He died July 2, 1864, soon after returning home.[13]

Thomas E. Corkhill, presiding elder of the Mt. Pleasant District, entered the army in the fall of 1862 as chaplain of the 25th Iowa Infantry. Returning home for health reasons in 1863, he found that his successor in Mt. Pleasant district had died. Corkhill resumed his former position.[14]

Alfred Brunson, born in Danbury, Connecticut February 9, 1793, went to Ohio in 1812 and joined the army under General Harrison. Eight years later, out of the army, he became a member of the Pittsburg Conference. Transferred to the Illinois Conference in 1833 and superintendent of the Chicago District, he presided over the first quarterly conference in the Dubuque Mission. In 1839 he gave up the ministry on account of poor health. In 1850 he re-entered the Methodist ministry, and served as chaplain for a year during the Civil War.[15]

Another older preacher, James H. White began preaching as a supply in the Ohio Conference in 1836. In 1853 he transferred to Iowa from the Pittsburg Conference. While a superannuate (retired), he was appointed chaplain of the 37th Iowa Volunteer Infantry which was known as the "grey-beard regiment," assigned to guard duty because it was made up of men too old for more active duty.[16]

Some of the preachers evidently believed that their services could be used to better advantage as soldiers or officers than as chaplains. John Orr helped recruit a volunteer company, of which he was then commissioned a First Lieutenant—Company I, 25th Iowa Infantry.[17]

Alpha J. Kynett, who is better known for his work as a leader in Church Extension, was an earnest patriot. During the Civil War he was on the staff of Governor Kirkwood, aiding in recruiting several companies, and active in sanitary and Christian Commission work. After the war he achieved fame by recruiting funds for building new churches.[18]

Stephen H. Henderson, a native of Tennessee, came to Iowa in 1845. He entered the army as Captain of Company A, 24th Iowa Infantry. Near the close of the war he was Colonel of the 44th Regiment.[19]

J. B. Casebeer was admitted on trial into the Iowa Conference in 1859 and transferred to the Upper Iowa Conference in 1864. In the meantime, he had spent two years (1862-1864) as Captain of Company D, 24th Iowa Infantry, leaving when he was wounded by the explosion of a shell. He returned to the Conference and served until 1888, but never fully recovered from his wounds.[20]

The form of slavery ended with the Civil War, but many of the problems related to it remained. The Negro people had been separated from their African languages and cultures, but had not fully acquired the American culture, and were for the most part illiterate. Many of them spoke English poorly. With freedom, they were set adrift. Many of the former slaves wandered about the country and finally found new homes. A few of them came into Iowa, and their efforts to adapt here form the background for a chapter section on race relations.

Before the war was over, the government created a new agency, the Freedman's Bureau, to deal with the problems of the ex-slaves. The bureau was discontinued July 1, 1869. The Freedman's Aid Society, an agency of the Methodist Episcopal Church, was created after the Civil War to provide education for the freed slaves and their children. This society did effective work for many years. The United Methodists of Iowa still give annually to the support of Rust College at Holly Springs, Mississippi, one of the schools started by this society.

RACE RELATIONS

The history of race relations in the United Methodist Church and its antecedent church bodies is a story of gradual movement from the common racial viewpoints of the early nineteenth century to a willingness, among the church membership as a whole, to recognize that people of all races have common human needs and rights. Prejudice has always been present, but voices have always been calling for mutual acceptance of all persons as children of God.

Racial problems have been complicated in the United States by a popular tendency to over-simplify our view of race, assuming sharp divisions. In an elementary school geography text used in Iowa around 1900 and earlier, we find humanity neatly divided into categories as follows:

3. The people living in different parts of the world may be divided into five Races: the *Caucasian,* or white race; the *Ethiopian,* or black race; the *Mongolian,* or yellow race; the *Malay,* or brown race; and the *American,* or red race.

4. The Caucasian, or white, race is superior to all others, and is the most numerous. It has a fair complexion, an oval face, with a high, rounded forehead, a symmetrical figure, an ample beard, and generally wavy hair varying in color.[21]

The same textbook classified the various peoples as barbarous, semi-civilized, or civilized. Its reference to religions had a distinctly Christian bias. The book presented ideas that are no longer generally accepted, but it is an example of what was being taught in the schools at the time and generally believed to be true. It painted the background against which the church taught.

The goal of the United Methodist Church in Iowa has been to create a society in which people of various groups can live, work, and worship side by side and respect one another. No one view has been held by all Methodists at any one time, but there has been a climate in the church which would make a member of the Ku Klux Klan uncomfortable.

The people of Iowa are sufficiently homogeneous in makeup that almost every viewpoint held by one group has been shared to some extent by others. The several sections of what is now the United Methodist Church used their influence to develop a respect for persons of all races. People with strong racial antipathies tend to look elsewhere for a church home, where they can be more comfortable.

When James S. Thomas, a black bishop, was assigned to the Iowa Area in 1964, some members of one church in South Iowa withdrew in protest, or at least, they quit attending services and supporting the church. When this writer arrived in 1967 as pastor of that church, members of the administrative board told him of the incident, and added the comment that those who withdrew had never been missed. They had not been attending often when they were members.

Iowa was considering application for statehood in 1844. A Constitutional Convention was called to prepare a constitution for the state-to-be. The convention members held views common to the rest of the country. An effort was made at that time to exclude free Negroes from living in Iowa. The idea was expressed that if doors were opened to the Negro, the policies of other states would drive the whole black population of the Union into Iowa.[22] If the church were to change attitudes to acceptance of all men as equal, it had a big job to do. First, the attitudes of church members had to change.

Following the Civil War, the country was confronted by many problems, but the one that concerns us here was the presence of thousands of homeless, mostly illiterate ex-slaves. In March, 1865, the Bureau of Refugees, Freedmen, and Abandoned Lands—better known as the Freedmen's Bureau—was established.

With the abolition of slavery, it was not just the federal government which assumed a responsibility for the welfare of the Freedmen. The churches also formed organizations to assist the freed slaves. In the Methodist Episcopal Church the Freedman's Aid Society was formed in 1866 for the purpose of "establishing and maintaining institutions of learning in the southern states among the Freedmen and others who have special claims upon the people of America for help in the work of Christian Education."[23]

Among the institutions organized was Rust College in Holly Springs, Mississippi. This college has had an important influence in Mississippi by training many young people who became teachers for public schools in that state.[24] It has also had a significant influence among Iowa Methodists. For many years, the Sunday nearest Lincoln's birthday has been observed in Iowa Methodist Churches as "Race Relations Day." At that time a special collection has been taken for Rust College. Usually a sermon on the topic of race relations has been preached. The cumulative effect of the sermons and the collections was to develop, among white Iowans, a feeling of concern for black Americans.

The Evangelical Association—one of the predecessor bodies of the Evangelical United Brethren Church, and still later, the United Methodist Church—had an interesting and perhaps frustrating experience with its efforts to aid the freed slaves. It was made up basically of German-speaking people. Its members had very little direct contact with black people. In a sense, they may have been isolated from some of the cultural viewpoints held by their English-speaking neighbors—by the barrier of language.

In the 1865 session of their annual conference it was voted:

par. 25 Resolved, that this conference constitute itself a society to devise means whereby to assist the emancipated colored people in their physical and spiritual needs.

par. 26 A committee was appointed to draw up a constitution for the proposed society and to report to the conference.[25]

Later, at the same session of the annual conference, the members realized that they had people who were interested, but they did not have machinery set up. Accordingly they resolved:

par. 63 Resolved, that as long as our Association does not begin a mission in the South, all goods be sent through the Chicago Society of the Freedman's Commission.

par. 64 Resolved, that the funds which the treasurer of this society has on hand be loaned on interest for a period of six months.[26]

Sometimes it is easier to pass resolutions than to implement them. Accordingly, four years later we find another session of the conference voting:

par. 53 It was resolved, that the missionary funds for the Freedman's Aid Society be loaned without interest for the church building project in Des Moines and that the note be retained by the missionary treasurer until the society requests the money.[27]

In the 1871 minutes of the conference the following notation appears:

par. 43 Resolved, that the note which the former Freedman's Society of this conference held against the Des Moines Church, be given it as a gift.[28]

The Freedman's Aid Society, which started in 1865 with good intentions, ended six years later with its assets being used to help build a church in Des Moines. This does not necessarily indicate a lack of concern for the black people in the South. At that time the population of Iowa was growing, and the Evangelical Association was organizing new congregations and building new church buildings every year. Their facilities were being strained by expansion within the state, without reaching into the South. Every year during the post-war period the annual conference minutes of the Evangelical Association show the church struggling with the problems incidental to forming small congregations of German-speaking people in Iowa.

The Methodist Protestant Church was another small denomination which dealt with the race problem in its own way. Never very numerous in Iowa, they met many of the same questions as the larger Methodist Episcopal Church. Apparently strong differences of opinion existed among the "M.P.s." In a history of that church in Iowa were found the following comments:

The debates on the colored question which had appeared in the Annual Conference record since 1849 led finally to a decision in 1857 whereby colored persons were pronounced eligible for Church membership, dependent upon the decision of the individual Classes or Societies.[29]

The road toward racial equality was still lengthy, but the first step had been taken.

Among the list of contributors to the first M.E. Church building fund in Iowa (1834) appear the names of three "colored" persons, believed to have been slaves. Blacks were integrated into the church to some small extent from the beginning.

In 1844 an Iowa Conference (M.E.) was organized. Out of 5,443 lay members at that time, twelve colored members were reported from five different local societies.[30] In 1845 an increase of 947 members included four who were colored. At the tenth session of the conference (1853), the M.E. Church in Iowa had twenty colored members.

The attitude toward the Indians was ambiguous, and there was less personal contact with them which might have led to church membership. One early Iowa preacher who put his thoughts into writing was Landon Taylor. He spoke of the Indians in terms which perhaps represented the thinking of many others:

> Yea, I believe them to be treacherous in every sense of the word, except in solitary instances; and yet I am fully satisfied that their association with the whites, copying their vices, purchasing their liquor, and swindled by their deception, has had much to do in giving a still darker shade to their degradation; and as they hold sacred the law revenge, is it a great wonder, after being so often deceived and imposed upon through government officials, that they were brought to despise government, and take matters into their own hands! They are a down-trodden and degraded race, of but little value in the world's history, and our business as a Christian nation is, not to make them worse, but to do all within our power to lift them up to a higher plane; and this can be done only in the exercise of justice, mercy, and truth.[31]

Progress has been made since the days of Taylor. The Methodist Church has been working since the Civil War to improve the conditions among the Indians and Negroes. Only in the earlier years were the races reported separately on membership rolls.

For more than a hundred years it has been impossible to determine even an approximate number of black members in predominantly white churches. The total Negro population in Iowa has never been large. In 1860 Iowa's Negro population was only 1,069. After the Civil War numbers increased, but the total never reached so must as one percent of the population until 1970, when the percentage climbed to 1.15.[32]

In 1865 the Iowa M.E. Conference offered its support to the program of the Freedman's Aid Commission, a governmental agency established at the end of the Civil War:

XII. Report on the Freedmen's Aid Commission

> Whereas, God has strongly set free four millions of human beings, long bound in the chains of an inquitous servitude, who, by every dictate of our religion, are claimants upon our sympathies and means, therefore,
> Resolved, That we will cordially welcome to our fields of labor the agents of the

Freedmen's Aid Commission, and will assist them in securing means for the moral and temporal well-being of the freedmen.

Abner Orr, Secretary[33]

Methodist conferences have always been generous in the passing of resolutions. These resolutions, when supported by the individual preachers and local churches, have gradually changed the attitudes of the people of the state. With help from Iowa Methodists schools for blacks were maintained in the South, and a more tolerant attitude developed in the North.

The Iowa Conference voted in 1866 to give its support to the Methodist Episcopal Church's own Freedman's Aid Society:

XI. Report on the freedmen
Whereas, God has broken the chains of human oppression and set at liberty four millions of bondsmen in this country, we feel it our imperative duty as a Church, to aid in the enlightenment of the Freedmen.
Resolved, that the time has come for the M.E. Church to direct its contributions for the education of the Freedmen, so that they shall be applied to the support of the schools in connection with our own Mission work.

2. That we hereby recognize and approve the "Freedmen's Aid Society of the M.E. Church," and pledge ourselves to the utmost of our ability to provide means for the furtherance of its object, and to bring the cause for which it labors before our Congregations, wherever practicable, during the Conference year.

I. P. Teter, Chairman[34]

As Negroes moved north during and after the Civil War, they found their places in Iowa communities. The old membership records of the Division Street Methodist Episcopal Church in Burlington (originally known as Ebenezer M.E. Church), which are now a treasured possession of the First United Methodist Church, record the names of eleven former Negro slaves who were received into the church on February 25, 1866. These ex-slaves later withdrew and formed the nucleus of the African Methodist Episcopal Church which was organized there. Some of the descendants of these people still live in Burlington, are members of the A.M.E. Church, and are proud of their ancestors' former connection with the Division Street Church.

The first Negro Methodist Episcopal Church in Iowa was formed in Des Moines in 1867 and named in honor of Bishop Burns, the first black bishop in the M.E. Church.

A number of Negroes settled in Oskaloosa. At first, as in Burlington, they worshiped with the whites. Finally they secured a frame church building for themselves and were listed in the Iowa Conference Minutes as Wesley Chapel.

There were always a few black members in predominantly white churches. Ben Grayson, a former lay member of the A.M.E. Church in Albia, was lay leader of the Albia United Methodist Church for several years.

The Fayette church has been proud of one of its members, Miss Susan Collins, a black girl who was brought to Fayette by her parents in 1866.

Around 1887 she went to Angola as a missionary teacher and served there many years. After retirement, she returned to Fayette, living there as an honored member of the community.

By 1964 racial attitudes in Iowa had developed to the point that Iowa Methodists were ready to extend an enthusiastic welcome to James Thomas, the North Central Jurisdiction's first black bishop. The episcopal committee of the 1964 Jurisdictional Conference had the responsibility for assigning the bishops to their respective areas. As that committee met to discuss the placement of each bishop, the Iowa delegation asked that Bishop Thomas be assigned to the Iowa Area. Each quadrennium after that he was invited back until he had served twelve years, the maximum length of time permitted by the Discipline of the church.

In the century following the Civil War Iowa had some black pastors serving black congregations. Since 1964, the Methodists in Iowa have accepted Korean, Japanese, Philippine, and black pastors into the conference to serve white or racially mixed congregations. The United Methodist Church is becoming cosmopolitan and interracial.

Temperance and Prohibition

The social problem which has aroused most concern among Methodist people, and on which they have been most agreed, is the use of beverage alcohol. Almost every Methodist has read the Bible story of Noah, the one man who, with his family, was considered worth saving from the flood. Noah survived the flood, only to get himself and his family into trouble with wine from the vineyard he planted.[35]

The Bible was written among people by whom the use of alcoholic beverages was accepted without much question, when used moderately, but drunkenness was condemned. The English and the Americans have not always shown the same restraint and social control as the Jewish people; in both England and America the use of alcohol has been and is a problem.

When the first settlers came across the Mississippi River into Iowa they were separated from many of the social restraints operating in the more settled places they had left. In an article appearing in the January, 1927 *Palimpsest,* Ruth Gallaher described conditions as they existed in Dubuque in 1835:

> The frontier along the Mississippi, like the frontier everywhere, attracted a lawless and turbulent element. Charles A. Murray, an English visitor at Dubuque in 1835, wrote that the barroom "was crowded with a parcel of blackguard noisy miners," but he added, "Theft is almost unknown; and though dirks are frequently drawn and pistols fired in savage and drunken brawls, I do not believe that an instance of larceny or house-breaking has occurred."[36]

Gallaher calls attention to the contrast provided by the Methodists:

> As early as 1834 a little group of Methodists erected at Dubuque the first

church building in Iowa. This little log church was "raised," we are told, "with few hands and without spirits of any kind"—a procedure apparently not according to the prevailing custom.[37]

Through the years the Methodists have fought against the use of beverage alcohol both by teaching against it and by striving to have the legislature pass laws regulating or forbidding its use. Methodist opposition to liquor has been a significant factor in Republican victories in Iowa politics from the Civil War until 1932.

The Republican Party was not only the "party of Lincoln," but in the nineteenth and twentieth centuries it was usually the "dry" party. It won many Iowa Methodist votes, regardless of other issues. In the campaign of 1860, when Nicholas J. Rusch was a candidate for Lieutenant Governor, feelings ran high. Rusch had voted for the beer and wine amendment to the state prohibition law of 1855. A Methodist minister is reported to have said he would rather vote for an advocate of slavery than for Rusch.[38]

The journals of the different Methodist conferences in the state reflect a common viewpoint among Methodists living in various sections. The 1860 *Upper Iowa Conference Journal* stated in its "Report on Temperance": "Resolved, That we recommend moral suasion and legal enactment, as the twin agencies for the banishment of Intemperance from the land."[39] The same year the Iowa Conference, which at that time included the southern part of the state, resolved that "each traveling preacher be required to preach upon the subject of temperance, at least once at each of his appointments, within the conference year."[40] This continuing emphasis on abstinence had its cumulative effect. However, Methodist views were not accepted by many others, and not always by all of its own members. A continuing controversy runs through Iowa history.

In the state's early years efforts were made to develop grape-growing and brewing as important industries. Des Moines had the largest distillery in the world. Mississippi and Missouri River towns profited from the liquor traffic. Yet sentiment in Iowa as a whole was anti-liquor, particularly in the rural areas.[41]

The Iowa constitution prohibited the sale of alcoholic beverages, "save ale, wine, and beer." The Iowa Methodists have usually been staunch prohibitionists, urging the prohibition of alcoholic drinks in all forms. A prohibitionary amendment to the state constitution was passed in the 1880 and 1882 sessions of the General Assembly. It was approved by the voters of the state and became effective July 28, 1882. The opponents of the amendment were quick to challenge it in the courts on the grounds that it had not been approved in identical form in the two sessions of the legislature.

A test case was brought in Davenport in October, 1882. The court decided against the amendment. The dry forces appealed to the State Supreme Court, which upheld the lower court. The dry forces were furious. A law was speedily passed by the legislature, known as "Clark's Law," which closed drinking places all over Iowa, except in Sioux City, where the so-called "liquor element" paid no attention to the law.[42]

Businessmen believed that closing the saloons would hurt their business and slow down the growth of Sioux City. Accordingly the business community sanctioned the violation, and by municipal action "licensed" places operated in direct violation of the state law. Once each month, each speakeasy operator was arrested on a charge of disturbing the peace by using loud, profane, and indecent language. In police court he would plead guilty and then pay a fine for his offense. He knew that if he did not plead guilty to the charge, he would be arrested for a liquor law violation and put out of business.[43]

The subterfuge seemed to work except that the pastor of the First Methodist Episcopal Church, Rev. George Haddock, was strongly opposed to the liquor traffic and believed that the law should be enforced. He kept track of the speakeasies and brought genuine liquor law charges against them. He preached temperance and law enforcement from the pulpit and also became prosecuting witness in the courts.[44] John F. Schmidt, a local Sioux City historian, states that:

> . . . he (Haddock) was threatened, insulted, and treated to all kinds of indignities, all of which he bore with "manly courage." He told his friends and his congregation that he expected to meet violence, and perhaps death, at the hands of the saloon element, but he saw his Christian duty and involved himself and his church in the community problem.
>
> Hissed by the lawless element, reviled by a portion of the local press, even discouraged by many of his clerical brethren, they, Rev. Haddock and his co-laborers, went straight ahead in their task of prosecuting, thinking of the end to be obtained—closing the Sioux City saloons. This was something the violators and their protectors had never seen before; the law had been violated and laughed at as a farce, but here were people willing to endure the persecutions, insults, and threats, who would not be stopped. It became evident that unless this preacher and his supporters could be stopped, in any way they could be, prohibition would come, even to Sioux City.[45]

A saloon-keeper association was organized with the stated objective to "whip Walker, Wood, and Haddock," who were witnesses for the state. A meeting was held in Holdenreid's hall, the evening of August 2, 1886. George Treiber, a German saloon-keeper, suggested that they hire two Germans to do the whipping. He had two Germans, Koschnitski and Granda, who would whip the preacher if they were paid to do it.

On the evening of August third, Haddock and the Rev. C. C. Turner rented a horse and buggy at Merril's livery stable on Water Street. They went to Greenville (a section of Sioux City) where they hoped to get some information to help them in their prosecution. In the meantime, the two Germans had been hired to whip Haddock and were waiting near the livery stable.

Word went down Fourth Street, and a crowd assembled. When Haddock returned from driving Rev. Turner home to the West Side, he saw the crowd waiting. Two men left the group and started toward him. One of them fired and Rev. Haddock fell, face down, on the muddy street. He died as a result of the assassin's bullet.

A grand jury indicted John Arensdorf, Harry L. Leavitt, Paul Leader, Fred Munchrath, Luis Plath, Alber Koschnitski, George Treiber, and Sylvester Granda. Some of them left town.

John Arensdorf was brought to trial March 23, 1887, charged with murder, which caused tremendous national excitement. Newspapers from Chicago and New York sent correspondents to Sioux City to cover the trial. The trial ended with a hung jury. Arensdorf was tried again in December. The verdict was "not guilty." [46]

Fred Munchrath was convicted of manslaughter in September, 1887, and sentenced to four years in prison. He was pardoned by the governor. [47]

A strong wave of sentiment demanding effective law enforcement swept over the state. Popular reaction to the death of Haddock is recorded in a story from LeMars:

Haddock Marker

At the time Rev. George C. Haddock was assassinated by the saloon element at Sioux City, and his remains were being conveyed through the state, over the Illinois Central Railroad, D. W. Held, of the LeMars German Methodist Episcopal Church, originated the idea of expressing sympathy by the tolling of every church bell, and that of the city fire department, while the train moved in and out of the city. This plan was carried out in full except by the Catholic Church, and the same was taken up by each town along the line of road over which his body passed, throughout Iowa. It was a truly befitting tribute to a grand life sacrificed on a temperance altar in Iowa. Though dead yet he speaketh in his influence. [48]

Governor Larrabee had not been very enthusiastic about enforcing the liquor law, but he interpreted the death of Haddock as a challenge to the law of the state. He called upon all sheriffs to enforce the law or suffer dismissal from office. The sheriffs responded so liberally that they soon had the jails packed. In order to make room, the governor began to issue conditional pardons to such as would pledge not to resume their illegal business.[49]

The Methodist ministers of the Northwest Iowa Conference which met following the death of Haddock approved memorial resolutions:

> Resolved, That we, the ministers of the Northwest Iowa Conference, standing here amid the solemnities of this memorial service, pledge to each other and to the ministers of the church of God throughout the world, to join in a crusade against the saloon curse, that shall know neither cessation nor abatement until, in God's good time, we join Geo. C. Haddock before the throne.

> Resolved, That in common with all thoughtful people, we charge upon the saloon the deep, crimson-dyed iniquity of George C. Haddock's taking off; and we earnestly invite and implore all ministers, all Christians, all lovers of humanity, our country, and of her laws, and all haters of anarchy and crime, to join us in our solemn pledge to wage an unceasing war of extermination against the saloon, the brewery, the distillery, and all breeding dens of murder and murderers.[50]

The death of George Haddock provided the dry forces of the state with a martyr, and this had its effect. George Haddock dead was more of a threat to the liquor forces than George Haddock alive. Over fifty years later, in 1937, First Methodist Episcopal Church of Sioux City dedicated an iron marker in the pavement at Fourth and Water Streets with a cross in the center and the words, "Haddock Died Here 8/3/1886."

After 1886 the trend was toward stronger enforcement of the temperance laws in Iowa, but many who believed in temperance did not think that personal morality should be legislated. This was more particularly true of church people in some denominations who did not regard moderate drinking as a moral question. The M.E. Church was not temperate in its opposition to intemperance. The resolutions passed at annual conferences gave evidence of the conviction that every political campaign was a one-issue race.

Bennett Mitchell, historian of the Northwest Iowa Conference and long-time presiding elder, made revealing comments. Regarding the Annual Conference of 1887, when the memory of Haddock was still fresh, he wrote:

> Quite a tilt was had over the report on temperance this year. As reported from the committee it was thought to smack of a partisan spirit. The language of the committee was slightly amended, not so as to blunt the point. Some brethren are awfully afraid that the church may become partisan. Well, when one party is right and the other wrong, how can it stand for the truth and not support the one and oppose the other? Party sinners should be rebuked as readily as individual sinners, and a party that stands for the right should be endorsed and supported as readily as an individual who stands for the right.[51]

Mitchell held views which were common among Methodists of the time. In his history are found indications that his viewpoint was not shared by all. Regarding the Annual Conference of 1895 he wrote:

On the matter of temperance we again passed loud resolutions. We declared that "no man or party would receive our suffrage unless pronounced in favor of the total prohibition of the liquor traffic in the state and nation." But Alas! like truckling politicians, more than half of the Conference went and voted at the next election for man and a party that stood for the mulct law, the enactment of which was, we said, a "great public crime and a base betrayal of every interest we hold dear. O, consistency, thou art a jewel," sometimes missing in a Methodist Conference.[52]

The Mulct Law to which Mitchell referred was an amendment to the old liquor control law and was approved by the legislature in January, 1894. By its provisions, cities of more than 5,000 population were allowed to operate saloons if petitions to that effect were signed by a majority of the voters in the last preceding election. Smaller cities and towns and whole counties could nullify the prohibitory law if petitions were signed by sixty-five percent of the voters in the county outside the larger cities.

The saloons that were thus permitted to operate were not really licensed to do business; instead, they were mulcted certain sums per month for violating what was still a state law. The minimum of such fines was fixed at $600 a year, and the penalties might be as much more as councils of cities and towns saw fit to impose.

What was popularly called the Mulct Law seemed contradictory and illogical, but it was sustained by the Supreme Court of Iowa, to the sorrow of the prohibitionists. The Mulct Law became popular for a time. One reason was that it was well enforced. Those who paid the high mulct fines saw to it they they had no competitors in the business. Politically it was such a satisfactory solution of what had been a troublesome issue that for many years the political parties dropped the liquor question out of their platforms.[53]

Although the political parties were very willing to dispose of a sticky question, the Methodist preachers were not so willing. Each year the annual conferences continued to attack the saloon and to preach temperance. The 1895 session of the Northwest Iowa Conference resolved:

We believe the mulct law of Iowa is a gross and wanton violation of the rights of the people, and notwithstanding that it was created by a so-called Christian Legislature, who was elected by a great army of Christian voters, it is nevertheless a great public crime, and a base betrayal of every interest we hold dear, and believe that those responsible for this legislation should be made to feel the public odium. . . .resolved,

First, That no man or party should receive our suffrage unless pronounced in favor of the total prohibition of the liquor traffic both in the state and nation.

Second, That we favor resubmission of a prohibitory amendment to our state constitution at a nonpartisan election to be held not sooner than the year 1897.[54]

In the latter part of the century two important temperance organizations were formed, and were supported enthusiastically by Iowa Methodists. The first was the Women's Christian Temperance Union (WCTU), organized in 1874. The second was an interdenominational organization formed in 1895— the Anti-Saloon League. Both had many Methodist members and received strong endorsement from the Methodist Conferences. The first national president of the League was an influential Methodist layman from Davenport. Hiram Price had been a businessman and local public official since 1844. He was elected to Congress in 1865, 1867, and 1877, and became national president of the Anti-Saloon League in 1895.[55]

Even the Anti-Saloon League was not always sufficiently militant to suit the Northwest Iowa Conference. Their 1898 session stated:

> We recognize in the Anti-Saloon League greater promise of ability to successfully unite all temperance elements and to create strong public sentiment against the saloon than in any other organization in the field.[56]

The State Superintendent of the League could see that many temperance people of the state were not entirely opposed to the Mulct Law, which was a form of local option. The same 1898 session of the Northwest Iowa Conference which had endorsed the League also was very critical of its leadership:

> Whereas the Rev. H. H. Abrams, the State Superintendent of the League, is reported by the papers throughout the state as saying in a public way that the Mulct Law as it is being enforced is coming "into favor with all classes of temperance people," and,
>
> Whereas, This statement has not been denied, or withdrawn by Mr. Abrams, nor repudiated by the League, therefore,
>
> Resolved, That we denounce the statement as false and wholly misleading, and we declare that the Mulct Law is a most iniquitous piece of legislation that has given the liquor traffic legal standing again in Iowa. We will stand on the platform that to legalize the liquor business in any form is sin.[57]

The Methodist Conferences of Iowa were never willing to accept the liquor traffic as a legitimate enterprise. Every year temperance sermons were preached in every church in the state, and resolutions were regularly approved stating in extreme terms the opposition to any compromise with Demon Rum. The 1906 session of the Upper Iowa Conference, in its report on Temperance, said in part:

> We recognize no victory as final until the whole traffic in intoxicating beverages shall be under complete subjection to the highest and best principles of temperance legislation.
>
> We heartily commend the organization and work of the Anti-Saloon League in its state and nationwide movement.
>
> We advise and exhort the voters of our church to give their suffrage only to such men to sit in our state legislature as are clean in life and who are recognized as holding the best temperance principles.[58]

It was hoped that the Eighteenth Amendment to the United States Constitution, ratified in 1919, would close all saloons in the country and forever settle the problem. The 1921 session of the Northwest Iowa Conference voted:

> We appreciate the splendid work done by the Anti-Saloon League of America in their fight to enforce the law against the liquor traffic. While victory is still on the side of the temperance forces, yet to conserve the results we need to strengthen our arms and realize that "eternal vigilance" is the price of liberty.[59]

By 1925 it was becoming apparent that national prohibition was not solving all social problems. Not everyone in the nation approved of the new law or was willing to obey it. The 1925 session of the Upper Iowa Conference noted that while

> ". . . we are grateful to Almighty God for the victories achieved thus far, for the cause of Temperance and Prohibition in the 18th Amendment to our National Constitution, we are made to know in many different ways that the war against strong drink is not yet over. The 'fight is still on.' "[60]

Those opposed to Prohibition did not accept settlement of the issue by constitutional prohibition, and repeal became a major issue in the 1932 national election. Other issues were important, but the Democratic Party urged repeal of the Eighteenth Amendment and won the election.

The first item in President Franklin D. Roosevelt's "New Deal" was the repeal. When the hold-over Congress met in December, 1932, the House passed a "bill to provide revenues by the taxation of certain non-intoxicating liquors," the same being 3.2 percentum beer. Congress thus declared that 3.2 beer is not intoxicating. The same Congress also passed legislation for repeal of the Eighteenth Amendment.

When the new Congress met in special session, the beer bill was passed on March 20, 1933. The repeal of the Eighteenth Amendment was ratified by an Iowa convention on June 20, 1933. The sale of distilled liquors was retained as a state monopoly to be administered by three commissioners in Iowa, with city councils and county supervisors authorized to issue permits for the sale of wine and beer.

The Upper Iowa Conference met June 21-26, 1933, at which time the committee on "State of the Country and Church" reported, "We recognize a strong move toward repeal of the eighteenth amendment, but we do not believe this represents the real heart of the masses of the American people." The Northwest Iowa Conference met September 26 to October 1 that same year, and in its report to the conference the Anti-Saloon League stated in part "that the fight will have to be made over, goes without debate. The Church and Christian forces have been whipped, but not defeated."[61]

At the 1948 session of the Upper Iowa Conference the Commission on the State of the Church reported: "Strong drink is the greatest single enemy of all that the Church stands for. We must oppose it with all our might. Christian people are earnestly exhorted to adopt a personal attitude of total abstinence."[62]

The United Methodist Church continues its opposition to intemperance through preaching and education, but is no longer a "single-issue" political lobby. More consideration is given now to the whole range of drug abuse.

War and Peace

Methodist people in Iowa have always been concerned about moral problems related to life in the military, whether in peace-time or war-time, and about war-connected problems for civilians as well. They have felt this concern to be appropriate despite the nation's constitutional separation of church and state. No church body elects representatives to Congress. No American bishop sits in the United States Senate as certain of the Anglican Bishops sit in the British House of Lords. However, the church can and does speak on moral issues, and its members, in their role as citizens, do vote. One may question whether they vote more as church members or as members of their political parties. The degree of the church's influence is hard to measure.

One of the basic objectives of the Christian churches of various denominations has been to promote peace and to prevent war. An article in the *Encyclopaedia Britannica* states, "International Peace has been regarded since the beginning of history as a blessing and its opposite, war, as a curse."[63] Although Methodist people have been concerned about issues of war and peace, they have not agreed upon what the Christian position truly is. Individuals have been ambivalent in their attitudes, and some persons have held different views at different stages in their lives.

The United Methodist Church has not been one of the traditional "peace" churches, such as the Quakers or the Church of the Brethren, but during the years between 1920 and 1940 the Methodist Episcopal Church passed resolutions against war as strong as, or stronger than, those of the "peace" churches. There were those in the church who regarded pacifism as the norm.

Between 1833, when the first Methodist preacher entered Iowa, and the present, the denominations which came together in the United Methodist Church have influenced, and been influenced by, the events of history. The United States fought a war with Mexico, a Civil War, a series of undeclared Indian Wars, a war with Spain, World War I, World War II, the Korean War, and the undeclared war in Viet Nam, besides using armed forces on various occasions for the advancement of the nation's foreign policy.

As the political situation has changed, so have the attitudes within the church. This has led to the passing of resolutions and the preaching of sermons intended to influence public opinion and to affect the course of events. A passage from the prophet Isaiah has been a popular sermon text:

He shall judge between the nations,
  and shall decide for many peoples;
And they shall beat their swords into plowshares,
  and their spears into pruning hooks;

Nation shall not lift up sword against nation,
neither shall they learn war any more.[64]

Sermons in the local churches and resolutions passed at annual conferences do not always indicate the thinking of the rank and file of the membership of the church. Discussing the Northwest Iowa Conference of the M.E.
Church, Bennett Mitchell, one of the key leaders, remarked:

> I sometimes think that if, by the passing of resolutions, the "crooked places" in
> this world could be made "straight" and the "rough places plain" our confer-
> ence could readily do the whole thing.[65]

In the middle years of the nineteenth century the churches were too busy
settling in the new state, converting sinners, and building churches to give
much, if any, attention to international affairs. The annual conference journals do not mention the Mexican War. The Civil War was an entirely different matter. Iowa Methodists looked upon the Union cause as a just cause,
which could and should be supported. When Ft. Sumter fell and President
Lincoln issued his call for volunteers, a recruiting station was established at
Dyersville in Dubuque County, Iowa. A group of men gathered, and the
pastor of the M.E. Church was called upon for a speech.

> After paying a fitting tribute to the flag and uttering strong words in support of
> Abraham Lincoln in his call for troops, he said: "Gentlemen, ours is a
> righteous cause, and should I go to war I would go to kill. Every time I lifted the
> rifle to my eye, I would raise a silent prayer to God to guide the ball to the heart
> of some one of my country's foes, and to have mercy on his soul."[66]

It is unlikely that very many of the preachers would have expressed themselves in quite so bloodthirsty a manner, and it is unlikely that even that one
would have done so in later years, when tempers had cooled. However, that
was not a temperate age. One wonders how such impassioned words could
have been remembered and recorded for posterity. The same Stephen Fellows, who in later years was a distinguished and honored preacher, university
professor, and historical writer, was the pastor of Dyersville at that time.[67]

Fellows does not make any judgment on the speech in his *History of the
Upper Iowa Conference,* written when he was much older. But he uses that
incident anonymously as an illustration of the feeling of the times. He also
states:

> It is not known that any member of the Conference wavered in his devotion to
> the flag. The people were so intensely loyal that they would not have received
> the Gospel from the lips of anyone who sympathized with the rebellion.[68]

Pacifism became an issue much later.

During the period after the Civil War little attention was given in church
conferences to questions concerning the military. The army was small and
not highly visible to the public. Except for the War with Spain (1898) and the
Indian Wars, the country was considered to be at peace.

Two resolutions dealing with the need for military chaplains were introduced and passed as the 1889 session of the Northwest Iowa Conference. The first was presented by Bennett Mitchell and R. H. Dolliver. Because of the prominence of these two men in the conference, it carried more weight than some other resolutions.

1. Whereas, the regular Army and Navy of the United States is recruiting from the young men of the country, And,
2. Whereas, the moral conditions (sic) of the Army and Navy as a whole is bad, And
3. Whereas, this condition is largely due to there being no moral standard required for admission into or promotion in the Army and Navy, to an almost total lack of Chapels and libraries, adequate Chaplain service and barracks where decent privacy is possible, which defects could be remedied by proper legislation on the part of Congress: Therefore
   Resolved That this Conference hereby ask the Presiding Elders of the several districts to call up this matter in the quarterly Conferences of the charges and secure, if possible, action favorable to the measure now pending in Congress in behalf of our soldiers and sailors known as "The Chaplaincy Bill," and instructions to have such action conveyed by the Recording Steward, or a Committee of the Conference, to the Representatives and Senators in Congress and that as religious teachers we urge the people to intercede with Congress to provide for the moral needs of the Army and Navy.[69]

The second resolution was similar to the first both in intent and in content.

World War I marked a great change in the life of America and its relations with the rest of the world. An increasing awareness of the moral and political effects of war, as well as its physical destruction, grew from the experiences of that conflict.

This writer remembers having been told by his father of neighbors' reactions to news of the outbreak of World War I in 1914. The dominant thought was thankfulness that the war was far away in Europe and could not affect them directly. The 1912 *Discipline* of the M.E. Church had a section on "The Church and Social Problems" which did not mention war.[70] The 1916 Journal of the Upper Iowa Conference (M.E.) had much to say about the temperance question which dominated Iowa politics at that time, but did not mention the war.

The 1914 Journal of the Iowa Conference (southeastern Iowa) included a committee report on the State of the Church which was adopted:

We deplore the European War—its suffering and slaughter, its arrest of progress and the Kingdom of God, and denounce it as a crime against God and man. We declare that Christianity which professes to love God and at the same time marches men in the name of God to war and slaughter, an emasculated and false Christianity. We declare that civilization a painted barbarism, that cries "God for my country" rather than my country for God; that affirms "Man exists for the government" rather than the government for man; and that drives men and nations to bloody strife, with the tragic and obstreperous buffoonery of an imperialism based on the political and discarded heresy of the "Divine right of kings."

We thank God that our nation is at peace with the world; that in the midst of great personal sorrow and the heavy burden incident to his high office, our Christian president has been sustained and guided into high statesmanship and lofty administration of world affairs. We pray God to use him to bring back world peace.[71]

As the war in Europe continued, it was impossible for America to avoid becoming emotionally involved in some way. An "Iowa Peace Society" was organized. It appealed to the churches for support. In the 1915 Journal of the Iowa Conference (M.E.) a report on the "State of the Country" mentioned it:

Your committee, to which was referred the communication of the Iowa Peace Society, submits the following for adoption:
1. We are in full sympathy with the object of the Iowa Peace Society and hail its advent as an expression of that deep undercurrent in American opinion which warrants the hope we indulge that our country shall avoid the horrors of war.
2. We further express it as our deep conviction that Christian statesmanship ought to discover a means of settlement for international disputes without resort to arms between and among civilized nations, and we feel that more than a century of peace with the land from which we wrested our independent national existence, with thousands of miles of unfortified frontier between us and their greatest colony, suggests the way.[72]

More was included in the above report, supporting the view that the United States could and should remain apart from the bloody European conflict.

When the United States was finally drawn into the war, the members of the Methodist Episcopal Church, in common with the rest of the country, found themselves forced to rethink their attitudes toward European homelands. The "Committee on the State of the Country" reported in the Northwest Iowa Conference Journal of the M.E. Church for 1917:

In view of the appalling world's catastrophy (sic) that confronts us a solemn responsibility rests upon the Christian church. A proper attitude towards these critical conditions is very essential. It is not easy to adjust our thinking to the unhappy turn events have taken. We cannot but express our deep regret that civilization is compelled to stagger beneath this terrible scourge of war. It has come to us as a distinct disappointment. We had set up our ideals of peace, we had perfected our plans of arbitration, we had committed ourselves to the rule of reason. To see all these fine schemes fall in the crash of battle cannot but depress our spirits. Our optimism has been undermined and our faith in the peaceable progress of society is sadly shaken.[73]

The dreams of peace seemed to have been swept away in the fervor of war.

We never know how accurately the resolutions passed at conferences reflect the secret thoughts of the individual members of a church, but some of the resolutions indicated a patriotic fervor that would not have been expected during the days of peace. One supposes that there may have been differences of viewpoint in 1917, as there had been in the years between 1861 and 1865.

The same year that the conference occupying the northwest fourth of the state passed the above resolution, the Iowa Conference in the southwest quarter passed a resolution which contained the following paragraphs:

> We urge our preachers to make their pulpits echo and re-echo with a patriotism so constructive as to counteract the destructive influences of hypocritical pacifist unthinking pro-Germans, and anarchistic agitators who shall find in Methodism a foe unrelenting and irresistible. . . .

> We commend the administration of President Wilson and we are proud of that quiet but efficient course of action which has landed a great army on the western battle front six months before our foes, the Huns, dreamed it could be done. We approve America's war aims, which when achieved, will take the crown from the head of every hereditary ruler and place the sceptre of power in the hands of the people, where it of right belongs.[74]

As the war continued, any voice of opposition to war seemed to have been silenced in the church, as well as outside it. In 1918 the Northwest Iowa Conference resolved that,

> Whereas the United States of America has made common cause with England, France, Italy and other nations of the world, who prize human liberty and achievements of Christianity, and is enlisted in the prosecution of a great war for the preservation of their historical heritage and for the extension to the oppressed people of the world everywhere; and

> Whereas, the call has gone forth from our President and those charged with the prosecution of the war; therefore be it

> Resolved, First, that we offer to God Almighty, the arbiter of the destinies of nations, our sincere gratitude for the success which He has already granted to our arms, and entreat that measure of Divine favor without which the successful conclusion of the war is impossible;

> Second, that we call upon all our people to render the fullest measure of their aid in ready compliance with every request for help, issuing from our government and in faithful and persistent prayer for the blessings of God to attend our efforts.[75]

Any objectivity, which is necessary for prophetic vision, appeared to have been lost; the church members were assured that God was on the Allied side and would assure victory to Allied armies. A pacifist was considered a hypocrite and/or a traitor.

Yet, even though the conference resolutions sounded so violent, there were other more moderate voices. In the same year that the above bellicose resolutions were passed, E. J. Shook, Superintendent of the Burlington District, stated in his report to the conference, "We must and we will win the war, but we are in danger of forgetting that it will be a poor victory unless we win in the *Name of Our Prince of Righteousness and Peace.*"[76] The contents of many sermons preached and discussions held in adult Sunday School classes were not recorded.

The minutes of the 1919 annual conferences do not tell much about the war. Much is said about the influenza epidemic, and there is some mention of the returning soldiers. One slight reference to the end of the war in the report of Upper Iowa University indicates that not everyone was carried away by a militaristic fervor.

> When the armistice was signed the War Department canceled its contracts with the colleges and demobilized all Student Army Training Corps, but invited the colleges to organize Officers Reserve Training Corps in their place. The Upper Iowa University did not think it wise to continue the policy of militarizing our colleges. [77]

The Northwest Iowa Conference received a committee report recommending that the peace treaty and the covenant of the League of Nations be ratified. One paragraph of the report states, "Knowing intimately the minds of the people who live in the northwest quarter of the State of Iowa, we are convinced that it is their earnest desire as well as our own that ratification be made without delay." [78]

Little regarding was appears in the conference journals during the 1920s, but the 1928 Journal of the Iowa Conference contains a report of the Committee on the State of the Church in which one paragraph says:

> We rejoice in the success of Secretary of State Kellogg's leadership in securing adherence of so many of the powers to the instrument which is to go down in history as the "Pact of Paris." This international agreement on the outlawry of war is a most important forward step on the pathway to world peace. We now favor world disarmament as rapidly as it is practically possible, and all such laws as shall make effective every agency and instrumentality looking more and more to the establishment of concord and cooperation among the nations of the earth. [79]

By the end of the 1920s there was a pronounced "peace movement" in the Methodist Episcopal Church, slowly growing at least since World War I. It was embodied in the sermons preached and in the lesson discussions of the young people's society—the Epworth League. The Northwest Iowa Conference of 1928 approved a report on World Peace, fairly well summarizing the "peace program" which continued until Pearl Harbor:

> Resolved,
> 1. That we are fully convinced that war is a supreme enemy of mankind and that its continuance means the suicide of civilization.
> 2. That if we hold war to be inevitable, we thereby repudiate our faith in the Lord, Jesus Christ, and the triumph of His gospel.
> 3. That we hold disputes between nations like disputes between individuals may be settled by judicial process.
> 4. That, while we recognize the need of an army and navy sufficient to serve as a police power for the protection of life and property on land and sea, we do renounce "War as an instrument of national policy" and set ourselves to create the will to peace, and pledge ourselves to mold the present youth of all races into a peace-loving generation.
> 5. That we commend the action of the last General Conference of our church, when it created a Commission of Peace and World Fellowship, and pledge our full co-operation with this commission.

6. That we pledge our support to all international treaties and compacts to the World Court and to all other external means which have been or will be created for the promotion of peace and the creation of good will.[80]

In 1931 the same Committee on World Peace proposed a program of agitation and education, looking toward a federal constitutional amendment outlawing war as a means of settling international difference.[81] Little consideration was given to the chance that some other nation might declare war on this country and commence hostilities.

Much of the peace agitation in the church of the 1920s and 1930s seemed irrelevant after the Japanese attack on Pearl Harbor in December, 1941. That event could not have been foreseen ten years earlier. A determined effort was launched to make the Methodist Episcopal Church into a "peace" church, the same as the Church of the Brethren and the Mennonites.

The Northwest Iowa Conference urged in 1930 that the R.O.T.C. be made optional in our state colleges instead of being a required course. The Iowa Conference stated that

> War is the supreme enemy of mankind and its continuance is the suicide of civilization. War is not inevitable and we would utterly repudiate our professed faith in our Lord Jesus Christ, the Prince of Peace, if we held that peace is not possible. We will think of peace, teach peace, talk peace, and will peace.[82]

The movement toward peace had little to say about the issues of international injustice which lead to wars, but concentrated on political agitation which would make it difficult, if not impossible, for the United States to engage in war. It was felt that if enough of the young men of America were to become pacifists and refuse to serve in the army under any circumstances, the politicians would find it impossible to take the country into war.

The Iowa-Des Moines Conference (M.E.), which at that time included the southern half of the state, resolved in 1936:

> We believe war, in any and all forms, to be unchristian and therefore, be it resolved that we are unutterably (sic) opposed to warfare as a method of settling any dispute. We will do everything within our power to discourage and prevent our entering war and will not willingly take part in war, except when it is, beyond any question of a doubt, a matter of defending our homes and our country.[83]

A program is suggested in the same report for implementing the above resolution. It urged that (1) every pastor preach at least one peace sermon in every church, (2) there should be one peace play produced in every church, (3) at least one lesson on peace should be presented in every Missionary Society or Ladies Aid Society, and (4) a "Prince of Peace" declamatory contest should be held in each church.

In both 1937 and 1939 the Iowa Des Moines Conference passed similar resolutions, with a stronger sense of urgency. The 1939 resolution advocated that "we ask for all conscientious objectors to military service the same immunity and treatment regardless of denominational affiliation," and "that we are united in opposing conscription of men as unchristian and undemocratic in a nation that refuses to draft capital in times of war."[84]

These resolutions passed only with long and impassioned debate. They did not reflect unanimity of conviction, but only a majority arrived at by parliamentary maneuvering. The Methodist Episcopal Church passed resolutions in favor of peace, but there was no consensus of how it could best be achieved.

In 1939 the Evangelical Church, which had been following a parallel track with the M.E. Church for many years, and which became part of the United Methodist Church in 1968, expressed great concern about the condition of the world. It stated, "We are opposed to war because it is not in harmony with God's will."[85]

The 1941 Northwest Iowa Conference (Methodist) passed resolutions which indicated an understanding of the fact that the United States was on the brink of war and that the conflict might not be avoided. The resolutions urged that "the Church, of which we are a part, set its face steadfastly against any form of propaganda or teaching which would indicate the spirit of hatred or of race discrimination, or rabid nationalism."[86] The church was asked to attempt seriously to reach its full quota of chaplains for the armed forces.

The 1941 session of the Iowa Conference of the Evangelical Church resolved,

> That every effort be put forth to defend those who, for conscience sake, cannot bear arms. As a Conference and as local churches, we will respect their position and plead in their behalf, if necessary, that their rights as "conscientious objectors" be recognized.[87]

As the country was drawn closer to war there seems to have been a unanimity of feeling against war—in principle—but an uncertainty as to whether it would be possible to remain aloof. The leadership of the church supported the right of the individual to express conscientious objection and to refuse military service. As is common in American life, the tendency was to seek simplistic solutions and to see every problem in black and white. On December 7, 1941, everything was changed. That which could not happen did happen. America was attacked without warning, and other countries declared war on the United States before Congress had had time to declare war against them. The United States was at war before having declared war. Many of the resolutions seemed irrelevant.

During World War II the churches were not carried away by the passions of war as they had been in World War I and the Civil War. Too many people remembered with shame some of the excesses of passion of World War I. The Committee on Christian Social Action of the Iowa Evangelical Conference reported in part,

> Through no choice of ours we are now actively engaged in war . . . We are aware of our own shortcomings and sins, as a nation, and that there are elements in our country from which we need to be purged. We would urge then the

necessity of humbly asking God's forgiveness and pray for a cleansing that will make us strong and the champions always of the right. While some voices in our nation call for hate, we must guard ourselves, and our people lest we give place in our hearts to the spirit of hatred and vengeance.[88]

In 1944 the Iowa Des Moines Conference of The Methodist Church established a Committee on Demobilization which was to make plans and to provide leadership in the restoration of the community to a peace-time status after the war. Plans were made for reintegrating the chaplains into the life of the church after their return home. This same conference expressed in 1945 the traditional Methodist opposition to peace-time conscription.

After the war ended the Iowa Des Moines Conference set forth a program for restoring world peace:

1. We must oppose peace-time conscription and all attempts to militarize the mind of America.
2. We should work for world-wide abolition of conscription and for general disarmament.
3. We should feed the hungry, clothe the naked, and give of our abundance to rebuild the devastated world.
4. We should oppose unilateral military aid to any country in the world.
5. We should oppose any effort to bypass or weaken the United Nations, for with all of its faults, it stands as man's best prospect for a workable political forum in the realm of international relationships.[89]

The undeclared war in Korea presented churches with a particularly difficult problem of conscience. From a legalistic viewpoint, this was not a war, but a police action, and could be excused as the Indian Wars had been. Also, American troops were fighting under the United Nations flag against an overt act of aggression. It was an unpopular war, not understood by those who did not grasp the military concept of a "limited war." In 1951 the District Superintendents' report to the South Iowa Conference of The Methodist Church had the statement,

The call to the armed forces of many parsonage sons, the decimation of our older youth groups, the vacant chairs in college classrooms, the sense of frustration on the part of multitudes of young people, call us to the building of a world order based on law, righteousness, and love.[90]

At that same session of the annual conference the Committee on Social Causes was disturbed, but was not so loud in its condemnation of the war because it was a police action in the name of the United Nations. The committee reported:

We stand with open minds before the troublesome decisions of world order. We recognize that all major nations share responsibility for the present disorder, but we are not so concerned to assess the blame as to work for the remedy. We seek a program to confine the fighting, bring about an armistice, and create the conditions of world order.[91]

Those against the war found themselves opposing, not those who favored war, but those who wanted to expand the war into a "general war" against both North Korea and China. The 1952 report of the Social Causes Committee contained a paragraph stating, "Hitler once said that he had the power to compel his enemies to imitate him. Stalin must possess that power, too. Fear of Communism compels us to imitate the Communists."[92] The 1953 Journal contained the statement, "We must not stop with renouncing war, we must strive to remove the causes of war," and went on to present a lengthy list of recommendations for action to bring about a more stable world society.[93]

The war in Viet Nam came as a conflict different from previous wars. The United States government became involved so gradually that confusion existed as to when the country was at war and when it was not. The Congress never declared war, and the president did not even declare "a state of emergency." The young men who had been conscripted for training and developing an effective reserve force were used to fight an undeclared war in an area where the nation's interests were unclear.

The Division of Peace and World Order of the South Iowa Conference reported in 1965:

Daily, our country deepens its military involvement in Viet Nam. The cost of the war effort has been steadily climbing until it has reached several million dollars a day and many lives . . . We urge a negotiated settlement of this war. We presume responsible terms that faithfully meet the needs and security of both sides. We commend the President in his request for "unconditional negotiations" and trust that this will be pursued.[94]

The struggle continued while Americans questioned whether we should be fighting a war on the other side of the world. By 1967 both the South Iowa and North Iowa conferences published a report that said in part,

The pursuit of "national policies" must never allow Christians to forget that all men are precious in the sight of God and we must abhor the suffering and killing in Southeast Asia, whether the victims be Americans, Viet Cong, or civilian Vietnamese. They are our brothers who are dying.[95]

The above report discussed the war at length, examining United States foreign policy, the need for East-West cooperation, and the military draft, and concluded with a statement which expressed the fears of many people.

We deplore the increasing tendency of our government to withhold and intentionally distort information released to the public. This practice constitutes a threat to the fabric of democratic government, and leads the public to distrust its political leaders and lose faith in the moral integrity of the nation.[96]

As the war was ending and a peace conference was held in Paris, a resolution was approved stating: "We rejoice in the effort of negotiation of the Viet Nam War in current Paris talks and commend the President of the United States for taking the initiative."[97]

The story of the progress within the United Methodist Church and the bodies which joined to form the present church has been tortuous and confusing. It has been a long journey from the militancy of the young preacher in 1861 who prayed for the death of his country's enemies to the strong opposition to the undeclared war in Viet Nam which appeared more than a century later.

It is probably fair to say that the United Methodist Church and its antecedents have had a significant part in the creation of a different climate of public opinion in America. This may help to develop a more peaceful community of nations. The United Methodist Church is not ready to give up hope of improving this world.

The Board of Christian Social Concerns presented to the 1970 session of the Iowa Annual Conference an "Interpretation of the Task of the Conference Board of Christian Social Concerns" which summarized the continuing debate over the role of the church as it faces the world's problems. A part of the report stated:

> Everyone recognizes that the church needs to be a reconciler under whose ministry different viewpoints can be discussed in Christian love and under the judgment of God. In these days, objective discussion of issues about which people care strongly is difficult. If polarization of views in church and society reaches the point where discussion cannot be held the church will have suffered a serious blow to its meaning and purpose. The church needs to be a prophetic reconciler in our times.[98]

Footnotes

1. Ruth A. Gallaher, "Slavery in Iowa," *The Palimpsest* Vol. XXVIII, p. 159.
2. Ibid., p. 160.
3. *Iowa Conference Journal Methodist Episcopal Church* 1850 p. 142.
4. *Iowa Conference Journal* M.E. 1856 p. 80.
5. *Upper Iowa Conference Journal* M.E. 1856.
6. *Iowa Conference Journal* M.E. 1856 p. 111.
7. Ibid., p. 111.
8. Aaron W. Haines, *Makers of Iowa Methodism* (Cincinnati: Jennings & Pye, 1900) pp. 53-55.
9. *Iowa Conference Journal* M.E. 1856 p. 106.
10. Haines, ibid., pp. 114-115.
11. Edmund H. Waring, *History of the Iowa Annual Conference of the Methodist Episcopal Church* (n.p., n.d.) p. 197.
12. Waring, ibid., p. 166.
13. Waring, ibid., p. 169.
14. Waring, ibid., p. 242.
15. Haines, ibid., pp. 21-22.
16. Haines, ibid., pp. 120-121.
17. Haines, ibid., p. 191
18. Haines, ibid., pp. 107-108.
19. Haines, ibid., pp. 150-151.
20. Stephen Norris Fellows, *History of the Upper Iowa Conference of the Methodist Episcopal Church* (Cedar Rapids: Laurance Press Co., 1907) p. 110.
21. *The Eclectic Complete Geography* (New York: Brugg & Co., 1883) p. 15.

22. Leland L. Sage, *A History of Iowa* (Ames, Iowa: The Iowa State University Press, 1974) p. 136.
23. *Encyclopedia of World Methodism*, Vol. I, pp. 882-883.
24. *Encyclopedia of World Methodism*, Vol. II, p. 2058.
25. *Iowa Conference Minutes*, Evangelical Association 1861-62, p. 47.
26. Ibid., p. 54.
27. Ibid., p. 99.
28. Ibid., p. 122.
29. R. E. Harvey, "Hail and Farewell! The Methodist Protestant Church in Iowa," *Annals of Iowa* Vol. 24, July 1942, p. 78.
30. *Yearbook of the Iowa Annual Conference of the Methodist Episcopal Church* 1844, p. 11.
31. Landon Taylor, *The Battlefield Reviewed* (n.p., n.d.) p. 179.
32. Sage, ibid., p. 173.
33. *Iowa Conference Minutes* M.E. 1865 p. 21.
34. *Iowa Conference Minutes* M.E. 1866 pp. 24-25.
35. Genesis 9:20-27.
36. Ruth A. Gallaher, "Religion and Morality," *The Palimpsest,* 8:28, January 1927.
37. Ibid.
38. Cyrenus Cole, *Iowa Through the Years* (Iowa City: The State Historical Society of Iowa, 1940) pp. 269-270.
39. *Upper Iowa Conference Minutes* M.E. 1860, p. 25.
40. *Iowa Conference Minutes* M.E. 1860, p. 27.
41. John F. Schmidt, *A Historical Profile of Sioux City* (Sioux City: Sioux City Stationery Co., 1969) p. 123.
42. Ibid., p. 123.
43. Ibid., p. 124.
44. Ibid., p. 124.
45. Ibid., p. 124.
46. Ibid., p. 125.
47. Ibid., p. 125.
48. *History of Woodbury and Plymouth Counties* (Chicago: Warner & Co., 1890) pp. 255-263.
49. Cole, ibid., pp. 371-372.
50. *Northwest Iowa Conference Journal* M.E. 1886, p. 28.
51. Bennett Mitchell, *History of the Northwest Iowa Conference 1872-1903* (Sioux City: Perkins Brothers Company, 1904) pp. 147-148.
52. Ibid., p. 220.
53. Cole, ibid., pp. 405-406.
54. *Northwest Iowa Conference Journal* M.E. 1895, p. 33.
55. Haines, ibid., pp. 82-83.
56. *Northwest Iowa Conference Journal* M.E., 1898, p. 34.
57. Ibid., pp. 34-35.
58. *Upper Iowa Conference Journal* M.E. 1906, p. 303.
59. *Northwest Iowa Conference Journal* M.E. 1921, p. 191.
60. *Upper Iowa Conference Journal* M.E. 1921, p. 242.
61. *Northwest Iowa Conference Journal* M.E. 1933, p. 155.
62. *Upper Iowa Conference Journal* Methodist 1948, p. 127.
63. *Encyclopaedia Brittanica,* Vol. 17 (Chicago: Encyclopaedia Brittanica Inc., 1964) p. 412.
64. Isaiah 2:4.
65. Mitchell, ibid., p. 53.
66. Fellows, ibid., p. 82.
67. Ibid., p. 194
68. Ibid., p. 83.
69. *Northwest Iowa Conference Journal* M.E. 1889, p. 32.
70. *1912 Methodist Episcopal Church Discipline,* par. 564.
71. *Iowa Conference Journal* M.E. 1914, p. 334.

72. *Iowa Conference Journal* M.E. 1915, pp. 471-472.
73. *Northwest Iowa Conference Journal* M.E. 1917, p. 261.
74. *Iowa Conference Journal* M.E. 1917, pp. 214-215.
75. *Northwest Iowa Conference Journal* M.E. 1918, pp. 414-415.
76. *Iowa Conference Journal* M.E. 1918, p. 339.
77. *Upper Iowa Conference Journal* M.E. 1919, p. 582.
78. *Northwest Iowa Conference Journal* M.E. 1919, p. 572.
79. *Iowa Conference Journal* M.E. 1928, p. 63.
80. *Northwest Iowa Conference Journal* M.E. 1928, pp. 52-53.
81. *Northwest Iowa Conference Journal* M.E. 1931, p. 487.
82. *Iowa Conference Journal* M.E. 1930, p. 352.
83. *Iowa Des Moines Conference Journal* M.E. 1936, p. 42.
84. *Iowa Des Moines Conference Journal* The Methodist Church, 1939, p. 649.
85. *Iowa Conference Journal,* The Evangelical Church, 1939, p. 60.
86. *Northwest Iowa Conference Journal,* The Methodist Church, 1941, p. 246.
87. *Iowa Conference Journal,* The Evangelical Church, 1941, p. 251.
88. *Iowa Conference Journal,* The Evangelical Church, 1942, p. 52.
89. *Iowa Des Moines Conference Journal,* The Methodist Church, 1947, p. 101.
90. *Iowa Des Moines Conference Journal,* The Methodist Church, 1951, p. 59.
91. Ibid., p. 100.
92. *Iowa Des Moines Conference Journal,* The Methodist Church, 1952, p. 103.
93. *Iowa Des Moines Conference Journal,* The Methodist Church, 1952, p. 108.
94. *South Iowa Conference Journal,* Methodist, 1965, pp. 168-169.
95. *South Iowa Conference Journal,* Methodist, 1967, p. 222.
96. Ibid., p. 223 and *North Iowa Conference Journal,* Methodist, 1967, p. 221.
97. *South Iowa Conference Journal,* Methodist, 1968, p. 241.
98. *Iowa Conference Journal,* United Methodist Church, 1970, p. 298.

13

Hospitals and Homes

Hospitals

Hospitals have traditionally made some provision for those who could not pay—one reason why churches have become involved with hospitals. This chapter concerns the hospitals in Iowa which have been built and administered by the Methodist Episcopal Church and its successors. The largest and best known is Iowa Methodist Medical Center in Des Moines.

Iowa Methodist Medical Center

IOWA METHODIST MEDICAL CENTER

In 1899 Theodore Gatchel, a Methodist layman serving as chairman of the conference committee on Deaconess Work, called the attention of the Des Moines Annual Conference to the need for a hospital in Central Iowa. He took the initiative in May of that year for calling together a group of Des Moines ministers and laymen, to discuss the need and to plan toward the creation of a hospital.

The hospital association was incorporated May 16, 1899, and the first annual meeting was held October 16, 1900. Iowa Methodist Hospital opened January 16, 1901, in a red brick building originally constructed as a private residence and later used to house Callanan College. James C. Callanan arranged for the Hospital Association to take over the property for $30,000, far less than its $65,000 value. Callanan also made an annuity agreement to return the $30,000 at his death.[1]

A hospital was something of a novelty around 1900, as most middle-class families cared for the sick at home. One room of the house was temporarily converted into a sickroom, and the doctor made house calls. Care was provided by members of the family, or by a "practical nurse." A hospital was regarded as a refuge for the poor, or a place to die. It took time for attitudes to change and for people to look to the hospital for care.

Iowa Methodist Hospital had thirty beds, and received six patients the first day. During the first three and one-half months it cared for fifty-four patients, one-third of whom were "free patients."[2]

The hospital had a school of nursing almost from the start. The first class graduated January 20, 1903. Nurses' training was not easy in the early days. Each nurse, on the average, cared for five patients in private rooms and seven in a ward. The janitor cleaned the corridor only, and nurses were expected to do the cleaning of patients' rooms and utensils. Not until 1909 were maids employed for dishwashing and cleaning.[3]

In a history of the hospital's first fifty years, a turbulent beginning period was noted. Six changes of superintendent took place during the first four years of operation. Miss Esther Pierson became superintendent in 1905, and held that position until 1912. Miss Pierson left to marry a Des Moines physician, a fact reflecting no disharmony in the administration of the hospital.[4]

In May, 1901, the first recorded reckoning showed the following expenses:

Pay for help	$250.	
Milk	32.	
Bread	15.	
Laundry	38.	
Drugs—Gibson	116.	
Meat	47.	
Grocery Bill	150.	
Gas, Elec. Lights, Fuel, Water, Etc.	100.	$748.[5]

A later entry showed that general sundry expenses had been omitted. Adding thirty dollars for sundries made the total $778. Of the fifty-four patients in the hospital in May, thirty-six paying patients provided income of $600.50. Eighteen patients were cared for without charge, accounting for a loss of $178.[6]

One expedient which saved expense was the selection of Dr. Raymond Cluen, a graduate of Drake Medical College, as the first intern at Iowa Methodist Hospital. He was a good pharmacist, and was asked to take charge of the medicines. He saved the hospital between $100 and $150 a month.[7] That seems small now, but it was important in 1901.

A registered pharmacist, Miss Alice Inhofe, was employed in 1910 to take charge of the "drug room" and to teach the nurses chemistry. She was a graduate of Highland Park Pharmacy School in Des Moines.[8]

More space was needed for expansion of the hospital in a short time. A new West Wing was built in 1910, but the space gained was soon found to be insufficient. A large East Wing was built in 1912 with $125,000 borrowed from the Massachusetts Life Insurance Company. Increasing costs made the debt a genuine burden, not paid in full until June 10, 1944. [9]

One wonders how Des Moines people would have managed without the benevolent institution. Tax-supported hospital facilities were inadequate for the number of indigent patients in the first two decades of this century. The modern Broadlawns General Hospital opened with a capacity of 150 beds in 1943.

Iowa Methodist Hospital used horse-drawn ambulances until the first motor-driven ambulance was bought in 1916. Such an ambulance was referred to as an "invalid's car." The hospital had a contract with the Gray Livery to care for the hospital-owned horses and vehicles. Of the $3.00 the patient was charged for use of the conveyance, the hospital received half and the livery barn half, with the hospital guaranteeing payment. [10]

Financial needs forced the hospital to raise its rates in 1911. The records do not show whether changes were made during the first decade, but the new rates called for $8.50 per week for a ward bed. The operating room fee was raised from $3.00 to $5.00 for minor surgery. No changes in charges for private rooms were mentioned. [11]

The service provided by a hospital calls for wholehearted support from the people of the church and the community served by the institution. From the beginning Methodist people responded when asked to contribute to the hospital. Appeals were made through "Financial secretaries," "field agents," and "corresponding secretaries" at various times. For many years the financial appeal was one of the duties of the chaplain. The hospital boards recommended that ministers be appointed to this special task by their annual conferences. [12] Beginning in 1901 the churches were asked to observe the first Sunday in February as Hospital Sunday.

Free care was offered to Methodist ministers and their wives from the time the hospital opened. In 1919 free care was extended to the ministers and wives of Swedish and German Methodist conferences in the state. [13] It is interesting to note how much free service was actually given to the needy. In 1909, 11% of the hospital's patients were cared for without charge; in 1911 the number had increased to 21% of 3,175 patients, and in 1913, 20% of 3,300 patients were free. [14]

The hospital bought its first x-ray machine for $1,517.07 in 1911, and employed Dr. Thomas Burcham as radiologist. In the second decade a pediatric department was also developed. A new maternity department opened March 8, 1922, stimulating a big increase in the number of hospital deliveries.

During the early years of the twentieth century Des Moines had to contend with a number of epidemics. A typhoid epidemic was caused by polluted water supplies in 1910-1911. In 1913 a smallpox epidemic developed. Vaccination was new then; nurses and interns had not been previously vaccinated. Despite the fact that they were all promptly vaccinated to prevent the spread of the epidemic, one of the interns was stricken with the disease.

Diphtheria and influenza epidemics raged in 1918 and 1919. The Des Moines Hospitals had to share some nurses with Camp Dodge, the army post north of the city.[15] After these epidemics, plans were made for care of other than surgical cases. The entire third floor was set aside for medical patients.[16]

In 1919 Iowa Methodist Hospital was listed as fifth in size among the fifty-four hospitals supported by the Methodist Episcopal Church in the United States. Two decades after the hospital was organized it was approved by the American College of Surgeons.[17]

Two men were the hospital's first chaplains—a retired minister, and a bricklayer who was a lay preacher. The Rev. Asbel Thornbrue and John Bailey were elected by the board of directors in July, 1911, to serve six months without pay.[18] In March, 1912, the Rev. Thornbrue was given a monthly stipend of $15. The Rev. Dilman Smith was elected chaplain in October, 1918, at an annual salary of $2,300. He held this position until his retirement in 1939.

Adequate support for the hospital was not always forthcoming from church people in the 1920s, when some pledged more than they were able to pay. The churches were also supporting other home and foreign mission projects, and five colleges in Iowa which had chronologically prior claim over the hospital.

Mere survival was a triumph in the period of the 1930s, but there was scientific progress, and on the financial front, the development of group hospitalization insurance. Depression years saw the hospital unable to continue its free service program.

In 1936, a report on free services covering a ten-year period showed that the hospital had given care totaling $138,658; yet gifts for free service, including those to the endowment fund, all food gifts, American White Cross offerings, and bequests, totaled only $125,168.[19]

Chaplain Dilman Smith reported that church people had given 19,000 quarts of fruits, jams, and jellies valued at $6,416.44 and eggs, linens, and other supplies valued at $1,679.28.[20]

A succession of minor administrative changes in the 1930s resulted from increased experience. Composition of the board evolved until it finally was made up of one-third Methodist ministers, one-third Methodist laymen, and one-third non-Methodist laymen.

Viewed superficially, Iowa Methodist's fourth decade (1931-1941) might appear to be a period without great accomplishment. However, there was a steady increase in scientific knowledge which improved the service offered by the hospital.[21] A contract with Iowa Hospital Service Incorporated (Blue Cross) was signed in 1939, making it easier for families to meet the costs of hospital care, and for the hospital to stay "in the black." In 1941 the total indebtedness on the hospital was reduced to $191,000.

A greatly reduced staff was left to maintain the hospital during World War II. For example, in 1941 Iowa Methodist had seventy graduate nurses, but only twenty-three in 1943. Eighty-five of the younger doctors on the staff entered the military services.

The Raymond Blank Memorial Hospital for Children was dedicated in 1944 as a memorial to Raymond Blank, son of the donors, Mr. and Mrs. A. H. Blank. During serious poliomyelitis epidemics in 1948 and 1950 the Blank Hospital part of Iowa Methodist was fully used. In 1948 a coordinated program for the School of Nursing was begun with Drake University. Work begun on the South Wing in 1949 was completed in 1950, and the wing was dedicated debt-free October 28, 1951. The new addition made fifty more beds available for general care, and twenty-eight for psychiatric care. A course in religious chaplaincy with Drake University was established in 1953. The new Younkers Center for Geriatric Rehabilitation received its first patients in 1958.

The 1960s and 1970s were a period of further progress in medical science and improvement in facilities provided by the hospital. The name was changed to Iowa Methodist Medical Center in 1975.

The addition of sixty-four positions brought the hospital staff numbers to over 400, representing every specialty of medical practice, in 1983. In that year over 21,000 patients were admitted for care at Iowa Methodist Medical Center, and more than 45,000 received care in the ambulatory department.

St. Luke's Methodist Hospital, Cedar Rapids

ST. LUKE'S METHODIST HOSPITAL—CEDAR RAPIDS

A hospital comes into being when someone sees the need and does something about it. The story is told that in 1883 a hobo fell from a train in Cedar Rapids and was seriously injured. He was carried to the city fire station barn, and the Rev. Samuel Ringold of Grace Episcopal Church was called to comfort the dying man. The minister was concerned about the lack of a hospital in the city. He preached a sermon on the subject in his church. Two parishioners—Sampson Bever and George Greene—responded by contributing land. This sparked a church-sponsored, fund-raising drive, with Methodists among the contributors. A ten-bed hospital was opened in Cedar Rapids in 1884 at a cost of $11,000.

The School of Nursing was founded in 1886 with Salome Beardsley as superintendent of the hospital and director of nursing. A three-story addition was built in 1902 in memory of Henrietta Dows. There were no elevators in the hospital. Patients either walked, or were carried, to the operating room.

Grace Episcopal Church deeded the hospital to the Upper Iowa Conference of the Methodist Episcopal Church in 1922, for one dollar and a promise to build another addition, and to contribute money annually to help maintain the hospital. Samuel Armstrong, a member of St. Paul's M.E. Church, donated $25,000. In 1926 a new 100-bed addition was opened, bringing the capacity to 165 beds.

During the farm depression of the 1920s St. Luke's hospital debt reached $370,000. Facing the financial critsis, employees of the hospital accepted a ten percent salary cut and gave up one-half of their annual vacation pay. The room rate at that time was $2.00 a day, $3.50 in maternity, with a 50¢ discount for cash payment at discharge. Very few people had hospital insurance.

A hospital auxiliary was organized in 1949, to provide fund-raising and volunteer service support. In 1951 what is now the center section of the hospital was added, increasing total capacity to 315 beds. One million dollars of the cost came from community gifts. The next year a psychiatric unit was opened on the second floor—the first such unit in Iowa.

The community responded again in 1960 to a fund-raising campaign, and the East Wing addition brought the hospital capacity to 400 beds, including a seventeen-bed Intensive Care Unit. A gift from the late Marshall Hardesty, former president of the hospital's board of directors, provided an Intermediate Cardiac Care Unit for ambulatory heart patients in 1966. A new West Wing, added in 1968, brought St. Luke's capacity to 620 beds and sixty bassinets. That year also saw the Skilled Nursing Facility opened to care for senior citizens.

The auxiliary raised funds in 1969 for a new Health Science Library, and a full-time physician staff manned the Emergency Department. In 1971 a joint Family Practice Residency program for smaller eastern Iowa communities was established in cooperation with the University of Iowa's College of Medicine.

A new diagnostic building was completed in 1974 to house a modern Emergency Department as well as departments of radiology and laboratory. The next year the hospital assumed the operation of a Family Health Center, providing clinical medical care to 10,600 low-income patients. A Dental Health Center also opened in 1975 to serve the needs of children from low-income families of the area.

The history of St. Luke's Hospital in Cedar Rapids is a story of development during a period when medical science was making spectacular progress. It has been challenging, as the community has had to feel its way, learning to identify and anticipate needs. At times the financial problems have inspired individual supporters to make genuine sacrifices.

Since 1922 the hospital has worked, first in the name of the Methodist Episcopal Church, next The Methodist Church, and now the United Methodist Church. But support has come from people of the Cedar Rapids community belonging to many different churches and synagogues or to no church. A church provides leadership, that the community may work together.

ST. LUKE'S REGIONAL MEDICAL CENTER—SIOUX CITY

Sioux City's first hospital was started at 17th and Pierce Streets in 1885 by Dr. William Jepson and the Women's Christian Association. It was known as the Samaritan Home. In 1908 Jepson founded another hospital at 14th and Jones Streets under the name of St. John's Hospital. At that time Sioux City had three Protestant-sponsored hospitals: Samaritan, St. John's, and the German Lutheran General Hospital.

In 1919 Dr. Jepson offered St. John's Hospital to the Northwest Iowa Conference of the Methodist Episcopal Church, on the condition that the conference establish an outstanding hospital in Sioux City. The doctor deeded the hospital building and a 280-acre farm north of the city in 1920, to provide an endowment.

The building was renovated and opened as a general hospital on October 20, 1920. The Conference Committee on Hospitals and Homes reported in 1921 that "Only a year has been necessary to prove the wisdom of the action of the Northwest Iowa Conference in opening the new Methodist Hospital in Sioux City."[22]

Samaritan Hospital and Methodist Hospital (formerly St. John's) merged as "Methodist Hospital" in 1922, and the Samaritan Hospital building was used until a new and larger building could be erected. A new Methodist Hospital building was constructed at 29th and Douglas Streets in 1925. This building is now (1984) used as St. Luke's educational building.

The Lutheran General Hospital had been organized in 1901-1902 by a number of individuals and congregations of Missouri Synod Lutheran

St. Luke's Regional Medical Center Sioux City

churches in Sioux City. They formed a Hospital Association which bought a frame building at 27th Street between Pierce and Nebraska Streets. A two-story brick addition was completed in 1902. A three-story addition was constructed in 1920. The $1.25 million addition of 1951-1953 provided fifty-five new beds.

Members of the American Lutheran Church and the Lutheran Church in America joined with the Missouri Synod members to organize the Lutheran Hospital Association in 1958, which then became the governing body of the hospital. Extensive remodeling of the hospital was undertaken in 1964.

The Lutheran Hospital (153 beds) merged with the Methodist Hospital (164 beds) to form St. Luke's Medical Center in 1966. St. Luke's Regional Medical Center is now sponsored jointly by the Lutheran Hospital Association of Sioux City and the Iowa Conference of the United Methodist Church. (In 1981 the hospital received the "Regional Hospital" designation.)

The two schools of nursing were merged in 1967. Ground was broken for a new Central Building in July, 1969, and in 1972 that building was opened. The Central Building was completed by the addition of the third and fourth floors in 1975, and in 1979 a replacement and expansion program was completed with the opening of the five-floor patient tower.

An $8.2 million building program to construct two more floors housing sixty-one new beds—including fifteen newly licensed beds—is expected to be completed by March, 1985. The new fifth floor will house the Mental Health Unit, replacing the MH Unit in the older East Building, and for the first time bringing MH patients into the mainstream of patient care. The new sixth floor will house the expanded Critical Care areas, including the enlarged Burn Unit, and will have larger rooms to allow greater use of state-of-the-art life-saving technology.

The Methodists and Lutherans of Northwestern Iowa have good reason to be proud of their hospital. As with all hospitals, many people of the area have made significant contributions, financial and otherwise, to the development and support of the hospital.

In addition to the three United Methodist hospitals which now serve the state of Iowa, others have played a part in providing medical care. These have been community enterprises to a large degree, supported financially by persons living in the communities where they are situated, but administered for a time with the help of the Methodist Episcopal Church.

GRAHAM HOSPITAL—KEOKUK

It is difficult to trace the whole story of the W. C. Graham Protestant Hospital in Keokuk. Inasmuch as its support came from the whole community, its connection with any one church was not stressed. A historical sketch of the Keokuk hospitals appearing in the Keokuk "Shoppers' Free Press" in 1974 makes no mention of any Methodist connection except that the Rev. H. L. Lindquist, pastor of Keokuk's Swedish Methodist Episcopal Church, was the first president of the board of trustees.[23]

Graham Hospital, Keokuk

One Hundred Years of Iowa Medicine, published to commemorate the centenary of the Iowa State Medical Society, states that in 1887 Mrs. W. C. Graham donated a building at the corner of 16th and Fulton Streets for use as a hospital. Mercy Hospital operated as a facility of the College of Physicians and Surgeons until the merger of the two medical schools in Keokuk in the year 1899.

The W. C. Graham Protestant Hospital Company was formed in 1890, and Mrs. Helen Comstock, heir of Mrs. Graham, deeded the property to the new corporation. Dr. F. B. Dorsey, secretary of the board, prevailed upon the Missionary Society of the First Methodist Episcopal Church to sponsor the hospital.[24] The presiding elder's report for the Iowa Conference Minutes of 1901 states that the hospital was under the management of the Deaconess Bureau of the Woman's Home Missionary Society, and open to receive patients.[25] In 1905 the hospital was deeded in fee simple to the Woman's Home Missionary Society.[26]

For a number of years the hospital continued operating efficiently with a Methodist Deaconess, Miss Mary Jackson, serving as superintendent. Each year a report was made to the Iowa Annual Conference by the Deaconess Board, and the hospital was often mentioned favorably in the presiding elder's report. Almost every year there was a full page advertisement in the conference journal which stated that the hospital was owned and managed by the W.H.M.S. of the M.E. Church. The advertisement appeared for the last time in 1927.

In 1928 the Rev. C. D. Loose, a pastor of the Keokuk Church, presented a proposition from the trustees of the Graham Hospital to offer the hospital to the conference. W. B. Keesey, Ottumwa District Superintendent, moved that the proposition be laid on the table. Thomas Osborn, Burlington District Superintendent, moved that a preacher be named to convey the conference's appreciation for the offer.[27]

Nothing more appears in the Conference Minutes regarding the hospital. It continued to serve the Keokuk community until it was merged into the Keokuk Area Hospital in 1979. A local history published in 1979 made no mention of the long-standing Methodist connection.

WEBSTER CITY HOSPITAL

A hospital which did not turn out well for the Methodists was Mercy Hospital of Webster City. The hospital was erected in 1902 by local people, and then offered to the Northwest Iowa Conference of the Methodist Episcopal Church, according to Bennett Mitchell in his *History of the Northwest Iowa Conference*. Discussing the 1902 session of the annual conference, he said:

Webster City Hospital

At this session a most generous proposition came to us from Mr. Jacob M. Funk of Webster City, in which he offered to give to the Conference an admirably planned hospital, then in course of erection at Webster City, together with the land upon which it was being erected—two acres, more or less—on condition that the Conference would agree to maintain the same for hospital use. We thanked Mr. Funk for his liberal offer and appointed a commission with power to act. The commission met soon after the adjournment of Conference and inquired carefully into Mr. Funk's offer and examined the grounds and the building, after which they accepted the gift on behalf of the Conference and devised and put in operation plans for conducting and maintaining the hospital.[28]

The hospital commission which was appointed in 1902 reported to the Conference the following year that they had examined and accepted Funk's offer. They had incorporated themselves under the name "Mercy Hospital of the Northwest Iowa Conference, Methodist Episcopal Church," and had elected a board of trustees.

Of the eighteen trustees, six were to hold office for one year, six for two years, and six for three years. Mr. J. M. Funk, L. A. McMurray, and Cyrus Smith were made life members, with power to name their successors, who in turn would name their successors, so on in perpetuity. Dr. Mitchell did not give a reason in his history for this arrangement, but it is safe to assume that this was to assure that the Webster City community would always be represented on the Board of Trustees.

Mitchell's book was published in 1903, so it does not tell the rest of the story. Something went wrong before long. The plans were not carried through as had been hoped. The 1903 Conference Journal contains an optimistic report which would indicate that the hospital was in operation. Some thought that Funk had intended to provide funds for the operation of the hospital, but he died suddenly in his room at Hotel Wilson, in Webster City. His will made no mention of the hospital. The institution was soon in serious financial difficulty.

In 1904 it seemed best to dissolve the ties between the conference and the hospital. A brief report in the Minutes does not appear to tell the whole story.

> In the judgment of this Commission it would be unwise to continue to operate the Hospital without having available at this time a suitable man for Superintendent.
>
> After thoroughly canvassing the matter your commission has been unable to find such a man who will consent to assume the responsibilities of the position. Therefore, the Commission recommends that the Board of Directors of the Hospital be instructed to dissolve the connection of the Northwest Iowa Conference with Mercy Hospital, according to the conditions or provisions of the deed from Jacob M. Funk to the Conference.[29]

The 1906 Minutes write perhaps the final word regarding the connection between the M.E. Church and her Webster City hospital. The report of the Hospital Committee states in part, "We recommend that inasmuch as the money amounting to $141.45 left in the hands of treasurer of Mercy Hospital of Webster City, was raised for hospital purposes, the said money be devoted to the work of the Iowa Methodist Hospital in Des Moines."[30]

In October, 1905, the Sisters of Mercy of the Dubuque Diocese of the Catholic Church agreed to operate the hospital. They continued until the Hamilton County Hospital was built and the old building abandoned in 1930. During the worst days of the Great Depression, a number of families moved into the building and lived there for several years, paying no rent. The old hospital building was finally torn down, with the demolition firm taking all the bricks and other usable materials.

Homes

One responsibility of every society is the proper care of old people who can no longer adequately care for themselves. Most would rather live in their own homes all of their lives, but that is not always possible. Living alone becomes increasingly difficult, and most modern homes are too small to accommodate three generations. Lawn mowing and snow removal become arduous chores. Some older persons living alone neglect their diet and as a result suffer from malnutrition. One answer for their need is the development of "retirement homes" by various churches, lodges, and private enterprise. The United Methodist Church has seven of these homes situated in different parts of Iowa, and each has its own history.

The Methodist Episcopal Church established a pension system in 1908, based upon years of ministerial service of all retired conference members, their widows and orphans. Near that time the Francis Home for retired ministers and widows of preachers was established in Indianola—a prologue to the development of the United Methodist retirement homes in Iowa. By 1912 the Francis Home was reported in prosperous condition with twenty-four guests and room for more.

However, the accidental death of the home's chief promoter, Dr. Fletcher Brown, had an adverse effect, and in 1914 the conference ordered the institution sold. The earnings from the proceeds were to be used for the relief of especially destitute cases among the conference claimants. The financial collapse of 1930 left much of the money in the frozen assets of closed banks, where it suffered shrinkage. The residue recovered was later applied to the proposed "Old People's Home" in Des Moines (Wesley Acres).

**Francis Home,
Indianola**

South Iowa Methodist Homes, Inc.

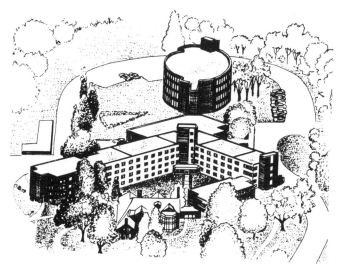

**Wesley Acres,
Des Moines**

WESLEY ACRES

Wesley Acres is the oldest of the three South Iowa Methodist Homes. The Conference Board of Hospitals and Homes recommended to the 1946 session of the South Iowa Conference that a corporation be formed to receive and invest funds for the establishment and maintenance of a "Home for the Aged" at such time and place as should later be decided by the conference. At a called session of the Annual Conference on January 7, 1947, a resolution was approved for the purchase of the "Chamberlain Estate," 3520 Grand Avenue in Des Moines for the future location of such a home.[31]

Prior to this time, the Area Headquarters had been located in the Old Colony Building at Tenth and Grand in Des Moines. The Iowa Farm Bureau bought the Old Colony Building, and the church headquarters had to be moved. For several years the Iowa Area Headquarters occupied a part of the space in the old Chamberlain mansion, which became the nucleus of Wesley Acres.

Wesley Acres opened officially in August, 1949, with five "qualified" members living in the old mansion. Six years later a sixteen-room, two-story residential building was completed, connecting to the mansion on the west. The Rev. George Dimmitt became Superintendent of Wesley Acres in 1956. He became manager of South Iowa Methodist Homes, Inc. in 1966, and continued until his retirement in 1975.

The Home for the Aged at 29th and University began its merger agreement with Wesley Acres in 1957. Three years later the Home for the Aged residents were among the first to move into a newly completed 100-room major addition to Wesley Acres. This addition included a dining room, main lounge, and 28-bed health center. That same year (1969) plans were begun for Heritage House in Atlantic, which was to become another of the South Iowa Methodist Homes, Inc. Halcyon House, a retirement home in Washington, also merged with Wesley Acres for administration. The name Wesley Acres, Inc. was changed to "South Iowa Methodist Homes, Inc." in May, 1963. This new organization included the three homes.

The Iowa Home for the Sightless, 1420 Penn Avenue, Des Moines, was merged into South Iowa Methodist Homes, Inc. in February, 1968, and nine sightless residents of the home moved into specially planned residential units at Wesley Acres. A fund for care of sightless residents was established.

Church-related retirement and nursing homes had for some time confronted a challenge to their property tax exempt status as charitable institutions. In 1970 the Iowa Supreme Court upheld their tax-exempt status as long as they provided an acceptable amount of free service. Wesley Acres met the test, and planning for growth could continue.

Sargent Hall, a major four-story addition to Wesley Acres was constructed in 1971. The E. I. Sargent Foundation was a major donor to this building, made up of fourteen one-bedroom efficiency apartments, with four guest rooms and one guest apartment.

Work commenced in 1973 on a new 54-bed Health Center which also included a Helpful Living area (twelve rooms), enlarged dining room and recreation room areas. This addition was completed in 1975.

HALCYON HOUSE

Halcyon House, a retirement home located in Washington, was built in 1959, and operated by the Home Association of Washington until it merged its administration with Wesley Acres in October, 1960. At that time it housed approximately twenty-five residents. A Task Force Study Committee was appointed in 1967; expansion plans were started in 1972. Phase I of the plans was completed in 1974 at a cost of $440,000, including twenty-eight apartments (ten studio, eight one-bedroom, and ten two-bedroom).

In 1977 Phase II was completed at a cost of about $1,113,000 with twenty-

**Halcyon House,
Washington**

two apartments. Included was a 22-bed Health Center, major office remodeling, and garage construction. Phase III was begun in 1978, including twenty-six large and four studio apartments, plus garage and a recreation center, named for Edmund D. Morrison, Jr., chairman of the management committee. The original building was renovated in 1982 at a cost of $460,000.

HERITAGE HOUSE

Some residents of Atlantic became concerned that they should have a retirement home in southwest Iowa. In 1962 they raised about $90,000, and Wesley Acres, Inc. provided interim funds during construction until a loan could be negotiated with Banco Mortgage Company. Heritage House of Atlantic was completed in November, 1963, at a cost of $1,500,000, and the first residents moved in. In 1979 ground was broken for Brookridge Apartments, Atlantic, containing nineteen two-bedroom and twelve one-bedroom apartments, and a thirty-one car garage.

By October, 1983, when Heritage House celebrated its twentieth anniversary, it had served 437 residents. At that time a study of a complete renovation of the Health Center was begun.

Heritage House,
Atlantic

Friendship Haven

During the 1940s while the attention of the world was centered on World War II, there were people in northwest Iowa who were dreaming of a home for older citizens. Clarence Wesley Tompkins, a Methodist minister, envisioned a home where retired persons might find comfort, Christian companionship, peace of mind, and security—a true home, which would be a satisfying replacement for the family home they had when younger.

The Northwest Iowa Conference ordered a study of the need and possibilities in 1945. In 1946 the conference accepted "Friendship Haven, Incorporated" with a Board of Trustees. Several sites were considered for the home. Among them were Storm Lake, Sac City, Eagle Grove, and Fort Dodge. After study, Fort Dodge was the unanimous choice of the board. The site was dedicated in 1947 while the annual conference was meeting in Fort Dodge. Clarence W. Tompkins was chosen as the first Executive Director. He "wore

Friendship Haven,
Ft. Dodge

the hats of promoter—expediter—builder—manager" of Friendship Haven until his retirement in 1972.

In the *Born a Promoter* booklet Dr. Tompkins related an experience which led to Friendship Haven's eventual national fame for its activities. "For three years I had feverishly flitted about the conference telling what sweet saintly souls would be living in Friendship Haven. The bubble burst. It seemed we had the world's worst gripers. . . . My dream castle came tumbling down." Dr. Gower put Tompkins in the hospital for a few days, during which he thought about the gripes. He realized that these were all the residents had to talk about. He resolved to encourage "every hobby under the sun," and some 110 activities resulted. Mrs. Florence Hilyard got fifty people involved with pottery making.

> Mr. Allen, the worst griper of them all, made a prize-winning sugaring kettle like they had in Vermont when he was a boy. Everyone fell over themselves praising him and he was converted and became the happiest man in the house. He confided to me that his parents had died when he was seven. He had knocked around for 70 years and this was the first time anyone had ever appreciated him.[32]

With gifts of ground from the Fort Dodge Betterment Foundation and some $125,000 from other donors, the Friendship Haven project was off to a flying start. Ground was broken in 1949 for the East Building, which was to be a three-story, four-winged structure. The first two wings were completed by 1950 and were dedicated at the session of the North Iowa Annual Conference by Bishop Charles W. Brashares and Dr. Karl P. Meister, head of the Board of Hospitals and Homes of The Methodist Church. The third wing was completed in 1952; the fourth, in 1953.

Soon there was "no more room in the inn" and it was decided that a second building should be constructed—this time with four stories and larger dimensions. The West Friendship Haven building was begun in 1955 and finished, one wing at a time, by 1960.

The infirmary sections of the two buildings served well, but the board and staff soon learned from experience that more capacity for care was needed. A six-story, 190-bed facility was under construction in 1964, and the completed building—the Tompkins Memorial Health Center—was consecrated in 1966. In 1975 eighteen more beds were added, making it a 208-bed facility. Areas for activities and physical therapy were also included in the 1975 addition.

The Chapel on the Hill was a gift from Stanford Griffith, Friendship Haven Architect, in memory of Mr. and Mrs. Frank Griffith and Mr. and Mrs. Friesth. In 1977 construction began for a garden-apartment area, with eleven one, two, and three-bedroom apartments. Each year since there have been additions and improvements. During 1983 seven new cottages were added to the complex for independent living, which brought the total to thirty-five, and at the end of that year, seven more were on the drawing board. At the end of 1983 Friendship Haven was serving over 550 residents at four levels of care.

Methodist Manor

The Iowa United Methodist retirement home on the north shore of Storm Lake was founded on December 18, 1959, by the Storm Lake Methodist Church. The local church entered into an agreement with Robert Swallum, executor for the estate of Dr. J. A. Swallum, to operate the local facility known as the Swallum Hospital and Gran Psychiatric Unit. At first Methodist Manor was under the direction and management of Friendship Haven, Methodist home at Fort Dodge. Operations began January, 1960, with a total of seventeen residents and one level of care. The original board of trustees consisted of the executive committee of Friendship Haven and several local persons.

In 1961 Methodist Manor expanded into two separate areas of service, residential and nursing care. By the end of that year it had a total of sixty

**Methodist Manor,
Storm Lake**

residents and patients. It was foreseen that the building would have to be remodeled to meet all of the needs. A utilization study of the facilities was made by the Griffith Company of Fort Dodge, who reported to the trustees that the facilities were not adequate and could not be remodeled to meet the needs of the people in the area.

Following the study, the relationship with Friendship Haven was severed, and a totally different board of trustees for the separate corporation of Methodist Manor was selected. An executive director, Roy Parker, was named, and served for six and one-half years. After his resignation, Blaine Donaldson was hired as administrator.

The nursing area was expanded in 1967 by the addition of two wings, which provided fifty more beds. A third wing was added in 1972, which brought the total beds in the Health Center to seventy-three. At that time the Health Center was divided into three separate areas of care, to provide for the needs of persons with different physical and mental ability. Each area had its own dining and all-purpose room. In 1973 the former Gran unit was completely gutted and remodeled, and in 1975 the former Swallum hospital building was also totally remodeled.

In 1979 Methodist Manor had seventy-three patients in the Health Center and eighty residents in the residential area, with seventy-seven employees providing four separate areas of care. In 1979 appraised value of Methodist Manor was $3,140,000, with a total indebtedness of $152,000. A long range planning committee worked with the building committee on plans to double the capacity.

A new patient wing for the Health Center complex was opened in 1981, together with a new multi-purpose room and a new lakefront entrance to the Health Center. During 1983 Methodist Manor provided 33,155 days of care in the Health Center, 13,140 days of which were subsidized care to people who could not afford to pay the full cost of care, and 25,833 days in the Residential Area, 4,026 of which were subsidized.[33]

Meth-Wick Manor

Meth-Wick Manor in Cedar Rapids developed as a joint project of the North Iowa Conference of The Methodist Church and the B. L. Wick Foundation of Cedar Rapids. The story began with Barthinius Wick, a Norwegian immigrant who came to the United States in 1876 as a twelve-year-old boy. He attended academies in Blairstown, LeGrande, and Iowa City, and earned his B.A., M.A., and law degrees from the University of Iowa. Mr. Wick moved to Cedar Rapids in 1894 to begin the practice of law.

Wick remained single and had no close relatives. Living alone, he learned the disadvantages of having no family in later life. During his latter years he drew his will so that his property could be used to establish a home where aged men could live in comfort with others who were congenial. The will provided for a foundation with five trustees who were to use the funds either alone, "or in cooperation with other bodies" to found such a home.

Meth-Wick Manor,
Cedar Rapids

Wick died in 1947. While the trustees were trying to determine the best way to implement the provisions of the Wick will, they kept the money invested in reasonably safe-but-growing corporation stocks and securities. By 1960 the original sum had more than doubled.

Representatives of the Board of Hospitals and Homes of the North Iowa Conference of The Methodist Church approached the Wick Foundation to discuss the possibility of establishing a home in Cedar Rapids together, making use of $500,000 or $600,000 of the foundation funds, the management experience of the church, and such money as it might secure from other sources. A contract was prepared, which provided that all five of the trustees of the foundation should also be trustees of the home.

Groundbreaking ceremonies were held on June 5, 1960, with ex-governor Robert D. Blue, chairman of the Board of Trustees, turning the first sod. The home began operations November 13, 1961, and by May 1, 1962, when the executive director wrote his report to the annual conference, fifty-one residents had moved in.

The 1964 report told of certain policy changes at Meth-Wick. One was an agreement with St. Luke's Hospital of Cedar Rapids, whereby the hospital operated the Health Center. This was mutually helpful to the hospital and the home. The Board of Trustees was able to prepare guidelines for the executive director regarding free and part-pay care. The home could extend services to several carefully screened Old Age Assistance recipients.

Meth-Wick Manor was formally adopted by the North Iowa Conference as a church-related institution in 1965. The home did not have an easy time, but with steady development and consistent support from friends difficult problems were solved. Meth-Wick received help each year from the annual conference, from the Wick Foundation, and from other friends.

Meth-Wick began a new program in 1975 for the elderly who were still living in their own homes or with relatives. The 1976 report to the Iowa Annual Conference described the new program.

Brendlewood is a pilot program founded by Federal Title XX funds. It is designed to accommodate fifteen or twenty persons in the community who are more or less isolated in their homes. It is a means of postponing institutional living.[34]

The 1980 report stated:

The Brendlewood Adult Day Care Center has become a model operation utilizing space in the lower level which is no longer certified for residential living. This additional service to some 35 older persons fills a great need in the community for persons who wish to remain outside of institutional living, but who could not, without this daily support system.[35]

The report for 1981, appearing in the 1982 conference journal, told of a $1,000,000 mortgage paid off in May. The twentieth anniversary year was marked by a quarter-million-dollar renovation of the fourth floor Health Center, and a $60,000 grant from the Hall Foundation, which permitted many improvements.

Western Home

Each of the United Methodist Homes in Iowa had a different origin. Western Home in Cedar Falls dates back to the General Conference of the Evangelical Church which met in Berlin, Ontario, Canada in 1903. Before then, nearly all of the denomination's institutions were located in the eastern United States. At that time it was decided to establish a home for the aged in the Middle West.

Several locations were considered, but at a meeting of the trustees held in Cedar Falls May 2, 1911, it was agreed to accept an offer made by Mr. G. A. Pfeiffer and Mrs. Anna Merner Pfeiffer: $20,000 and the site of the old

Western Home,
Cedar Falls

Pfeiffer home in Cedar Falls. The gift was made in memory of their parents, Mr. and Mrs. Henry Pfeiffer and Mr. and Mrs. John Merner.

Work commenced on the building in August, 1911, and was completed the following spring. The first building was modest in size, but adequate for the time. At every meeting of the board the need for a larger home was discussed, but not until the summer of 1923 was a fireproof, modern addition built. This addition had forty rooms, a chapel, a large kitchen, two dining rooms, and an electric elevator. It enabled the home to care for seventy-two persons, which seemed sufficient for years to come, but the fact that more rooms were needed soon became evident.

On Christmas Day, 1928, Mr. and Mrs. Henry Pfeiffer and Mrs. G. A. Pfeiffer gave $60,000 toward another addition. This unit provided thirty-six rooms, another elevator, an up-to-date laundry, two solariums, a diet kitchen, and two nurses' stations. Built at the cost of $100,000, it was dedicated November 3, 1929, and named the "Barbara Pfeiffer Sunshine Ward."

In May, 1958, the North Wing was completed. This provided for fifty more people, a spacious lounge, an automatic elevator, and sitting rooms. At the same time a brick, six-stall garage was built.

The Northwest Wing costing $461,000 was completed in the summer of 1963. Sixty more residents could be accommodated. In 1967 it was thought that the close proximity of staff would assure quality care, so a building was constructed to the north of the existing building, to house employees. Because this idea did not accomplish the hoped-for result, the building was converted to retirement living in 1971.

The 10th Street addition was erected in 1969 to provide a more efficient kitchen and an attractive dining room, as well as ten more resident rooms. This brought the capacity of the home to 278.

An apartment building with four units of "Independent Living Retirement Apartments" was built in cooperation with the First United Presbyterian Church of Cedar Falls in 1977. Plans were made for additional units as funds became available.

Since its beginning in 1912, Western Home, as a nonprofit agency, has been providing a service to the elderly. It now serves an average of 240 persons a day at four levels of care. The home is able to subsidize the support of many who are unable to pay the entire cost themselves.

Footnotes

1. *A Brief History of Iowa Methodist Hospital* (Des Moines: Iowa Methodist Hospital, 1952) n.p.
2-21. Edith M. Bjornstad, *Wings in Waiting* (Des Moines: Iowa Methodist Hospital, 1952), pp. 10-101 passim.
22. *Northwest Iowa Conference Journal* 1921 (Methodist Episcopal Church) p. 192.
23. *Shoppers Free Press* (Keokuk: Shoppers Free Press, Inc., Oct. 27, 1979) p. 1.
24. Walter L. Bierring, Ed., *One Hundred Years of Iowa Medicine* (Iowa City: The Athens Press, 1950) p. 384.

25. *Iowa Conference Journal* 1901 (Methodist Episcopal Church) p. 127.
26. *Iowa Conference Journal* 1905 (Methodist Episcopal Church) p. 144.
27. *Iowa Conference Journal* 1928 (Methodist Episcopal Church) p. 29.
28. Bennett Mitchell, *History of the Northwest Iowa Conference* (Sioux City: Perkins Brothers Company, 1904) pp. 279-280.
29. *Northwest Iowa Conference Journal* 1904 (Methodist Episcopal Church) p. 46.
30. *Northwest Iowa Conference Journal* 1906 (Methodist Episcopal Church) p. 170.
31. *Iowa Des Moines Conference Journal* 1947 (The Methodist Church) pp. 25-26.
32. Clarence W. Tompkims, *Born a Promoter* (Fort Dodge: By the Author, 1984) p. 20.
33. *Iowa Conference Journal* 1984 (The United Methodist Church) p. 46.
34. *Iowa Conference Journal* 1976 (The United Methodist Church) p. 38.
35. *Iowa Conference Journal* 1980 (The United Methodist Church) p. 44.

14

Special Ministries

The United Methodist Church in Iowa reaches out beyond its home base to serve in special ministries. Other chapters discuss the hospitals and homes and the church colleges. In this chapter a look will be taken at a variety of special ministries "beyond the local church."

CHAPLAINCIES

One of the ministries beyond the local church is that of the chaplains. Such situations as service in the armed forces and stays in hospitals or prisons call for a special ministry.

Traditionally, the churches have provided chaplains for the armed forces, although the program was not well understood until the First World War. During the Civil War (1861-65) Methodist chaplains served in both the northern and southern armies. They were men of their times, who believed strongly in the justice of their cause, but were present primarily to preach the gospel, to strengthen men facing personal temptations, and to bring comfort in suffering. The Methodist Episcopal Church of Iowa sent its full share. Some of the chaplains are mentioned by name in previous chapters.

The Military Chaplaincy became an established institution in the public mind during the two World Wars. Approximately 325 Methodist chaplains served in the U.S. Army and Navy, in the first World War. Some of them were from the four Iowa Conferences of the Methodist Episcopal Church. The Evangelical and United Brethren Churches also provided chaplains.

During World War I a number of ministers served with the Y.M.C.A., accompanying the army and providing religious services. In later years one of them indicated to this writer that he considered himself to have been an army chaplain at that time. The 1918 *Upper Iowa Conference Journal* lists seven ministers as appointed to army service with the Y.M.C.A. under "Special Appointments" and five as chaplains.

The 1918 *Northwest Iowa Conference Journal* lists five chaplains and six men with the Y.M.C.A. The Iowa Conference had five appointed as chaplains in the U.S. Army. Seven were appointed to "service in the army." The nature of the service is not stated in the *Journal*, but some may have been with the Y.M.C.A. The Des Moines Conference reported six chaplains and nine men with the Y.M.C.A. in 1919. The *Journal of the Evangelical Association* that year reported fourteen in the U.S. Army, but did not indicate whether any were chaplains. Two were with the Y.M.C.A.

Between the World Wars the United States Army was small and had correspondingly few chaplains. By World War II the military chaplain's work was clearly defined so that he could not be assigned any tasks that would interfere with his religious duties. He no longer had to be recreation officer or manage the Post Exchange. The 1944 *Journal of the Iowa Des Moines Conference* (Methodist Church) listed fifteen in the military chaplaincy. Upper Iowa listed seven in the army or navy chaplaincy; Northwest Iowa, thirteen.

Since World War II the chaplains have received more specialized training as counselors. In 1942 the Council of Bishops created a Commission on Chaplains as an interim agency to recruit, endorse, and give general oversight to the work of the chaplains in the armed forces and federal agencies. The 1944 General Conference officially established a Commission on Chaplains. The commission became a "Division of Chaplain and Related Ministries" of the General Board of Higher Education and Ministries in 1972, with the same responsibilities as before. In 1984 the Iowa Conference had twelve chaplains in the armed forces, four in the Veterans' Administration, eleven in hospitals, and two in United Methodist retirement homes.

The hospital chaplaincy has been a developing field of service, with growing appreciation for the contribution of chaplains to the health-care team. The first chaplains to serve Iowa Methodist Hospital are described in the chapter on hospitals: Rev. Asbel Thornbrue, a retired minister, and John Bailey, a brick-layer who was also a lay preacher. They both served six months without pay. In March, 1912 Thornbrue was given a monthly stipend of $15.

Rev. Dilman Smith was elected chaplain in 1918 with an annual salary of $2,300. He held the position until his retirement in 1939. During that period the chaplain's duties included maintaining liaison with the churches, raising funds, and contacting prospective nursing students. Counseling with the patients was only a part of his work, limited by the fact that his other duties kept him out of town much of the time. Much later the hospital chaplaincy became a recognized specialty in the Christian ministry, requiring specialized training.

Clinical Pastoral Education (CPE) had its beginning about 1925. Since then there has been progress in development of better training, along with the development of standards and accreditation of training programs. The Association for Clinical Pastoral Education (ACPE) represents various religious groups and exists to foster CPE as a part of theological education.

In 1951 Rev. Russell Striffler became the first chaplain of Iowa Methodist Hospital in Des Moines to devote his full time to work with patients and their families and train others for hospital chaplaincy. A course in religious chaplaincy was established with Drake University in 1953. Chaplain Striffler served in Des Moines until 1970, when be became Director of Chaplaincy and Chaplain Supervisor at St. Luke's Hospital in Cedar Rapids.

St. Luke's Regional Medical Center in Sioux City has a dual history, being a joint project of the Methodists and the Lutherans. At first, the pastoral care of the patients and their families in the Lutheran Hospital was a responsibility of the Missouri Synod Lutheran Industrial Chaplain, who also served a variety of institutions in Sioux City. Rev. Rudy Oudheusden was called in 1965 as a full-time staff chaplain in the hospital.

Chaplaincy services were first provided on a part-time basis in Sioux City's Methodist Hospital. Chaplain Robert Chapler had been in the U.S. Army Chaplaincy from 1942 to 1946. He was then assigned to the church in Sergeant Bluff and to the hospital chaplaincy, dividing his time between the two. In 1949 he was assigned to the hospital full-time, holding that position until his retirement in 1962.

Rev. Oscar Rees came to the Methodist Hospital in 1962 and served until he retired in 1983. The Lutheran and Methodist hospitals of Sioux City merged in 1966 to form St. Luke's Medical Center. Chaplains Oudheusden and Rees carried on co-operative chaplaincy programs in the two separate buildings. When the new building was opened in 1972, they combined their programs, serving as co-directors until 1982 when Rev. Steve Pohlman was appointed Director of Chaplaincy Services. The hospital is now able to give both "basic" and "advanced" CPE.

Since 1970 Rev. Russell Striffler has been Director of Chaplaincy and Chaplain Supervisor at St. Luke's Methodist Hospital in Cedar Rapids. R. Thomas Steward came as Associate Chaplain in Pastoral Care and Counseling in 1981. At present (1984) Chaplain Striffler and Rev. Robert P. Rogers are supervisors and are able to offer both basic and advanced CPE.

The Protestant chaplain in each of the three Veterans' Administration hospitals in Iowa (1984) is a member of the Iowa Conference of the United Methodist Church.

Iowa United Methodist congregations joined those of eleven other denominations in the state in a concerted effort to finance a third chaplain at Iowa State Penitentiary at Fort Madison by taking a special offering in 1984. The goal was to raise $100,000 as seed money to hire a full-time chaplain for a minimum of three years. Dr. Alferd Wilken, Chairman of the Iowa Inter-Church Agency for Peace and Justice Chaplaincy Commission, explained that the prison had two full-time chaplains trying to serve the needs of some 950 inmates. Since minority races comprised twenty-five percent of the prison population, the commission recommended that the third chaplain be of a minority race. Repeated efforts to obtain state funding for a third chaplain had failed.

DES MOINES AREA URBAN MISSION

The Des Moines Area Urban Ministry was established in 1968, with Rev. L. R. Keck as "Urban Minister at Large." Its purposes were to: (a) enable local churches and individuals to identify, clarify, and execute appropriate strategies to meet recognized needs of the community; (b) facilitate communication between local congregations, existing ministries, and the church at each level of organization; (c) develop mutual lines of accountability between congregations, existing ministries' staff members, and the church at each level of organization.

Rev. Kenneth Finneran, who was appointed Des Moines Urban Minister in 1971, reported that during 1972 major action included co-ordination of United Methodist ministries in the city—Bidwell-Riverside Center, Inner City Cooperative Parish, Iowa National Esther Hall, Wesley Acres home for elderly, Wesley Center City Parish, Wesley Foundation, and the work of the urban minister. Besides financial support of several of these ministries or their projects, monetary aid was given to the Door-of-Faith Mission (rehabilitation of alcoholic and indigent men), to the Enabler-Developer-Director for the Center for Study and Application of Black Theology, and to the Urban Religious Coalition.

Workshops were held to relate local churches more closely to a comprehensive urban missional plan. Employment was identified for action corporately, resulting in a "Supportive Friends in Employment" project. Around 275 inner city children were fed daily at four Breakfast Program Centers in 1973, with supportive relationships emphasized. An outstanding achievement reported in 1975 was the Pre-Trial Support Project (function of Black Community Worker), with pre-trial release and rehabilitation of forty-five women, five youth, and one man. Empowerment of community groups, reported in 1978, included Spanish-speaking and Native American programs, public hunger programs, and the Young Women's Resource Center.

Rev. Chester L. Guinn became Des Moines Urban Minister February 2, 1979, after Rev. Finneran left to take the position of Executive Director of Crossroads Urban Center at Salt Lake City, Utah. Among highlights Guinn reported for 1981 were: Black community radio station KUCB founded, two-day workshop at Drake for ethnic youth interested in entering law school, a full-time minister to Hispanics appointed (Roberto Mariano), and problem-solving for refugees.

1982 was judged "an unusually productive year" in which "Our Community Kitchen" free meal program began operation, serving 600 to 800 weekly. Joe Anna Cheatom received the Martin Luther King Jr. award for establishing radio station KUCB, and Robert A. Jackson Sr. was chosen by Governor Robert Ray to be the recipient of the Senior Citizen Community Service Award.

Philip Carver, "The Justice Troubador," who was added to the staff in 1982 made ninety-three presentations attended by 7,253 persons in 1983, to help congregations understand the church's witness within the city. Urban Minister Guinn hosted nineteen half-hour "Spotlight on Faith" shows for WHO-TV besides preaching or speaking on sixty-two occasions. Included where sharing from a fact-finding tour of Honduras and Nicaragua. The Hispanic ministry under Director Verne Lyon became a significant feature of the Hispanic community during 1983.

The bylaws of the Urban Mission Council were revised in 1984, and membership of the council was expanded to include one pastor and one lay person from each Des Moines metropolitan area United Methodist Church. This was intended to increase visibility of the council's activities and spur a growing interest in Urban Mission programs throughout the church community.

BIDWELL-RIVERSIDE CENTER

As has been pointed out by some observers, Bidwell-Riverside Center has a double line of heritage. The first line began with Des Moines' first Methodist deaconess in 1893 and others who began work in 1894. With a $75,000 bequest from Major A. V. Bidwell, a home for the deaconesses was established at 1155 West 9th Street. In 1900 the Iowa Bible Training School was organized and conducted as a part of the Deaconess Home, with its first class of five graduating in 1901, and all five graduates going into special work under the Woman's Home Missionary Society.

Miss Hannah K. Binau, a deaconess who was to be involved with the teaching and activities of the Iowa Bible Training School and the Bidwell Social Service Center for nearly forty years, became supervisor of supply work in 1915. On February 12, 1923, Bible Training School students occupied a new building which had been erected at 921 Pleasant Street. It was dedicated May 27th by Bishop Homer C. Stuntz. The school continued until 1931. During its three decades 230 young women were graduated, and most entered full-time Christian vocations.

In 1931 the Bible Training School building became Iowa National Esther Hall, a home away from home for business women and students. It also housed the Bidwell Social Service Center, an outgrowth of the practical work in the Training School under Miss Binau's direction, and a conference project of the former Woman's Home Missionary Society (one of the predecessors of the Woman's Society of Christian Service).

Bidwell-Riverside's second line of heritage came through the organization for Sunday School for the children of "Boxtown" in 1909 by Miss Flora Taylor of the Tenth Street Methodist Church and Miss Mabel Hopkinson of the Scott Street Methodist Church. These deaconesses served an area where homes were made largely of tarpaper-covered packing boxes secured free from department stores. Mexican and Spanish-speaking families lived in this area.

In 1910 the Conference Home Missionary Society rented a cottage on Granger, and the following year L. M. Mann gave a lot at S.E. 14th Street Court and Hartford. The building was known as Riverside Mission, and later as Riverside Community House. Students from the Iowa Bible training School received practical experience there. The location in a flooded area, the need for more space, and other factors led to moving the building in 1947 to 1203 Hartford. A basement added more space for activities with all age groups.

Better economic conditions gradually changed the type of work needed. Under the direction of Rev. and Mrs. Ray Tribble, the Sunday School work was merged with Jordan Methodist Church. A bus carried the children to the new Sunday School program in the church. Miss Binau's retirement in 1954 and changes in Esther Hall plans caused the Bidwell Social Service Center to be merged with the Riverside Community Center. The name was changed to Bidwell-Riverside Center.

**Bidwell-Riverside
Center**

Hanna Binau

Bidwell-Riverside Extension work was organized near the slaughter houses and city dump in October, 1954. A building was rented at 801 S.E. 26th Court, and Miss Effie Lawton, deaconess, gave part-time help to the Tribbles in carrying on a program of sewing classes, pre-school work, and used clothing distribution.

By 1955 the need for additional space became so great that the Women's Society of Christian Service of the South Iowa Conference accepted the responsibility of an addition to the Bidwell-Riverside Center building. The complete project was dedicated in April, 1957.

The purpose of Bidwell-Riverside Center is "to enlist interest in and provide opportunity for individual and group development, irrespective of sex, religion, national origin, or color; to strengthen family relationships, and to work toward community leadership which will assist in living within a Christian and democratic frame of reference, also to develop program with the needs of the people in mind, thus providing a channel for Christian witness."

Among the programs offered are pre-school and summer programs for children; outreach, emergency food pantry, thrift shop, latch-key, summer youth recreation, and parenting workshop for families; Golden Oaks for senior citizens and Bid-You-Well line for homebound; sewing guild, Christmas sharing, afternoon-out child care, high school equivalency, English as second language study, community kitchen, grow-your-own vegetables, classes in living skills, and Artists of Asia program.

The Center's bylaws require that a third of the board members represent United Methodists, one-third represent the neighborhood, and one-third represent the community at large.

HAWTHORN HILL

The Bidwell-Riverside section of this chapter tells the history of the Iowa Bible Training School and the Bidwell Social Service Center, which operated from 1923 until 1931 in the building now serving as Hawthorn Hill, also the use of the building as Iowa National Esther Hall 1931-1970. The name was changed to Hawthorn Hill in 1974, and young men were invited to residency after a Des Moines Community Survey showed that housing was needed in the area.

Hawthorn Hill

According to Lois Watson, president of Hawthorn Hill Board 1974-1976, "more single rooms were made available, something not offered elsewhere, and the program change was successful with the support of Iowa Methodist Medical Center's need for housing for medical students. . . . During all this time, social changes were occurring which affect housing desires of young adults. Iowa law provides adulthood at age 18. Many social changes have affected the appeal of dorm-type housing—the apartment and car boom; less parental influence; the fast food era—all these moves toward independence and changing lifestyles influenced the possibility of continuing a residence of this size when the costs of building maintenance were continually rising. On November 10, 1976 the Board of Directors voted to close Hawthorn Hill as a residence and proceed to dissolve the corporation."

New Articles of Incorporation for Hawthorn Hill as a multi-ministry facility were adopted at the annual conference of 1979. Rev. Robert Crum, Executive Director, listed goals in the 1980 conference report: (1) to provide a center for multi-ministry activities and programs for the Des Moines area urban ministries; (2) to provide an ecumenical and conference-wide retreat center; (3) to host special events and celebrations; (4) to provide temporary shelter for individuals on a need and/or emergency basis; (5) to serve as an active and on-going advocate for downtown senior citizens; (6) to create an ecumenical center for the continuing education of laity and clergy; and (7) to establish a free theological research lending library, principally for the Midwest. A 1981 information report classified the hospitality of Hawthorn Hill as "intergenerational, interracial, and international."

At the time of the 1982 report the Community Kitchen, sponsored by the Urban Mission Council, prepared 200 nutritious meals daily at Hawthorn Hill for delivery to two meal sites, made emergency rations available, and provided lunches for the needy. Collection and distribution of clothing for Indo-Chinese refugee mothers and children and Hispanic refugees and migrants was carried out in cooperation with the Des Moines Hispanic Ministry. Women and children referred by the Family Violence Center and the Door-of-Faith Mission for Women were being housed temporarily as need arose. Parolees and ex-offenders, through the Safer Foundation, worked in the maintenance department, and a Prisoner's Fellowship support group met weekly at Hawthorn Hill. Among educational programs offered were English as a Second Language, and the Shepherd Center for senior citizens.

Hawthorn Hill's team of "volunteers, senior citizens, handicapped, in-kind, part-time, and full-time staff is on call 24 hours a day, seven days a week." Hawthorn Hill is supported in part by the Iowa Conference of the United Methodist Church. Approximately two-thirds of its funding comes from other sources, including supportive groups and individuals.

FORT DODGE URBAN MINISTRY

The Fort Dodge Urban Ministry's predecessor, Mission-in-the-Valley, was begun as a ministry to a depressed area in the Fort Dodge flood plain. The expanded Fort Dodge Urban Ministry was so organized in 1966 that it would be amenable to the Annual Conference Board of Missions, with one-half of its board of directors to be nominated by the mission board. As reported five years later in the 1971 *Journal of the Iowa Annual Conference,* the Fort Dodge Urban Ministry had "become an ecumenical action tool for the churchmen in the wider Fort Dodge community."

In addition to major support from United Methodists, broader support and involvement was obtained through the Metro Council including some seventy persons from twenty-two churches of seventeen denominations, according to the 1971 report. A day-care center, education, job training and opportunities for the vocationally handicapped, legal aid, housing problems, rights advocacy, and supportive service to out-of-state students at the community college were among the concerns.

Entering its eighth year of service in 1973, the Fort Dodge Urban Ministry was relocated from 326 11th Avenue S.W. to 1318 10th Avenue S.W., directly north of Pleasant Valley School. In his report that year Director Alvin B. Moore mentioned busing youths to high school, conducting a week-day ethnic school for two-to-five-year-olds, a breakfast program, tutoring, and a recreation program. He noted funding from Lutherans, Episcopalians, and the Covenant Church of America, as well as United Methodists, in the 1974 report.

Twenty Fort Dodge business firms endorsed the work of the Urban Ministry as the first step in a city-wide drive for local funding in 1976. Growing out of concern for improvement of communication between the police department and black residents, a community get-together was promoted in 1979. Prizes and foods to serve were donated by businesses. Between 500 and 600 people from over the city gathered to share enjoyment and friendship. A local radio station gave a $150 guitar as a prize, and broadcast live from the scene. Executive Director James Lockman reported that $850 was raised by the event to benefit the urban ministry's programs.

On January 1, 1982 the Fort Dodge Urban Ministry became the sponsoring agency for a Family Support Program with referrals to come through the Department of Social Services. Two day-care programs—Ethnic School Day Care and Aunt Nancy's Day Care—were operating, with eighty percent of the children from low-income families. Nutrition and education/recreation activities programs served different groups of children at two sites—First United Methodist Church and Pleasant Valley School. A three-day Bible camp was sponsored.

In making the 1984 report Director Lockman cited the interracial work force of twenty blacks, nine whites, and one Oriental as one of the most significant aspects of the Fort Dodge Urban Ministry.

URBAN MINISTRY IN THE QUAD CITIES—CHURCHES UNITED OF SCOTT AND ROCK ISLAND COUNTIES

The Quad City School of Religious Studies and Leadership Development was begun in 1969 to increase skills and knowledge of minority pastors. Grants from the John Deere Foundation and the Moline Foundation were used. Workshops for community and agencies in dialogue brought together thirty-six different agencies. Cluster groups of ministers in or near the Model City Area were organized.

The Urban Ministry Task Force was activated January 20, 1972, at the close of the annual meeting of Churches United. Twenty-two members were involved, and met monthly until June 1. Rev. Clarence Savoy served the first nine months of 1972 as Urban Minister and laid a foundation for the continuing program. Through a special grant from the Iowa Conference of the United Methodist Church and the Muscatine District of that conference a new program in motivational training was implemented in the Scott County jail beginning in 1974. A trained counselor visited the jail daily and met with small groups of inmates for one hour each. Using tapes, group techniques, and individual counseling, he explored with them the motivations for their criminal behavior and the alternate motivations toward socially constructive behavior.

Thomas N. Kalshoven, Executive Director, reported significant achievements in 1975 for Metropolitan Issues (formerly Urban Ministry) including: helping to deal with police-community tensions, consumer advocacy in local and state health planning councils, graduation of six from Quad Cities School of Religious Studies (program to enhance black leadership), aid for about 1,000 persons per month through the Food Pantry system, leading the development of a council on crime and delinquency (citizen input), and running a Friendly Town program.

Total funding by denominational contributions from eleven judicatories was reported in 1980. Emphasis was on jail ministry, nursing home visitation of people who had no other visitors, food pantries, and advocacy in areas of health planning, jail construction, women's rights, and minority issues.

Severe unemployment in the Quad Cities area in 1983-84 demanded the attention of the urban ministry to causes and results of the problem. Food pantries increased in number and quantity by fifty percent over 1982. Expansion of the summer migrant program for people harvesting food in the area was underway. Ministry to single persons was also a growing program.

THE URBAN MINISTRY OF GREATER WATERLOO

The 1971 *Iowa Annual Conference Journal* contained a report of purpose and plans for urban ministry in Waterloo, which would enable the church to be in action so that its community might become the place where persons, not property, receive priority; people, not profit, are valued most; all may find a chance for fulfillment. The Strategy Council was made up of representatives of all the United Methodist Churches in Waterloo, Cedar Falls, and Evansdale, with an Urban Minister set free to minister by not being assigned to a local congregation. Rev. Stanley Kennedy directed the urban ministry at Waterloo from 1971 to 1982.

A consultation was planned for the fall of 1971 with urban ministers and workers from the Episcopal, Roman Catholic, and Lutheran churches, and Jimmie Porter from the Black Enabler Program, funded by the United Presbyterian Church. A two-storefront building in the black business community was received as a gift to the United Methodist Church.

Early in 1972 a loan fund for the poor was established, to be administered by a committee of low-income people. It aided persons in need during emergency situations. During a period of tension that year, when members of the black community sought equal educational opportunity for their children and equal economic opportunity for all people, a sit-in at the Central Administration Building of the school system and the picketing of a local shopping plaza took place. The Urban Ministry endeavored to function as interpreter and reconciler, with a "significant group of ministers meeting weekly to discuss the community's needs." Urban seminars were sponsored for several groups, to give exposure to hurting parts of the community.

Following an area-wide 1973 Urban Consultation with consultative help from the Office of Urban Ministry of the Board of Global Ministry of the United Methodist Church, five task forces were formed to attempt: (1) the establishment of a half-way house for women offenders; (2) establishment of a referral agency to help people find help; (3) increased support of the Questryst Youth Center; (4) low income housing; (5) establishment, sensitizing, and training of a group of committed persons to support the racial minorities in their quest for justice and equality. An event of 1973 in which the urban ministry was involved was the election of the first black to a city council seat.

1974 saw significant follow-up from the task forces. A group that became the Community Corrections Council was named responsible for half-way house facilities. Funding was sought for a referral agency. The housing task force sensitized the community to responsibility toward low-income persons and families. A member of the task force on racial minorities became a representative on the board of a neighborhood center. An Annual Conference grant of $1,000 to the Human Development Fund made possible a recreational program for young people at Logandale Apartments, and the city also became involved. A similar grant from the Waterloo District of the United Methodist Church was used to meet emergency needs.

In its eighth year (1975) two community organizations were founded through Urban Ministry—Minority Alcoholism, and Friends of the Accused. Linkage with a number of health and welfare organizations in the community made ministry more effective.

The Urban Minister, Stanley Kennedy, directed a multicultural camp, sponsored by the United Methodist Church in 1979. United Methodist Women of Waterloo Districts provided camp scholarships for inner-city children.

When Rev. Kennedy became a District Superintendent in 1982, Rev. Donald L. Carver succeeded him as Urban Minister. Carver's 1984 report noted special attention to interpretive ministry to local churches across the state, classes, and seminars or workshops. Rev. Carver and Jim Porter of the Black Enabler Program were part of a weekly broadcast—For Your Information—over KBBG radio. Support was given in 1984 to a newly formed organization, Neighborhood East Waterloo Project. Crises of persons and families due to economic stagnation consumed a major amount of urban ministry time and effort, with response to over 300 families.

WALL STREET MISSION, SIOUX CITY

C. E. Robinson and Prof. Joseph G. Hobson were founders and key workers of Sioux City's Wall Street Mission beginning in 1890. Afternoon Sunday School and chapel services in the Worcester School building served Native Americans and the foreign-born of eighteen nationalities. A sewing school was organized in 1893.

**Wall Street Mission,
Sioux City**

Rapid expansion of activities in the second decade of the mission included boys' sloyd work (manual training), girls' industrial work and gymnasium class. Boys' gymnasium, library, medical dispensary, cooking class, basket weaving, Legal Aid Society, home nursing class, night school, and day nursery. Deaconess Kathryn Troyer arrived in 1905 to be superintendent of the girls' industrial work, and Rev. Horace L. Houghton was appointed as the mission's first resident pastor in 1908. He was succeeded by Rev. Maurice E. Levitt, supply pastor, in 1911.

Mary Wendzillo Patrick recalled in an interview,

> Our neighborhood was like the United Nations. We were like one big happy family. The hub of our activities was the Wall Street Mission. Mr. Levitt had deaconesses come for Bible study and then would put out clothes for us to take if needed. He had a dispensary and doctors would come to look us over. There was something going every afternoon and evening after school. Morningside College kids would come to help, and sometimes would take us on hikes to South Ravine and on picnics. . . . Everything I ever learned about the Bible I learned at the mission Sunday School, not at my own church. . . .[1]

Rev. John Perry Hantla came in 1919 to begin his forty years' service as Wall Street Mission superintendent. When the senior Dr. Hantla retired in 1959, his son—Dr. John Paul Hantla—was appointed superintendent. As he continued to meet the challenges of the position in 1985, the unusual father-son record of dedicated service in special ministry already totaled sixty-five years.

Rev. George L. Search founded the Helping Hand Mission in 1906 to provide lodging and Christian astmosphere for the homeless and unemployed in Sioux City. For fifty-two years this mission and its "Church of the Crowded Ways" ministered to those in distress. It merged with the Wall Street Mission in 1958-59. Property and assets of Helping Hand were vested in the corporation and trustees of Wall Street Mission.

The Wall Street Mission's Harriet Ballou Day Nursery and Neighborhood Center were serving over 250 children and youth by 1922, with clubs, classes, crafts, sports, interest groups, and "multi-activities." Goodwill Industries developed as the "Industrial Arm" of Wall Street Mission's service to the community beginning in 1923. The Blind Shop was founded by Guy Deuel in 1927, and several social clubs for persons with various types of handicaps were organized in 1928. The Crystal Lake Camp site was purchased in 1929. It was to become a summer camping facility for thousands of underprivileged children and handicapped persons through the years.

The first Christmas Shoe Party for needy school children was held in 1942. This became an annual event of increasing proportions, with referrals of children from the surrounding Siouxland area, as well as those from the city. Children were measured for shoes several weeks before the December 24 party at which they received hand-knitted mittens, socks, and treats, as well as shoes. Eleven hundred children were outfitted in 1973. Youth and adult volunteers from Sioux City District churches participated in the annual distributions.

A rehabilitation center was developed in 1947 with Dr. John Perry Hantla as first president of the board of directors and Miss Marie Marietta, formerly of Goodwill, as executive director. Harriet Ballou New Hope Center for the severely retarded, the Evaluation and Work Adjustment Center, and an opportunity center in cooperation with the Association of Retarded Children of Woodbury County were all in operation during the mission's eighth decade (1961-1970).

WACO (Work Activity Company) evolved from the former Harriet Ballou New Hope Center as a self-help program, funded by the National Division of the Board of Global Ministries of the United Methodist Church, the Iowa Department of Social Services, and local donations. WACO's relationship with Wall Street Mission ended in 1979 with its expansion and withdrawal to different quarters.

To keep pace with the activities of Wall Street Mission, the building at 314 S. Wall had been enlarged in 1901 and again in 1910. Hobson Hall was erected in 1927. The first industrial building was constructed in 1935; the second unit in 1947; the third in 1952; and a fourth in 1963.

The location of Interstate Highway 29 through the Wall Street Mission district in 1958-59, and resettlement of families who lived in the Mission area to other parts of the city, brought about numerous adjustments of programs and procedures for Wall Street Mission-Goodwill.

A disastrous fire March 26, 1973 destroyed one-fourth of the industrial complex. In February, 1976 the Wall Street Mission occupied a new 77,000 square-foot facility, free from architectural barriers, at 3100 W. 4th Street. The Rehabilitation Center was now adjacent to both War Eagle Village (a

Mission-owned low-income housing development built in 1971) and Wesley Willard Residence (a structured residential facility for Goodwill trainees), built in 1973. Pheasant Acres for low-income elderly and handicapped residents was ready in 1979.

The year 1979 proved financially difficult for Goodwill Industries when inflation, the increase in the federal minimum wage (amounting to $80,000 per year 1979-81), and substantially less earned revenue necessitated curtailing of jobs and services, with fewer persons receiving employment, training, and rehabilitation services.

After many years' service the Church of All Nations had voted itself out of existence at its Quarterly Conference in 1951. Only one adult who attended still lived in the shrinking neighborhood around the mission after new highway location. For a time the building was used as a chapel for Goodwill employees and trainees.

Sioux City Journal Photo

The Hantlas with Bishop Thomas and John Moore.

In 1980 Dr. John Paul Hantla proposed that a pioneer church building be recycled as a "Chapel of All Nations" in celebration of Wall Street Mission's 90th year, and in honor of J. G. Hobson, C. E. Robinson, Guy Deuel, George L. Search, Ryal Miller, Mr. and Mrs. Gust Soderberg, Mrs. Nellie Hobson Long, Sam Cohen, Martha May Younglove, Mrs. Carlotta C. Chrisman, "Pop" Jenks, and Dr. John Perry Hantla—all Godfearing people dedicated to serving mankind and the Mission. The former United Methodist Church of Richland, South Dakota's building (erected 1885) was acquired, moved, and restored as the chapel for Goodwill Industries and for Sunday services at the Mission at 3100 W. 4th Street.

GOODWILL INDUSTRIES OF DES MOINES, INC.

An Area Goodwill Industries Commission reported to the Iowa-Des Moines Annual Conference in 1954 a number of locations in Iowa "where a Goodwill Industries could get underway," but was frustrated in its effort during the year that followed, despite "untold phone calls, miles of travel, and scores of meetings." A national survey had determined that Des Moines had 2,800 handicapped residents, with only six percent of them receiving any kind of service in sheltered workshops or on-the-job training.

After various obstacles were overcome, a charter was granted June 9, 1955 to the Goodwill Industries of Des Moines, Iowa. Funding, a qualified director, and a suitable plant were all needed. At the 1956 Annual Conference, a glowing report mentioned a generous Federal Aid Grant for equipment, and a mortage grant from the Home Missions Board, as well as support from local churches; the calling of Ted Grob Jr. as director; also the acquisition of a store at 417 E. 6th and a warehouse at 612 E. Locust. The factory was set up at 325 E. 5th. The Kiwanis Club and the Boy Scouts aided in Goodwill Bag placements.

According to the 1957 conference report, Des Moines Goodwill progressed the fastest of any United States unit in 1956-57, when 73,564 employment hours were given 424 different handicapped persons. The 1962 report urged that (1) Goodwill Industries continue as a Conference Advance Special, (2) that churches use speakers from Goodwill, (3) that one member of the local church Commission on Missions be designated by the chairman to have special responsibility for promoting the work of Goodwill in the local church.

Although 192 handicapped people were employed and/or trained under the leadership of Executive Director Alexander J. Waugh in 1964-65, over 300 applications for Goodwill's services had to be turned down because of space, equipment, and fund limitations. A new $500,000 Rehabilitation Center, constructed at 2550 E. Euclid, was occupied early in 1968. Churches were asked to increase their support through Advance Specials to include $27,000 needed for construction of the chapel in the new building. Strong emphasis on transitional employment (developing clients for graduation to jobs in competitive fields of business and industry) was stressed in 1968 and 1969 reports of the work under Executive Director Lester C. Stoehr.

The Iowa Annual Conference Commission's visit to the Des Moines facility was reported in 1974. They observed that,

> One noticeable aspect of Goodwill Industries today is the changing pattern of the collectable items they receive. With the increasing of garage sales . . . there is less usable material sent to Goodwill Industries, making it necessary for them to explore other types of activity for the employment of clients. There is an increasing number of consignments of small assembly type jobs . . . from various industries.[2]

GOODWILL INDUSTRIES AT COUNCIL BLUFFS

Goodwill Industries' presence at Council Bluffs has been intermittent, usually connected with the Omaha, Nebraska Goodwill. In 1956, Mr. Luff

Payne was a part-time executive director at Council Bluffs. Boy Scouts assisted with bag distribution. In 1957, seventeen handicapped persons were employed, one small pick-up was in use, and $2,174 of processed materials were sold. The Council Bluffs Goodwill Industries informed the South Iowa Annual Conference of its intention to modernize and to explore the possibility of obtaining "nuisance" contract work from industrial firms.

The "first annual report" to South Iowa Conference from the Iowa-Nebraska Goodwill Industries was assembled in 1965. Seventy-two Iowans received service that year. Dr. W. W. Steinmetz, P. E. Heineman, and Leo M. Ungar were Iowans on the Board of Trustees. Some financial support was received from the South Iowa Conference.

The Omaha-Council Bluffs Goodwill Industries was visited by the Iowa Annual Conference Commission in 1971. Under a management agreement plan Nebraska Goodwill Industries reopened a workshop for the handicapped in Council Bluffs—Area XIII Rehabilitation Center at 612 S. Main Street—in April. All new equipment was installed in a completely renovated building.

HILLCREST FAMILY SERVICES

An organization called "The Women's Rescue Society" operated a home in Dubuque for unmarried mothers and their babies for some years before 1914. In that year, when the home was to be closed for lack of funds, the building was offered to any Protestant group which would maintain it. Anna B. Cook, a Methodist deaconess, shouldered the responsibility with the assistance of St. Luke's Methodist Episcopal Church and other Protestant churches.

**Hillcrest Family
Service**

The institution located at 2005 Asbury Road was renamed Hillcrest Baby Fold. In 1951 it was reported that an average of thirty-three infants and children were being sheltered annually, with part of the support provided by the North Iowa Conference of the Methodist Church. As years have passed, the institution's name has been changed several times, emphasizing the broadening of its services.

"Hillcrest Children's Services" was the new name approved at the North Iowa Annual Conference of 1963, along with revised Articles of Incorporation. Hillcrest enrolled in the Associate Program of the Child Welfare League of America the following year, and began to secure professionally trained caseworkers so that services could be improved. By the time of Executive Director Donald R. Osborne's report in 1970, Hillcrest had become the first church-related agency in Iowa to receive a funded contract from a federal agency, for providing such services as family life education and family planning to a number of counties.

Osborne's 1971 report began with the statement, "Hillcrest is the only child care and family service agency in Iowa sponsored by the Iowa Conference of the United Methodist Church and the Synod of Iowa, United Presbyterian Church, U.S.A." Hillcrest achievements noted at that time included development of a purchase-of-service program in Cedar Rapids and Linn County and selective use of unwed mothers in adoptive study groups, as well as casework, counseling, and healing ministry of a holistic nature.[3]

Hillcrest Services to Children and Youth assumed management of two Dubuque County group homes—Delhi for boys and Fenelon for girls—in July, 1972. During 1973-74 the changing social climate caused Hillcrest's board and staff to revise their long-range planning, with immediate establishment of a special education learning center for residents of the group homes and Hillcrest House, as one phase of the plan.

Clients numbering 8,182 were served by Hillcrest Family Services in 1983—the most served in any year since its founding. Family, Marriage, and Individual Counseling—Family Planning—Chemical Dependency Program—Family Life Education—Unwed Parent Services—Supplemental Food Program—Residential Treatment for Disturbed Youth—Adult Group Home Care—and Crisis Intervention Service were offered. Proceeds from a "New Horizons" funding campaign made it possible to purchase a new group home in Iowa City, to remodel a facility in Cedar Rapids, and to build an extension to Wesley Place, a residential treatment center for boys in Dubuque.

IOWA GREAT LAKES MINISTRY

Since 1973 the Iowa Great Lakes Ministry has been directed by a pastor appointed to it by the Iowa Annual Conference. The program began in a small way in the 1950s and was centered in a coffee house at Arnolds Park in the early 1960s. Since the mid 1960s, it has featured the summer bar ministry of seminarians. Rev. Merlin R. Mather served as director from 1973 to September 1, 1977, when he was succeeded by Rev. Richard Viney.

Described as a "ministry of presence," coordination of the volunteer chaplain efforts of area pastors, patient advocacy at the hospital, and various kinds of counseling are among functions undertaken. Financial support has come from the Iowa Conference of the United Methodist Church, the regional branch of the Presbyterian Church, local churches, and individuals.[4]

UNITED METHODIST MEN

Goals to communicate the emphasis in a new United Methodist Men's ministry, and to provide resources and leadership, were expressed in 1974. Charges were requested to include in their lists of officers the representative of men's ministry in each church. In addition to district retreats, a Purdue-like United Methodist Men's program for the Iowa Conference United Methodist Men was projected for 1976. July 9-11 were the dates selected for the men's conference on the theme "Bicentennial Wesleyan Renewal," at C. Y. Stephens Auditorium in Ames. Seven hundred men attended, with Bishops Thomas and Ensley among the inspirational speakers.

At the time of the 1977 report to Annual Conference, Iowa had forty-one chartered United Methodist Men's organizations. Eighty-one were chartered by 1979, with 2,176 members across the conference and a total of $45,703 contributed to projects.

A highlight of the men's activity was the 1983 trip made by twenty men with Bishop Clymer to view projects in Ghana. Nine thousand dollars were raised for a pick-up truck for Rev. Ray Howland to use in promoting the Selp-Help Tractor Foundation. United Methodist Men also supported the *Upper Room* WATS Line Prayer Ministry.

Russell J. Kruse, Conference President, reported a twelve percent increase in the number of chartered United Methodist Men's fellowships during 1983. The All Iowa Men's Convocation III was held on the theme "I Believe" at Simpson College in July, 1983, with an attendance of 216. Those present considered the convocation "a spiritual happening."

IOWA UNITED METHODIST FOUNDATION

An Iowa Methodist Foundation was authorized by annual conference action in 1952, but a corporation was not formed until 1957. The purpose of the foundation is to provide a legally constituted body to solicit, receive, and administer funds of every kind for the use and benefit of the various religious, educational, and benevolent works and/or organizations related to the United Methodist Church in Iowa, or in any other place in the world.

Board members elected by the annual conference are five laymen, five laywomen, and five clergy, with five more representatives elected from the agencies: one from the hospitals and Hillcrest Family Services; one from the colleges; one from the retirement homes; one from the camps and retreat centers; and one from the board of pensions. Financial support for operation of the foundation comes from the conference dollar.

Comparatively little activity was reported up to the time of the 1975 Iowa Annual Conference. It was recommended in 1975 that a full-time director be employed beginning in 1976, and Rev. Mearle Griffith was appointed as of

January 1. He served until April 1, 1977. The Iowa United Methodist Foundation experienced outstanding first-year growth, and was commended by the National Association of United Methodist Foundations. Eleven pilot wills programs were conducted.

Griffith's successor, Gordon Danielson, became executive director in September, 1977. He referred to the foundation as "a new creation," for it had been reorganized by the 1977 annual conference.

Among highlights reported in 1980 was the April seminar for several hundred Iowa United Methodists in Ames on Life/Estate Planning, with Dr. Neil Harl as lecturer. The seminar served as a springboard for additional training around the state through Director Danielson's individual counseling and presentations at local churches, sub-districts, districts and conference meetings. The foundation awarded a number of scholarships to outstanding United Methodist youth.

It was noted in the 1984 report that activities of the foundation include such services as administration of trust funds, writing annuities, custody of scholarship funds, financial counseling, and education of local congregations.

Footnotes
1. Louise Zerschling, "Never a Dull Moment on South Bottom," *The Sioux City Sunday Journal,* April 19, 1981, p. B-1.
2. *Journal of the Iowa Annual Conference of the United Methodist Church*, 1974, Vol. 1, p. 24.
3. *Journal of the Iowa Annual Conference of the United Methodist Church,* 1971, p. D-63.
4. William Simbro, "Seminary Students Show Ministry to Patrons of Great Lakes Bars," *Des Moines Sunday Register,* August 12, 1984, p. 3-B.

15

Schools and Colleges

Louis A. Haselmayer

Methodism was born in the academic setting of Oxford University. Students shared a voluntary program of personal piety, spiritual discipline, Bible study and church renewal. This "method" was practiced within collegiate walls. John and Charles Wesley never lost their esteem for learning and scholarship. John Wesley remained a Fellow of Lincoln College, Oxford, until his death. His goal for religious dedication and theological insight is captured in an oft quoted statement, "Let us unite the two so long divided—knowledge and vital piety."

As Methodism spread from the British Isles to overseas colonies, the emphasis on education became an essential factor in the missionary outthrust. Persons needed to be able to read the Word of God in order to enter into a genuine relationship with Jesus Christ. Literacy and education were parts of a missionary concern to establish academic institutions.

The westward movement of settlers and missionaries across Pennsylvania, Ohio, Indiana, Illinois and Iowa resulted in church effort for schools and colleges.

Such collegiate activity in Iowa predated the organization of the first Iowa Annual Conference. These efforts were initially directed to elementary and secondary work since there were no public schools in the 1840s. At least one of these schools never achieved collegiate status. The others gradually evolved from elementary/secondary curricula into baccalaureate work and then the academy instruction was eventually discontinued.

Each institution was initiated under local leadership in specific communities. These groups included ministers and lay persons of the Methodist Episcopal Church with the support of tiny congregations as organizational undergirding. These persons sought or intended to seek affiliation with or sponsorship by Annual Conferences. But there was never any overall Conference strategy to determine where these colleges should be located. Local efforts in existing centers of population, motivated by a need for formal education, were the driving impulses. Colleges came into existence as settlement moved from the eastern to the western border of Iowa in different decades.

The five surviving Iowa colleges related to the United Methodist Church constitute a kind of crazy quilt pattern of local effort from the 1840s in southeast Iowa to the 1890s in northwest Iowa. They are related to the development of Methodism in an historic series of Annual Conferences authorized at different dates over the century as well as to a fluctuating sequence of mergers and realignment and redistribution of Annual Conference areas.

Although each of these colleges demonstrates the educational concern of Methodism, they are all independent institutions, privately incorporated under charters from the State of Iowa. They are not owned, operated, or totally funded by United Methodist Annual Conferences. They are not part of a formal Conference educational system. It is a misnomer to call them "Church Colleges" since there is no vested interest of either Church or Conference. They are "related" in a variety of ways to an Annual Conference. The phrase "church-related" is a more accurate title.

This church-relatedness is effective in specific forms. The Charter or Articles of Incorporation contain a reference to the United Methodist Church. Each Board of Trustees has a designated number of members who are elected by the Annual Conference or appointed by the Resident Area Bishop. Each college provides an annual report to the Annual Conference through the Conference Division of Higher Education and Campus Ministry. Each college receives an annual grant of money for operating expenses from the Annual Conference. The grant, however, represents only a fraction of the total income of each college. The academic programs provide a Department of Religion with courses in Biblical literature and other religious studies. A chaplain is appointed by the college, ordinarily an ordained minister of the United Methodist Church, with responsibility for campus religious life and corporate worship. The social codes, priority values and ways of life of each college reflect the relationship to the United Methodist Church.

The colleges respond to the national church through the Commission on Higher Education of the Board of Education and by voluntary membership in a National Association of Schools and Colleges of the United Methodist Church. Each is accredited as a viable educational institution with a valid church relationship by the University Senate of the United Methodist Church. University Senate accreditation is the basis for official status as an institution of the United Methodist Church.

Relationship in diverse ways, co-operative activities and a consciousness of Christian identity are the marks of the United Methodist church-related colleges.

Ten colleges in Iowa since 1842 have had a relationship with various Methodist, Evangelical, and United Brethren Annual Conferences. Four of these no longer exist. One continues without any church relationship. One preparatory school never achieved collegiate status and closed in the 1920s. Since these schools came into existence at different times and under the auspices of different Annual Conferences, it will be best to discuss them in a roughly chronological order of origin within each sponsoring Annual Conference.

The Iowa Conference (1844-1932)

1. THE IOWA CITY COLLEGE: 1842-1847

The Rev. George B. Bowman, pastor of the Methodist Episcopal Church, Iowa City, pushed for the establishment of a college in 1842. A charter was obtained from the Illinois Territorial Legislature which stated that "said College should be under the auspices of the Methodist Episcopal Church, with power to confer all degrees in the arts and learned professions."[1]

The first (1844) session of the Iowa Annual Conference in Iowa City adopted this proposed institution and approved the local board of trustees. It turned down at the same time an application for sponsorship from the Mt. Pleasant Collegiate Institute, fifty miles south.[2]

The Iowa City College held its first classes in 1845 with James Harlan as president. Harlan, a recent graduate of Indiana Asbury University (now DePauw University), had been invited to Iowa City for this purpose. The college existed only two years. In 1847 James Harlan became the first State Superintendent for Schools in Iowa and the Iowa City College closed its doors.[3]

2. IOWA WESLEYAN COLLEGE:1842-

Mount Pleasant, Iowa, was platted as part of Illinois Territory in 1834. In 1836 a Methodist Episcopal circuit rider was preaching in a log cabin and in 1843 the Rev. Isaac I. Stewart organized the first Quarterly Conference of about forty members. Among this group of lay persons arose a desire to establish a school.

On February 17, 1842, sixteen incorporators from that group obtained from the Illinois Territorial Legislature a charter for the Mt. Pleasant Literary Institute with the provision that "said institution shall be under the charge of the Methodist Episcopal Church, but there shall be no religious tests for the admission of students."[4] Nothing came of this effort.

One year later in February, 1843, a group of twenty men, including the original sixteen leaders, incorporated in the Henry County Court House under a document to establish the Mt. Pleasant Collegiate Institute and made provision to place it "under the patronage and control of the Annual Conference of the Methodist Episcopal Church, in the bounds of which it is located,"[5] even though there was no organized Iowa Annual Conference at the time.

Land was donated. An educator and Methodist lay preacher, Aristides J. Huestis, was engaged as director and together with the Rev. Isaac I. Stewart began a fund drive to erect a two-story building (now Pioneer Hall) and begin classes by 1845.[6]

In 1844 the Iowa Annual Conference was authorized for "all the Iowa Territory." The first organizational session in Iowa City was held on August 14, 1844. The incorporators of Mt. Pleasant Collegiate Institute presented a request for approval as the school of the Conference. But the Conference extended the approval to another venture, the Iowa City College.[7]

Old Main

The James Harlan Home Iowa Wesleyan Campus

The same resolution was presented to the Conference in 1845 and a visiting committee was appointed to report back in 1846. By the meeting of the 1849 Annual Conference, the Iowa City College had gone out of existence. The Mt. Pleasant Collegiate Institute was accepted but no funds were allocated for its support. [8]

The association with the Iowa Annual Conference continued unbroken into the Iowa-Des Moines Conference in 1932; the South Iowa Conference in 1958 and the Iowa Conference of the United Methodist Church in 1968.

In 1852 James Harlan, former president of the Iowa City College and now a member of the Iowa Bar, became president of the Institute. He proposed the seeking of a new charter from the State of Iowa changing the name to Iowa Wesleyan University, the introduction of a full level baccalaureate program, and the construction of a second building. The new charter was obtained in 1855 and the three-story brick building completed in the same year.[9] It still serves the college as Old Main and was totally restored in 1981.

James Harlan became United States Senator in 1855 and Secretary of the Interior under Andrew Johnson. He maintained his home in Mt. Pleasant until his death in 1899, serving the college as a trustee, interim president, and professor. His home after retirement from the Senate is today owned by Iowa Wesleyan College and maintained as a museum—the James Harlan Home.[10]

The baccalaureate program resulted in the granting of the first B.A. degree in 1856 and the first B.A. to a woman student in 1859. The Academy was maintained, however, until 1917.[11]

On January 21, 1868, seven women students formed the P.E.O. Sisterhood in a room in Old Main. This has grown into an international women's educational organization of over 200,000 living members. The founding spot is maintained by the college as a P.E.O. Shrine.[12]

In 1912 the name was changed to Iowa Wesleyan College and no further attempts were made to develop professional schools.[13]

Iowa Wesleyan in 1872 took leadership in establishing the Mt. Pleasant German College to serve the needs of pastors and students of German-speaking Methodist Episcopal congregations and conferences. The Mt. Pleasant German College merged in 1909 with Central Wesleyan College, Warrenton, Missouri, and the land and buildings reverted to Iowa Wesleyan College.[14]

Iowa Wesleyan was served by distinguished presidents of whom the most outstanding was J. Raymond Chadwick (1950-1961) under whose leadership four buildings were constructed, curriculum revised, faculty expanded, library resources enriched and the endowment fund increased. The college library (1968) is dedicated to his memory.

The Upper Iowa Conference (1856-1948)

1. CORNELL COLLEGE:1852-

The establishment of Cornell College, Mount Vernon began while this community was still located in the Iowa Annual Conference. The leadership came from the Rev. George B. Bowman, circuit rider and later presiding elder. He had been instrumental in the earlier, short-lived Iowa City College. He was affectionately known as Elder Bowman over the years. His idea was well supported by local residents who were members of the Methodist Episcopal Church.[15]

In 1852 the Iowa Annual Conference accepted fifteen acres of land in Mt. Vernon and agreed to provide support for the Mt. Vernon Wesleyan Seminary to be erected there, with Elder Bowman as the agent for fund raising.[16]

The first building was completed in November, 1854, and the school opened as an elementary/secondary institution, with the Rev. Samuel N. Fellows as principal and two faculty members. It was called the Iowa Conference Seminary with a local board of trustees. The name was changed later in

1854 to Cornell College, in honor of William W. Cornell of New York, a generous benefactor, and Articles of Incorporation were issued.[17]

The first (1856) session of the Upper Iowa Annual Conference passed a resolution to ". . . adopt Cornell College, located at Mount Vernon and formerly known as Iowa Conference Seminary, as their college, and they hereby pledge themselves to its patronage and support."[18] It remained in relationship to the Upper Iowa Annual Conference until the 1948 merger of the Upper Iowa and Northwest Iowa Annual Conference as the North Iowa Conference, and continued into the Iowa Annual Conference of the United Methodist Church in 1968.

Collegiate instruction was introduced and the first B.A. degrees were granted in 1858. Cornell College had a history of steady growth and stable administration during the extended presidency of William Fletcher King (1865-1908). He is memorialized today in the King Chapel and the King Scholarship Program. At the time of the completion of the chapel in 1882 a large window was given by and dedicated to Elder George Bowman and he is also remembered in Bowman Hall (1885), the first residence hall.[19]

Great benefactors in the 1930s were Mr. and Mrs. Henry Pfeiffer, New York, who provided successive gifts for a variety of capital purposes.[20]

William Fletcher King Memorial Chapel, Cornell College

2. UPPER IOWA UNIVERSITY: 1854-1928

A second institution of the Upper Iowa Conference resulted from local effort in Fayette, Iowa. In 1854 a group of citizens under Colonel Robert Alexander proposed the idea of a school. Building operations started for the Fayette Seminary. An unsuccessful approach was made to the Iowa Annual Conference in the fall of 1855. Work continued and on March 12, 1856, Articles of Incorporation were drawn and the sponsorship of the newly organized Upper Iowa Annual Conference was obtained. The Fayette Seminary opened for instruction on January 7, 1857, with William H. Poor as principal.[21]

The name was changed to Upper Iowa University on July 15, 1858, and the Rev. Lucius H. Bugbee was elected the first president on July 31, 1859. Collegiate work had been introduced on December 27, 1857.[22]

A long-term president was John W. Bissell (1873-1899) who provided stable leadership. But the problems of providing support for two colleges became more intense for the Upper Iowa Annual Conference during the first decades of the 1920s.[23]

College Hall
Upper Iowa

Additional difficulties arose in 1927 when Upper Iowa University lost its North Central Association academic accreditation and the Science Hall was destroyed by fire in December of the same year.[24] A possible merger with Cornell College was in the discussion stage during April, 1928, but this did not materialize.[25] Upper Iowa University decided to drop its church-related status and continue as an independent college. The Upper Iowa Annual Conference in September, 1928, voted "that Upper Iowa University not be included in payment from educational funds and that hereafter the Conference would support and maintain but one college, Cornell at Mt. Vernon . . . UIU from now on would be operating as an independent college."[26]

The March, 1929, catalog of Upper Iowa University contained no reference to the Methodist Episcopal Church and affirmed that "while it is Christian in all its teachings, it is non-sectarian in spirit and control."[27] It has continued in that status to the present day.

3. EPWORTH SEMINARY: 1857-1923

The third educational effort of the Upper Iowa Annual Conference was Epworth Seminary which never achieved collegiate status, offering only secondary academic work.

The Journal of the 1856 Upper Iowa Annual Conference indicated that plans were underway for a seminary at Epworth, Dubuque County and approval was given for this work to continue.[28]

In 1857 Epworth Seminary was formally organized by a group of local Methodist Episcopal leaders in a single brick building. The first classes were held in the fall of 1857 with John Pollock as principal and the seminary operated until 1866 when it passed into private hands. In 1870 Epworth Seminary was repurchased by the local Methodist Episcopal group with John H. Rigley as principal, and shortly afterwards a chapel was constructed.[29] The Epworth Seminary Bulletin for June, 1907, a semi-centennial history, indicated that there was a four-year secondary course leading to a diploma but no college level work.[30]

The Epworth Seminary terminated the Conference relationship in 1923. It became the Epworth Military Academy with an independent board of trustees. There was a continuing discussion in 1924, 1925, and 1926 regarding the exact relationship of the academy and its property to the Upper Iowa Annual Conference. It was noted in the 1928 Journal of the Upper Iowa Conference that Epworth Military Academy had closed and that its property had been disposed of through a bankruptcy sale to a Dubuque bank.[32]

Western Iowa Conference (1860-1864)

SIMPSON COLLEGE: 1860-

In a number of central Iowa communities in the mid-century there were local groups of lay persons and ministers who sought to begin seminaries or schools for elementary/secondary education. The most successful effort arose in Indianola, Warren County, platted and designated as the county seat in 1849.[33]

Administration Building
Simpson College

In 1860 plans to establish an Indianola Seminary were in the talking stage within a group that included members of the Methodist Episcopal Church. This group approached the newly organized Western Iowa Annual Conference in 1860 for approval of the Indianola Male and Female Seminary. Sponsorship was granted with the proviso "That the enterprise shall not be pecuniarily embarrassed, and that this Conference will not be responsible in any way, for any funds necessary for the future prosecution of the enterprise."[34]

A curriculum of elementary, secondary, and normal education was announced in an 1861 Bulletin and classes were offered in the 1860-1861 academic year. The name was changed in 1866 to the Des Moines Conference Seminary in the light of proposed realignment and change of name for the Conference itself.[35]

Collegiate level work was introduced in 1866 with the appointment of the Rev. Samuel Milton Vernon as president. President Vernon, an 1867 graduate of Iowa Wesleyan University, served until 1868. He was succeeded by Alexander Burns, a former faculty member and vice president of Iowa Wesleyan University. During the next decade until 1878 he held office, providing stable leadership and physical growth.[36]

It was felt that a new name was necessary to indicate the character of the college and in 1867 it became Simpson Centenary College. The double name served to honor Bishop Matthew Simpson, a distinguished Methodist Episcopal leader and church historian whose 1878 *Cyclopaedia of Methodism* would be a landmark reference work. The name also took into account the centennial of the organization of Methodism in the United States. In 1884 the title was shortened to Simpson College.[37] Bishop Matthew Simpson is also memorialized by the Simpson Room for history and archives in the current college library.

The Conference relationship continued from the Western Iowa Annual Conference into the Des Moines Annual Conference in 1864, the Iowa-Des Moines Annual Conference in 1932, the South Iowa Conference in 1958 and the Iowa Annual Conference of the United Methodist Church in 1969.

A distinguished former student who spent his first two years at Simpson College was the black scientist George Washington Carver whose biological research gained world renown. The Carver Hall of Science is a memorial to him.[38]

In 1942 a major gift from Mr. and Mrs. Henry Pfeiffer, New York spurred a massive fund drive and capital campaign which resulted in fifteen new buildings in the next years.[39] Indianola has remained a small county seat town, but its proximity to Des Moines, fifteen miles away, has contributed to the suburban-urban character of its collegiate life.

Northwest Iowa Conference (1872-1948)

MORNINGSIDE COLLEGE: 1890-

When the Northwest Iowa Annual Conference was organized in 1872 there was discussion of the founding of an educational institution. The first ideas were advanced in 1882 and by 1887 several sites, including Sioux City, were mentioned. The 1889 Conference indicated that it would consider bids for sponsorship from local groups in the area. [40]

The Sioux City group of prominent businessmen under the leadership of the Rev. R. C. Glass, local pastor, and the Rev. Wilmot Whitfield, presiding elder, initiated plans. Articles of Incorporation for the University of the Northwest were drawn on December 27, 1889. These envisaged a grandiose university of seven colleges under a board of managers who would be members of the Methodist Episcopal Church. Construction of a first building was in progress in the spring of 1890 and classes were held at Grace M.E. Church in September, 1890, with Wilmot Whitfield as president. [41]

A Commission of the Conference appointed to examine the structure and finances of the university was asked to report to the 1891 Conference. Financial problems were soon evident, although the building was completed in January, 1891, and classes moved to that spot for the spring semester. A graduating class was presented in 1891. [42]

Conference sponsorship was delayed as members questioned the viability of the school. In the summer of 1892 the Rev. William Brush became president. [43]

In 1894 the Annual Conference decided to begin its own work, independent of the University of the Northwest, and passed resolutions to create a board of trustees for a new school to be called Morningside College. The University of the Northwest ceased operations, and the property went into the hands of the sheriff. [44]

On June 11, 1895, the directors of the planned Morningside College determined to purchase the land, building and foundations of a second building of the defunct University of the Northwest. Through this action, Morningside College became a reality as a Conference sponsored institution. Two students who had completed academic work at the former school formed the first graduating class of Morningside College. [45]

The relationship with the Northwest Iowa Annual Conference was continued into the merger with the Upper Iowa Annual Conference in 1948 as the North Iowa Annual Conference and then into the Iowa Annual Conference of the United Methodist Church in 1969.

Capable, aggressive leadership began in 1897 with the election of Wilson Seeley Lewis, former principal of the Epworth Seminary, as president. He served more than a decade until 1908 when he was elected a bishop of the Methodist Episcopal Church. He introduced a well planned educational program and an extensive building program. Lewis Hall, the administration building, is named in his honor. [46]

In 1914 there was a merger with the Charles City College, Charles City, Iowa, a former college of the Northwest German Conference. Its liquidated assets of $100,000 were added to the Morningside College Endowment Fund. Academic and music equipment was brought to Sioux City and several faculty members joined the Morningside College staff. In September 1958

Charles City College Hall on Morningside College Campus

the Conservatory of Music was remodeled by the alumni of the former Charles City College and named the Charles City College Building.[47]

A long presidency was that of Earl A. Roadman—twenty years beginning in 1936. A substantial building program was completed between 1948 and 1966. Morningside College is the only urban church-related college of the United Methodist Church in Iowa.[48]

The Iowa Evangelical United Brethren Conference (1946-1968)

The Iowa Evangelical United Brethren Annual Conference presented a complex union of separate groups, some of which were English-speaking and some of which were German-speaking.

The Church of the United Brethren in Christ held a first Iowa Annual Conference in 1845. The Evangelical Association organized a first Annual Conference in 1861; the United Evangelical Church in 1894. (The Evangelical Association and the United Evangelical Church formed The Evangelical Church in 1927.) These were merged into the Evangelical United Brethren Church in 1946 and continued until the corporate union with The Methodist Church in 1968, to form the United Methodist Church. At that time Evangelical United Brethren and Methodist churches, pastors and institutions were assigned together into a single Iowa Annual Conference.

Educational efforts shared by the district Conferences in Iowa and adjacent states eventually became a single academic institution—Westmar College, Le Mars, Iowa.

1. WESTERN COLLEGE: 1857-1918

Western College was founded at Shueyville, Linn County, Iowa on January 1, 1857, by the United Brethren in Christ. It was moved to Toledo, Iowa in 1881 and renamed Leander Clark College in 1906. It merged with Coe College, Cedar Rapids, a Presbyterian sponsored school in 1918. Its alumni files and other records were deposited with York College, York, Nebraska, founded by the Church of the United Brethren in Christ, and eventually moved to Westmar College, Le Mars, Iowa in 1955.[49]

2. WESTMAR COLLEGE: 1900-

In 1900 there were activities to establish a college in Le Mars, Iowa. The Northwestern Normal School and Business College begun by Professor Jacob Wernli in 1887 was in existence and a Le Mars Normal School Association was begun in 1892. That group helped to erect the first building. The property was obtained by leaders of the United Evangelical Church and on April 12, 1900, a new institution, Western Union College, came into being with H. H. Thoren as president.[50]

The first building was completed in 1901 and today is named Thoren Hall in honor of the first president. In 1921 a residence hall was named for the founder of the original school as Wernli Hall. Long-term presidents were Charles A. Mock (1911-1930) and David O. Kime (1932-1955). The decade

Thoren Hall at Westmar College

of the 1940s saw considerable building expansion including the Charles A. Mock Library.[51]

The name of Western Union College was changed to Westmar College in 1948 because of constant public confusion with the Western Union Telegraph Company.[52]

In 1886 the Church of the United Brethren in Christ of Nebraska purchased the Gibbon Collegiate Institute in Gibbon from the Baptists and moved the school to York, Nebraska under the new name of York College. In 1931 Kansas City University was merged with York College. Kansas City University had been the result of several earlier mergers of Avalon College, Gould College, Lane University and Campbell College. York College became the depository of files and alumni records of these earlier institutions.[53]

The Administration Building of York College was burned to the ground in 1951 and some property titles became unclear. As a result York College was united with Westmar College in 1955, together with all of the combined records. The name of Westmar College was retained.[54]

The 1968 formation of the United Methodist Church from the previous Methodist Church and Evangelical United Brethren Church brought Westmar College into the Iowa Conference of the United Methodist Church. Until 1968 Westmar College had been sponsored by and received support from the national Evangelical United Brethren Church as well as from twenty Annual Conferences in the Midwest. It was now related to the United Methodist Church only through the Iowa Annual Conference.

German Methodist Episcopal Conferences

Missionary work among German speaking immigrants to the Midwest was carried out by Methodist Episcopal activity. It resulted in local churches with German speaking pastors and services conducted in the German language. These were originally part of English speaking Annual Conferences, but after the 1860s such local churches were organized into German speaking Annual Conferences. Because of the scattered character of the work, such Annual Conferences frequently crossed state lines. Various German Annual conferences sponsored or established academic institutions in which secondary, collegiate and theological training were offered in the German language. The major mission was to provide clergy for the German speaking congregations.

Northwest German Conference (1868-1933)

This Conference organized in 1868 included German congregations of northern Illinois and northern Iowa. When it was dissolved in 1933, the Illinois and Iowa churches and pastors were assigned to English speaking Annual Conferences in the separate states.

THE CHARLES CITY COLLEGE: 1868-1914

The Annual Conference initiated in 1868 in Galena, Illinois the North-West German-English Normal School as a secondary academic effort. The curriculum was expanded in 1880 to include collegiate work and theological training and the name became the German-English College of Galena. In 1887 the presidency was assumed by Friedrich Schaub who served until 1914 —the entire period of the college's existence. In 1890 the college was moved to Charles City, Iowa, an area of the Northwest German Annual Conference, and renamed the Charles City College. [55]

A building was erected in 1893, some financial security was obtained, and work continued on the college level until 1913. The German language was gradually dropped as the medium of instruction and the institution served a dwindling number of students, chiefly in business courses and music instruction. The Northwest German Annual Conference and the Northwest (English) Annual Conference covered the same Iowa territory and Morningside College, Sioux City was the sponsored college of the Northwest Conference. A plan of merger was effected in 1914.

The Charles City College assets were liquidated to about $100,000 and designated as "The Northwest German Conference Fund of Morningside College." The library, science and music equipment were moved to Sioux City and several faculty members, including Friedrich Schaub, joined the Morningside faculty.

In September, 1958, the Alumni of Charles City College raised funds to remodel the Morningside Conservatory of Music, which was then re-dedicated as the Charles City College Building with a bronze plaque listing the names of the donors. It remains the visible memorial to the previous college.

St. Louis German Conference and West German Conference (1864-1925; 1864-1933)

A Southwest German Annual Conference was created in 1864. In 1878 it was subdivided into the St. Louis German Annual Conference, to include areas of western Illinois, eastern Iowa, eastern Missouri, and the West German Annual Conference for western Missouri, Kansas, and Nebraska. The St. Louis German Annual Conference continued as a corporate entity until 1933 at which time the local churches, pastors and institutions were merged into adjacent English speaking Methodist Episcopal Conferences.

THE MOUNT PLEASANT GERMAN COLLEGE: 1872-1909

The Mount Pleasant German College (Das Deutsche Kollegium) began as a joint effort of Iowa Wesleyan University, Mount Pleasant, Iowa, and officials of the Southwest German Annual Conference. [56]

In 1870 the presidency of Iowa Wesleyan University was assumed by the Rev. Dr. John Wheeler who had been president of Baldwin University, Berea, Ohio, where a dual arrangement with German Wallace College had been effected. He led the negotiations for a similar academic venture. The

Mt. Pleasant German College

Southwest German Annual Conference had already established Central Wesleyan College, Warrenton, Missouri, but was open to the concept of another college.

Iowa Wesleyan University made an offer of campus land, provided some financial support for a building, offered free tuition for German College students at Iowa Wesleyan as well as an exchange of faculty. Courses were to be offered in the German language on the secondary, collegiate and theological level. The collegiate work was heavily dependent upon Iowa Wesleyan. German College students became involved in Iowa Wesleyan social and extracurricular activities. Qualified German College students obtained the Iowa Wesleyan baccalaureate degree as well as the German College diploma or certificate. The German College faculty members provided the Department of German at Iowa Wesleyan.

Some 400 to 500 students were enrolled in the German College over the years 1873-1909, of whom 179 received a German College diploma and 63 an Iowa Wesleyan B.A. degree. Fifty-six students obtained the German College theological diploma.

The single building completed in 1873 remained the only academic facility, since many classes, including all in science, were offered in Iowa Wesleyan College buildings. The German College Chapel was built in 1902 and also served as the church for the local German speaking congregation. Pastors were German College faculty members. Students lived in private homes and organized eating clubs.

Faculty recruitment posed a problem since there were at first very few German speaking pastors who possessed a college degree. Most of the faculty were drawn from other German speaking colleges and in later years from German College alumni. Some distinguished German Methodist Episcopal scholars did serve the institution over the decades.

The outstanding president was the Rev. Dr. Edwin Stanton Havighorst (1898-1908). He was a graduate of the German College, Iowa Wesleyan University and the Boston University School of Theology.

Enrollment was difficult to maintain after the turn of the century as the use of the German language in local churches and homes began to decline. The St. Louis German Annual Conference found the burden of supporting two colleges a difficult task. There was discussion of a merger of the Mt. Pleasant German College and Central Wesleyan College, Warrenton, Missouri in 1905. It was determined upon in 1908 and became effective in 1909 when the college closed.

The land and buildings reverted to Iowa Wesleyan University, in accord with the terms of the original grant. The small endowment fund of $30,000 was divided between Iowa Wesleyan University and Central Wesleyan College. The library of 10,000 German books, as well as academic equipment, was moved to Warrenton, Missouri. A handful of students transferred to Central Wesleyan but the largest number dropped out or entered Iowa Wesleyan. Faculty members moved to either Central Wesleyan College or Baldwin Wallace College. One faculty member who had been president during the final year, the Rev. Dr. Henry G. Leist, joined the Iowa Wesleyan faculty as professor of religion and German and later served as academic dean until his retirement in 1936.

The German College Building was used at Iowa Wesleyan chiefly for work in physics and music. In 1910 the German College Ex-Studenten Bund placed a commemorative tablet over the entrance to the German College Building. This building was razed in 1961 to make space for a new Hall of Science. Original bricks and the commemorative tablet were erected into a monument on the spot as a designated memorial to the Rev. Rudolph Havighorst and the Rev. Dr. Edwin Stanton Havighorst, leading presidents.

The German College Chapel was removed in 1926 after it had suffered very severe roof damage. In 1961 Iowa Wesleyan College was given a very extensive collection of German-American Methodist archives by the late Rev. Dr. Zwingli F. Meyer, Crete, Nebraska. It was accepted at a formal academic convocation in 1973 on the 90th Anniversary of the founding of the German College and is housed as the Zwingli F. Meyer Collection in the Iowa Wesleyan College Library. It is available for research purposes.[57]

Central Wesleyan College, Warrenton, Missouri, survived with great difficulty. There was an increasing loss of students speaking the German language. It continued as an English speaking college of the English speaking Conference after the dissolution of the West German Annual Conference in 1933. It was reduced to junior college status and quietly terminated in 1941. Its archives and records are stored at Northeast Missouri State University, Kirksville, Missouri. A Central Wesleyan College Alumni Association holds an annual gathering in Warrenton and has established an historical room in the local United Methodist Church.[58]

Footnotes

1. Stephen Norris Fellows, *History of the Upper Iowa Conference of the Methodist Episcopal Church 1856-1906* (Cedar Rapids: 1907) p. 53.
2. Charles J. Kennedy, *History and Alumni Record of Iowa Wesleyan College 1842-1943* (Mt. Pleasant: 1942) pp. 14, 92, n. 11, n. 12.

3. Louis A. Haselmayer, *History and Alumni Record of Iowa Wesleyan College 1842-1967* (Mt. Pleasant: 1967) p. 10.
4. Ibid., p. 8.
5. Ibid.
6. Ibid., p. 9.
7. Ibid., p. 10.
8. Ibid.
9. Ibid, p. 11.
10. Louis A. Haselmayer, *The Harlan-Lincoln Tradition at Iowa Wesleyan College* (Mt. Pleasant: 1977) pp. 8-11, 13-16, 27.
11. Haselmayer, *History*, ibid., p. 14.
12. Ibid., p. 20.
13. Ibid., p. 30.
14. Ibid., pp. 17, 29.
15. Fellows, ibid., pp. 53, 56.
16. Marjorie Medary, "The History of Cornell College 1853-1953," *The Palimpsest,* XXXIV, No. 4 (April 1953) pp. 146-148.
17. Ibid., p. 157.
18. Fellows, ibid., p. 53.
19. Medary, ibid., pp. 153, 158, 183.
20. Ibid., pp. 163, 189.
21. Fellows, ibid., pp. 54-59.
22. Ibid., p. 59.
23. M. H. Alderson, "Upper Iowa University," *The Palimpsest,* XLVI, No. 3 (March 1965) p. 149.
24. Ibid., p. 169.
25. *Cedar Rapids Evening Gazette* April 30, 1928.
26. Alderson, ibid., p. 170.
27. Ibid., p. 170.
28. Fellows, ibid., p. 62.
29. Ibid.
30. *Epworth Seminary Bulletin,* June 1907.
31. *Dubuque Telegraph Herald,* Undated clipping. *Directory of Epworth Seminary Alumni and Former Students 1857-1923* (Mimeograph: 1968).
32. *Upper Iowa Conference Journal,* 1923, pp. 570-572; 1924; 1925; 1926, p. 396; 1928, p. 49.
33. Ruth M. Jackson, "Southwest Iowa Methodist Seminaries," *Proceedings of Historical Society of the North Central Jurisdiction of the Methodist Church,* July 1967, no pagination.
34. Ibid.
35. Ibid.
36. Ibid.
37. Ibid.
38. "Simpson College" *Encyclopedia of World Methodism,* p. 2160.
39. Ibid.
40. Robert McDonald, "The Struggle for Education in Northwest Iowa: University of the Northwest 1889-1895," *Annals of Iowa,* Third Series, XXXIX, No. 7, p. 481.
41. Ibid., pp. 482, 483.
42. Ibid., p. 487.
43. Ibid., p. 492.
44. Ibid., pp. 494, 496.
45. Ibid., p. 496.
46. Ida Belle Lewis, *Bishop Wilson Seeley Lewis* (Sioux City: 1929).
47. Louis A. Haselmayer, "Charles City College," *Encyclopedia of World Methodism,* p. 452.
48. *Morningside College Catalog,* 70th Anniversary Issue.
49. A. E. Wilken, "The Iowa Conference of the Evangelical United Brethren Church," *1970 Journal Iowa Annual Conference of the United Methodist Church,* p. 361.
Henry W. Ward, *History of Western-Leander Clark College 1856-1911* (Dayton, Ohio: 1911).

50. "Westmar College," *Encyclopedia of World Methodism* "History," *Westmar College Catalog 1958,* pp. 20-21. A. Q. Larsen, "A Short History of Westmar College," *Proceedings of North Central Jurisdiction Historical Society of the United Methodist Church 1975,* p. 1.
51. Larsen, ibid., pp. 1-3.
52. Ibid., pp. 3, 21.
53. Ibid., pp. 5-6.
54. Ibid., p. 6.
55. Louis A. Haselmayer, "Charles City College," *Encyclopedia of World Methodism,* p. 452. This is the only printed account and is based upon archives of Charles City College in the Morningside College Library.
56. Louis A. Haselmayer, "German Methodist Colleges in the West," *Methodist History II,* No. 4 (July 1964) pp. 35-43. Includes a complete bibliography of sources. Cf. also Louis A. Haselmayer, "The Mt. Pleasant German College" in *Encyclopedia of World Methodism.*
57. Haselmayer, ibid., p. 41.
58. Ibid., p. 42.

Bibliography

I. General articles on Conferences, Institutions, Persons, Simpson, Matthew, *Cyclopaedia of Methodism* (Philadelphia: 1875). *Encyclopedia of World Methodism,* Edited by Nolan B. Harmon 1974.

II. Conference Histories

Haines, Aaron, W. *The Makers of Iowa Methodism* 1900.

Waring, Edmund H., *History of the Iowa Annual Conference of the Methodist Episcopal Church,* 1910.

Fellows, Stephen Norris, *History of the Upper Iowa Conference of the Methodist Episcopal Church 1856-1906* (1907).

Mitchell, Bennett, *History of the Northwest Iowa Conference 1873-1903* (1904).

Gallaher, Ruth, *A Century of Methodism in Iowa 1844-1944* (1944).

Haselmayer, Louis; Morris, James; Wilken, A. E.; Mac Cannon, R. R., "History of United Methodism in Iowa 1844-1970," *1970 Journal of Iowa Annual Conference.*

Harvey, R. E., "Historical Sketch of the Des Moines Conference of the M.E. Church, 1832-1860," *Annals of Iowa,* Third Series, XXV, No. 3, January, 1944, pp. 192-228. "Des Moines M.E. Conference Growth," *Annals of Iowa,* Third Series, XXV, No. 4, April, 1944, pp. 282-312. "War Years of Des Moines, M.E. Conference," *Annals of Iowa,* Third Series, XXVII, No. 1, July, 1945, pp. 44-61. "Imperial Expansion of M.E. Church," *Annals of Iowa,* Third Series, XXVII, No. 2, October 1945, pp. 119-150. "Des Moines Reduces Area," *Annals of Iowa,* Third Series, XXVIII, No. 4, April 1947, pp. 287-329.

Deaver, Leonard E., *One Hundred Years with Evangelicals in Iowa* (1944).

Douglas, Paul T., *The Story of German Methodism* (1939).

Ferguson, Dwayne L., *A Brief History of the Iowa Conference of the Evangelical United Brethren Church* (1967).

Kriege, Otto E., *Geschichte des Methodismus* (1909).

Trailblazers, Centennial of the Iowa Conference of the Evangelical United Brethren Church (1961).

Magaret, E. C. et al., *Jubilaumsbuch der St. Louis Deutschen Konferenz* (1904).

St. Louis German Conference 1879-1926 Final Minutes (1925).

Henke, E. W. et al., *Geschichte der Nordwest Deutschen Konferenz* (1913).

Yearbook and Journal of Tenth Annual Sessions of Chicago-Northwest Conference of the Methodist Episcopal Church (1933).

Kriege, Otto E. et al., *Souvenir der West Deutschen Konferenz der Bischoplichen Methodistenkirche* (1906).

West German Conference, Methodist Episcopal Church Final Minutes (1926).

III. Individual Colleges

A. *Iowa City College*

Fellows, Stephen Norris, *History of the Upper Iowa Conference of the Methodist Episcopal Church 1856-1906* (1907).

Haselmayer, Louis A., *History and Alumni Directory, Iowa Wesleyan College 1842-1967* (1967).

Kennedy, Charles J., *History and Alumni Record, Iowa Wesleyan College 1842-1942* (1942).

B. *Iowa Wesleyan College*

Hancher, John W., *Historical Sketch and Alumni Record of Iowa Wesleyan University* (1905).

Wilson, Ben Hur, *Historical Sketch and Alumni Record of Iowa Wesleyan University* (1917).

Kennedy, Charles J., *History and Alumni Record of Iowa Wesleyan College 1842-1942* (1942).

Haselmayer, Louis, A., *History and Alumni Directory, Iowa Wesleyan College 1842-1967* (1967).

Haselmayer, Louis A., *The Presidents of Iowa Wesleyan College* (1967).

Haselmayer, Louis A., "The Mt. Pleasant Collegiate Institute: A Struggle for Existence," *Annals of Iowa,* XXXIX, No. 3, Winter, 1968.

Haselmayer, Louis A., *The Harlan-Lincoln Tradition at Iowa Wesleyan College* (1977).

C. *Cornell College*

Medary, Marjorie, "The History of Cornell College," *The Palimpsest,* XXXIV, No. 4 (April, 1953).

The Quinquennial Register and Alumni Record of Cornell College (Mount Vernon, Iowa: December, 1913).

Cornell College 1853-1903 A Record of the Celebration of the Fiftieth Anniversary of the Founding of the College (Mount Vernon, Iowa).

D. *Upper Iowa University*

Alderson, M. H., "Upper Iowa University," *The Palimpsest,* XLVI, No. 3 (March, 1965).

Upper Iowa University Alumni Register, 1939.

E. *Epworth Seminary*

Fellows, Stephen Norris, *History of the Upper Iowa Conference of the Methodist Episcopal Church 1856-1906* (1907).

Epworth Seminary Bulletin 1907.

File of miscellaneous printed, duplicated and newspaper items in United Methodist Archives at Iowa Wesleyan College.

F. *Simpson College*

Jackson, Ruth M., "Southwest Iowa Methodist Seminaries," *Proceedings of Historical Society of the North Central Jurisdiction of the Methodist Church, July, 1967.*

G. *Morningside College*

McDonald, Robert L., "The Struggle for Education in Northwest Iowa: University of the Northwest 1889-1895," *Annals of Iowa,* Third Series XXXIX, No. 7.

Tweito, Thomas E., "A College in a Cornfield," *The Palimpsest,* XXV, No. 25 (November, 1944).

Lewis, Ida Belle, *Bishop Wilson Seeley Lewis* (1929).

Morningside College Catalog, 70th Anniversary Issue.

H. *Western College (Leander Clark College)*

Ward, Henry W., *History of Western-Leander Clark College* (1911).

I. *Westmar College*

"History," Westmar College Catalog (1958).

Larsen, A. Q. "A Short History of Westmar College," *Proceedings of the Historical Society of the North Central Jurisdiction of the United Methodist Church* (1975).

J. *Charles City College*

Haselmayer, Louis A., "Charles City College," *Encyclopedia of World Methodism* (1974).

Archives of Charles City College in Morningside College Library.

K. *Mount Pleasant German College*

Haselmayer, Louis A., "Das Deutsche Kollegium," *Annals of Iowa*, XXV, No. 3 (Winter 1960).

Haselmayer, Louis A., *History and Alumni List of the Mt. Pleasant German College 1873-1903* (1963).

Haselmayer, Louis A., ed., *The Life Memories and Day Book of Wilhelm Balcke (1847-1926)* (1963).

Haselmayer, Louis A., "German Methodist Colleges in the West," *Methodist History,* II, No. 4 (July 1964).

16

Educational Ministries

SUNDAY SCHOOLS—CHURCH SCHOOLS

John Wesley's "Sunday School" in Georgia in the 1730s and Robert Raikes' Sunday Charity School for teaching the three R's to poor English children who worked weekdays in factories during the 1780s are referred to as predecessors of the Sunday Schools which developed in the 1780-1800 period in the United States. Katy Furguson, a black woman, established a Sunday School in New York City in 1793.

The first Sunday School Union was formed in 1816 to "promote, coordinate, and improve" independent efforts to teach religion. Iowa's early Sunday Schools were generally Union-style, with pupils and teachers of various denominations involved. It has been observed that the Union Sunday School movement was built upon a "lowest common denominator Protestantism," based on Bible study.

To give one example, Grandma Booth's Sunday School "out upon the prairie" in 1872 drew nine children, who walked up to three miles to reach the Jackson School building—about a mile from where the town of Moville in Woodbury County was organized fifteen years later. Teacher and children sang such favorites as "The Sunday School Army" and "Around the Throne of Heaven" without benefit of accompaniment, and shared the "old, old story" from the Bible. The school was carried on as a Union Sunday School until the last few years of the 1880s when United Brethren and Congregational people constructed buildings in the community, worshiped separately, and founded denominational Sunday Schools.

In 1901 Methodists were said to be "the most prominent people in Sunday School work." The Iowa State Sunday School Association—an "incorporated interdenominational institution" through which the Protestant Sunday Schools of Iowa united "to carry the open Bible by the hand of the trained teacher to every boy, girl, man, and woman in Iowa"—was a part of the International Sunday School Association (1905-1922). It was said to cultivate the spirit of cooperation, while at the same time developing "denominational loyalty." The association promoted cradle rolls, home departments, graded lessons, young people's and adult Bible classes, teacher training, evangelism, missionary instruction, systematic giving, temperance instruction, pledge signing, and regular worker's meetings.

Older United Methodists today may remember the Bible picture cards used in kindergarten and primary classes, with a Golden Text to be memorized. They may also recall the popularity of "Classmate," "Sunday School

Advocate," "Trails for Juniors," "Boys and Girls," or "My Book" when these were available.

Materials prepared cooperatively by a number of Protestant denominations in the 1950s had wide acceptance in Iowa. Observation Schools and Laboratory Schools, where certified teachers demonstrated techniques with classes of children from the host church, attracted eager participants. The instruction in both Sunday classes and Vacation Church Schools was upgraded. The name "Church School" was adopted to cover a concept larger than Sunday School; it embraced weekday, night, or outdoor sessions, as well as Sunday classes.

The 1964 Iowa Area summer laboratory school at Newton drew large attendance of church school teachers and staffers from both North and South Iowa when the "New Curriculum" of Christian studies for Methodist children was introduced. As the "lab" school participants reported to their local churches back home, the design for Methodist Curriculum for Children suggested that in the broadest sense Christian nurture is concerned with what God has revealed through redemptive action and the implication of this redemptive action for man in the whole field of relationships. The broad scope of the curriculum was divided into five major areas: Life and Its Setting; The Reality of God; The New Life in Christ; Vocation (Discipleship); The Church (Christian Community). All areas were rooted in the Bible.

District literature seminars, led by those who had been at the Newton lab school, inspired teachers to try packets of teaching aids containing such helps as time lines, maps, art prints, and audio-visuals. "Team teaching" grew in popularity as commissions on education and counseling teachers in local churches recruited women and men willing to learn with their pupils. Parents were urged to be involved with their children's Christian development.

Launching of a new Youth Curriculum in South Iowa and North Iowa Methodist conferences and the Iowa Conference of Evangelical United Brethren in 1968 was reported by Milton R. Vogel, Donald D. Frank, and Anne Hartsuck, at the 1969 Iowa Uniting Conference. The report also forecast the appointment of a new program staff for Christian Education.

The 1971 report of the Board of Christian Education, signed by Arthur B. Campney, Chairman, pointed out that the board

is elected by the Annual Conference to foster and direct a plan of Christian Education that encourages an experience of Christ and the development of well-rounded Christian character. To this aim each local church through the work areas on Education and the Council on Ministries seeks to: enable persons to possess their heritage, guide the development of persons, and equip persons for their responsibilities.[1]

The Division of Local Church Education assumed the responsibility of the former Board of Christian Education in 1975. Training was provided for youth ministry, and a Media Festival was held to help persons learn to use media in a creative manner. The "Learning Center" was continued during

Annual Conference, promoting use of programmed learning and portable learning centers. The Division offered Small Membership Church Consultant Training at a number of locations in 1983. Kaleida-Quest materials—Justice Shalom with the emphasis on Peace—were prepared.

Two Intro-80s workshops were held in Des Moines with leadership from Nashville, to give district teams an overview and orientation for a new curriculum for children, youth, and adults, available in the fall of 1982. One hundred eighty-eight district trainers then held eighty-three workshops throughout the conference, to acquaint church school teachers and leaders with the potential afforded by the materials. A Church School Growth and Renewal Workshop with follow-up workshops in the districts was a feature of 1984.

An interesting ecumenical development took place in 1984 when United Methodists, the Des Moines Catholic Diocese, the United Church of Christ, the Episcopal Church, and Baptists agreed to form the Iowa Religious Media Services. It was their intent to pool libraries of films, videotapes, film strips, print materials, and the like from church media centers, and to share production equipment by 1986. Each denomination agreed to pay an annual fee of forty cents per member to operate a combined media center. Don Mendenhall, a member of the state program staff for United Methodists, was chosen chairman of the board. A "stronger ecumenical image" for Iowa churches was predicted by religious leaders.

CAMPS—OUTDOOR EDUCATION

The evolution of our church camps—from pioneer camp meetings to Epworth League Institutes and Bible Conferences and on to the varied opportunities currently listed by the Iowa Annual Conference's Division of Camps and Extended Ministries is a thrilling story. As a long-range study report stated in 1972, "Camping is continuing Christian education of-and-beyond the local church whether it is in a tent, cabin, lodge, retreat center, motel or

Clear Lake Campground Tabernacle

church basement, and whether it be a trail hike, a bus trip, or an overnight retreat."

Three of the camp grounds in the northern half of the state trace their roots back to early camp meetings. About 1877 camp meetings were held on the "Old Camp Grounds" known as Methodist Hill on the northwest edge of Clear Lake. In 1896 the Clear Lake Chautauqua Association was formed. Epworth League Institutes were held in P. M. Park, just east of the present camp grounds.

Rev. Clyde Baker's dream of a permanent camp ground became a reality in 1924, when the present site was purchased. Its purpose has always been: Gather more understanding of Christ and go forth to serve others in the cause of Christ. In 1977, some 700 people celebrated the 50th anniversary of the operation of the present camp grounds, with Bishop Webb preaching and the Confirmation Campers recognized. Since 1927, when the grounds were platted, they have been dotted by cabins owned by churches and private residents.

Riverview Camp Tabernacle

Riverview Park at Cedar Falls claims the distinction of being the "oldest continual camp meeting in Iowa." The early camp meetings, beginning in 1893, had been held by the Iowa Conference (Evangelical) at Chautauqua Park in Waterloo, east of Cattle Congress Grounds, but the coming of "noisy summer attractions" nearby made a change of location desirable. Land was purchased on the banks of the Cedar River, and lots were sold on a 99-year lease basis. The name Riverview Park was adopted, and the grounds were dedicated in August, 1917.

The United Brethren in Christ rented the grounds for the first time in 1929 for a ten-day Christian Education program. In 1930 the United Brethren bought thirty-three lots west of Riverview Park, known as Riverbluff Park, by action of the Iowa Conference.

When the Riverview tabernacle was declared unsafe because city and state fire-safety regulations could not be met in 1978, a new building was planned and constructed. The new tabernacle was dedicated and given debt-free by the Cedar Falls Bible Conference to the United Methodist Church in 1979. Following a revitalization consultation with Dr. Paul Diettrich of Naperville,

Illinois, the board adopted a new mission statement: Riverview Park, as an extension of the mission of the United Methodist Church, is a center for physical, mental, and spiritual renewal. Riverview's 90th Year of Christian Continuing Education for ministers and lay persons of the Iowa Conference was celebrated in 1983 with Bishop Wayne Clymer preaching at the opening worship.

A Sheldon District (Northwest Iowa Conference, M.E.) Camp Meeting was held in Arnolds Park, West Lake Okoboji in 1914, with 1,049 participants. A commission was appointed to find a permanent location. Several offers were considered before forty heavily timbered acres owned by the Brownell family, at the north end of the lake, were purchased. Lot prices were kept low to permit preachers and families to own property, and this Sheldon District project was established in 1915 under the leadership of District Superintendent D. A. McBurney, Rev. S. H. Turbeville (pastor of the Spirit Lake church), and Rev. O. M. Bond of the Spencer church.

Arch at Methodist Camp, Okoboji

Spirit Lake Beacon Photo

Incorporation was accomplished in 1920, and the announcement for 1921 declared, "This Camp Meeting is the creation of the Northwest Iowa Conference of the Methodist Episcopal Church, but all people are cordially invited to enjoy it. The tabernacle seats 2,000!"

The 1930s saw the development of the Okoboji Summer Music Camp adjacent to Methodist Camp and under the direction of Paul MacCollin of Morningside College. Musical appearances by the students and faculty became an important part of the annual Bible Conference. Dr. Margaret Kidder prepared an historical booklet for the 50th anniversary of Methodist Camp in 1965, using as one resource a scrapbook kept in the Northwest Iowa Conference Archives at the college.

Besides accommodating the Bible Conference and Summer Assemblies, the three northern camp grounds were popular sites for Epworth League Institutes (later Youth Fellowship) and camping periods, attracting high school and older youth. Eventually camping experience for junior highs, elementary age groups, families, and single adults were included. Additional sites—Dolliver Park at Fort Dodge, Stone Park Boy Scout Camp near Sioux City—were used for some of the mid-twentieth-century camp sessions.

A master plan to develop Pictured Rocks Camp near Monticello was accepted by the North Iowa Annual Conference (Methodist) in 1960. Morris Steffenson was employed as director for 1961-1962, and the camp began operating with seven different camping periods scheduled, each limited to fifty youth plus adult workers. In 1971 a total of 4,708 "camper days" were logged, including use of winterized lodges.

The development of camping programs in southern Iowa was along different lines than in northern Iowa. South Iowa does not have large natural lakes such as Clear Lake and Okoboji, and did not develop camp grounds with privately owned cottages. Instead, the Senior Epworth League Institutes met on the campuses of Iowa Wesleyan and Simpson colleges. The organization for junior high camps rented space in various state parks, and held their camps at such locations. The first of these camps was organized by Rev. W. M. Doughty and met in Lake Aquabi State Park south of Indianola.

The Iowa Des Moines Conference scheduled fourteen camps and institutes in six locations in 1954. Southern Iowa camps have been held at Springbrook State Park, Lake Darling, and Camp Dodge, as well as Lake Aquabi State Park. In 1953, a tract of 55.7 acres suitable for a camp-site (Wesley Woods) adjoining Lake Aquabi State Park on the west side of the lake was purchased and work begun to develop it. Methodist Student Fellowship volunteers from nine Iowa colleges and universities and one Nebraska college aided with work camps in April, 1956.

In 1959 a tract of 100 acres was bought in Montgomery County between Villisca and Stanton, adjoining Lake Viking State Park. The site was developed with volunteer labor and named "Camp Aldersgate." Seventy-five men from neighboring communities turned out for the first workday, and twenty-five more on the second. Also in 1959, 104 acres were acquired along the Skunk River north of Lockridge in Jefferson County, to become "Camp Golden Valley."

Sixty acres of virgin timber south and west of Winterset were given to the Iowa Annual Conference by Mrs. Armena Brownell, with several restrictive clauses. The tract was named Camp Fellowship Forest, and used for Scout and pioneer camps.

The Iowa Annual Conference of 1979 directed that the bishop appoint a Camp Fiscal Responsibility Task Force to report in 1980. Statements from the preamble to the 1980 report showed the seriousness with which the task force chaired by Beverly Everett had approached its task:

> The history of Christian Education in the out-of-doors in Iowa Methodism, in the Evangelical United Brethren Church, and later in United Methodism has been both visionary in its day and a victim of its inflationary times. It has benefited greatly from the thousands of camper days' worth of devoted volunteers,

lay and clergy alike, and yet because of its tendency to grow physically and pro-grammatically in all directions at once, it is now increasingly difficult to keep both the vision for its potential and the necessary structure of support in a financially healthy state.

The task force appointed by Bishop Lance Webb at the mandate of the 1979 Annual Conference began its work in August of 1979, and has continued steadily through to report completion in March of 1980. It has perused all preceding studies of the past decade, has initiated and evaluated its own research as well as that of the Division of Camps and Extended Ministries.[2]

The review of preceding studies included a long-range study authorized by the annual conference in 1970, and a professional study by Bone and Associates 1975-1976.

In addition to fulfilling the conference directive by bringing in a suggested plan for disposing of three sites (Aldersgate, Pictured Rocks, and Riverview Park) in 1981, the Division of Camps and Extended Ministries brought a substitute proposal which recommended the retention of all sites and the continuation of the funding plan adopted by the 1980 Annual Conference— that in 1982 the sites receive $100,000; 1983-1990 they receive $200,000 annually. The substitute proposal was adopted, and the sites enabled to make a variety of improvements such as sewer repairs, road maintenance, new restrooms, upgrading of buildings, and replacement of worn-out equipment.

Attendance at the conference camp events during the summer of 1981 was up 13.7% over 1980. As the Clear Lake camp flyer, "On Down the Road," noted in April, 1983:

> The Iowa Conference of the United Methodist Church in Iowa sparked a new surge of spirit and commitment to our camping program in 1981. We have expanded our organized camps and the campgrounds ministry not only at Clear Lake, but on all seven of our Conference properties throughout the state.

Among the camping opportunities listed for 1985 were the week-long elementary and junior high resident camps, pioneer, senior citizen, sports, wilderness canoeing, river canoeing, bicycling, music, visual arts, family, winter fun, Colorado backpack, youth mission, exceptional person, horse ranch, single parents, leadership development, gospel music, Native American, day, farm, and work camps, also the Bible Conferences.

WESLEY FOUNDATIONS

The Wesley Foundation is the educational ministry of the United Methodist Church on the campus of a state-supported or independent college or university. Four Wesley Foundations are located in Iowa, serving the United Methodist students at the University of Iowa in Iowa City, Iowa State University in Ames, the University of Northern Iowa in Cedar Falls, and Drake University in Des Moines.

Many students living away from home for the first time indicate a United Methodist religious preference, even though they have not been involved in

Wesley Foundation Iowa State University

church activities in their home communities. On the campus, through the Wesley Foundation, some of them find "a church home away from home," become acquainted with Christian friends, and eventually become active in the church. Other denominations have similar student centers.

Before 1913, the pastor of the church in the college town was expected to care for the Methodist students attending the state schools, but his primary responsibility was always to his permanent, local congregation. The beginnings of a more complete ministry through a student pastor (later called a campus minister) is described in the chapter on the Upper Iowa Conference.

The first Wesley Foundation was established at the University of Illinois in 1913. About that time the Methodist Episcopal Church in Iowa was starting its student work on the university campuses. L. F. Townsend of the Upper Iowa Conference was appointed in 1913 to be Student Pastor at the University of Iowa and William Hints was assigned to the same work at Iowa State College in Ames, by the Des Moines Conference. Financial support came from all four of the English-speaking conferences in the state. Rev. Nelson P. Horn was appointed director of an Inter-Church School of Religion at Iowa State College, a position be held until 1921. The Iowa campus ministries were soon known as "Wesley Foundations," and date their histories from 1913, though Illinois may have used the name first.

The building of a home for the Wesley Foundation next to a campus was sometimes a problem when the congregation was made up of students and only a few permanent residents. The Collegiate Methodist Episcopal Church in Ames started an addition west of the sanctuary before World War I to house the program for students. A ground floor was completed with a temporary roof, but two World Wars and the Depression of the 30s prevented completion of the building for many years. Finally in 1956 the building was finished.

The Wesley Foundations in Iowa City and Ames provided such good service that the potential was soon seen for similar work on the campus of Iowa State Teachers' College in Cedar Falls. The Upper Iowa Conference Committee on Education stated in 1920:

> We approve of the action of this Board (Wesley Foundation Board) in appointing a committee to investigate the needs of the Methodist Episcopal Church in Cedar Falls in caring for the Methodist constituency in the State Teachers' College. We recommend that the request of the committee from that church for aid in the support of a resident deaconess, to the extent of two-thirds of her salary, be provided by the Wesley Foundation.[3]

The Wesley Foundations Board acted quickly. Although in the Journal of the Northwest Iowa Conference and the Journal of the Iowa Conference one reads that they "commend the work to be started during the next year," the Upper Iowa Conference Journal said,

> We commend the work inaugurated and accomplished at our State Teachers' College at Cedar Falls this year and approve the effort of the Wesley Foundation to carry on the work of that center and its plans for the future of that work.[4]

The Wesley Foundation was already off to a flying start in a third state school.

The 1959 Journal of the South Iowa Conference reported the 1958 establisment of a new Wesley Foundation on the Drake University campus in Des Moines with Miss Ann Adams as full-time director. Housed in a frame building located in the heart of the campus, the Drake University Wesley Foundation differed from the other Iowa Wesley Foundations, which had their programs built around congregations meeting weekly for worship. Since Grace Methodist Church was near the Drake campus, an additional Sunday morning service seemed unneeded. A change came about almost thirty years later (1984) when several Protestant Campus Ministers planned with students to provide a weekly service on campus.

In 1959—the year that the Drake Wesley Foundation began—the University of Iowa had 2,438 Methodist students, Iowa State had 2,661, the University of Northern Iowa had 1,035, and Drake University had 703. By 1966 there were 198 accredited Wesley Foundations in the nation.

Several pastors have had outstanding length of service in Wesley Foundation work. Rev. G. S. (Sam) Nichols, pastor of Collegiate M. E. Church, was also Director of Wesley Foundation at Ames for twenty-five years. Rev. Dean Walters was Wesley Foundation Minister at Ames fourteen years (1953-1977), and had also served as Wesley Foundation Director at Emporia, Kansas (1947-1950) and Brookings, South Dakota (1950-1953). Current directors of Wesley Foundations having long records of service are Rev. David Schuldt in his fifteenth year at Iowa City and Rev. Robert T. Ellis in his eleventh year at Cedar Falls.

Footnotes

1. *Journal of the Iowa Annual Conference* 1971, p. D-24.
2. *Journal of the Iowa Annual Conference* 1980, p. 221.
3. *Upper Iowa Conference Journal (M.E.)* 1920, p. 84.
4. *Upper Iowa Conference Journal (M.E.)* 1921, p. 243.

17

Other Methodist Brethren

"Methodism is a family of Churches" was a statement made by William Arthur, a nineteenth century Wesleyan.[1] The Wesleyan movement which began in England in the eighteenth century has spread around the world, taking various institutional forms at different times and places. Many bodies in America are part of the movement. They cannot be ignored in a study of Iowa Methodism. Each has influenced, and been influenced by, the United Methodist Church or its antecedents. Preachers and laymen have transferred easily from one body to another. Some ministers now serving in the Iowa Conference of the United Methodist Church have enriched the conference by having transferred from one of these sister denominations.

THE FREE METHODIST CHURCH

The Free Methodist Church grew out of a reform movement in the Genesee Conference of the Methodist Episcopal Church in the mid-nineteenth century. The reformers called for a return to strict observance of the Methodist rules on attendance at Class Meetings, family prayers, singing by the congregation, plainness of dress, simplicity and spirituality in worship, freedom for the slaves, freedom from oath-bound secret societies, and free seats in the churches.

Genesee Conference leaders called for a spirit of moderation and compromise, but were not inclined to practice what they preached. The 1850s were not a time of tolerance and true compromise in American life.

The spokesman for the reformers was Rev. E. T. Roberts. As a result, he and a few of his followers were expelled from the M.E. Church in 1858. He appealed his case to the General Conference of 1860, but the members seemed interested in other matters and gave his appeal no attention. It was rejected on a technicality, and he was out of the church.

Meanwhile, several hundred lay sympathizers with Roberts had been expelled from their local churches. On August 23, 1860, at Pekin, New York, the Free Methodist Church was organized, and Roberts was elected its first superintendent.

The Free Methodist Church has developed a world-wide missionary program and has been very "evangelistic" in its outreach, though it is not a large denomination. By 1969 it had 69,623 lay members and 1,771 preachers in the United States, and a similar number spread through other countries.

The beginnings of Free Methodism in Iowa moved westward from Illinois, as did other branches of Methodism. The 1867 session of the Illinois

Conference appointed W. B. Tracy to "Northern Iowa." However, he had poor health and died at work.

A footnote to the statistical tables of the Illinois Conference for 1868 states that "the figures for Galva, Winnebago, and Freeport Circuits include missionary appointments in Iowa." That same list of appointments contained three in the state of Iowa: Fairfield, W. F. Manley; DeWitt, B. F. Doughty; Cedar Rapids Mission, Isaac Bliss.[2]

The General Conference of 1874 ordered the formation of an Iowa Conference. Accordingly, in 1875 the Iowa Annual Conference of the Free Methodist Church was organized at Birmingham in Van Buren County. General Superintendent Edward Payson Hart presided. The conference was divided into two districts, the Waterloo and Fairfield Districts.

The Iowa Conference grew, and for a while was subdivided, but now includes the whole state. The 1980 conference minutes reported twenty-four congregations with 871 full members, 212 preparatory members, 107 junior members, and 29 preachers, making a total of 1,219 members.

Through the years many Methodist preachers of several denominations have been trained in Asbury Theological Seminary at Wilmore, Kentucky, which is associated with the Free Methodist Church.

THE WESLEYAN METHODIST CHURCH

The Wesleyan Methodist Church of America was founded in 1843 by Methodist Episcopal members who withdrew because they felt the mother church had gone too far in attempting to hold the church together by compromise over the slavery issue. The Methodist Episcopal Church had expressed strong opposition to slavery and had provided disciplinary rules for dealing with slave-holders who might be, or might want to become, members of the M. E. Church. However, as Methodism spread into the South, the issue became controversial.

By 1830 the slavery question was inflammatory. Many leaders in the church sought to limit debate in the interest of harmony. But opposition to slavery was the uniting element which drew together ministers who, for various reasons, wanted to reform the church. At the 1840 session of the General Conference the efforts of bishops to restrain debate on the issue of slavery backfired. The movement begun as anti-slavery also became anti-episcopacy.

As a result, members began to leave the M. E. Church in 1841. The first Wesleyan Methodist Conference was organized in Michigan that year. Orange Scott, J. Morton, and L. R. Sunderland withdrew from the M. E. Church in 1842, and published in the the first edition of *The True Wesleyan* their reasons for withdrawal.

In February, 1843, these men met with Luther Lee and L. C. Matlack to prepare plans for a new denomination. They issued a call for a general convention at Utica, New York, beginning May 31, 1843. This convention created a denominational structure with a *Discipline,* and adopted the name, "The Wesleyan Methodist Church." The new church grew and prospered.

The convention had placed Iowa and Wisconsin Territories in the Miami Conference. At the first General Conference (1844) Iowa became part of the Wisconsin Conference. The Iowa Territory was assigned to the Illinois Conference in 1848. Four years later Iowa constituted a Wesleyan Methodist Conference.[3]

The first session of the Iowa Conference was held in the Union School House near Montezuma in Poweshiek County, with Daniel G. Cartwright as first president. Cartwright had withdrawn from the M. E. Church in 1838 in sympathy with republicanism in church government and opposition to slavery.[4]

For four years beginning in 1867 a West Iowa Conference was maintained. It was discontinued in 1871, but reformed in 1877. In 1891 it was discontinued a second time. Because of some dissension in Minnesota, a number of churches withdrew from the denomination in 1904. The Minnesota churches remaining loyal became a part of the Iowa Conference.[5]

The Wesleyan Methodist Church made its own distinctive contribution to the religious life in Iowa, though it never became a large denomination. It began a new chapter at the time of the merger with the Pilgrim Holiness Church and formation of "The Wesleyan Church" June 26, 1968.

PILGRIM HOLINESS CHURCH

After the close of the Civil War a wave of religious and moral indifference engulfed the country. Perhaps it could be described as a sort of emotional fatigue after years of a great moral crusade. The mainstream churches were a bit less willing to challenge "the world." Many who had not been converted in traditional ways joined the church. The Class Meeting became less significant, though still active. The old-time camp meeting, as described in the *Autobiography of Peter Cartwright,* began to lose its influence in church life. Many of the preachers, as well as sincere members of the church, became concerned.

In the post-war years the holiness movement gained influence with strong support from Methodists. However, the mainstream of Methodism did not exhibit enough enthusiasm to satisfy the holiness people. They were led to form new organizations of their own, in much the way that the Methodist societies in England evolved into a separate church without that intention.

Elmer T. Clark wrote in *Small Sects in America* that the Pilgrim Holiness Church dated from 1897, when the Rev. Martin W. Knapp, a Methodist minister, gathered a dozen people in his Cincinnati home and organized the International Apostolic Holiness Union. He believed Methodists had deserted certain Wesleyan landmarks which he deemed important. It was not his plan to organize a new sect, but rather to be a "leaven" which would influence congregations. Nevertheless, his group became an independent denomination. Like the Nazarenes, this group grew by joining with similar, like-minded groups.

After several name changes the denomination was called the International Apostolic Holiness Church in 1913, but following a 1919 merger with the

Holiness Christian Church, the name was the International Holiness Church. In 1922 the International Holiness Church merged with the Pentecostal Rescue Mission and the Pilgrim Church (a schism from the Nazarenes) to form the Pilgrim Holiness Church. Successive additions to the Pilgrim Holiness Church were the Pentecostal Brethren in Christ (1924), the People's Mission Church (1925), and the Holiness Church (1946).

The Wesleyan Methodist Church merged with the Pilgrim Holiness Church June 26, 1968, taking the name "The Wesleyan Church." In 1984 there were forty local churches with 4,176 lay members in the Iowa-Minnesota District.

THE CHURCH OF THE NAZARENES

The Church of the Nazarenes is one of the larger religious bodies growing out of the nineteenth century holiness movement in America. A number of similar bodies sprang up almost simultaneously at various places in the United States near the end of that century. They soon found it desirable to join together.

The first union assembly of churches from the East and the West met in Chicago in October, 1907, and formed the Pentecostal Church of the Nazarene. Representatives of the Holiness Church of Christ attended the General Assembly in Chicago that year, but had no power to act. The next year the second General Assembly convened with the Holiness Church of Christ at Pilot Point, Texas, and planned a union. On October 8, 1908, the union was consummated under the name "Pentecostal Church of the Nazarene." The work "Pentecostal" was dropped from the name in 1919.

Since then, other holiness churches have joined with the Nazarenes, and the denomination has grown. This story is told in detail in Section I of the Manual of the Church of the Nazarene. The increase has been not only by mergers, but by an enthusiastic, evangelistic spirit permeating the church. Many persons have joined because they did not feel satisfied in other local churches.

Both ministers and laymen have transferred between the United Methodist Church and the Church of the Nazarene and felt at home. Some ministers now serving in the Iowa United Methodist Church commenced their ministry with the Nazarenes. The Iowa District of the Nazarenes had 6,630 members in 76 churches in 1983, with 124 ordained elders, which included 31 licensed ministers, 21 retired, and 5 in the connectional assignments.

THE AFRICAN METHODIST EPISCOPAL CHURCH

The African Methodist Episcopal Church (A.M.E.) was the first national organization established by blacks in North America, growing out of a small prayer band conducted in St. George's Methodist Episcopal Church in Philadelphia.

The desire of the black members to escape paternalistic control and discrimination experienced in St. George's inspired a group, under the leadership of Richard Allen, to withdraw in 1787 and form the Free African

Society, a semi-autonomous church. They erected a building, dedicated in 1794 by Bishop Francis Asbury of the M.E. Church.

That congregation became the nucleus of African Methodism, despite its continuing under the jurisdiction of the M.E. Church. Asbury ordained Allen as deacon in 1799, and as elder in 1816. The same year Allen learned Negro congregations had been formed in New York, New Jersey, Delaware, and Maryland. Sixteen congregations came together, formed the African Methodist Episcopal Church, and on April 10, 1816, elected him their first bishop.

In 1964 the denomination had 5,878 local churches, including some in Iowa.

THE AFRICAN METHODIST EPISCOPAL CHURCH ZION

The African Methodist Episcopal Church Zion dates its history from 1796, but that date marks a new chapter in the story of the experiences of black Methodists. The earlier history of this church is not easily secured since the leaders left few written records.

The A.M.E. Zion grew out of prayer groups in the John Street M.E. Church in New York City, in a manner similar to the A.M.E. Church's growth out of St. George's in Philadelphia. David H. Bradley stated in the *Encyclopedia of World Methodism,* "Contrary to common belief, the movement of these Africans toward the establishment of a Negro Church appears not to have been one of protest, but of expediency."[6]

Conversations concerning merger between the A.M.E. Church and the A.M.E. Zion have taken place repeatedly, almost since their beginning. After the Civil War the Colored Methodist Episcopal Church (now named Christian Methodist Episcopal Church) was included in these talks. A century later in 1965 a General Commission on Union was appointed to plan toward union. The commission set 1975 as a target date for merger between themselves, and 1980 as a target date for merger with the United Methodist Church. The black Methodist denominations are also involved in union talks with the Consultation on Church Union, an ecumenical body.[7] The A.M.E. Zion Church has one congregation and seventy-five members in Iowa.

CHRISTIAN METHODIST EPISCOPAL CHURCH

The Christian Methodist Episcopal Church was formed soon after the American Civil War as the "Colored Methodist Episcopal Church." At the beginning of the Civil War the M.E. Church South had 207,000 Negro members. Because of the disruption during the war there were only 78,000 at its end. At the 1866 General Conference of the M.E. Church South representatives of the Negro members asked for a separate organization.

The first General Conference of the Colored Methodist Episcopal Church was held December 15, 1870. The new church did not have an easy time, but received help, both financial and otherwise, from the members of the mother church, especially for educational work. The C.M.E. has been distinguished in the field of higher education, having organized six major institutions:

Paine College, Augusta, Georgia; Texas College, Tyler, Texas; Lane College, Jackson, Tennessee; Miles College, Birmingham, Alabama; Mississippi Industrial College, Holly Springs, Mississippi; and Phillips School of Theology, Atlanta, Georgia.

The name of the church was changed on January 3, 1956, to the Christian M.E. Church. It has been an active participant in world-wide ecumenical and interdenominational movements and has been a member of the Consultation on Church Union since 1967.

The C.M.E. Church is not numerous in Iowa but has 2,598 churches nationally, with 466,718 members. In Iowa there is one church, with seventy-five members.

Footnotes

1. *Encyclopedia of World Methodism* Vol. II p. 1553 (Nashville: The United Methodist Publishing House, 1974).
2. William T. Hogue, *History of the Free Methodist Church of North America* Vol. II p. 6 (Chicago: The Free Methodist Publishing House, 1915).
3. *The Iowa Conference Centennial 1853-1953* (Published by the Iowa Conference of the Wesleyan Methodist Church in America).
4. E. H. Waring, *History of the Iowa Annual Conference of The Methodist Episcopal Church* p. 88 (n.p., 1909).
5. *Iowa Conference Centennial,* ibid.
6. *Encyclopedia of World Methodism* Vol. I, ibid., p. 66.
7. *Encyclopedia of World Methodism* Vol. II, ibid., p. 1712.

EPILOGUE

Old dreams still rule
the trenches of our valor,
and the melody lingers on;

wanderers are we all,
never quite arriving,
always only striving.

While marveling at what time has wrought,
pause to reflect on
what is yet to be;

'mid these grasses and computers,
lift ever high the torch that gives the life
to mission high fulfilled.

To Whom It May Concern
"between two rivers."

—Carl Stiefel
Burlington, Iowa
January, 1986

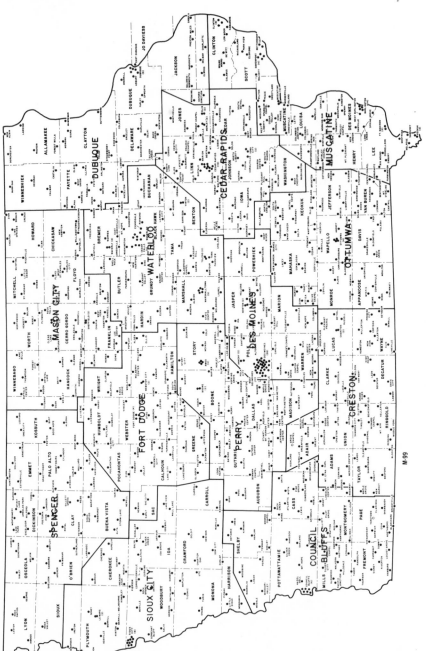

CHURCHES OF THE IOWA CONFERENCE
THE UNITED METHODIST CHURCH

prepared for Iowa United Methodist Communications
by the Town and Country Division, Board of Global Ministries
drawn by Dane Crossett, Jr., February, 1983

M-99

GLOSSARY

(Glossary entries are adapted largely from the 1980
Book of Discipline of the United Methodist Church.)

Accepted supply. Formerly a local preacher regularly appointed to a charge.

Administrative Board. The primary administrative body of the local church (formerly Official Board).

Appointment. Annual appointment of all ministerial members of Annual Conference, unless on sabbatical leave, disability leave, leave of absence or retired.

Apportionment. An amount assigned to a local church.

Associate member, ministerial. A minister in the itinerant ministry of the church who has not met all of the requirements of full ministerial membership of the Annual Conference—can be ordained Deacon and can vote on matters before the Conference except on three questions reserved for the full members.

Bishop. A general superintendent. An elder elected to the office of bishop by a Jurisdictional or Central Conference and duly consecrated by other bishops.

Cabinet. The resident bishop and the district superintendents.

Charge, Pastoral. One or more local churches, governed by a single Charge Conference.

Circuit. Two or more local churches which are joined together for pastoral supervision, constituting one pastoral charge.

Class Meetings. A system whereby church members were organized in small groups for prayer, Bible study, and sub-pastoral care.

Conference, Annual. The basic administrative body in the United Methodist Church.

Conference Claimants. Retired ministers, surviving spouses of ministers and surviving dependent children are claimants upon annual conference retirement funds.

Conference, General. The legislative body for the entire Church, meeting every four years. It is composed of elected lay and ministerial members, in equal numbers, from all of the Annual Conferences.

Conference, Jurisdictional. The representative regional body, of which there are five in the United States, composed of an equal number of lay and ministerial delegates from the Annual Conferences within the jurisdictional boundaries, meeting every four years. It elects bishops to serve in that jurisdiction.

Connectional, Connectional Principle. The principle that all United Methodists and United Methodist congregations are connected in a network of conciliar and legal relationships. This and the appointive system, in which the bishop has final authority, constitute two of the most distinctive features of United Methodist polity.

Cooperative Parish or Ministry. Two or more pastoral charges or local churches, having coordinated programs and organization.

Council on Ministries. Primary planning and correlating agency.

Deacon. An Annual Conference probationary or associate member who has been ordained deacon.

Deaconess. A woman commissioned by a bishop to serve in any capacity not requiring full clergy rights.

Diaconal Minister. Professional or full-time minister who has been consecrated—often for Christian Education, evangelism, music, church business administration, communication, health and welfare, church and community work, etc.

Discipline (The Book of Discipline of The United Methodist Church). The official published statement (revised quadrennially) of the Constitution and laws of the Church, its rules and procedure, and a description of administrative agencies and their functions.

District Superintendent (Earlier Presiding Elder). A minister appointed by the bishop to administer the work within a district.

Elder. Itinerant minister in full connection within an Annual Conference, having been ordained an elder. This is the highest ministerial order.

Episcopacy. General superintendents.

Itineracy (also spelled itinerancy). The system by which ministers are appointed to their charges by the Bishop and are under discipline to accept such an appointment.

Jurisdiction. A major regional division within the United States, composed of several Annual Conferences.

Laity. From *laos*, meaning "people of God"—lay persons, not of the ordained ministry.

Larger Parish. A number of congregations working together using a parish-wide administrative board, council on ministries, etc.

Local Orders. Formerly ordination of a local preacher (not a Conference member) as local Deacon or local elder.

Local Pastor. A layman regularly appointed to serve as a pastor.

Local Preacher. Formerly one licensed to preach, who might or might not be appointed to a charge.

Location, Honorable. The voluntary termination of an ordained minister's membership in an Annual Conference. Such action carries no moral stigma.

Member, Annual Conference. Annual Conference membership is composed of an equal number of lay and ministerial members.

Ordination. The act of conferring ministerial orders, presided over by a bishop.

Presiding Elder. Now district superintendent.

Probationary Member. A person received as a probationary member of an Annual Conference.

Quarterly Conference. Now Charge Conference or Church Conference—the governing body of the pastoral charge.

Social Creed. A summary statement of Social Principles adopted by the 1976 General Conference to be emphasized in every United Methodist Congregation. In 1908 a Social Creed was adopted by the Methodist Episcopal General Conference.

Social Principles. A prayerful and thoughtful effort of the 1976 General Conference to speak to the human issues in the contemporary world from a sound biblical and theological foundation as historically demonstrated in United Methodist tradition (1980 *Discipline*, pp. 86-104).

Superannuated. Formerly a retired member of the Annual Conference.

Supernumerary. Ministerial leave of absence.

Trustees. The official body with the responsibility of acquisition, sale, maintenance, and management of church property.

World Service. The basic benevolences of the Church, approved by the General Conference and apportioned through the Annual Conference to the local churches.

IOWA UNITED METHODIST LISTINGS ON THE
NATIONAL REGISTER OF HISTORIC PLACES

In the Heritage Hill Historic District of Burlington:

St. Paul's (German) Methodist Episcopal Church, 7th & Washington Streets; built 1868-69, now serving the community as Arts for Living Center.

First United Methodist Church, N. 5th & Washington; successor to 1838 "Old Zion" Methodist Episcopal, 1858 Ebenezer Methodist Episcopal, and 1868-69 St. Paul's German Methodist Episcopal; built 1889.

In Mount Pleasant:

Old Main, Iowa Wesleyan College Campus; built 1855.

Harlan-Lincoln House 101 W. Broad Street; first occupied by Harlan family 1873.

In Mount Vernon Historic District:

Entire campus of Cornell College, founded 1853.

William Fletcher King Memorial Chapel, built 1875-76.

United Methodist Chuch building dedicated 1900, on site of second building which was constructed 1851.

Bethel Church, Morning Sun, 1855—limestone relic of frontier religious (Methodist) development in Iowa.

First United Methodist Church, Rock Rapids, built 1895-96.

Thoren Hall, Westmar College Campus, LeMars, 1910 building.

In Des Moines:

First United Methodist Church, 10th & Pleasant Streets; built 1906.

Burns Memorial United Methodist Church, 811 Crocker Street; congregation organized 1866, building acquired 1930.

Palmyra Methodist Episcopal Church, T 77 N 4 22 W NE of NW ¼ Sec. 31, Warren County; 1867-1870 building replaced first church, organized 1853.

Washington Prairie Methodist Church, T 97 N R 8 E, SW ¼ of Sec. 1, Winneshiek County; "Mother Church" of Methodism in Norway, built 1863-68; congregation established by Ole Peter Petersen, who took Methodism back to his home country, Norway.

St. John's United Methodist, 1325-9 Brady Street, Davenport; built 1902.

Charles City College Hall, Morningside College, Sioux City, built 1891 as Main Building for the University of the Northwest; later the Conservatory of Music for Morningside College; renamed for Charles City College, which merged with Morningside.

Note: Listing of eligible buildings on the National Register of Historic Places is initiated by the owners, who approach the Office of Historic Preservation in the Iowa State Historical Department at Des Moines.

SESSIONS AND OFFICERS OF
IOWA CONFERENCE M.E. CHURCH

No.	Time	Year	Place	Bishop	Secretary
1	August 14-19	1844	Iowa City	Morris	H. W. Reed.........
2	Sept. 3-8	1845	Burlington	Morris	H. W. Reed.........
3	Sept. 2-7	1846	Bloomington	Hamline.........	H. W. Reed.........
4	Sept. 1-7	1847	Mt. Pleasant	Waugh	Joseph Brook ......
5	August 23-28	1848	Dubuque	Morris	H. W. Reed.........
6	August 8-13	1849	Ft. Madison	Janes	Landon Taylor ......
7	August 7-12	1850	Fairfield........	Hamline........	J. G. Dimmitt ....
8	August 6-11	1851	Davenport	Waugh	M. H. Hare ....
9	Sept. 29 to Oct. 4 ..	1852	Burlington	Ames	Joseph Brooks .....
10	Sept. 28 to Oct. 4 ..	1853	Oskaloosa	Scott	Joseph Brooks .....
11	Sept. 27 to Oct. 4 ..	1854	Dubuque	Morris	H. W. Reed.........
12	Sept. 26 to Oct. 2 ..	1855	Keokuk	Simpson	Joseph Brooks .....
13	Sept. 24-30	1856	Mt. Pleasant	Janes	Joseph Brooks .....
14	Sept. 24-26	1857	Des Moines	Ames	Joseph Brooks .....
15	Sept. 8-14	1858	Fairfield........	Morris	E. L. Briggs ....
16	Sept. 7-12	1859	Muscatine	Simpson	E. H. Waring ....
17	Aug. 29 to Sept. 3 ..	1860	Oskaloosa	Janes	E. H. Waring ....
18	Aug. 21-26	1861	Burlington	Scott	E. H. Waring ....
19	Sept. 10-15	1862	Washington.....	Baker	E. H. Waring ....
20	Sept. 9-14	1863	Newton	Ames	E. H. Waring ....
21	Sept. 14-19	1864	Keokuk	Janes	E. H. Waring ....
22	Sept. 27 to Oct. 2 ..	1865	Mt. Pleasant	Janes	E. H. Waring ....
23	Sept. 26 to Oct. 1 ..	1866	Knoxville	Ames	E. H. Waring ....
24	Sept. 18-23	1867	Ottumwa	Scott	E. H. Waring ....
25	Sept. 3-7	1868	Burlington	Janes	E. H. Waring ....
26	Sept. 1-6	1869	Muscatine	Thompson	E. H. Waring ....
27	Sept. 28 to Oct. 3 ..	1870	Albia	Ames	E. H. Waring ....
28	Oct. 4-9	1871	Mt. Pleasant	Ames	E. H. Waring ....
29	Oct. 9-13	1872	Oskaloosa	Andrews	E. H. Waring ....
30	Sept. 17-21	1873	Washington.....	Bowman	E. H. Waring ....
31	Sept. 16-21	1874	Bloomfield	Haven..........	E. H. Waring ....
32	Sept. 15-21	1875	Keokuk	Merrill	E. H. Waring ....
33	Sept. 6-12	1876	Ottumwa	Wiley	George N. Power....
34	Sept. 5-10	1877	Fairfield........	Ames	George N. Power....
35	Sept. 4-16	1878	Brooklyn	Foster	George N. Power....
36	Sept. 3-9	1879	Burlington	Harris	George N. Power....
37	Sept. 8-13	1880	Centerville......	Hurst	George N. Power....
38	Aug. 31 to Sept. 5 ..	1881	Knoxville	Merrill	George N. Power....
39	Sept. 6-11	1882	Muscatine	Wiley	George N. Power....
40	Sept. 5-10	1883	Burlington	Simpson	George N. Power....
41	Sept. 3-9	1884	Ottumwa	Foster	George N. Power....
42	Sept. 10-15	1885	Mt. Pleasant	Ninde	George N. Power....
43	Sept. 2-7	1886	Washington.....	Bowman	George N. Power....
44	Sept. 7-12	1887	Newton	Merrill	George N. Power....
45	Sept. 5-10	1888	Oskaloosa	Goodsell	George N. Power....
46	Sept. 4-9	1889	Burlington	Warren.........	George N. Power....
47	Sept. 4-8	1890	Grinnell	Joyce	George N. Power....
48	Sept. 2-7	1891	Muscatine	Foss...........	George N. Power....
49	Sept. 7-12	1892	Washington.....	Andrews	George N. Power....
50	Sept. 6-11	1893	Mt. Pleasant	Mallalieu	C. L. Stafford ....
51	Sept. 12-16	1894	Fairfield........	Fowler	C. L. Stafford ....
52	Sept. 11-16	1895	Ottumwa	Foster	C. L. Stafford ....
53	Sept. 9-14	1896	Knoxville	Newman	C. L. Stafford ....
54	Sept. 8-13	1897	Oskaloosa	Fitzgerald	C. L. Stafford ....
55	Sept. 28 to Oct. 3 ..	1898	Montezuma	Vincent	C. L. Stafford ....
56	Sept. 27 to Oct. 2 ..	1899	Mt. Pleasant	McCabe	C. L. Stafford ....
57	Sept. 19-24	1900	Bloomfield	Walden	John C. Willits......
58	Sept. 18-24	1901	Newton	Merrill	John C. Willits......
59	Sept. 17-22	1902	Keokuk 1st Ch. ..	Hamilton	John C. Willits......
60	Sept. 9-14	1903	Muscatine	Mallalieu	John W. Potter .....
61	Sept. 7-12	1904	Sigourney	McDowell	John W. Potter .....
62	Sept. 6-11	1905	Albia	Warren.........	John W. Potter .....
63	Sept. 5-10	1906	Grinnell	Goodsell	John W. Potter .....
64	Sept. 4-9	1907	Burlington	Cranston	John W. Potter .....
65	Sept. 2-7	1908	Ottumwa	Quayle	John W. Potter .....

66	Sept. 8-13	1909	Winfield	Spellmeyer	John W. Potter .....
67	Sept. 7-12	1910	Pella...........	Wilson	John W. Potter .....
68	Sept. 6-7	1911	Fairfield	Cranston	W. A. Longnecker ...
69	Sept. 4-9	1912	Newton	Hughes, E. H. ...	W. A. Longnecker ...
70	Sept. 3-8	1913	Oskaloosa	Shepard	W. A. Longnecker ...
71	Sept. 2-7	1914	Ft. Madison	Shepard	W. A. Longnecker ...
72	Sept. 1-6	1915	Centerville.....	Stuntz	W. A. Longnecker ...
73	Aug. 30 to Sept. 4 ..	1916	Mt. Pleasant	McConnell......	W. A. Longnecker ...
74	Sept. 5-10	1917	Washington.....	Cooke	W. A. Longnecker ...
75	Sept. 4-9	1918	Bloomfield	Hughes, M. S. ...	W. A. Longnecker ...
76	Sept. 2-8	1919	Muscatine	Stuntz	W. A. Longnecker ...
77	Sept. 1-6	1920	Grinnell	Stuntz	W. A. Longnecker ...
78	Sept. 7-12	1921	Mt. Pleasant	Stuntz	W. A. Longnecker ...
79	Sept. 13-18	1922	Keokuk	McConnell......	W. A. Longnecker ...
80	Sept. 5-10	1923	Newton	Stuntz	W. A. Longnecker ...
81	Sept. 10-15	1924	Fairfield	Keeney.........	W. A. Longnecker ...
82	Sept. 9-13	1925	Mt. Pleasant	Thirkield	P. M. Conant ....
83	Sept. 1-5	1926	Montezuma	Keeney.........	P. M. Conant ....
84	Aug. 31 to Sept. 5 ..	1927	Burlington	Burns	P. M. Conant ....
85	Sept. 12-16	1928	Osklaloosa	Leonard	P. M. Conant ....
86	Sept. 4-9	1929	Ottumwa	Leete	P. M. Conant ....
87	Sept. 3-7	1930	Knoxville	Lowe	P. M. Conant ....
88	Sept. 9-13	1931	Muscatine	Leete	P. M. Conant ....

SESSIONS AND OFFICERS OF
DES MOINES CONFERENCE M.E.

	DATE	PLACE	BISHOP	SECRETARY
1	Aug. 22, 1860	Indianola	Edmund S. Janes	E. M. H. Fleming ....
2	Sept. 4, 1861	Council Bluffs	Levi Scott	E. M. H. Fleming ....
3	Sept. 3, 1862	Chariton	Osmund Baker	E. M. H. Fleming ....
4	Sept. 2, 1863	Winterset	Edward R. Ames	Chas. C. Mabee ....
5	Aug. 31, 1864	Clarinda	Edmund S. Janes	Jas. F. Goolman ....
6	Aug. 30, 1865	Osceola	Matthew Simpson	H. B. Heacock ....
7	Aug. 22, 1866	Boonesboro	Edward R. Ames	H. B. Heacock ....
8	Sept. 19, 1867	Des Moines	Davis W. Clark	H. B. Heacock ....
9	Aug. 20, 1868	Council Bluffs	Matthew Simpson	Henry H. Oneal ....
10	Aug. 26, 1869	Indianola	Davis W. Clark	Henry H. Oneal ....
11	Aug. 31, 1870	Montana	Edmund S. Janes	Henry H. Oneal ....
12	Sept. 21, 1871	Sioux City	Edward R. Ames	Henry H. Oneal ....
13	Sept. 25, 1872	Chariton	Edward G. Andrews ...	Henry H. Oneal ....
14	Sept. 10, 1873	Winterset	Thomas Bowman	Henry H. Oneal ....
15	Sept. 9, 1874	Des Moines	Gilbert Haven	Henry H. Oneal ....
16	Oct. 6, 1875	Indianola	Stephen M. Merrill ...	Henry H. Oneal ....
17	Sept. 28, 1876	Red Oak	Randolph S. Foster ...	Henry H. Oneal ....
18	Sept. 12, 1877	Boonesboro	Edward R. Ames	Henry H. Oneal ....
19	Sept. 18, 1878	Atlantic	Jesse T. Peck	Wm. T. Smith ....
20	Aug. 27, 1879	Des Moines	William L. Harris	Wm. T. Smith ....
21	Sept. 22, 1880	Chariton	Edward G. Andrews ...	Wm. T. Smith ....
22	Sept. 14, 1881	Indianola	John F. Hurst	James Lisle ....
23	Sept. 13, 1882	Winterset	Isaac W. Wiley	James Lisle ....
24	Sept. 12, 1883	Clarinda	Matthew Simpson	James Lisle ....
25	Sept. 10, 1884	Red Oak	Edward G. Andrews ...	M. D. Collins ....
26	Sept. 17, 1885	Des Moines	Cyrus D. Foss	M. D. Collins ....
27	Sept. 9, 1886	Council Bluffs	Thomas Bowman	M. D. Collins ....
28	Sept. 14, 1887	Des Moines	Stephen M. Merrill ...	Wm. H. W. Rees........
29	Sept. 12, 1888	Creston	Daniel A. Goodsell ...	Wm. H. W. Rees........
30	Sept. 11, 1889	Denison	Henry W. Warren	Jno. R. Horswell ....

31	Sept. 17, 1890	Indianola	Isaac W. Joyce	Jno. R. Horswell ....
32	Sept. 16, 1891	Des Moines	Cyrus D. Foss	Jno. R. Horswell ....
33	Sept. 14, 1892	Perry	Edward G. Andrews ...	A. W. Armstrong ....
34	Sept. 13, 1893	Audubon	W. F. Mallalieu	A. W. Armstrong ....
35	Sept. 5, 1894	Shenandoah.......	Charles H. Fowler	A. W. Armstrong ....
36	Sept. 25, 1895	Indianola	William X. Ninde	A. W. Armstrong ....
37	Sept. 23, 1896	Corydon	J. P. Newman	W. Stevenson ....
38	Sept. 22, 1897	Guthrie Center.....	J. N. FitzGerald	W. Stevenson ....
39	Sept. 14, 1898	Creston	J. H. Vincent	W. Stevenson ....
40	Sept. 13, 1899	Denison	I. W. Joyce	W. Stevenson ....
41	Sept. 12, 1900	Boone............	J. M. Walden	W. Stevenson ....
42	Sept. 11, 1901	Chariton	Stephen M. Merrill	W. Stevenson ....
43	Sept. 10, 1902	Jefferson	John W. Hamilton	W. Stevenson ....
44	Sept. 16, 1903	Indianola	W. F. Mallalieu	W. Stevenson ....
45	Sept. 21, 1904	Atlantic	W. F. McDowell	C. J. English ....
46	Sept. 14, 1905	Osceola	H. W. Warren	C. J. English ....
47	Sept. 12, 1906	Des Moines	Earl Cranston	C. J. English ....
48	Sept. 11, 1907	Council Bluffs	Daniel A. Goodsell....	I. N. Woodward ....
49	Sept. 9, 1908	Clarinda	Henry Spellmeyer	I. N. Woodward ....
50	Sept. 15, 1909	Ames	Joseph F. Berry	A. E. Slothower ....
51	Sept. 7, 1910	Perry	John W. Hamilton	A. E. Slothower ....
52	Sept. 13, 1911	Shenandoah.......	Thomas B. Neely	A. E. Slothower ....
53	Sept. 11, 1912	Boone............	Edwin H. Hughes	M. R. Talley ....
54	Sept. 10, 1913	Mount Ayr	Frank M. Bristol	M. R. Talley ....
55	Sept. 9, 1914	Atlantic	Charles W. Smith	M. R. Talley ....
56	Sept. 8, 1915	Des Moines	Frank M. Bristol	M. R. Talley ....
57	Sept. 6, 1916	Glenwood	Homer C. Stuntz......	Fred N. Willis ....
58	Sept. 19, 1917	Indianola	Homer C. Stuntz......	Fred N. Willis ....
59	Sept. 18, 1918	Jefferson	Matthew S. Hughes ...	Fred N. Willis ....
60	Sept. 17, 1919	Des Moines	Homer C. Stuntz......	Fred N. Willis ....
61	Sept. 15, 1920	Winterset	Homer C. Stuntz......	R. M. Shipman ....
62	Sept. 14, 1921	Red Oak	Homer C. Stuntz......	R. M. Shipman ....
63	Sept. 20, 1922	Chariton	Homer C. Stuntz......	R. M. Shipman ....
64	Sept. 12, 1923	Ames	Homer C. Stuntz......	R. M. Shipman ....
65	Sept. 17, 1924	Clarinda	F. T. Keeney	R. M. Shipman ....
66	Sept. 16, 1925	Atlantic	Wm. F. Anderson	R. M. Shipman ....
67	Sept. 22, 1926	Perry	Wm. F. McDowell.....	R. M. Shipman ....
68	Sept. 14, 1927	Shenandoah.......	F. T. Keeney	R. M. Shipman ....
69	Sept. 12, 1928	Boone............	F. D. Leete	R. M. Shipman ....
70	Sept. 18, 1929	Indianola	Thos. Nicholson......	R. M. Shipman ....
71	Sept. 10, 1930	Council Bluffs	F. D. Leete	L. L. Weis ....
72	Sept. 9, 1931	Creston	E. G. Richardson	Guy F. Fansher ....

SESSIONS AND OFFICERS OF
IOWA-DES MOINES CONFERENCE M.E.

	DATE	PLACE	BISHOP	SECRETARY
1	Sept. 20-26, 1932	Des Moines, Grace .	Leete	P. M. Conant ....
2	Sept. 21-24, 1933	Des Moines, First ..	Leete	P. M. Conant ....
3	Sept. 18-24, 1934	Burlington, First ...	Waldorf	P. M. Conant ....
4	Sept. 18-23, 1935	Des Moines, Grace .	Leete	P. M. Conant ....
5	Sept. 16-21, 1936	Des Moines, First ..	Oxnam	P. M. Conant ....
6	Sept. 15-20, 1937	Newton...........	E. H. Hughes	P. M. Conant ....
7	Sept. 13-19, 1938	Fairfield	Oxnam	L. L. Weis ....
8	Sept. 12-15, 1939	Burlington, First ...	Magee	L. L. Weis ....

IOWA-DES MOINES CONFERENCE OF THE METHODIST CHURCH

	DATE	PLACE	BISHOP	SECRETARY
1	Sept. 15-17, 1939	Burlington, First ...	Magee	L. L. Weis ....
2	Sept. 10-15, 1940	Des Moines, Grace .	Magee	L. L. Weiss and F. G. Barnes ....
3	June 10-15, 1941	Atlantic	Magee	F. G. Barnes ....
4	June 9-14, 1942	Mount Pleasant	Magee	F. G. Barnes ....
5	June 9-13, 1943	Des Moines, First ..	Magee	F. G. Barnes ....
6	June 7-11, 1944	Des Moines, Grace .	Magee	E. W. Frohardt ....
7	June 6-8, 1945	Des Moines, First ..	Brashares	E. W. Frohardt ....
8	June 5-9, 1946	Mount Pleasant	Brashares	E. W. Frohardt ....
9	June 11-15, 1947	Des Moines, Grace .	Brashares	E. W. Frohardt ....
10	June 9-13, 1948	Des Moines, First ..	Brashares	E. W. Frohardt ....
11	June 8-12, 1949	Muscatine, First ...	Brashares	R. M. Shipman ....
12	June 7-11, 1950	Shenandoah.......	Brashares	R. M. Shipman ....
13	June 6-10, 1951	Ottumwa	Brashares	R. M. Shipman ....
14	June 11-15, 1952	Council Bluffs	Brashares	R. M. Shipman ....
15	June 10-14, 1953	Des Moines, Grace .	Ensley	R. M. Shipman ....
16	May 26-30, 1954	Oskaloosa	Ensley	R. M. Shipman ....
17	June 9-14, 1955	Des Moines, First ..	Ensley	R. M. Shipman ....
18	June 7-12, 1956	Mt. Pleasant.......	Ensley	R. M. Shipman ....
19	June 9-13, 1957	Des Moines, Grace .	Ensley	M. C. Shupe ....
20	June 22-26, 1958	Ames, Collegiate...	Ensley	M. C. Schupe ....

Name changed to
SOUTH IOWA CONFERENCE OF THE METHODIST CHURCH

	DATE		PLACE	BISHOP	SECRETARY
21	June 14-18, 1959		Des Moines, First ..	Ensley	M. C. Schupe ....
	Nov. 12, 1959	(Special)*	Des Moines, Grace .	Ensley	M. C. Shupe .....
22	June 19-23, 1960		Indianola	Corson........	M. C. Shupe ....
23	June 11-15, 1961		Des Moines, Grace .	Ensley	M. C. Shupe ....
24	June 17-21, 1962		Newton, First......	Ensley	Carl E. Wilson....
25	June 9-13, 1963		Des Moines, First ..	Ensley	W. W. Steinmetz ..
	Oct. 16, 1963	(Special)*	Des Moines, First ..	Ensley	W. W. Steinmetz ..
26	June 21-25, 1964		Mt. Pleasant, First..	Ensley	W. W. Steinmetz ..
27	June 13-17, 1965		Des Moines, Grace .	Thomas	W. W. Steinmetz ..
28	June 19-23, 1966		Indianola, First	Thomas	W. W. Steinmetz ..
29	June 11-15, 1967		Des Moines, First ..	Thomas	W. W. Steinmetz ..
30	June 10-14, 1968		Ames, Collegiate...	Thomas	W. W. Steinmetz ..

SESSIONS AND OFFICERS OF
THE NORTHWEST IOWA CONFERENCE M.E.

	Place	Date	Presiding Bishop	Secretary
1	Fort Dodge	Sept. 18, 1872	Andrews	B. C. Hammond ......
2	Yankton, Dak. T.	Sept. 25, 1873	Bowman	J. A. Potter ....
3	Algona	Sept. 24, 1874	Haven	J. A. Potter ....
4	Fort Dodge	Sept. 29, 1875	Merrill	J. A. Potter ....
5	Le Mars	Oct. 11, 1876	Foster	J. A. Potter ....
6	Webster City	Sept. 27, 1877	Andrews	J. A. Potter ....
7	Cherokee...........	Sept. 25, 1878	Peck	J. A. Potter ....
8	Sioux City	Oct. 2, 1879	Harris	C. B. Winter ....
9	Fort Dodge	Sept. 16, 1880	Warren	C. B. Winter ....
10	Algona	Sept. 29, 1881	Hurst	C. B. Winter ....

#	Location	Date		Name	Minister
11	Sheldon	Sept.	28, 1882	Bowman	C. B. Winter
12	Le Mars	Sept.	26, 1883	Simpson	C. B. Winter
13	Spirit Lake	Sept.	24, 1884	Andrews	S. P. Marsh
14	Storm Lake	Sept.	24, 1885	Foss	F. H. Sanderson
15	Webster City	Sept.	23, 1886	Foster	F. H. Sanderson
16	Sioux City	Sept.	28, 1887	Merrill	F. H. Sanderson
17	Ida Grove	Sept.	26, 1888	Goodsell	F. H. Sanderson
18	Algona	Sept.	25, 1889	Warren	F. H. Sanderson
19	Spencer	Sept.	17, 1890	Fowler	F. H. Sanderson
20	Fort Dodge	Sept.	16, 1891	Ninde	F. H. Sanderson
21	Cherokee	Sept.	27, 1892	Andrews	F. H. Sanderson
22	Sioux City, Grace	Sept.	27, 1893	Mallallieu	F. H. Sanderson
23	Le Mars	Sept.	26, 1894	Merrill	D. M. Yetter
24	Webster City	Oct.	2, 1895	Joyce	D. M. Yetter
25	Eagle Grove	Sept.	30, 1896	Fitzgerald	D. M. Yetter
26	Ida Grove	Sept.	23, 1897	Walden	E. S. Johnson
27	Emmetsburg	Sept.	21, 1898	Vincent	O. K. Maynard
28	Sioux City, First	Sept.	20, 1899	Merrill	E. S. Johnson
29	Spencer	Sept.	26, 1900	Hurst	E. S. Johnson
30	Algona	Oct.	2, 1901	Joyce	E. S. Johnson
31	Clear Lake	Oct.	1, 1902	Hamilton	E. S. Johnson
32	Sioux City, Whitfield	Oct.	7, 1903	Fowler	E. S. Johnson
33	Sac City	Sept.	28, 1904	McDowell	E. S. Johnson
34	Sheldon	Sept.	27, 1905	Warren	E. S. Johnson
35	Fort Dodge	Sept.	19, 1906	Cranston	E. S. Johnson
36	Sioux City, First	Sept.	18, 1907	Goodsell	T. S. Bassett
37	Rockwell City	Sept.	23, 1908	Spellmeyer	T. S. Bassett
38	Estherville	Sept.	22, 1909	Berry	T. S. Bassett
39	Spencer	Sept.	20, 1910	Wilson	T. S. Bassett
40	Sioux City, Grace	Sept.	20, 1911	Cranston	T. S. Bassett
41	Storm Lake	Oct.	2, 1912	Bristol	E. S. Johnson
42	Webster City	Oct.	1, 1913	Shepard	E. S. Johnson
43	Forest City	Sept.	30, 1914	Quayle	E. S. Johnson
44	Fort Dodge, First	Oct.	6, 1915	Bristol	E. S. Johnson
45	Spencer	Oct.	4, 1916	Stuntz	J. B. Walker
46	Algona	Sept.	26, 1917	Stuntz	J. B. Walker
47	Estherville	Sept.	25, 1918	Hughes, M. S.	J. B. Walker
48	Sioux City, First	Oct.	1, 1919	Stuntz	J. B. Walker
49	Humboldt	Sept.	29, 1920	Stuntz	J. B. Walker
50	Storm Lake	Sept.	28, 1921	Hughes, E. H.	J. B. Walker
51	Fort Dodge, First	Oct.	4, 1922	Richardson	J. B. Walker
52	Sioux City, Grace	Sept.	26, 1923	Stuntz	J. B. Walker
53	Rockwell City	Oct.	1, 1924	Keeney	J. B. Walker
54	Le Mars	Sept.	30, 1925	Waldorf	J. B. Walker
55	Sioux City, Grace	Sept.	29, 1926	McDowell	J. B. Walker
56	Webster City	Sept.	28, 1927	Keeney	J. B. Walker
57	Cherokee	Sept.	26, 1928	Leete	J. B. Walker
58	Eagle Grove	Sept.	25, 1929	Nicholson	J. B. Walker
59	Storm Lake	Sept.	24, 1930	Wade	J. B. Walker
60	Estherville	Sept.	22, 1931	Lowe	M. D. Bush
61	Sioux City, Grace	Sept.	27, 1932	Leete	M. D. Bush
62	Humboldt	Sept.	23, 1933	Leete	M. D. Bush
63	Algona	Sept.	26, 1934	Magee	M. D. Bush
64	Spencer	Oct.	2, 1935	Leete	M. D. Bush
65	Fort Dodge, First	Sept.	29, 1936	Oxnam	M. D. Bush
66	Sioux City, Grace	Sept.	28, 1937	Oxnam	M. D. Bush
67	Sac City	Sept.	27, 1938	Flint	M. D. Bush
*68	Webster City	Sept.	26, 1939	Magee	M. D. Bush

*At this session the Declaration of Union was made and The Northwest Iowa Conference of the Methodist Episcopal Church formally and legally became The Northwest Iowa Conference of The Methodist Church on September 29, 1939. The 68th session was the last which was entertained on the Harvard plan.

	Place	Date	Presiding Bishop	Secretary
69	Sioux City, First	Sept. 24, 1940	Magee	W. E. Ellison ....
70	Estherville..........	Sept. 23, 1941	Magee	W. E. Ellison ....
71	Storm Lake	Sept. 22, 1942	Magee	W. E. Ellison ....
72	Fort Dodge, First	Sept. 22, 1943	Magee	W. E. Ellison ....
73	Sioux City, Grace	Sept. 20, 1944	Brashares	W. E. Ellison ....
74	Estherville..........	Sept. 19, 1945	Brashares	W. E. Ellison ....
75	Eagle Grove	Sept. 19, 1946	Brashares	W. E. Ellison ....
76	Fort Dodge	Sept. 17, 1947	Brashares	W. E. Ellison ....
77	Cherokee...........	Sept. 22, 1948	Brashares	W. E. Ellison ....
*	Cedar Rapids	June 21, 1949	Brashares	W. E. Ellison ....

*Final session for effecting Merger with the Upper Iowa Conference, to form the North Iowa Conference.

SESSIONS AND OFFICERS OF
THE UPPER IOWA CONFERENCE M.E.

	Place	Date	Presiding Bishop	Secretary
1	Maquoketa	Aug. 27, 1856	E. S. Janes	L. Taylor ....
2	Marion	Sept. 9, 1857	E. R. Ames	E. Skinner ....
3	Lyons..............	Aug. 25, 1858	T. A. Morris	S. P. Crawford ....
4	Iowa City	Aug. 24, 1859	E. S. Janes	L. Taylor ....
5	Dubuque	Aug. 29, 1860	O. C. Baker	R. W. Keeler ....
6	Marshalltown	Sept. 18, 1861	L. Scott	R. W. Keeler ....
7	McGregor	Sept. 10, 1862	E. S. Janes	R. W. Keeler ....
8	Davenport	Sept. 16, 1863	E. R. Ames	R. W. Keeler ....
9	Waterloo	Sept. 21, 1864	L. Scott	R. W. Keeler ....
10	Tipton	Sept. 13, 1865	M. Simpson	C. G. Truesdell .....
11	Decorah............	Sept. 12, 1866	E. R. Ames	C. G. Truesdell .....
12	Iowa City	Sept. 18, 1867	E. S. Janes	C. G. Truesdell .....
13	Anamosa	Sept. 3, 1868	M. Simpson	C. G. Truesdell .....
14	Independence.......	Sept. 22, 1869	D. W. Clark	R. W. Keeler ....
15	Cedar Falls	Sept. 7, 1870	E. S. Janes	R. W. Keeler ....
16	Clinton	Sept. 27, 1871	E. R. Ames	R. W. Keeler ....
17	Vinton	Sept. 25, 1872	I. W. Wiley...........	R. W. Keeler ....
18	Cedar Rapids	Oct. 1, 1873	E. G. Andrews........	J. W. Clinton ....
19	Charles City	Sept. 30, 1874	G. Haven	J. W. Clinton ....
20	Dubuque	Sept. 22, 1875	S. W. Merrill	J. W. Clinton ....
21	Maquoketa	Sept. 21, 1876	R. S. Foster..........	J. W. Clinton ....
22	McGregor	Oct. 3, 1877	E. R. Ames	J. W. Clinton ....
23	Marshalltown	Oct. 2, 1878	J. T. Peck	J. W. Clinton ....
24	Davenport	Sept. 24, 1879	W. L. Harris..........	J. W. Clinton ....
25	Osage	Oct. 1, 1880	E. G. Andrews........	S. W. Heald ....
26	Waterloo	Sept. 21, 1881	J. F. Hurst	S. W. Heald ....
27	Cedar Rapids	Sept. 20, 1882	I. W. Wiley...........	S. W. Heald ....
28	Marion	Sept. 19, 1883	M. Simpson	S. W. Heald ....
29	Mason City	Oct. 1, 1884	T. Bowman	S. W. Heald ....
30	Toledo	Oct. 1, 1885	H. W. Warren	S. W. Heald ....
31	Cedar Falls	Sept. 20, 1886	R. S. Foster..........	S. W. Heald ....
32	Clinton	Oct. 3, 1887	W. F. Mallalieu	S. W. Heald ....
33	Vinton	Oct. 3, 1888	C. D. Foss	S. W. Heald ....
34	Iowa City	Oct. 2, 1889	W. X. Ninde..........	S. W. Heald ....
35	Decorah............	Oct. 8, 1890	S. M. Merrill	S. W. Heald ....
36	Davenport	Sept. 30, 1891	J. P. Newman	S. W. Heald ....
37	Hampton	Oct. 5, 1892	E. G. Andrews........	S. W. Heald ....
38	Maquoketa	Oct. 4, 1893	J. M. Walden	S. W. Heald ....
39	Charles City	Oct. 3, 1894	T. Bowman	S. W. Heald ....
40	Mason City	Oct. 6, 1895	C. H. Fowler	S. W. Heald ....
41	Independence.......	Oct. 7, 1896	J. N. Fitzgerald	S. W. Heald ....

42	Dubuque	Oct.	6, 1897	H. W. Warren	S. W. Heald ....
43	Marion	Oct.	5, 1898	J. H. Vincent.........	S. W. Heald ....
44	Waterloo	Oct.	4, 1899	C. C. McCabe	S. W. Heald ....
45	Osage	Oct.	3, 1900	J. F. Hurst...........	S. W. Heald ....
46	Vinton	Oct.	2, 1901	S. M. Merrill	S. W. Heald ....
47	Marshalltown	Sept.	24, 1902	D. A. Goodsell	S. W. Heald ....
48	Cedar Rapids	Sept.	23, 1903	C. H. Fowler	W. H. Slingerland .....
49	Davenport	Oct.	5, 1904	I. W. Joyce	W. H. Slingerland .....
50	Hampton	Sept.	27, 1905	L. B. Wilson	W. H. Slingerland .....
51	Maquoketa	Oct.	3, 1906	Earl Cranston	W. H. Slingerland .....
52	Cedar Falls	Oct.	9, 1907	W. F. McDowell	W. H. Slingerland .....
53	Mt. Vernon	Oct.	7, 1908	W. S. Lewis	W. H. Slingerland .....
54	Mason City	Sept.	29, 1909	J. F. Berry	W. H. Slingerland .....
55	Charles City	Sept.	14, 1910	J. W. Hamilton	W. H. Slingerland .....
56	Waterloo	Sept.	20, 1911	T. B. Neely	W. H. Slingerland .....
57	Marshalltown	Sept.	25, 1912	E. H. Hughes	W. H. Slingerland .....
58	Tipton	Sept.	24, 1913	F. M. Bristol	W. H. Slingerland .....
59	Cedar Rapids	Sept.	23, 1914	W. A. Quayle.........	W. H. Slingerland .....
60	Dubuque	Sept.	15, 1915	H. C. Stuntz	W. H. Slingerland .....
61	Waterloo	Sept.	25, 1916	F. J. McConnell	W. H. Slingerland .....
62	Iowa City	Sept.	26, 1917	R. J. Cooke	W. H. Slingerland .....
63	Clinton	Oct.	2, 1918	M. S. Hughes	W. H. Slingerland .....
64	Charles City	Sept.	24, 1919	H. C. Stuntz	S. C. Bretnall ....
65	Oelwein.............	Sept.	22, 1920	H. C. Stuntz	S. C. Bretnall ....
66	Davenport	Sept.	28, 1921	H. C. Stuntz	S. C. Bretnall ....
67	Mason City	Sept.	27, 1922	E. G. Richardson	S. C. Bretnall ....
68	Marion..............	Oct.	3, 1923	H. C. Stuntz	S. C. Bretnall ....
69	Osage	Sept.	24, 1924	F. T. Keeney	S. C. Bretnall ....
70	Mt. Vernon	Sept.	23, 1925	W. F. Anderson.......	S. C. Bretnall ....
71	Marshalltown	Sept.	22, 1926	E. H. Hughes	E. A. Baker ....
72	Cedar Falls	Sept.	21, 1927	F. T. Keeney	E. A. Baker ....
73	Vinton	Sept.	19, 1928	F. D. Leete	E. T. Gough ....
74	Dubuque	Sept.	18, 1929	F. D. Leete	E. T. Gough ....
75	Davenport	Sept.	23, 1930	Titus Lowe	E. T. Gough ....
75	Cedar Rapids	Sept.	23, 1931	Edgar Blake	E. T. Gough ....
77	Mason City	June	22, 1932	F. D. Leete	E. T. Gough ....
78	Dubuque	June	31, 1933	F. D. Leete	E. T. Gough ....
79	Waterloo	Sept.	12, 1934	E. L. Waldorf	E. T. Gough ....
80	Cedar Rapids	Sept.	25, 1935	F. D. Leete	E. T. Gough ....
81	Marshalltown	Sept.	23, 1936	G. B. Oxnam	J. W. Clinton ....
82	Waterloo, Grace	Sept.	15, 1937	G. B. Oxnam	E. A. Sabin ....
83	Cedar Falls	Sept.	21, 1938	J. Ralph Magee.......	E. A. Sabin ....

SESSIONS AND OFFICERS OF
THE UPPER IOWA CONFERENCE OF THE METHODIST CHURCH

	Place	Date	Presiding Bishop	Secretary
84	Clinton	Sept. 20, 1939	J. Ralph Magee.......	H. H. Dill ....
85	Hampton	Sept. 17, 1940	J. Ralph Magee.......	H. H. Dill ....
86	Iowa Falls	Sept. 9, 1941	J. Ralph Magee.......	H. H. Dill ....
87	Waterloo	Sept. 15, 1942	J. Ralph Magee.......	H. H. Dill ....
88	Davenport	June 16, 1943	J. Ralph Magee.......	H. H. Dill ....
89	Iowa City	June 14, 1944	J. Ralph Magee.......	H. H. Dill ....
90	Mt. Vernon	June 20, 1945	C. W. Brashares	H. H. Dill ....
91	Mt. Vernon	June 19, 1946	C. W. Brashares	H. W. Farnham ....
92	Dubuque	June 17, 1947	C. W. Brashares	H. W. Farnham ....
93	Mt. Vernon	June 22, 1948	C. W. Brashares	H. W. Farnham ....
*	Cedar Rapids	June 21, 1949	C. W. Brashares	H. W. Farnham ....

*Final session for effecting Merger with Northwest Iowa Conference, to form the North Iowa Conference.

NORTH IOWA CONFERENCE OF THE METHODIST CHURCH

	Place	Date	Presiding Bishop	Secretary
94	Cedar Rapids, St. Paul's.....	June 22, 1949	C. W. Brashares ...	W. E. Ellison......
95	Fort Dodge, First	June 21, 1950	C. W. Brashares ...	H. A. Walker......
96	Waterloo, Grace	June 20, 1951	C. W. Brashares ...	H. A. Walker......
97	Davenport, St. John's	June 18, 1952	C. W. Brashares ...	H. A. Walker......
98	Mt. Vernon, Cornell Col......	June 17, 1953	F. G. Ensley	H. A. Walker......
99	Sioux City, M'side Col......	June 11, 1954	F. G. Ensley	H. A. Walker......
100	Fort Dodge, First	June 17, 1955	F. G. Ensley	H. A. Walker......
101	Mason City, First	June 17, 1956	F. G. Ensley	H. A. Walker......
102	Waterloo, First	June 16, 1957	F. G. Ensley	H. A. Walker......
103	Cedar Rapids, St. Paul's.....	June 15, 1958	F. G. Ensley	H. A. Walker......
104	Mason City, First	June 21, 1959	F. G. Ensley	H. A. Walker......
105	Marshalltown, First	June 12, 1960	F. G. Ensley	H. A. Walker......
106	Sioux City, Grace	June 18, 1961	F. G. Ensley	H. A. Walker......
107	Mt. Vernon, Cornell Col......	June 10, 1962	F. G. Ensley	H. A. Walker......
108	Fort Dodge, First	June 16, 1963	F. G. Ensley	H. A. Walker......
109	Cedar Rapids, St. Paul's.....	June 14, 1964	F. G. Ensley	H. A. Walker......
110	Waterloo, First	June 20, 1965	J. S. Thomas......	H. A. Walker......
111	Mason City, First	June 12, 1966	J. S. Thomas......	H. A. Walker......
112	Davenport, St. John's	June 18, 1967	J. S. Thomas......	H. A. Walker......
113	Sioux City, M'side Col.......	June 3, 1968	J. S. Thomas......	H. A. Walker......

SESSIONS AND OFFICERS OF
THE IOWA ANNUAL CONFERENCE OF
THE UNITED METHODIST CHURCH

No.	Date		Place	Resident Bishop	Secretary
126	June 8-12, 1969		Des Moines	J. S. Thomas	R. R. MacCanon ..
127	June 14-19, 1970		Des Moines	J. S. Thomas	R. R. MacCanon ..
	May 22, 1971	(Special)*	Des Moines	J. S. Thomas	W. T. Miller ......
128	June 4-7, 1971		Des Moines	J. S. Thomas	W. T. Miller ......
	May 20, 1972	(Special)*	Ames	J. S. Thomas	W. T. Miller ......
129	June 9-13, 1972		Des Moines	J. S. Thomas	W. T. Miller ......
	May 19, 1973	(Special)*	Des Moines	J. S. Thomas	W. T. Miller ......
130	June 8-12, 1973		Des Moines	J. S. Thomas	W. T. Miller ......
	May 18, 1974	(Special)*	Des Moines	J. S. Thomas	W. T. Miller ......
131	June 14-18, 1974		Des Moines	J. S. Thomas	W. T. Miller ......
	May 17, 1975	(Special)*	Des Moines	J. S. Thomas	Susan J. Terry....
132	June 13-17, 1975		Des Moines	J. S. Thomas	Susan J. Terry....
	May 22, 1976	(Special)*	Des Moines	J. S. Thomas	Susan J. Terry....
133	June 11-15, 1976		Des Moines	J. S. Thomas	Susan J. Terry....
	May 14, 1977	(Special)*	Des Moines	Lance Webb	Susan J. Terry....
134	June 3-7, 1977		Des Moines	Lance Webb	Susan J. Terry....
	May 6, 1978	(Special)*	Des Moines	Lance Webb	Susan J. Terry....
135	June 3-7, 1978		Des Moines	Lance Webb	Susan J. Terry....
136	June 2-6, 1979		Des Moines	Lance Webb	Susan J. Terry....
137	June 7-11, 1980		Des Moines	Lance Webb	Susan J. Terry....
138	June 6-10, 1981		Des Moines	Wayne K. Clymer ..	Susan J. Terry....
139	June 4-8, 1982		Des Moines	Wayne K. Clymer ..	Susan J. Terry....
140	June 3-7, 1983		Des Moines	Wayne K. Clymer ..	Susan J. Terry....
	April 28, 1984	(Special)*	Des Moines	Wayne K. Clymer ..	Susan J. Terry....
141	June 1-5, 1984		Des Moines	Wayne K. Clymer ..	Susan J. Terry....

FOREIGN LANGUAGE CONFERENCE SESSIONS
HELD WITHIN IOWA

(The foreign language Methodist Episcopal Conferences were not limited to Iowa in their area and membership. The following are the sessions held within the bounds of Iowa.)

No.	Date	Place	Presiding Bishop	Secretary
Northwest Swedish Conference (1877-1893)				
8	1884	Burlington	Foster	C. G. Nelson
9	1885	Dayton	Bowman	C. G. Nelson
Norwegian-Danish Conference (1880-1943)				
5	1884	Forest City	Foster	Christian Trieder
18	1897	Forest City	Vincent	L. A. Larson
28	1907	Forest City	Goodsell	R. F. Wilhelmsen
49	1928	Forest City	E. H. Hughes	Ole Rohrstaff
St. Louis German Conference (1879-1925)				
3	1881	Burlington	Hurst	William Koeneke
8	1886	Muscatine	Foster	William Koeneke
12	1890	Burlington	Joyce	C. B. Addicks
21	1899	Mt. Pleasant	McCabe	C. B. Addicks
22	1900	Burlington	Hurst	C. B. Addicks
31	1909	Burlington	Spellmeyer	E. Weiffenbach
35	1913	Muscatine	Smith	E. Weiffenbach
44	1922	Muscatine	Leonard	E. Weiffenbach
Northwest German Conference (1864-1880)				
10	1873	Charles City	Andrews	E. E. Schuette
14	1877	Charles City	Ames	E. E. Schuette
Chicago-Northwest Conference (1924-1932)				
4	1927	Charles City	Smith	W. F. Belling

* * *

No Lexington (Black) Conference Sessions were held in Iowa.

IOWA CONFERENCE OF THE METHODIST PROTESTANT CHURCH
(1846-1939)

Year	Place	President	Secretary
1846	Iowa City	Wm. Patterson	A. L. Gray
1847	Winchester (Van Buren County)	Wm. Patterson	A. Parish
1848	Burr Oak Ridge (Cedar County)	Wm. Patterson	T. Snider
1849	Cedar Rapids	J. K. Dawson	C. D. Gray
1850	Winchester	J. K. Dawson	Erastus Hoskins
1851	Oskaloosa	Alex Colwell	Erastus Hoskins
1852	Montezuma	Alex Colwell	Erastus Hoskins
1853	Marshall (Henry County)	J. K. Dawson	Erastus Hoskins
1854	Winchester	F. A. Kirkpatrick	Erastus Hoskins
1855	Ashland (Wapello County)	George Wheatley	Erastus Hoskins
1856	Montezuma	Wm. G. Scott	Erastus Hoskins
1857	Oskaloosa	George Wheatley	Erastus Hoskins
1858	Genoa Bluffs (Iowa County)	A. A. Kerran	W. E. DeGarmo
1859	Richwood (Henry County)	John Mason	George Wheatley
1860	Peoria (Mahaska County)	John Mason	W. E. DeGarmo
1861-1868	Conference Journals Lost		

Year	Place	President	Secretary
1869	New London (Henry County)	J. B. Hiles	J. W. Murphy
1870	Winsell Chapel (Jefferson County)	E. S. Brown	W. B. Harrington
1871	Osceola	J. L. Turner	H. H. Workman
1872	Mt. Carmel (Mahaska County)	Wm. Remsburgh	H. H. Workman
1873	New London	Wm. Remsburgh	H. H. Workman
1874	Osceola	Wm. Remsburgh	H. H. Workman
1875	Hixon's Grove (Jasper County)	E. S. Brown	H. H. Workman
1876	Wheeling (Marion County)	E. S. Brown	H. H. Workman
1877	New London	E. S. Brown	H. H. Workman
1878	Lynn Grove Chapel (Jasper County)	Wm. Remsburgh	H. H. Workman
1879	Colo	W. W. Huddleston	H. H. Workman
1880	Marne	W. W. Huddleston	H. H. Workman
1881	Ohio (Iowa County)	Wm. Remsburgh	J. W. Murphy
1882	Hixon's Grove	Wm. Remsburgh	J. W. Murphy
1883	Osceola	J. A. Bolton	J. W. Murphy
1884	Union Chapel (Selma Circuit)	?	J. W. Murphy
1885	Virginia Chapel (Tipton Circuit)	E. S. Brown	J. W. Murphy
1886	Olivet (Mahaska County)	Josiah Selby	J. W. Murphy
1887	Keswick	Josiah Selby	J. W. Murphy
1888	Osceola	W. W. Huddleston	J. W. Murphy
1889	Bussey	W. W. Huddleston	J. W. Murphy
1890	Buena Vista Chapel (Polk County)	Wm. Remsburgh	J. W. Murphy
1891	Ladora	W. Sparks	J. W. Murphy
1892	New London	W. Sparks	J. W. Murphy
1893	Mapleton (Monona County)	S. J. Geddes	J. W. Murphy
1894	Ohio Chapel (Iowa County)	E. S. Brown	J. W. Murphy
1895	Rhodes	E. S. Brown	J. W. Murphy
1896	Conference Journal lost		
1897	Sully Chapel (Jasper County)	James Kirkwood	J. W. Murphy
1898	Nichol's Station (Muscatine County)	James Kirkwood	J. W. Murphy
1899	Bussey	James Kirkwood	J. W. Murphy
1900	Keswick	S. J. Geddes	J. W. Murphy
1901	Ottumwa	S. J. Geddes	J. W. Murphy
1902	Collins	S. J. Geddes	J. W. Murphy
1903	Osceola	S. J. Geddes	J. W. Murphy
1904	Ladora	S. J. Geddes	J. W. Murphy
1905	Downey (Cedar County)	E. S. Brown	J. W. Murphy
1906	Bussey	E. S. Brown	J. W. Murphy
1907	New London	C. J. Nutt	J. W. Murphy
1908	Keswick	C. J. Nutt	J. W. Murphy
1909	Rhodes	C. J. Nutt	J. W. Murphy
1910	Keokuk	C. J. Nutt	J. W. Murphy
1911	Farrar	C. J. Nutt	J. W. Murphy
1912	Osceola	Albert H. Linder	W. H. Betz
1913	Ladora	Albert H. Linder	W. H. Betz
1914	St. Anthony	C. J. Nutt	W. H. Betz
1915	New London	C. J. Nutt	W. H. Betz

IOWA-MISSOURI CONFERENCE OF
THE METHODIST PROTESTANT CHURCH

Year	Place	President	Secretary
1916	Ohio Church (Iowa County)	W. H. Betz	L. M. Cooper
1917	Harmony Church (Ravenswood, Missouri)	W. H. Betz	J. S. Wood
1918	Osceola	J. C. Leonard	J. S. Wood
1919	Downey	J. C. Leonard	Frank Butterfield
1920	Keswick	J. C. Leonard	Frank Butterfield
1921	Beulah Church (New London Circuit)	J. C. Leonard	Frank Butterfield
1922	Powersville, Missouri	J. C. Leonard	Frank Butterfield
1923	Millersburg	C. J. Nutt	Frank Butterfield
1924	Osceola	C. J. Nutt	A. M. Kopf
1925	Farrar	C. J. Nutt	A. M. Kopf
1926	Ladora	C. R. Green	E. C. Lepper
1927	Luray, Missouri	C. R. Green	E. C. Lepper

Year	Place	President	Secretary
1928	Marne	C. R. Green	E. C. Lepper
1929	Keokuk	C. R. Green	W. H. Betz
1930	New London	C. R. Green	W. H. Betz
1931	Harmony Church (Ravenswood, Missouri)	W. H. Betz	Hugh E. Williams
1932	Osceola	W. H. Betz	Hugh E. Williams
1933	Newton	W. H. Betz	Hugh E. Williams
1934	Keswick	W. H. Betz	Hugh E. Williams
1935	Luray, Missouri	W. H. Betz	Hugh E. Williams
1936	Attica	Hugh E. Williams	W. H. Betz
1937	Bussey	Hugh E. Williams	W. H. Betz
1938	Farrar	Hugh E. Williams	W. H. Betz
1939	New London	Hugh E. Williams	W. H. Betz

NORTH IOWA CONFERENCE OF THE METHODIST PROTESTANT CHURCH (1858-1874)

Note: This conference was small and had many problems. The records presented below are incomplete and may contain errors.

Year	Place	President	Secretary
1858		William Patterson	J. J. Watson
1859		William Patterson	
1860		J. J. Watson	
1861		J. J. Watson	R. B. Groff
1862		J. A. Bolton	R. B. Groff
1863		Joel Dalby	R. B. Groff
1864		Joel Dalby	Josiah Selby
1865			Josiah Selby
1866		W. Purvis	Josiah Selby
1867		Wm. Remsburgh	Josiah Selby
1868		Josiah Selby	
1869		G. M. Scott	John W. Murphy
1870			
1871		G. M. Scott	
1872		G. M. Scott	
1873		J. A. Bolton	
1874		F. A. Kirkpatrick	

IOWA CONFERENCE OF THE EVANGELICAL ASSOCIATION

Date	Place	Chairman	Secretary
1861	Grandview	W. Orwig	Jac. Keiper
1862	Grandview	Jos. Long	R. Dubs
1863	Lisbon	Jos. Long	R. Dubs
1864	Dubuque	J. J. Escher	R. Dubs
1865	East Prairie, Minnesota	Jos. Long	J. Hammetter
1866	East Prairie, Minnesota	J. J. Escher	R. Dubs
1867	Grandview	Jos. Long	R. Dubs
1868	Cedar Falls	J. J. Escher	Jac. Nuhn
1869	Belle Plaine	J. J. Escher	Jac. Nuhn
1870	Blairstown	J. J. Escher	Jac. Nuhn
1871	Ackley	J. J. Escher	H. Brauer
1872	Grandview	J. J. Escher	C. C. Pfund
1873	La Porte	J. J. Escher	C. C. Pfund
1874	Ackley	J. J. Escher	C. C. Pfund
1875	Belle Plaine	J. J. Escher	J. F. Berner

1876	Floyd Valley	R. Dubs	J. F. Berner
1877	La Porte	J. J. Escher	J. F. Berner
1878	Waterloo	Thos. Bowman	C. C. Pfund
1879	Ackley	J. J. Escher	C. C. Pfund
1880	Cedar Falls	R. Dubs	J. F. Berner
1881	Fort Dodge	J. J. Escher	J. F. Berner
1882	Dubuque	Thos. Bowman	J. F. Berner
1883	Trumbuls Grove, Waverly	R. Dubs	J. F. Berner
1884	Ackley	Thos. Bowman	E. J. Schultz
1885	Dysart	Thos. Bowman	E. J. Schultz
1886	Cedar Falls	J. J. Escher	E. J. Schultz
1887	Waterloo	R. Dubs	J. F. Berner
1888	Floyd Valley	R. Dubs	J. F. Berner
1889	Silver Creek	J. J. Escher	C. C. Pfund
1890	Ackley	Thos. Bowman	C. C. Pfund
1891	Dubuque	Thos. Bowman	C. C. Pfund
1892	Dysart	J. J. Escher	E. Nolte
1893	La Porte	Wm. Horn	E. Nolte
1894	Waverly	S. C. Breyfogel	E. Nolte
1895	Cedar Falls	Thos. Bowman	E. Nolte
1896	Sumner	J. J. Escher	E. Nolte
1897	Van Horne	Wm. Horn	E. Nolte
1898	Ackley	S. C. Breyfogel	A. L. Hauser
1899	Lu Verne	Thos. Bowman	A. L. Hauser
1900	Des Moines	J. J. Escher	A. L. Hauser
1901	Radcliffe	S. C. Breyfogel	E. Schroeder
1902	Cedar Falls	Wm. Horn	E. Schroeder
1903	Dysart	M. Gruener	E. Schroeder
1904	Waverly	Wm. Horn	E. Schroeder
1905	Sumner	S. C. Breyfogel	E. Schroeder
1906	Fort Dodge	Thos. Bowman	E. Schroeder
1907	La Porte	Wm. Horn	E. Schroeder
1908	Dubuque	S. C. Breyfogel	E. Schroeder
1909	Council Bluffs	Wm Horn	E. Schroeder
1910	Van Horne	Thos. Bowman	E. Schroeder
1911	Waterloo	S. P. Spreng	E. Schroeder
1912	Cedar Falls	Wm. Horn	L. W. Bock
1913	Ackley	S. C. Breyfogel	L. W. Bock
1914	Dysart	Wm. Horn	L. W. Bock
1915	Lu Verne	S. P. Spreng	F. I. Haas
1916	Hubbard	G. Heinmiller	F. I. Haas
1917	Cedar Falls	S. C. Breyfogel	F. I. Haas
1918	Story City	L. H. Seager	F. I. Haas
1919	Radcliffe	S. P. Spreng	F. I. Haas
1920	Council Bluffs	G. Heinmiller	F. I. Haas
1921	Dumont	S. C. Breyfogel	F. I. Haas
1922	Van Horne	L. H. Seager	F. I. Haas
1923	Waterloo, First	S. P. Spreng	F. I. Haas
1924	Sumner	S. C. Breyfogel	F. I. Haas
1925	Dysart	J. F. Dunlap	F. I. Haas
1926	Story City	M. T. Maze	F. I. Haas
1927	Cedar Falls	L. H. Seager and J. F. Dunlap	F. I. Haas
1928	Le Mars	S. P. Spreng	G. H. Bamford
1929	Des Moines, First	M. T. Maze	G. H. Bamford
1930	Cedar Rapids, First	J. S. Stamm	G. H. Bamford
1931	Waterloo, First and Calvary	L. H. Seager	G. H. Bamford
1932	Dumont	L. H. Seager	G. H. Bamford
1933	Manly	L. H. Seager	G. H. Bamford
1934	Des Moines, First	L. H. Seager	G. H. Bamford
1935	Cedar Falls	C. H. Stauffacher	G. H. Bamford
1936	Story City	C. H. Stauffacher	G. H. Bamford
1937	Clinton	C. H. Stauffacher	G. H. Bamford
1938	Le Mars	C. H. Stauffacher	G. H. Bamford
1939	Hubbard	C. H. Stauffacher	G. H. Bamford
1940	Cedar Rapids, First and Second	C. H. Stauffacher	G. H. Bamford
1941	Meservey	C. H. Stauffacher	G. H. Bamford
1942	Dysart	C. H. Stauffacher	G. H. Bamford
1943	Manly	C. H. Stauffacher	G. H. Bamford
1944	Marshalltown, First and State Street	C. H. Stauffacher	G. H. Bamford
1945	Des Moines, First	C. H. Stauffacher	G. H. Bamford
1946	Waterloo, Calvary	J. A. Haehlen	G. H. Bamford

1947	Cedar Falls	C. H. Stauffacher	G. H. Bamford........
1948	Story City	C. H. Stauffacher	G. H. Bamford........
1949	Le Mars	C. H. Stauffacher	G. H. Bamford........
1950	Waverly...........................	C. H. Stauffacher	G. H. Bamford........
1951	Des Moines, First.................	C. H. Stauffacher	G. H. Bamford........

DES MOINES CONFERENCE OF EVANGELICAL ASSOCIATION

Date	Place	Chairman	Secretary
1876	Blairstown	R. Dubs	W. Klinefelter........
1877	Lisbon...........................	J. J. Escher	E. B. Utt.............
1878	Colo.............................	Thos. Bowman	E. B. Utt.............
1879	Afton............................	R. Dubs	W. J. Hahn ....
1880	Grandview........................	R. Dubs	J. H. Yaggy ....
1881	Blairstown	Thos. Bowman	J. H. Yaggy ....
1882	Des Moines.......................	J. J. Escher	E. B. Utt.............
1883	Afton............................	R. Dubs	E. B. Utt.............
1884	Cedar Rapids	Thos. Bowman	E. B. Utt.............
1885	Des Moines.......................	Thos. Bowman	B. H. Niebel
1886	Columbus Junction	J. J. Escher	B. H. Niebel
1887	Belle Plaine	R. Dubs	B. H. Niebel
1888	Cedar Rapids	J. J. Escher	B. H. Niebel
1889	Afton............................	R. Dubs	S. A. Walton ....
1890	Des Moines.......................	E. B. Utt.............	S. A. Walton ....
1891	Anita	J. J. Escher	S. W. Kilinger ....
1892	Creston	Thos. Bowman	J. H. Yaggy ....
1893	Story City	S. C. Breyfogel	J. H. Yaggy ....
1894	Des Moines.......................	J. J. Escher	J. H. Yaggy ....
1895	Maxwell..........................	Wm. Horn	L. N. Day ....
1896	Morning Star, Pierson	Thos. Bowman	J. H. Yaggy ....
1897	Story City	Thos. Bowman	J. H. Yaggy ....
1898	Creston...........................	S. C. Breyfogel	J. H. Yaggy ....
1899	Des Moines.......................	J. J. Escher	J. H. Yaggy ....
1900	Buffalo	Wm. Horn	J. H. Yaggy ....
1901	Morning Star, Pierson	Thos. Bowman	J. H. Yaggy ....
1902	Audubon..........................	S. C. Breyfogel	Chas. P. Lang ....
1903	Des Moines.......................	Wm. Horn	L. N. Day ....
1904	Viola Center	Thos. Bowman	L. N. Day ....
1905	Pierson	Wm. Horn	L. N. Day ....
1906	Audubon..........................	Wm. Horn	L. N. Day ....
1907	Des Moines.......................	S. C. Breyfogel	L. N. Day ....
1908	Creston...........................	S. P. Spreng	L. N. Day ....
1909	Viola Center	Wm. Horn	L. N. Day ....
1910	Story City	Thos. Bowman	L. N. Day ....
1911	Green Mountain	S. C. Breyfogel	L. N. Day ....
1912	Cedar Falls	Wm. Horn	L. N. Day ....

DES MOINES CONFERENCE, UNITED EVANGELICAL CHURCH

Date	Place	Chairman	Secretary
1891	Lisbon	D. H. Kooker	S. A. Walton ....
1892	Cedar Rapids	W. M. Stanford	S. A. Walton ....
1893	(nothing listed)		
1894	Colo.............................	C. S. Haman	S. A. Walton ....
1895	Nora Springs	R. Dubs	S. A. Walton ....
1896	Otter Creek.......................	W. M. Stanford	S. A. Walton ....
1897	Belle Plaine	W. M. Stanford	E. B. Utt.............

1898	Zearing	R. Dubs	E. B. Utt
1899	Floyd	R. Dubs	E. B. Utt
1900	Iowa Center	W. M. Stanford	E. B. Utt
1901	Cedar Rapids	R. Dubs	E. B. Utt
1902	Colo	W. M. Stanford	Chas. Pickford
1903	Zearing	H. B. Hartzler	Chas. Pickford
1904	Marshalltown	W. F. Heil	Chas. Pickford
1905	Center Point	H. B. Hartzler	Chas. Pickford
1906	Harlan	W. F. Heil	Chas. Pickford
1907	Afton	H. B. Hartzler	J. G. Walz
1908	Lisbon	W. F. Heil	J. G. Walz
1909	Zearing	H. B. Hartzler	J. G. Walz
1910	Cedar Rapids	W. F. Heil	J. G. Walz
1911	Marshalltown	U. F. Swengel	J. G. Walz
1912	Anita	W. H. Fouke	C. H. Stauffacher
1913	La Porte City	U. F. Swengel	C. H. Stauffacher
1914	Zearing	W. H. Fouke	C. H. Stauffacher
1915	Manly	U. F. Swengel	C. H. Stauffacher
1916	Marshalltown, State Street	W. H. Fouke	C. H. Stauffacher
1917	Des Moines	U. F. Swengel	C. H. Stauffacher
1918	Grandview	W. H. Fouke	J. G. Walz
1919	Colo	W. F. Heil	J. B. Meloy
1920	Center Point	M. T. Maze	J. B. Meloy
1921	Lisbon	M. T. Maze	J. B. Meloy
1922	Marshalltown, First	M. T. Maze	J. B. Meloy
1923	Afton	M. T. Maze	G. H. Bamford
1924	Zearing	J. F. Dunlap	G. H. Bamford
1925	Cedar Rapids, Zion	M. T. Maze	G. H. Bamford
1926	Belle Plaine	S. P. Spreng	G. H. Bamford
1927	Cedar Falls	J. F. Dunlap	G. H. Bamford

NORTHWESTERN CONFERENCE, UNITED EVANGELICAL CHURCH

Date	Place	Chairman	Secretary
1899	Floyd	R. Dubs	K. Kaupp
1900	Ackley	R. Dubs	K. Kaupp
1901	Otter Creek	R. Dubs	K. Kaupp
1902	Le Mars	R. Dubs	J. H. Mayne
1903	East Prairie, Minnesota	W. F. Heil	K. Kaupp
1904	Stanton	H. B. Hartzler	K. Kaupp
1905	Ackley	W. F. Heil	K. Kaupp
1906	Nora Springs	H. B. Hartzler	K. Kaupp
1907	Defiance	H. B. Hartzler	K. Kaupp
1908	Le Mars	H. B. Hartzler	K. Kaupp
1909	Odessa, Minnesota	H. B. Hartzler	K. Kaupp
1910	Kimball, Minnesota	W. F. Heil	K. Kaupp
1911	Floyd	U. F. Swengel	K. Kaupp
1912	Defiance	W. H. Fouke	B. F. Zuehl
1913	Nora Springs	U. F. Swengel	B. F. Zuehl
1914	Nerstrand, Minnesota	W. H. Fouke	B. F. Zuehl
1915	Le Mars	U. F. Swengel	B. F. Zuehl
1916	Lafayette	W. H. Fouke	B. F. Zuehl
1917	Stanton	U. F. Swengel	B. F. Zuehl
1918	Slayton, Minnesota	W. H. Fouke	B. F. Zuehl
1919	Nora Springs	W. F. Heil	B. F. Zuehl
1920	Nerstrand, Minnesota	M. T. Maze	B. F. Zuehl
1921	Rands	M. T. Maze	J. J. DeWall, Jr.
1922	Lafayette	M. T. Maze	B. F. Zuehl
1923	Le Mars	M. T. Maze	B. F. Zuehl

THE IOWA CONFERENCE OF UNITED BRETHREN IN CHRIST

Date	Place	Chairman	Secretary
1845	Wm. Thompson Home	John Russell	
1846	Columbus City	J. J. Glossbrenner	
1847	Wm. Thompson Home	B. R. Hanby	
1848	Joel Shively Home	B. R. Hanby	
1849	Lisbon	David Edwards	
1850	Clark's Point	J. J. Glossbrenner	
1851	Henry Thompson Home	Jacob Erb	
1852	Knoxville	J. J. Glossbrenner	
1853	Lisbon	Lewis Davis	
1854	Anamosa	Lewis Davis	
1855	Muscatine	J. J. Glossbrenner	
1856	Lisbon	J. J. Glossbrenner	
1857	West Union	Lewis Davis	
1858	Western College	Lewis Davis	
1859	Lisbon	Lewis Davis	
1860	West Union	J. J. Glossbrenner	
1861	Otterbein Chapel	Solomon Weaver	
1862	Lisbon	Jacob Markwood	
1863	Western College	Jacob Markwood	
1864	Mt. Pleasant	Jacob Markwood	
1865	Lisbon	Jacob Markwood	
1866	Lisbon	J. Kurtz	
1867	Lisbon	D. K. Flickinger	
1868	Muscatine	Jacob Markwood	
1869	Lisbon	John Dickson	
1870	Prairie Chapel	John Dickson	
1871	Western College	John Dickson	
1872	Lisbon	John Dickson	
1873	Olin	J. J. Glossbrenner	
1874	Western College	J. J. Glossbrenner	
1875	Lisbon	J. J. Glossbrenner	
1876	Castalia	J. J. Glossbrenner	
1877	Toledo	Milton Wright	
1878	Lisbon	Milton Wright	
1879	Western College	Milton Wright	
1880	West Union	Milton Wright	
1881	Cedar Rapids	Jonathon Weaver	
1882	Toledo	Jonathon Weaver	
1883	Lisbon	Jonathon Weaver	
1884	No Session		
1885	Toledo	Jonathon Weaver	
1886	Cedar Rapids	E. B. Kephart	
1887	Muscatine	Nicholas Castle	
1888	Lisbon	John Dickson	
1889	Bristow	Jonathon Weaver	
1890	Toledo	Nicholas Castle	
1891	Cedar Rapids	E. B. Kephart	
1892	Lisbon	John Dickson	
1893	Bristow	Jonathon Weaver	
1894	Muscatine	Nicholas Castle	
1895	Toledo	J. W. Hott	
1896	Ottumwa	H. W. Hott	
1897	Sumner	E. B. Kephart	
1898	Monticello	Nicholas Castle	
1899	Lisbon	Nicholas Castle	
1900	Cedar Rapids	Nicholas Castle	
1901	Muscatine	Nicholas Castle	

THE DES MOINES CONFERENCE OF UNITED BRETHREN IN CHRIST

Date	Place	Chairman	Secretary
1853	Lisbon	Lewis Davis	
1854	Knoxville	Lewis Davis	
1855	Attica	J. J. Glossbrenner	
1856	Polk City	J. J. Glossbrenner	
1857	Columbus City	Lewis Davis	
1858	Newburn	Lewis Davis	
1859	Newburn	Lewis Davis	
1860	Gosport	D. K. Flickinger	
1861	UB Chapel	Jacob Markwood	

THE NORTH IOWA CONFERENCE OF UNITED BRETHREN IN CHRIST

Date	Place	Chairman	Secretary
1862	Lisbon	Jacob Markwood	
1863	Chickasaw	Solomon Weaver	
1864	Colesburg	Jacob Markwood	
1865	West Union	Jacob Markwood	
1866	Plum Creek	I. K. Statton	
1867	Taylorsville	D. K. Flickinger	
1868	Cedar Falls	Jacob Markwood	
1869	Girard (sic) Church	John Dickson	
1870	Colesburg	John Dickson	
1871	Washington Church	John Dickson	
1872	Mountain Grove	John Dickson	
1873	West Union	J. J. Glossbrenner	

THE EAST DES MOINES CONFERENCE OF UNITED BRETHREN IN CHRIST

Date	Place	Chairman	Secretary
1862	Libertyville	Jacob Markwood	
1863	Salem Church	Jacob Markwood	
1864	Washington	Jacob Markwood	
1865	Stone's Chapel	Jacob Markwood	
1866	Chillicothe	William Davis	
1867	Columbus City	D. K. Flickinger	
1868	Salem Church	E. B. Kephart	
1869	Washington	John Dickson	
1870	Newburn	John Dickson	
1871	Columbus City	John Dickson	
1872	Washington	John Dickson	
1873	Salem Church	J. J. Glossbrenner	
1874	Ainsworth	J. J. Glossbrenner	
1875	Bethel Church	J. J. Glossbrenner	
1876	Columbus City	J. J. Glossbrenner	
1877	Ainsworth	Milton Wright	
1878	Fry Chapel	Milton Wright	
1879	Zion Center	Milton Wright	
1880	Fry Chapel	Milton Wright	
1881	Salem Church	E. B. Kephart	

1882	Columbus City	E. B. Kephart	
1883	Ainsworth	E. B. Kephart	
1884	Moravia	E. B. Kephart	
1885	Keota	Nicholas Castle	
1886	Pleasant View	E. B. Kephart	
1887	Columbus City	Jonathon Weaver	
1888	Selection	John Dickson	
1889	Uniondale	E. B. Kephart	
1890-1901	No listings		
1902	Olin	E. B. Kephart	
1903	Moravia	G. M. Mathews	
1904	Garwin	G. M. Mathews	
1905	Letts	G. M. Mathews	
1906	Castalia	W. M. Weekley	
1907	Toledo	W. M. Weekley	
1908	Bristow	W. M. Weekley	
1909	Gladbrook	W. M. Weekley	
1909	Des Moines, Castle (Special Session)	W. M. Weekley	

THE WEST DES MOINES CONFERENCE OF
UNITED BRETHREN IN CHRIST

Date	Place	Chairman	Secretary
1862	Panora	Jacob Markwood	
1863	Avon	Jacob Markwood	
1864	West Union	Jacob Markwood	
1865	Panora	Jacob Markwood	
1866	Pleasant View	J. Wilson	
1867	Fremont City	D. K. Flickinger	
1868	Hopkins Grove	C. S. Jones	
1869	No listing		
1870	Brush Ridge	William Jacobs	
1871	Sheep Farm, Page County	John Dickson	
1872	Panora	John Dickson	
1873	Blair Chapel	J. J. Glossbrenner	
1874	Union	J. J. Glossbrenner	
1875	Fremont City	J. J. Glossbrenner	
1876	Ollerbury Church	J. J. Glossbrenner	
1877	Norwood	Milton Wright	
1878	Pleasantville	Milton Wright	
1879	Van Meter	Milton Wright	
1880	Dale City	Milton Wright	
1881	Avon	Jonathon Weaver	
1882	Davis City	Jonathon Weaver	
1883	Scranton	Jonathon Weaver	
1884	Des Moines	Jonathan Weaver	
1885	Hoskins Grove	E. B. Kephart	
1886	Avon	Nicholas Castle	
1887	Van Meter	John Dickson	
1888	Des Moines	Jonathon Weaver	
1889-1901	No listings		
1902	Des Moines, Castle	G. M. Mathews	
1903	Des Moines, Summit	G. M. Mathews	
1904	Jamaica	G. M. Mathews	
1905	Des Moines, Castle	W. M. Weekley	
1906	Ames	W. M. Weekley	
1907	Des Moines, Summit	W. M. Weekley	
1908	Lake City	W. M. Weekley	

THE IOWA STATE CONFERENCE OF
UNITED BRETHREN IN CHRIST

Date	Place	Chairman	Secretary
1909	Des Moines, Castle	W. M. Weekley	
1910	Toledo	W. M. Weekley	
1911	Waterloo	W. M. Weekley	
1912	Vinton	W. M. Weekley	
1913	Albia	H. H. Fout	
1914	Des Moines, Summit	H. H. Fout	
1915	Des Moines, Castle	H. H. Fout	
1916	Toledo	H. H. Fout	
1917	Waterloo	C. J. Kephart	
1918	Webster City	C. J. Kephart	
1919	Cedar Rapids	C. J. Kephart	
1920	Des Moines, Miller	C. J. Kephart	
1921	Des Moines, Castle	C. J. Kephart	
1922	Des Moines, Miller	C. J. Kephart	
1923	Des Moines, St. Andrews	C. J. Kephart	
1924	Albia	C. J. Kephart	
1925	Cedar Rapids	A. B. Statton	
1926	Des Moines, Miller	A. B. Statton	
1927	Muscatine	A. B. Statton	
1928	Ames	A. B. Statton	
1929	Marshalltown, Bethany	A. B. Statton	
1930	Toledo	A. B. Statton	
1931	Des Moines, St. Andrews	A. B. Statton	
1932	Waterloo, Graves	A. B. Statton	
1933	Moville	A. B. Statton	
1934	Albia	A. B. Statton	
1935	Webster City	A. B. Statton	
1936	Cedar Rapids, St. Andrews	A. B. Statton	
1937	Des Moines, St. Andrews	A. B. Statton	
1938	Albia	V. O. Weidler	
1939	Des Moines, Miller	V. O. Weidler	
1940	Vinton	V. O. Weidler	
1941	Muscatine	V. O. Weidler	
1942	Waterloo, Graves	V. O. Weidler	
1943	Des Moines, St. Andrews	V. O. Weidler	
1944	Des Moines, St. Andrews	V. O. Weidler	
1945	Albia	V. O. Weidler	
1946	Waterloo, Graves	V. O. Weidler	

THE IOWA CONFERENCE (UB) OF
EVANGELICAL UNITED BRETHREN

Date	Place	Chairman	Secretary
1947	Chariton	V. O. Weidler	
1948	Des Moines, St. Andrews	V. O. Weidler	
1949	Albia	V. O. Weidler	
1950	Muscatine	V. O. Weidler	
1951	Des Moines, St. Andrews	D. T. Gregory	

SESSIONS AND OFFICERS OF
IOWA CONFERENCE E.U.B. CHURCH

(For a list of the Sessions of the Iowa Conference (Ev) and predecessor Conferences, see Journal of 1951, page 99.)

(For a list of the Sessions of the Iowa Conference (UB) and predecessor Conferences, see Journal of 1951, page 170.)

No.	Date		Place	Chairman	Secretary
108	May	2-6, 1951	Des Moines, First	C. H. Stauffacher	G. H. Bamford
109	May	6-9, 1952	Cedar Falls, First	C. H. Stauffacher	G. H. Bamford
110	May	6-10, 1953	Des Moines, First	C. H. Stauffacher	R. R. MacCanon
111	May	5-9, 1954	Cedar Falls, First	D. T. Gregory	R. R. MacCanon
112	May	3-6, 1955	Des Moines, First	L. L. Baughman	R. R. MacCanon
113	May	1-4, 1956	Waterloo, First	L. L. Baughman	R. R. MacCanon
114	May	7-10, 1957	Dysart	L. L. Baughman	R. R. MacCanon
Sp.	Sept.	4, 1957	Cedar Falls, First	L. L. Baughman	R. R. MacCanon
115	May	6-9, 1958	Cedar Rapids, Sharon	L. L. Baughman	R. R. MacCanon
116	May	5-8, 1959	Des Moines, First	L. L. Baughman	R. R. MacCanon
117	May	3-6, 1960	Fort Dodge, First	L. L. Baughman	R. R. MacCanon
118	May	2-5, 1961	Cedar Falls, First	P. W. Milhouse	R. R. MacCanon
119	May	1-4, 1962	Cedar Rapids, Salem	P. W. Milhouse	R. R. MacCanon
120	May	6-10, 1963	Story City	P. W. Milhouse	R. R. MacCanon
121	May	4-7, 1964	Hubbard	P. W. Milhouse	R. R. MacCanon
122	May	3-6, 1965	Waterloo, First	P. W. Milhouse	R. R. MacCanon
123	May	2-5, 1966	Ames	P. W. Milhouse	R. R. MacCanon
124	May	1-4, 1967	Fort Dodge, First	P. W. Milhouse	R. R. MacCanon
125	May	13-16, 1968	Nevada	P. W. Milhouse	R. R. MacCanon

For a history of the Iowa Conference (former EUB) and its predecessor Conferences see the *Proceedings of the Iowa Conference*, 1968, pp. 102-107.

Index

The following abbreviations are used to save space: